BC

The Economics of
Fisheries Management

The Economics of Fisheries Management

Revised and enlarged edition

Lee G. Anderson

The Johns Hopkins University Press
Baltimore and London

The Johns Hopkins University Press
701 West 40th Street
Baltimore, Maryland 21211
The Johns Hopkins Press Ltd., London

The paper used in this publication meets the minimum requirements of
American National Standard for Information Sciences—Permanence of
Paper for Printed Library Materials, ANSI Z39.48-1984.

Library of Congress Cataloging-in-Publication Data

Anderson, Lee G.
  The economics of fisheries management.
  Bibliography: p.
  Includes index.
  1. Fisheries—Economic aspects. 2. Fishery
management—Economic aspects. I. Title.
SH334.A53 1986   338.3'727   85-24061
ISBN 0-8018-3253-5 (alk. paper)

To Sheila, Bronwyn, and Pearce,
my best friends

Contents

Figures and Tables

Tables

Acknowledgments

To be complete, I would have to acknowledge every author listed in the bibliography as well as many other individuals from whom I have heard presentations or with whom I have had discussions on fisheries economics and management. I will only mention Gardner Brown, Colin Clark, Virgil Norton, Giulio Pontecorvo, Brian Rothschild, Anthony Scott, Robert Stokes, Ivar Strand, and especially James A. Crutchfield and thank them for their help over the years. I would also like to thank those who read the first edition and shared their reactions with me. Clive Southey read a draft of the first edition, and Richard Bishop and Gordon Munro read parts of the draft for the second edition; I am very grateful for their specific comments. Rich's were especially detailed and stimulating. I am also grateful to Frederick W. Bell for permission to quote freely from his work on the lobster fishery. Last but not least, I would like to thank the many secretaries who assisted me on the first edition and specifically Ruth Leo, who, with the assistance of Jeffrey Leggett, did all the clerical work for the second edition.

Introduction

When the first edition of this book was published in 1977, it was the only one of its kind. There was a large literature on the economic aspects of the fisheries exploitation, but there was no single source where the interested reader could find an extensive discussion of the subject. One of the goals for writing the book was to draw the material together, fill in some of the gaps, and present the results for a general audience of individuals interested in the rational exploitation of fisheries, not just for economists. Since 1977 the literature on fisheries economics has increased significantly. There have been many scientific articles, some addressing new areas and others improving the work in earlier papers, with much of the analysis for both types being presented in a rigorous mathematical economics format. One topic that has received special attention is the theoretical and applied aspects of various types of regulations. Besides these individual papers, a number of general fisheries economics books have been published, many within the last two years.

Another change that has occurred since the first edition was written is the institutional arrangement under which nations can manage their marine fisheries. Through both unilateral action and international negotiation at the United Nations Convention of the Law of the Sea, exclusive economic zones have been created; these have granted the sole right to manage fisheries to coastal states. As a result, many fisheries that were up for grabs or subject to the difficulties of international management now have the potential for beneficial management.

If I were to have given full coverage to all of the additions to the literature and the changes in institutional arrangements in revising this book, I would have been in for a monumental task and the product would have been a very large volume indeed. I have not taken that route, however. For one thing, there are a number of references where much of the literature on the general and specific effects of extended fisheries jurisdiction on economic aspects of fisheries management can be found in a single source. For example, Cunningham, Dunn, and Whitemarsh (1985) present an excellent discussion of the specifics of the new management regimes in many countries since the advent of the extended fisheries zones. See also Anderson (1977b, 1982a). Therefore, these issues will not be discussed here. It is important to realize, however, that, without this institutional change, the probability of implementing management programs based on the concepts in this book would be much smaller.

Although I have tried to take into account the additions to the literature, I have placed some limits here as well, but mostly on the manner of presentation rather than on the range of topics. This book has been almost completely rewritten, taking the recent literature into account, but the emphasis on presenting the material in a way that will be accessible to a wide range of readers has been maintained. For one thing, mathematics has been kept to a minimum. For those who desire it, Colin W. Clark has published a second book (Clark 1985a) that, in a combination with his now-classic 1976 volume and his other works—many of them coauthored with Gordon Munro, presents a rigorous treatment of optimal fisheries utilization. The topics, the issues, and the conclusions contained here will be essentially the same as those in the more rigorous treatment; only the manner of presentation will be different. The issues to be covered are complex, however, and in order to do them justice, the analysis is often quite difficult. Although the first edition was written for the "diligent non-economist," I must admit that the required diligence for the second will likely increase.

While the revised book has the same general format as the first edition, new topics include recreational fisheries, fisheries development, and the share system of remuneration. The general discussion has also been expanded to give more explicit attention to different types of biological models and to situations other than one fleet harvesting a single independent fish stock. There is also a more extensive coverage of the concept of user cost and of the various types of fishery regulations. Finally, there is additional material on developing and operating a fisheries management program.

In one of the earlier works on the economics of fisheries, H. Scott Gordon felt the need to include the following paragraph in his introduction (Gordon 1953, 443):

An apology is perhaps necessary. This paper is written for a mixed audience so far as economic theory is concerned. There will perhaps be those who are thoroughly familiar with the devices that are employed in the following pages and, to them, some of the explanation and proofs given will be exasperatingly elementary. Others may have had no formal training in modern economic theory and for them it is necessary to include sufficient explanation so that the argument may be followed. I have tried to solve this dilemma by including only the barest amount of explanation necessary to complete the reasoning without taking anything for granted. I am afraid that the result is neither fish, flesh nor fowl, but perhaps it will nevertheless be a synthetic protein with some food value, and not entirely unpalatable at that.

My attitude and approach are similar to those of Gordon. I have included a brief chapter on basic economic concepts for those who feel the need for them, and the discussion in the rest of the book is more detailed than would be the case in a book aimed solely at economists. Nevertheless, the subject at hand is basically economic in nature, and it would be a disservice to "water down" the material. While presupposing no prior knowledge of economics, it does require an interest in the economic aspects of the complex problem of fisheries management, supported by a good-humored willingness to take the time to master a few basic economic concepts. The trained economist, on the other hand, will find the going somewhat easier and should find a rewarding vein of pay dirt in the extensive coverage of the economics of common-property resources.

Conversely, to the fisheries biologist the discussions of the reproductive biology of fish stocks may appear elementary and the analysis somewhat simplistic. My goal, however, has been to provide an adequate framework for the economic analysis to follow without getting bogged down in finer theoretical points.

The fact that I discuss mainly the economic aspects in no way implies that these are the most important of the many facets of fisheries management. The interplay of these elements will be discussed wherever possible, but in the interest of keeping the book a manageable length, the reader is asked to forgive what may appear to be a cavalier treatment of other aspects as he reads on to see how economic considerations fit into the overall picture. This is, after all, a book on the economic theory of fisheries exploitation.

Economics can be defined as the study of the optimal allocation of scarce resources among unlimited wants. Individuals, families, and societies normally all face the same puzzle: how to allocate limited means or resources among unlimited wants, given the state of technological knowledge, in such a way that their welfare or happiness, however measured, is maximized. For society as a whole, the traditional assumption in economic analysis is that the value of goods and services produced annually is the correct measure of welfare, where value is determined by an individual's willingness to pay. For our purposes then, economics can be defined as the study of the allocation of society's scarce resources so as to maximize the value of production. It is with respect to this definition that terms such as *efficiency* and *optimal allocation* or *suboptimal allocation* of resources should be interpreted—an efficient or proper allocation being one that maximizes the value of production. The reader is asked to bear this in mind, because the conclusions to follow may appear strange, simplistic, or just plain wrong if some other connotation is placed on these terms.

The logic behind the above criteria is that, if resources can be reallocated such that the value of production increases, then at least one person can be made better off (i.e., can receive a higher-valued consumption bundle) without making anyone else worse off, and hence such a reallocation is justified. Admittedly there may be difficulties in obtaining such a redistribution of product, and this point will be discussed in detail below, especially during the analysis of regulation.

Several interrelated points should be made at this juncture. First, by placing emphasis on willingness to pay in the definition of efficiency, one must accept the existing distribution of income among the members of society as the proper one. A change in distribution will change the willingness to pay for, and hence the value of, certain goods, which will lead to a change in the make-up of the proper allocation of resources. For example, shifting income from the rich to the poor will probably mean that more resources will be used to produce small housing units and less will be used for yachts. The effect that this assumption will have depends upon how one views the propriety of the existing distribution, especially in relation to current institutional programs to redistribute it.

Second, using maximization of the value of production is not as crass and materialistic as it might appear. Logically, clean air and a pleasant mountain meadow suitable for hiking and meditation are services that should be included in total production in addition to such goods as steel, automobiles, etc. Admittedly there are difficulties in measuring people's willingness to pay for these special goods, but conceptually they are a part of the problem. And finally, the emphasis on efficiency as defined here does not have to be absolute. A society may choose to use other criteria dealing with income distribution, regional employment, or other social or strategic phenomena. Even so, economic efficiency criteria are valuable in demonstrating the economic costs that will be incurred in achieving other types of maxima. This point will receive separate treatment in chapter 4.

Common usage of the word *economics* usually implies that it deals only with profit and loss, but this is a very narrow view. True, profits and losses are important to resource allocation, because in a perfectly operating market economy the search for profit and the avoidance of losses will lead to a proper allocation, given the income distribution. But, as the above discussion demonstrates, economics is much more than this, and it is this broader view that will be taken throughout this book.

In view of this definition of economics, fishery economics can be defined as the study of the optimal allocation of resources to a fishery in such a way that the value of production is maximized. Alternatively, this can be expressed as the study of the optimal allocation of all resources, including the fishery, in such a way that society's welfare is maximized. Although the subject at hand is the fishery, other resources and other individuals who are not directly associated with fishing are thus seen to be crucial to our discussion, and this is one focal point of the book. The study will cover not only how and why an unregulated fishery will allocate resources in a suboptimal manner but (more important) what the optimal allocation *should* be, in view of standard economic analysis.

Of the book's seven chapters, the first presents a brief introduction to the basic principles of economics important to the study of fisheries and offers a more extended treatment of what is meant by economic efficiency and how it is achieved in a freely competitive economy. This will provide a frame of reference that (while unrealistic on its own because, as defined, there is no such thing as a freely competitive economy) is very useful in analyzing the problem at hand when properly adjusted and correctly interpreted. Those with training in economics may wish to skip or skim this rapidly. Others may want to supplement it by referring to basic economics books. When the economic concepts introduced here are used in later discussion, reference is made to this chapter; therefore, a third alternative is to start with chapter 2 and refer to the opening chapter only when a more complete understanding of any concept is desired. Please do not be afraid of the graphs in this chapter and throughout the text. Since this is a book on the economics of fisheries, the tools of the economist must be used; and any economic workman keeps well-sharpened graphical analysis at his fingertips for the building and presenting of economic models. Properly used, it can aid tremendously in the discussions to follow. Moreover, each graph that follows is accompanied by explanatory text.

Chapters 2 and 3 contain the main economic analysis. Initially, simple population dynamics and simplifying economic assumptions are used to describe the concept of maximum economic yield of a fishery and why an unregulated fishery will not operate at that level. To make the discussion more realistic, some of these assumptions are then relaxed, and the effects on the analysis are considered. Chapter 3 deals with the economics of the individual fishing unit, with implications of a variable price of fish, and with fisheries as part of the whole economy as well as with recreational fishing and fisheries development.

One of the most important concepts developed in chapters 1, 2, and 3 is the idea of an equilibrium in a fishery; it will be worthwhile to discuss it very briefly here. An equilibrium in any system occurs when there is no tendency for change. In the economic part of a fishery, there will be an equilibrium if the profits of the vessels are high enough that none wants to cease fishing but yet low enough not to encourage individuals to obtain vessels and start fishing. If conditions remain unchanged, the number of vessels will not change. In the biological part of a fishery, there will be an equilibrium if the amount caught each year just equals the natural growth of the fish stock. If conditions remain the same, the size of the stock will not change. A general equilibrium, or what is sometimes called a bionomic equilibrium, will occur in a fishery when an economic and a biological equilibrium occur simultaneously. Along with the problem of common property, this extra dimension provided by the absence or presence of a biological equilibrium is one of the things that makes fishery economics deserving of special study.

Chapter 4 moves on into the more intricate economic models of fishery exploitation, considering the effects of more complex population dynamics and the concepts of a maximum social yield and an international maximum economic yield. In addition, there are discussions of formal dynamic models and of the share system of crew remuneration. In chapter 5, the discussion moves beyond the analysis of a single fleet harvesting an independent fish stock to a range of cases that more closely mirrors real world fishery exploitation.

Chapter 6, a general discussion of types of fishery regulation, focuses primarily on their economic aspects and on economical ways of implementing them. Chapter 7 provides a brief introduction to some recent empirical studies and shows how the theory of the previous chapters can be used to provide useful information.

It should be noted that the book is designed to serve a wide variety of purposes. The reader who wants merely a brief overview of the subject can begin with chapter 2 and read whatever parts of chapters 3 and 4 that are of interest, using the reference in chapter 1 to bolster any weaknesses in his economic background. He may then move on to the appropriate corresponding sections of chapter 6. Finally, he can glance through chapter 7 to discover some applications of the model. A more intensive reader may choose to explore further into chapter 3 and to carry on into chapters 4 and 5. The distance he covers will depend upon how deeply he wants to delve into the subject. Also, for those instances where the book is to be used as a text for a fisheries management or an economics of natural resources course, I have included a series of study questions for chapters 2 through 6.

The Economics of
Fisheries Management

1

Basic Economics

Demand, Supply, and Economic Equilibrium

Demand Curves

Demand and supply curves, two basic tools in the economist's kit, are fairly well understood among noneconomists but perhaps deserve sharper definition. A demand curve shows the amount of a good that will be demanded over a specified time period at various prices, if other influences remain constant. This curve is generally assumed to be downward sloping, indicating that more will be purchased per period if the price is lowered, as indicated in figure 1.1. The vertical axis represents price measured in terms of dollars; the horizontal axis represents quantity demanded per period of time. The time element is important: to say that five units will be demanded at a price of $9.00 is almost meaningless unless it is known whether this is five units per day, per week, per year, etc.

Note that if price should fall from $9.00 to $8.00, the quantity demanded increases from 5 to 6. Only price must change; otherwise one cannot be sure what variable has caused the resultant increase in quantity demanded. (Other possibilities might be changes in incomes, in tastes, or in prices of other goods.) Therefore, in talking about a demand curve, these other considerations must be assumed as constant, or the shape and position of the entire curve will be affected. For example, assume that the good under consideration is Ford automobiles. If the price of all other cars increases by $3,000, the demand curve for Fords will shift to the right as consumers who would normally have purchased other cars will now buy Fords, and more will be sold at every price. On the other hand, if clean, convenient, rapid, and safe mass transportation becomes available at a low price, the demand for Fords will shift to the left. The effects of changes in tastes and incomes can be handled in a similar fashion. Increases in income and favorable changes in taste will shift the curve to the right, while decreases and unfavorable changes will shift it to the left. For some special goods, changes in income will have the opposite

1

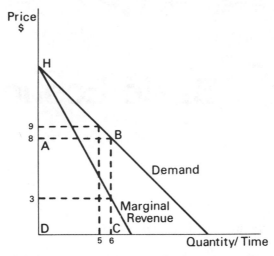

Figure 1.1. *Demand and Marginal Revenue Curves.*   The demand curve shows how many units of a particular good will be purchased per period of time at various prices, all else equal. The marginal revenue curve shows the increase in revenue that is obtained by the sale of the last unit. For example, the marginal revenue of the sixth unit is $3.00.

effect. For example, it is conceivable that, as a family's income goes up, it may buy less macaroni at every price, but such a case is the exception.

A demand curve exists for each good for each individual (or family) in an economy, its shape and position determined by income, tastes, and the prices of other goods. The market demand for a good is the horizontal summation of all of the demand curves for the individuals, and its shape and position in turn depend upon the composite of tastes, the distribution of income, and the prices of other goods.

One reason the demand curve of an individual is thought to have a negative slope is the law of diminishing marginal utility. Very simply, this economic law states that, as more and more units of a particular good are consumed, the value of each succeeding one decreases. Therefore, an individual will buy more of a certain good during a specified period only if the price is lowered. The market demand curve will exhibit a negative slope for the same reason and also because, as price decreases, not only will existing purchasers buy more but new purchasers will enter the market.

The demand curve shows how many units of a good will be sold per period at various prices. Alternatively, it shows the highest price per unit that can be obtained on the market for various outputs per period. For instance, in figure 1.1, at a price of $9.00, five units will be demanded each period. Or to look at it the other way, if a producer were to sell five units each period, the market price would be $9.00. In this sense the demand curve can be thought of as an average revenue curve, because it shows the average return to the firm for selling various amounts per period.

Another concept that will be useful in later analysis is *marginal revenue:* the change in total revenue provided by a change in production and sale of a unit of output. If a firm with the demand curve in figure 1.1 produces five units of output, the price of each will be $9.00, for a total revenue of $45.00. If the firm produces one more unit of output, the price falls to $8.00 and total revenue for the six units increases to $48.00. Whereas the price of the last unit sold is $8.00, the marginal revenue is only $3.00; $8.00 is gained by selling that extra unit, but $5.00 has been lost by the reduction in price—$1.00 for each unit that was previously sold at the higher price.

The curve labeled marginal revenue in figure 1.1 shows the relationship between this and quantity sold. Note that at every level of output, marginal revenue is less than price. It becomes negative at the point where the reduction in revenue caused by the decrease in price exceeds the increase due to the sale of an extra unit.

Although the two words are sometimes used in common, *demand* and *need* have separate meanings in economics. A demand is a need backed by purchasing power. The poor may have a need for more food but, given the way our market economy has distributed income, they do not have the money to purchase it. This point is important because, in all that follows, demand curves are used as indicators of what people are willing (and able) to pay for goods and hence what their relative values are. Granted, a change in income distribution may lead to a change in demand curves. Economists often take the existing distribution of income as given since they have no basis for selecting another. They then work to show how the economy can do better even if we are not free to change overall income distribution. Using the current distribution is a value judgment, just the same.

The market demand curve can thus be used to express the value to society of any level of production. In figure 1.1 note that, at a price of $8.00, six units would be sold per period. Total revenue from such a sale would be $48.00 per period. Therefore, the value to society of six units of production per period is at least $48.00, as represented by the area of rectangle *ABCD* in the figure. Actually, however, the value is greater than this. Notice that if the price were to increase to $9.00, five units would still be purchased; thus the consumers of these units place a value of at least $9.00 on each unit. At a price of $8.00 they are actually getting a bonus of at least $1.00, and this economists call *consumer's surplus*. It is the difference between the amount a person would be willing to pay for an item and what he actually has to pay for it in the market. Since the demand curve represents the maximum that will be paid for any quantity, the area between the demand curve and the price line represents consumer surplus. When six units are purchased at a price of $8.00, consumer surplus is represented by the area of triangle *ABH*. The total value to society of six units of production per period is the total revenue engendered by its sale, plus the consumer surplus. This is represented by the area of *HBCD*, the area under the demand curve to the left of six units of production.

Supply Curves

The supply curve can be defined in much the same fashion as the demand curve; it shows the amount of a good that will be offered for sale during a specified period at various prices, other influences on production held constant. It is normally thought to be upward sloping, indicating that more will be offered for sale at higher prices. The amount of a certain good offered for sale is also affected by such other considerations as the state of technology and the costs of inputs. The better the technology and the lower the input prices, the more will be offered for sale at every price, and vice versa.

To understand a supply curve, one must also look at the production function and the cost curves of a firm. The production function is the relationship between the amount of inputs used and the amount of output that results. Costs incurred in the production of goods include a "normal" return on investments of time and assets, as based upon an average over the whole economy. Total costs can be broken down into two categories; fixed and variable. Fixed costs remain constant regardless of the level of output; for example the purchase price or rent on a machine is the same regardless of production. On the contrary, variable costs are directly related to the level of output. For example, the costs of raw materials and maintenance increase with production. Just how variable cost changes with production can be ascertained from the production function by determining the types of inputs that must be increased and by how much to expand the level of production. Using this information and the prices of the variable inputs, the relationship between output and variable cost can be determined. Economists have shown that this relationship will always be of a predictable nature due to what they call the law of diminishing productivity. This economic law, sometimes called the law of diminishing returns, says that, as more variable inputs are added to a production process, the increase in production will shrink. Therefore, variable costs will increase and at an accelerating rate, as output is expanded. After the law of diminishing marginal productivity sets in, each additional unit of output will require more and more inputs for its production and will thus cost more than the previous one.

This information is displayed in a manner useful to our analysis in figure 1.2. The axes are the same as for the demand curve. The curve labeled marginal cost shows how total cost changes as production increases. For example, at four units of output, marginal cost is $7.00. This means that producing the fourth unit increased total costs by $7.00. The curve is upward sloping to the right because, due to the law of diminishing marginal productivity, each additional unit of output increases cost more than does the previous one. The two other curves in the diagram are the average variable cost curve and the

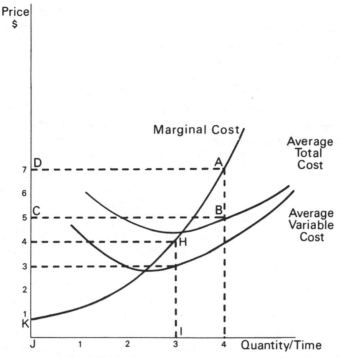

Figure 1.2. *Average and Marginal Cost Curves.* The average cost curve shows how average costs vary as output per period of time increases. The marginal cost curve shows the increase in cost that results from increasing output per period by one unit. For example, the marginal cost of producing the third unit is $4.00.

average total cost curve. The difference between the two is average fixed cost, which gets smaller as output increases because fixed cost is thus spread over more units. They both have a modified V shape, initially downward sloping due to decreases in average fixed cost but then turning upward, again due to the law of diminishing marginal productivity. If each additional unit increases total cost more than the previous one, this eventually will make up for the decreasing average fixed costs, and so average costs will increase. A point crucial to our analysis is that the marginal cost curve will always pass through the minimum of both the average curves. The logic behind this is as follows. If the last or marginal unit costs less to produce than the average of all previous units, then average cost must fall. On the other hand, if the marginal unit costs more to produce than the average of all previous units, then average costs will increase. Therefore, as long as the marginal cost is below an average cost, be it total or variable, the average will decrease, while if marginal cost is above the average, then the average must increase, which means that the marginal cost curve must intersect the average curves at their minimums.

One other aspect of the marginal cost curve that will be useful in the discussions to follow is that the area under the curve represents the total cost at that particular output. For example, in figure 1.2 the total cost of producing an output of three units equals the area of the polygon *KHIJ*. The logic behind this is that, since marginal cost is that of producing the last unit, the area under the curve must be the sum of costs for all individual units.

The above description of the cost curves of an individual firm is admittedly very brief. The interested reader may want to refer to much expanded explanations in other books listed in the bibliography, or he may elect simply to accept on faith that the laws of production will yield cost curves, as pictured in figure 1.2. Average variable cost and average total cost will initially decrease as output per period increases, but eventually they will rise. Marginal cost will for all practical purposes always be upward sloping and always intersect the average cost curves at their minimums.

The supply curve of the firm is simply that portion of the marginal cost curve lying above the average variable cost curve. Firms are in business to make a profit, so they will expand their production per period as long as the cost of doing so is less than the revenue earned. For example, at a price of $7.00, the profit-maximizing firm will produce four units of output per period. If it were to produce fewer, profit would not reach its maximum, since marginal cost at lower output levels would be less than the price. Expanding output by one more unit would gain more revenue than it would cost; therefore, it pays to expand output. On the other hand, to expand beyond four units would increase costs more than revenue. The latter would go up by $7.00 per unit, but the increase in cost beyond the fourth unit would be greater than that.

The same type of analysis applies at other price levels: the profit-maximizing firm will operate where price equals marginal cost. However, while this policy guarantees that profit will be as large as possible, it does not insure that it will be positive. To return to our examples, at a price of $7.00, the profit-maximizing output is four units. The average cost, including a normal return, of producing four units is only $5.00, resulting in a pure economic profit of $2.00 per unit. Total economic profit can be represented by the area of rectangle *ABCD* in figure 1.2. However, suppose that the price is equal to marginal cost where the latter crosses the minimum of the average total cost curve; then price will merely equal the average total cost, and economic profit will be reduced to zero. The firm will still be making a normal return so it will remain in operation. Any further reduction in price, however, will mean that it will equal marginal cost at a point where average cost is greater than price. This is the case in figure 1.2 when price is equal to $4.00. Note that, since average variable cost is only $3.00, in the short run it still makes sense for the firm to stay in operation. If it stops production completely, it will have to pay the fixed costs. But if it produces three units of output, it will earn $1.00 per unit above average variable costs—an insufficient sum to cover fixed costs completely, but better than not meeting them at all. In other words, as long as the firm can cover its out-of-pocket expenses it should remain in business. In the long run, however, if the price remains low, it would do better to sell its production facility, to cancel its leases, or to take similar steps toward stopping production all together.

Since the firm will produce at that point where price equals marginal cost as long as it is above average variable cost, this portion of the marginal cost curve is the supply curve of the firm. The industry or market supply curve is the horizontal summation of the marginal cost curves of all of the firms in a particular industry.

Economic Equilibrium

Figure 1.3 presents both a market demand and a market supply curve, and their point of intersection determines the equilibrium for price and quantity of the good in question. Recall from above that the market demand curve is the sum of the demand curves of individual consumers. Equilibrium occurs where price is $7.00 and output is four units per period, because producers are selling all they want to at that price at the same time that consumers are

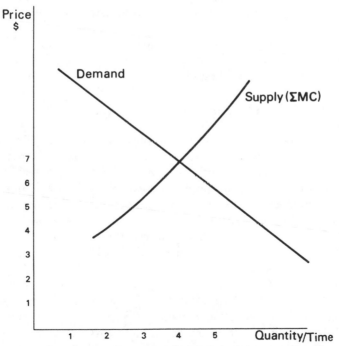

Figure 1.3. *Demand and Supply.*   The equilibrium price and quantity is determined by the intersection of the market demand and the market supply curves. In this case it occurs at a price of $7.00 and an output of four units per period of time.

purchasing all they want; thus both the price and the amount of production are stable. At no other price would this be true. At a higher price, producers would be willing to supply a larger quantity than consumers would purchase, and conversely at a lower price consumers would be willing to buy more than producers will want to sell.

Because the actions of buyers and sellers guarantee that this point will be reached, it is known as a stable equilibrium. If for some reason the price were to increase, the fact that more would be offered for sale than people would be willing to buy would motivate producers to lower prices back toward the equilibrium level. Such a decrease would cause consumers to buy more and producers to manufacture less, thus restoring equilibrium. On the other hand, if prices were to fall, an increased desire to purchase goods coupled with a decrease in production would create a situation where many who wanted to buy the good at the existing price would not be able to do so. They would therefore tend to bid up the price, and producers, observing many willing customers competing for their relatively small amounts of output, would more than likely up their asking price. As prices went up, the quantity demanded would again decrease and the quantity supplied would increase, thus restoring the original equilibrium. These movements away from the equilibrium price should be distinguished from changes in the shape or position of either the demand or the supply curve, since they lead to new equilibrium points for price and quantity.

In summary, demand and supply combine to determine equilibrium price and output. However, the logic behind these curves is somewhat more intricate than may appear at first glance.

The Operation of a Firm in a Competitive Industry

The above analysis of demand and supply glosses over many details of the determination of equilibrium price and quantity. To describe them more fully requires a closer consideration of the actions of the individual firm in a competitive industry. For our purposes, a *competitive industry* implies that enough firms are included so that no one of them can change industry supply enough to affect the price; that firms can enter and leave the industry with no restrictions; and that information as to prices is accessible to all. Assuming, for simplification, that all firms in an industry are identical, we can identify the operation of all on a single set of cost curves.

The operation of the individual firms and of the industry as a whole is represented in figure 1.4. Part a depicts the cost curves of a representative firm, while part b illustrates the demand and supply of the industry. In this context, it is most useful to consider the demand curve to be an average revenue curve. The price, or average revenue per unit sold at any point in time, is determined by the intersection of the market demand curve and the sum of the individual firms' marginal costs curves. If the number of firms is such that

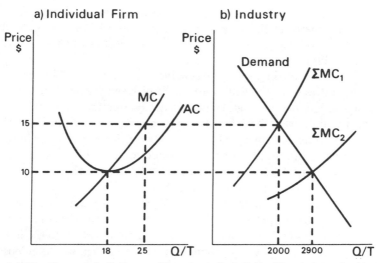

Figure 1.4. *The Firm and the Industry.* The price to the individual firm is determined by the intersection of the market demand and supply curves. The firm, in order to maximize profits, must operate where marginal cost is equal to this exogenously determined price.

ΣMC_1 is the industry supply curve, then the price will be $15.00. Since each firm is small relative to the whole industry and cannot affect price, it will accept $15.00 as a given price or a given return per unit and will produce 25 units of output per period. Industry output will be 2,000 units, and each firm will be making an economic profit since price is above average cost. At this point, other firms will be motivated to enter the industry and to take advantage of greater-than-normal profits. The industry supply curve now moves to the right, because the summation of cost curves embraces a larger number of firms. The industry price will therefore decrease as the industry supply curve intersects the market demand curve farther to the right. New entry will continue until price falls so that it intersects the marginal cost curve of the individual firm at the minimum of its average cost curve, at which level price will equal average cost and all firms will be earning only a normal profit. In terms of the diagram, entry of firms will continue until ΣMC_2 is the relevant industry supply curve. If for any reason the industry supply were to be to the right of this, firms would not be making normal profits at their profit-maximizing outputs; as a result, some firms would, in the long run, leave the industry and the supply curve would shift to the left until the losses were eliminated.

At this point the industry would be in a long-run equilibrium. Each firm would maximize its profit by producing 18 units for a total industry output of 2,900 units. Since new firms would no longer have incentive to enter the industry, nor would existing firms have reason to change the amount they produce, industry output would remain static.

In a perfectly competitive economy, all industries operate in the same way. Greater than normal returns attract investors to an industry while losses turn them elsewhere. In this way resources are shifted from one industry to another, and equilibrium for the whole economy occurs when all industries are in equilibrium.

Note that, due to the profit-maximizing behavior of individual firms, a purely competitive economy will produce the proper amount of each good at the lowest average cost possible. Firms will always operate where price equals marginal cost and, given the demand curve, the price represents what the last unit is worth to the consumer. Therefore, when price equals marginal cost, the last unit being produced has a market value equal to the cost of producing it. If any more is produced, marginal cost will be greater than price; that is, the last unit costs more than it is worth. If any less is produced, someone is willing to pay more for an extra unit than the cost of producing it. Therefore, the point where price equals marginal cost is actually the economically efficient amount of production. Extra resources are not allocated to the industry unless the value of the resulting production is greater than would be possible if they were used in any other industry. And since the entry or exit of firms from an industry will always guarantee that each firm is operating at the minimum of its average cost curve, this proper amount will be produced as cheaply as possible. It will be demonstrated later that this optimal allocation of resources does not occur in a perfectly competitive fishery.

The Production Possibility Curve, Indifference Curves, and General Economic Equilibrium

The Production Possibility Curve

Economics is the study of the allocation of scarce resources to fulfill unlimited wants. It investigates how the limited amounts of land, labor, capital, natural resources, and entrepreneurial ability available at any given time can be combined to best satisfy the desires of society. How a market economy achieves these ends can be described by the use of a simple model consisting of a production possibility curve and a set of indifference curves.

An example of a production possibility curve (hereafter called a PP curve) is pictured in figure 1.5. Assuming that an economy can produce only two goods, meat and wool, the PP curve shows the various combinations of these goods that can be produced during a specified amount of time, given the number and types of resources and the current state of technology. Alternatively, it shows the maximum amount of one good that can be produced during a period, given that a specified amount of the other is also produced. For example, if all resources are used to produce wool in the most efficient fashion, then 10 units will be produced. However, if six units of meat are produced, then only seven units of wool can be attained. A properly operating economy must produce a bundle of goods that lies directly on the PP curve. If

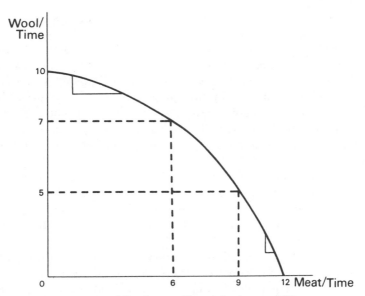

Figure 1.5. *The Production Possibility Curve.* The production possibility curve represents the possible combinations of products that an economy can produce in a given period of time with the existing supply of resources and capital equipment, and the state of technology. The only way for an efficiently operating economy to get more of one good is to reduce its production of another.

production falls inside the curve, resources are being wasted because more of at least one good can be turned out without affecting existing production. It would be impossible for the economy to operate outside the curve.

The curve is concave to the origin; that is, it becomes steeper as more meat is produced. The different inputs are not equally suitable to the production of meat or of wool. As more wool is produced, less satisfactory inputs must be used, and more of them will be required to produce each extra unit. The effect of this is demonstrated if we note that, when a small amount of meat is being produced, a reduction in wool output results in a substantial increase in meat. However, when meat production is near its maximum, the same reduction in wool output leads to only a small increase in meat. (Note the small triangles at both ends of the PP curve.)

The concept of opportunity cost can easily be explained by way of the PP curve. Note that if the economy is producing six units of meat and seven of wool, the only way it can increase its output of meat to nine is to decrease wool production to five. Only by a transfer of inputs from one product to the other can this be achieved. In this case, the opportunity cost of three units of meat (the increase from six to nine) is two units of wool (a decrease from seven to five). Notice also that the shape of the curve dictates that the opportunity cost of either good increases as more of it is produced.

The important concept of opportunity cost thus indicates that cost is not stated best in terms of dollars and cents but rather in terms of things that must be foregone. The dollar cost of an item is essentially a measure of the value of the things foregone.

For practical applications it should be stressed that movements along the PP curve are long-run phenomena. A reduction of wool production will permit an increase in meat only after some time lag has allowed the resources to be switched. For example, if, by government decree, the production of wool were to be cut from seven units to five on June 1, then on June 2 the economy would more than likely be producing five units of wool but only six of meat. Only after months, maybe years could the resources formerly used in wool be adapted to meat.

The PP curve for a nation represents the various combinations of goods that it has the ability to produce. But which combination will it produce? The answer depends in part on tastes, income distribution, and the type of economy. In a perfect market economy the composite desires of consumers will dictate what is produced.

This can be demonstrated in the following manner. Producers will provide that combination of goods that maximizes profit. Since we are talking about all producers combined, profit maximization occurs when revenue is maximized, given that all the resources are used properly. Total revenue depends on the relative prices for the two goods and on the actual amounts of each produced. Ignoring for the moment how relative prices are determined, total revenue for all the producers in our hypothetical economy can be represented by the following equation:

$$TR = P_m \cdot M + P_w \cdot W \qquad (1.1)$$

P_m and P_w represent the price of meat and wool, respectively, and M and W represent the units of the two goods that are produced. Given the prices, profit-maximizing producers will produce that combination of M and W which results in a maximum TR. In terms of the normal equation for a straight line, the above can be written as

$$W = \frac{TR}{P_w} - \frac{P_m}{P_w} M \qquad (1.2)$$

TR/P_w is the vertical intercept and $-(P_m / P_w)$ is the slope of the line. Three total revenue lines and a PP curve are drawn in figure 1.6. All the lines have the same relative prices, but TR_3 has a greater total revenue than does TR_2. Similarly, the revenue on TR_2 is greater than that on TR_1. Actually, there is a whole family of TR lines, one for each possible total revenue. Producers will operate at that point on the PP curve that will be on the highest possible TR line. Therefore, given the relative prices represented by the slopes of the TR curves, the producers in this economy will maximize total revenue by producing M_2 units of meat and W_2 units of wool. They cannot produce any combination on TR_3, and although they can produce two combinations on TR_1, the other mix will earn a higher revenue.

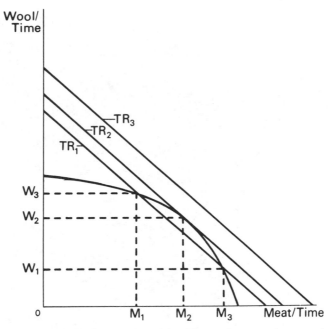

Figure 1.6. *Maximizing the Value of Production.* The maximum total revenue from sales at given prices will occur at that point on the production possibility curve where the ratio of the prices is equal to the slope of the curve.

At the production point, the slope of the PP curve will be equal to the slope of the *TR* line. Therefore, the slope of the PP curve at that point will be equal to $- (P_m / P_w)$.

Indifference Curves

Since relative prices are determined by the actions of buyers and sellers, we must also look on the consumption side of the market behavior. The indifference curve is a tool used by economists to study consumer behavior. Each curve is a locus of points representing combinations of goods that yield equal satisfaction to the consumer. Two such curves are plotted in figure 1.7. Actually, there is a curve through every point in the graph. Since points A and B lie on the same indifference curve, six units of wool and four units of meat will give the same amount of satisfaction or welfare as would five units of wool and seven units of meat. In other words, if the consumers are at point B, a decrease of three units of meat can be compensated for by an increase of one unit of wool. Since I_2 represents a higher level of satisfaction than does I_1, the bundle of goods represented by point D yields more satisfaction than do those at A and B. Similarly, any combinations of goods below I_1 will yield less satisfaction.

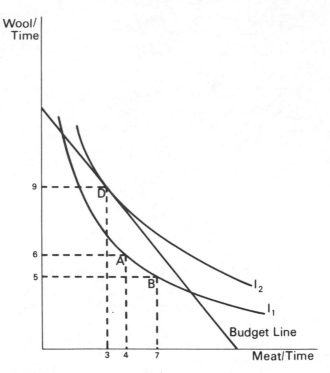

Figure 1.7. *The Indifference Curve and the Budget Line.*   Consumer satisfaction will be maximized at that point on the budget line that touches the highest indifference curve possible. At this point the slope of the indifference curve will equal the ratio of the prices.

The curves for normal goods are always downward sloping, indicating that if the amount of one good is decreased, total satisfaction can remain unchanged only if the amount of the other is increased. The slope of the curve at any one point measures the willingness to trade one good for the other at that particular consumption bundle. Indifference curves are convex to the origin (i.e., they become less steep as the amount of meat consumed per period increases) because, as people get more and more of one good, they require increasingly larger amounts of it to compensate them for equal reductions of the other. The exact curvature and position of the family of indifference curves depend upon the tastes and income distribution of the economy.

Given a certain amount of money to spend, consumers will buy that combination of goods yielding the highest satisfaction. The straight line in figure 1.7 is a budget constraint line, representing the various combinations of goods that can be purchased with the size of the budget and relative prices predetermined. The larger the budget, the farther the budget line will be from the origin. The slope of the line indicates the price ratio. Note that the budget line is somewhat analogous to the total revenue line.

The budget line in figure 1.7 indicates that consumers will maximize their welfare by purchasing consumption bundle D because no other point available to them is on a higher indifference curve. At this point, the slope of the indifference curve equals the price ratio.

General Equilibrium

Since revenue earned by producers eventually ends up as earnings to consumers, the total revenue line is also the budget constraint for an economy. The economy will be in equilibrium when producers are willing to supply the same amount of goods as consumers wish to purchase. This can be graphically portrayed by juxtaposing a set of indifference curves with a PP curve, as in figure 1.8. The only possible equilibrium point is B, where the slope of the PP curve equals the slope of the indifference curve at that point. The equilibrium price ratio will be the slope common to both curves. Notice that, at the equilibrium point, welfare reaches its maximum, given the production possibilities of the economy. That is, I_2, the indifference curve through point B, is the highest one that can be reached, given the PP curve. Note also that, be-

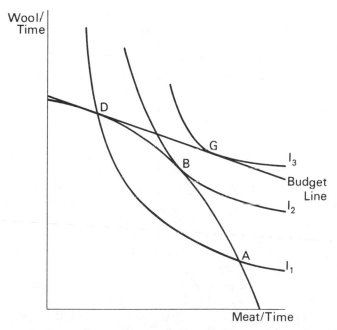

Figure 1.8. *General Equilibrium in an Economy.* A general market equilibrium will occur when, at the existing prices, the production bundle that will maximize revenue for producers will also maximize consumer satisfaction. This will occur where the production possibility curve touches the highest indifference curve possible. Therefore, in a "perfectly" operating market economy, consumer satisfaction will be maximized.

cause the slope of the PP curve is equal to the slope of the indifference curve at B, the opportunity cost of one good in terms of the other is just equal to the ratio at which people are willing to trade these goods. What people are willing to pay in terms of foregone consumption is equal to what the good cost in terms of foregone production. In this flexible priced model, this is equivalent to the maximization of the value of production, where value is based on willingness to pay.

To see why point B is an equilibrium and why a free market economy will always operate there, consider the following. Assume that the price ratio is such that the producers wish to operate at point D. Given that level of income, consumers will wish to purchase bundle G (an impossibility, given the PP curve), which contains more M and less W. This increased demand for meat will bid its price up, while the decreased demand for wool is causing its price to fall. As the slope of the price line $-(P_m / P_w)$ becomes steeper, producers will adjust production accordingly until point B is reached. Similarly, if the price ratio happened to lead to production at point A, the action of consumers would change the price ratio until point B was reached. At that point, everything produced is being sold, no further pressure is exerted on prices, and the economy has no impetus to move from point B.

It has been shown that a market-oriented economy will base its decisions of what to produce chiefly on the desires of the consumers, who always try to buy the consumption bundle that maximizes their welfare. In seeking to earn the largest returns to themselves by satisfying the market demand, profit-conscious suppliers will also produce the bundle that best serves the welfare of the economy. As the analysis to follow will demonstrate, the open-access fishery will not operate so as to maximize the welfare of the economy.

Present Value

The present value of a stream of future income is an important economic concept that allows for comparisons of money at different points in time. There will be cause to use it during the discussion of the proper intertemporal management of a fishery.

Money to be received in the future is not the same as a similar amount received today, since money in hand can be loaned out at interest. The interest rate (sometimes called the discount rate) can therefore be used as a means of comparing the value of money at different points in time. For example, if the interest rate is 5 percent, it is clear that $105 to be achieved a year from now will be no more valuable than $100 received today, since (other aspects of the market held constant) the $100 can be loaned out at interest to return $105 at the end of a year. Further, today's $100 is as valuable as $110.25 two years in the future, since the $105 earned by the end of the first year would return an additional $5.25 interest in the second year. As a corollary, $105 to be received a year from now, plus $110.25 two years from now, would yield a present value of $200.

To use simple algebraic terms, the amount of money available at the end of one year (call it X_1) when X dollars are loaned out at r percent will be:

$$X_1 = X(1 + r)$$

For the amount of money available at the end of two years, the equation reads:

$$X_2 = X(1 + r)(1 + r) = X(1 + r)^2$$

Similarly, the value at the end of three years will be:

$$X_3 = X(1 + r)^3$$

In general, then, we say that the amount of money available after loaning X dollars out at r percent for n years will be:

$$X_n = X(1 + r)^n$$

Solving this equation for X yields:

$$X = \frac{X_n}{(1 + r)^n}$$

which shows the relationship between the values of money in the future and in the present: X_n dollars n years from now is worth only X dollars in the present, because X dollars loaned out at the existing interest rate will return X_n dollars after n years. In formal terms, X is the present value of X_n dollars n years from now. For example, the present value of $2,500 five years from now at a 5 percent interest rate is:

$$\frac{\$2500}{(1.05)^5} = \frac{\$2500}{1.2762} = \$1958$$

A higher discount rate would lead to a lower present value, and vice versa.

The present value of a stream of income in the future is the sum of the present values of each of them. For example, the present value of $100 a year every year for the next four years starting right now is:

$$\$100 + \frac{100}{1.05} + \frac{100}{(1.05)^2} + \frac{100}{(1.05)^3}$$

This simplifies to:

$$\$100 + \$95.23 + \$90.70 + \$86.38 = \$372.31$$

Notice that the present value of the $100 is lower, the farther in the future it will be received.

In general, the equation for the present value of a stream of future income is:

$$P.V. = X_0 + \frac{X_1}{(1 + r)} + \frac{X_2}{(1 + r)^2} + \frac{X_3}{(1 + r)^3} \cdots + \frac{X_n}{(1 + r)^n}$$

The subscript refers to the number of years in the future and r is the interest rate.

A Final Word on Economic Models

The economic models presented here contain many simplifications. For instance, contrary to our assumptions, many industries in our economy actually are comprised of only a few large firms, each of which can therefore influence price by changing its supply. Also, firms cannot enter and leave industries as easily as has been assumed, and any economy obviously does produce more than two goods. Nonetheless, these models not only are useful for providing concise descriptions of certain economic concepts but are also surprisingly accurate in predicting behavior of the players on the economic stage and also in formulating policy recommendations. When specific situations to be analyzed are completely at odds with the assumptions, the models of course have to be changed accordingly.

Readers interested in a more complete description of the theoretical economics discussed only briefly here may find the following a very good reference:

Paul Samuelson, and William D. Nordhaus. 1985. *Economics, Twelfth Edition*. New York: McGraw-Hill.

2

Fundamentals of Fisheries Economics

Introduction

What is a fishery? There is no generally accepted definition, but for purposes of this study a fishery can be thought of as a stock or stocks of fish and the enterprises that have the potential of exploiting them. For precision in the discussions that follow, unless otherwise specified, the introductory analysis will be in terms of a fleet that exploits only one biologically independent stock. More realistic but more complex situations will be discussed in later sections. With regard to the stock of fish, the crucial variables to consider are its size and growth rate, the latter of which is dependent upon reproduction, individual growth, and mortality. For the enterprises, total fishing effort and catch and the costs and revenues associated with them are the primary variables. Fishing effort deserves further comment at this point. Sometimes called fishing power, it is a measure of the number of boats (in some cases the number of traps, etc.), their catching power, their spatial distribution, the time spent fishing, the skill of the crew, etc. Obviously this is a complex concept, the exact formulation depending upon biological and economic characteristics of the fishery involved. At this point it is only necessary to conceive of it as the effect of the factors of production that are applied to the stock. Some of the problems involved in obtaining a useful proxie for effort for empirical studies will be discussed in the context of the analysis to follow. This chapter will develop the basic elements of an economic analysis of a fishery, using elementary concepts of population dynamics as the basis.

The Production Function in a Fishery

Recall from chapter 1 that a production function is the relationship between the amount of inputs used and the amount of resultant product. In terms of a fishery, it is the relationship between the effort applied and the fish caught. We will talk about two kinds of production functions, and both will be important to the analysis that follows. The short-run production function or short-run yield curve is the relationship between catch and effort for a given population level. The long-run production function, or sustainable yield curve, is the relationship between effort and the amount of catch that can be harvested period after period without affecting the stock. The purpose of this section will be to derive basics of these two curves and to explain their meaning in more detail. Knowing their biological and technical underpinnings will make the analysis to follow more meaningful.

The production function in a fishery depends on the reproductive biology of the fish stock. (A fish stock does not necessarily include all the fish of a particular species. More than one biologically independent stock of any species may exist.) A simple biological theory of population dynamics is the Schaefer logistic analysis, where the growth of the fish stock measured in weight is assumed to be a function of its size in weight (see Schaefer 1954, 1957a, 1959). Because this assumption is useful in describing the main relationships involved, it will be used in spite of its somewhat limited applicability. It should be noted, however, that other types of growth can and do occur. For instance, in the Gulf of Mexico shrimp fishery, there is an annual crop of shrimp the size of which is dependent upon varying ecological factors but not significantly upon the previous year's population. Further, even when the Schaefer analysis does hold, a model designed for a specific fishery will not necessarily hold for any other. Bearing these points in mind, let us proceed with a general description of this type of growth. Other types will be discussed in chapter 4.

The biomass of an unexploited fish stock will tend to increase at various rates, depending upon its size, and will grow toward some maximum weight that, once reached, will be maintained. This population size will be termed the *natural equilibrium size*.

Salinity, temperature, prevailing currents, numbers and feeding habits of other species of fish, the amount of radiated solar energy, the rate of photosynthesis, and the rate at which mineral elements are replaced are some of the vitally important environmental parameters in determining this natural equilibrium size and the rate of growth in approaching it. In the following analysis these factors will be assumed constant, although in some cases the influence of changes in them will be considered. Given these parameters, the three components in the growth rate of a fish stock are: (1) recruitment, the biomass weight of fish entering the catchable population during the time period; (2) individual growth, the biomass weight of the growth of individual fish within the population during the time period; and (3) natural mortality, the biomass weight of fish lost from the population due to natural death and predation during the time period. For purposes of discussion, assume the time period to be one year. Recruitment and individual growth add to the stock size while mortality diminishes it.

In the Schaefer analysis, it is assumed that the net increase in biomass of a fishery as a function of population, taking all three of the above relationships into consideration, can be depicted as a bell-shaped curve, as in figure 2.1. (Ignore for the moment the broken lines.) The horizontal axis measures population size and the vertical axis growth per period, both in terms of weight. For instance, when the population equals P_3, net increase in size or growth will equal F_3. At small stock sizes, the net effect of recruitment and individual growth is greater than natural mortality, and natural increase is positive and increases with stock size. At some intermediate level the rate of growth begins to fall off as the stock continues to grow, because mortality

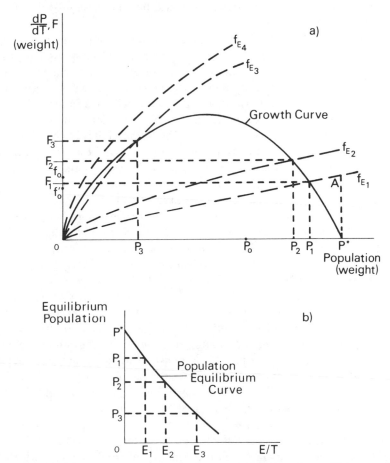

Figure 2.1. *Population Equilibrium Analysis.* For any level of effort, the equilibrium population will occur at that size where the catch rate is equal to growth. At higher levels of effort, the catch curve is shifted up. As diagrammed in this simple case, therefore, the equilibrium population size decreases as effort increases. The population equilibrium curve in figure 2.1b is derived from the relevant intersections in figure 2.1a.

becomes relatively more powerful. Eventually a point will be reached where recruitment and individual growth are just balanced by natural mortality, and stock growth will cease. The strengths of these different forces may vary according to the species, but in general the growth curve will retain its bell shape, although in some cases the right-hand side may asymptotically approach the horizontal axis in a more or less skewed manner. This case will be discussed in chapter 4.

According to the figure, $P*$ is the stock size where recruitment and individual growth are just matched by natural mortality. Therefore, population size will no longer increase, and this will be the natural equilibrium population. At any smaller population, growth will continue and so population size will increase. At larger populations, there will be a negative growth rate and so population size will fall.

In an actual fish stock, the growth rate at any level of population will vary over some range. Therefore, this growth curve should be thought of as an average over time. In fact, it should be thought of as an average with a high degree of variability, primarily due to the wide dispersion of recruitment. Similarly, the natural equilibrium population size will be a range rather than a point. In the interest of simplification, this distinction will sometimes be ignored in what follows. However, one of the fundamental issues of fisheries utilization is the year-to-year variability in stock size and the effect, if any, of human predation on this variability. Bearing these points in mind, the Schaefer growth curve is still a useful frame upon which to build the analysis. More complicated issues will be covered in later sections.

When man begins to exploit any fishery, he becomes another predator to disturb the population equilibrium. A new equilibrium then will be achieved at that level of population where the net increase in weight from natural factors just equals the net decrease due to fishing mortality. At any point in time, catch or fishing mortality will be a function of (1) the amount of fishing effort, as defined above, that man applies to the fishery, and (2) the size of the stock. For any given population size, the higher the effort, the larger will be the catch; and for any given level of effort, the larger the population, the larger will be the catch. Graphically, then, mortality due to fishing can be plotted as a function of effort if population is held constant or as a function of population if effort is held constant. Obviously, the shape and position of either curve will change if the constant is changed. During the course of this explanation, we will have reason to use both of these types of curves.

Since catch varies with the level of effort, a different equilibrium population size will result at each level of effort. This is important because effort is a variable controlled by man. Catch is a function of stock size and effort, but since equilibrium stock size is a function of effort, then sustainable yield is a function of effort only. It will prove useful then in this description of the sustainable yield curve to analyze in more detail the relationship between effort and equilibrium population size. It can be derived by use of the growth curve and the set of curves that shows how man-made mortality (or catch) varies with population. This is done in figure 2.1. The four dotted curves represent the amount of fishing mortality measured in weight that will occur during the period at various population sizes, each for a different level of effort. (It is legitimate to plot these catch functions and the growth curve on the same diagram because in both cases the independent variable is population size and the dependent variable is a change in biomass measured in weight over a given period.) For instance, if population is equal to P^*, at fishing level E_1 (which is assumed to be less than E_2, catch will be f_0 units. Similarly, if population were P_1, the catch would be F_1.

If man exerts E_1 units of effort over an extended period of time, the population will reach a new equilibrium at P_1. To see this, note that at population level P^* the catch for the period would be f_0. Since population growth is zero at P^*, population will fall by the amount of the catch. For the sake of argument, let the new population be P_2. At this population, catch will be f_0' and net natural increase will be F_2. Since catch is less than natural growth for the period, the population will increase. This type of fluctuation will continue until population P_1 is reached. At higher levels of population, growth will be less than catch, so population will decrease; at lower levels, growth will be greater than catch, so population will increase. At P_1, however, catch just equals growth, and so stock size will not change. All of the above assumes a constant level of effort of E_1. If it increases to E_2, the population will be in equilibrium at P_2, because only there will growth equal catch for the given level of effort. Likewise, the equilibrium population size for E_3 is P_3.

For each level of effort, then, there is an equilibrium population size. As long as the curves are as drawn in figure 2.1a, an inverse relationship is established between effort and equilibrium population size. The curve that plots the relationship (call it the population equilibrium curve) is shown in figure 2.1b.

The catch obtained from a level of effort and its corresponding equilibrium population is called a sustainable, or a sustained, yield. It is sustainable because population size will not be affected by fishing, since catch is replaced by natural increase. Therefore, the same level of effort will yield the same catch in the next period. The locus of points representing sustainable yield catches for each level of effort is called the sustainable, or sustained, yield curve. For our hypothetical fishery, such a curve is shown as the solid line in figure 2.2a. The vertical axis measures catch in weight, and the horizontal axis measures effort. (E_1, E_2 and E_3, like F_1, F_2, and F_3, are analogous to those explained for figure 2.1a.)

As a demonstration of the meaning of the curve, consider the following. At E_1 the point F_1 is a sustainable catch because F_1 is also the growth rate for P_1, the equilibrium stock size when effort equals E_1. A more complete description of the derivation of this curve is contained in the appendix to chapter 3, but for the moment note that, as effort increases, sustainable catch at

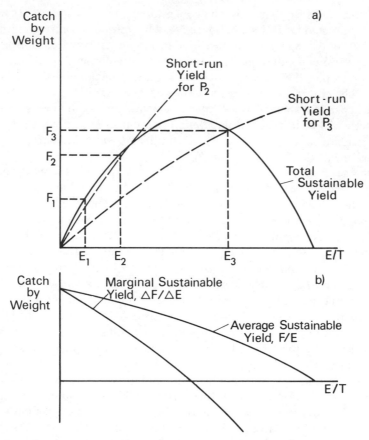

Figure 2.2. *The Sustainable Yield Curves.*   The total sustainable yield curve shows the catch that will be forthcoming from any given level of effort once the equilibrium population size for that level of effort has been achieved. P_3 is the equilibrium population size for E_3 units of effort. The average and marginal sustainable yield curves follow directly from total sustainable yield.

first rises but ultimately falls. Basically, this is for reasons already explained: as effort increases, the equilibrium level of population falls; and as population falls, the natural growth that has at first increased will ultimately decline. And since sustained yield equals natural growth, as effort is increased, sustained yield will at first increase but will ultimately decline. Specifically, an increase in effort from F_1 to E_2 reduces the equilibrium population size but accelerates natural increase and so sustainable yield increases. On the other hand, an increase in effort in the neighborhood of E_3 reduces the stock in the range where it will cause natural growth to decrease, and so sustainable yield will decrease. (For the moment assume that, if effort expands far enough, sustainable yield will fall to zero since the population will be destroyed. Several sections of chapter 4 deal with more realistically complicated assumptions, but our present task is to become familiar with the basic workings and conclusions of the model, leaving refinements for later consideration.)

The sustainable yield curve shows the relationship between effort and total sustainable yield. While this total is an important concept, the economic analysis to follow focuses largely on average sustainable and marginal sustainable yields. Curves for these are plotted in figure 2.2b. Notice that average sustainable yield, which is sustainable yield per unit effort or F/E, falls continuously until it reaches zero at the same level of effort as does total sustained yield. Marginal sustained yield, which is the change in sustained yield due to a change in effort (or $\Delta F/\Delta E$ where Δ represents "a change in"), is positive but declining at low levels of effort, reaches zero at the level of effort that obtains maximum sustainable yield, then turns negative, and becomes increasingly so at higher levels of effort. This means that, at lower levels of effort each additional unit of effort applied to the fishery will add a positive increment to the catch, although the size of this increment lessens as the total amount of effort is increased and that, beyond maximum sustainable yield, additional units of effort actually decrease sustainable catch.

It should be pointed out that the size of the average fish caught decreases as effort expands, due to the increased probability of catch before full individual growth can occur. This can have an effect on the economic analysis to follow if price varies with size of individual, but it will be ignored here. For a more detailed discussion of this point and its ramifications see Gates (1974).

In the economic analysis to follow, the sustained yield curve will be considered the long-run production function of the fishery. That is, it will show the quantity of fish that can be "produced" on a sustained basis at various levels of effort. The temporal aspect of the curve should be remembered, however: changes in effort will lead to a change in the equilibrium level of population, but time will elapse before that new equilibrium is reached. This means, for example, that if effort is increased from E_1 to E_2, only after the population has adjusted will the yield change from F_1 to F_2. Immediately after the increase in effort, catch will increase slightly and will only gradually approach F_2 as the stock size decreases (see below).

In cases where this time lag is important to our discussion, yield curves for specified levels of population will be used as short-run production functions for the fishery. The dotted curves in figure 2.2a are examples, showing the catch that will be forthcoming from given levels of population for various levels of effort. (They are the reverse of the catch and population curves for specified levels of effort used in figure 2.1a.) A different curve is needed for each population size; of the two shown, the higher is for the larger population. P_2 and P_3 are the same as in figure 2.1.

Since a sustainable yield occurs where catch equals the natural growth of the fish stock, these curves will intersect the sustainable yield curve at the level of catch equal to the growth rate for the specified population. For example, population P_3 has a growth rate equal to F_3 (see figure 2.1a), but F_3 is also the catch that will be forthcoming when E_3 units of effort are applied to that population. Therefore, operating on the short-run yield curve for P_3 at E_3 units of effort will lead to a sustainable yield, so this point will lie on the sustainable yield curve. Similarly, population P_2 has a growth rate of F_2; when E_2 units of effort are applied to that population, the catch will equal the growth rate, and this point on the short-run yield curve for P_2 will also, therefore, appear on the sustainable yield curve.

These curves can be used to describe more fully the process of moving from one point on the sustainable yield curve to another. Consider a fishery operating on the sustainable yield curve at E_3 units of effort. Catch and growth will equal F_3, and population will equal P_3. If effort were decreased to E_2 then, for a stock size of P_3, catch would fall to an amount slightly greater than F_1. (See the short-run yield curve for P_3 in figure 2.2a.) Given the population, this implies a short-run decrease in catch. Therefore, population must increase, since catch will be less than growth at P_3. Population will continue to grow until it reaches P_2, because when E_2 is applied to that population, catch will equal growth again. The absolute size of growth and catch will have changed because of the change in the level of population, but they will still be equal to each other. An increase in effort from E_3 will cause catch to exceed growth at P_3, so population will decrease until it again reaches an equilibrium.

This is the process by which the population adapts to changes in the level of effort. At a sustainable yield, catch equals growth, but when effort is changed, the size of the catch varies from that equality. Therefore, population size will change until a new equilibrium is established at the point where growth again becomes equal to catch.

The sustainable yield curve, its average and marginal curves, the short-run curves for given populations, and the process of moving from one point on the sustainable yield curve to another will all be keys to unlock the economic concepts in the following discussions. To be sure of their usage, the reader may find it helpful at this point to redraw the diagrams on scratch paper, studying their interrelationships.

It should be remembered, in all that follows, however, that these are at best only average relationships. The growth rate and equilibrium population sizes of even a single stock of fish is a very complex phenomenon that cannot really be pinned down to a precise mathematical function and perhaps can only be expressed in stochastic terms. One should not read too much into the above as far as man's ability to control the biomass. There are so many other environmental factors affecting recruitment, individual growth, and natural mortality that they often can overpower any effect a change in man-made mortality can have on the net growth of a stock. Nevertheless, the concepts of these sections can prove extremely useful if interpreted with care.

The Basic Economic Model of a Fishery

The Open-Access Equilibrium Yield

It has been shown that a fish stock will reach an equilibrium population level for a given amount of effort. The purpose of this section is to show how the costs and revenues of fishing will determine an equilibrium level of effort. A main part of the analysis is the linkage between the process of determining the equilibrium level of effort and the process of arriving at an equilibrium population size. It will also be shown that the amount of effort provided by an unregulated fishery will be suboptimal to the welfare of society as a whole. The remaining sections of this chapter will expand and clarify the basic points raised.

The following model presents the fundamentals of the analysis of an unregulated fishery open to the exploitation of many similar boats. Using the sustained yield curve derived above and the simplifying assumption that the price of fish and the cost of effort are constant, the long-run relationship between total revenue and effort and total cost and effort are pictured in figure 2.3a. As in chapter 1, cost includes a normal return to labor and capital.

It will be assumed that industry cost is equivalent to opportunity cost. In some fisheries, however, this may not be the case. Such things as fuel, bait, and food for the crew could easily be put to use in other segments of the economy, so market price is a good measure of their opportunity cost. This is not so, however, for much of the labor force in the fishing industry. Many fishermen are not equipped for other types of work, and, additionally, they are geographically isolated from other sources of employment. The incomes received from fishing are usually not a good measure of their opportunity cost but are often just the amount necessary to keep them working. This amount may vary among individuals, but it is a function of the age, pride, risk-taking tendencies, and other personal attributes of fishermen and of the amount of welfare payments or retraining and/or relocation aid available to those who decide to quit fishing. The opportunity cost of the labor as far as the economy is concerned is a function of average age and skill levels of the fishermen, of unemployment in the local area and in the nation, and of existing industries in the local area. In terms of formal economic analysis, as discussed in the introduction and chapter 1, it represents the larger of two sums: (1) the value, in terms of consumers' willingness to pay, of what that labor will produce in its next-best alternative without retraining, and (2) the net value of what it could produce after retraining, taking into account the cost of retraining and the expected useful life of the newly attained skill. It should be obvious that, at best, such a measure will not be easy to attain and that almost insuperable problems are posed by any attempt to measure opportunity costs over time in assessing the proper intertemporal use of the fish stock.

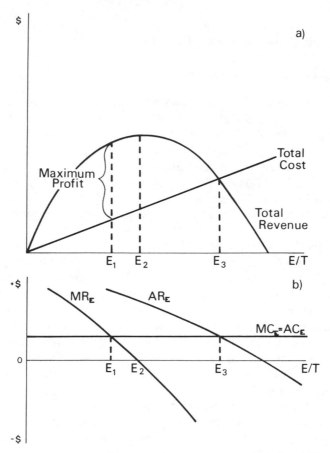

Figure 2.3. *Open Access and Maximum Economic Yield.* Open-access equilibrium yield occurs at E_3 where total revenue is equal to total cost (i.e., where average revenue equals average cost). Maximum sustainable profit occurs at E_1, where the difference between the total revenue and total cost curves is a maximum. This will occur where the marginal revenue curve intersects the marginal cost curve.

If opportunity cost is less than the income of labor, then industry cost will overestimate opportunity cost and the policy implications of what follows will have to be modified appropriately.

To return to the main argument, the total revenue curve has the same shape as the sustained yield curve because the constant price of fish implies that total revenue varies directly with catch. The cost curve is a straight line, indicating that cost for the fishery as a whole increases in direct proportion to effort. In other words, each additional boat, when operated in the most efficient manner, can be added to the fishery at the same cost as was the previous one. Both curves are long-run phenomena: the revenue curve being based on the sustained yield curve, and the cost curve assuming that extra effort is produced by new boats operating in an efficient manner rather than by existing boats expanding their effort.

The curves for marginal revenue, average revenue, and marginal cost associated with these total curves are pictured in figure 2.3b. Marginal revenue, which shows the change in revenue resulting from a change in the production of effort, is downward sloping because the marginal catch per unit of effort decreases as greater intensity of fishing develops. Average revenue, which shows revenue per unit at each level of effort, is downward sloping because average catch per unit of effort declines under the same conditions. These revenue curves are, in effect, monetized versions of the yield curves in figure 2.2. The marginal cost curve, which shows the change in cost due to a change in effort, is, by assumption, constant and therefore equal to average cost per unit of effort.

With no regulation, the equilibrium level of effort in the fishery will be E_3, where total revenue equals total costs. It is also the point where average revenue per unit of effort equals average cost per unit of effort. To see why this is an equilibrium, consider any level of effort to the left of E_3. Total revenue for the fishery as a whole is greater than total cost; therefore, each boat will earn profits. To put it another way, to the left of E_3, average revenue per unit of effort is greater than average cost per unit of effort. This state of affairs will not only encourage existing boats to expand their effort; it will also motivate new boats to enter the fishery. Now consider a level of effort greater than E_3, where total costs are greater than total revenues. The boats will be suffering losses. Average cost per unit of effort will be greater than average revenue per unit; therefore, each boat will decrease its effort, and some may leave the fishery. (A more complete discussion of this process of entry and exit will be found in the next section.) Since effort will tend to increase below E_3 and to decrease above it, the equilibrium level of effort in an open-access fishery will settle at this point, hereafter to be referred to as the open-access equilibrium yield.

Since any point on the sustained yield curve is a biological equilibrium, the yield thus established will provide equilibrium in both an economic and a biological sense. It can be called a bionomic equilibrium. The level of effort will not change unless price or cost changes; and as long as effort remains constant, the population will not change.

The above analysis, which draws on the sustained yield curve, provides an overly simple picture of open-access exploitation because it ignores the year-to-year changes in the process of obtaining an equilibrium. This equilibrium may be only a theoretical construct that, if taken too literally, may provide a confusing basis for understanding fisheries management. It will be useful, both for its own sake and as a preface to discussing optimal management, to look at the dynamics of fisheries utilization.

Recall that a fish population does not adjust immediately to a change in effort but may take several periods to do so. More precisely, stock size one year in the future depends upon the cumulative effects of natural mortality, individual growth, recruitment, and fishing mortality, and only in those cases where their net effect is zero will stock size remain the same. Also, boats do not enter or leave a particular fishery instantaneously. If a particular fishery is providing profits to the boats involved, interested observers may delay entry to make sure that it was not just a lucky year; or they may need some time to obtain a boat and begin to fish. Thus profits may exist for several periods with no significant impact on effort. Comparably, once a fishery begins to suffer losses, individual boats are even more hesitant to leave. Among several reasons for this, the first is purely economic: as long as nothing else can be done with the boats—and if returns are large enough to pay for the variable costs (gas, repair of nets, etc.) and still provide some return to the boat owner—it makes sense to continue to fish. He will not be covering all of his costs, but he would lose even more by shutting down completely. (This is analogous to the discussion in chapter 1 of how the supply curve of a firm is represented by the marginal cost curve above average variable costs.) Also, the fisherman may be a gambler waiting for the big catch, or he may be "romantically" tied to the sea. Since the fishery can be in true equilibrium only when no tendency exists for either the population or the amount of effort to change, it is useful to consider how changes in these variables take place.

By adding the short-run revenue curves that correspond to the short-run production curves discussed above, it is possible to investigate in a rather simplistic form the dynamic aspects of reaching an equilibrium in an open-access fishery (see chapter 4 for a more formal discussion of dynamics). Figure 2.4 resembles those used earlier except for the addition of short-run revenue curves, R^*, R_2, R_3, and R_4. The first of these shows the relationship between revenue and effort, given that the population is in long-run natural equilibrium, or level P^* in figure 2.1. This revenue curve is derived directly from the short-run yield curve when population equals P^*. The short-run revenue curves, R_2, R_3, and R_4, correspond to populations P_2, P_3, and P_4 (the latter of which is not shown in figure 2.1 but is smaller than P_3). The sustained revenue curve is derived from the sustained yield curve. Figure 2.4 is similar to figure 2.2a except that the yield curves (both the sustained yield and the yields for particular populations) are expressed in monetary terms.

The following is a hypothetical case of the exploitation of a fishery, taking into account these dynamic aspects and the extra problems they can cause. When the fishery is first exploited, since the stock is at the natural equilibrium population, R^* is the relevant revenue curve for the period. Effort will tend to expand toward E_4, where the curve for short-run revenue intersects that for cost. For the sake of argument, assume that, during the first period, effort is somewhere between E_3 and E_4. Since the natural growth rate is zero at P^* and yet a positive catch results from this range of effort, stock size will decrease. Meanwhile, effort is earning a profit and so will provide an incen-

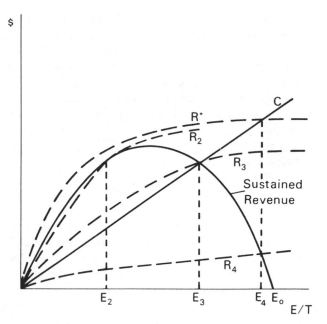

Figure 2.4. *Simple Dynamics.* A biological and economic equilibrium occurs if, at the existing level of effort, catch equals growth so the population will not change and at the same time revenue equals cost so the amount of effort will not change. If either of these conditions does not hold, then the population size or the level of effort will change.

tive for more boats to enter the fishery. At this disequilibrium point, population will be falling and effort will tend to rise.

Now assume that in the next period the population falls to P_3 so that R_3 becomes the short-run revenue curve. Also assume that effort increases to E_4, and recall that a short-run yield curve intersects the sustained yield curve at that level of effort which will obtain a catch equal to the growth rate at that particular population size. The same analysis holds true for sustained and short-run revenue curves. Therefore, since R_3 intersects the sustained revenue curve at E_3, the combination of a population of P_3 and an effort of E_4 will lead to a catch greater than growth, and population will continue to fall. Effort will now also tend to diminish, since cost is greater than revenue at this combination of effort and population (i.e., R_3 lies below the cost curve at E_4). As the next step, assume that the following period finds population falling to P_4 but that fishermen decide to stick it out for another year and so effort does not change.

At this combination of effort and population, the fishery will be operating on the sustained revenue curve; thus, population will not change. The continued losses, however, will increase the trend towards lower levels of effort. To make a long story short, suppose that it now falls to E_3, where catch will fall below natural growth rate and so stock size will increase, causing the short-run revenue curves gradually to approach R_3. At this combination of effort and population, E_3 and P_3, biological and economic equilibrium will occur simultaneously. Catch will equal growth, so the population will not change; and revenue will equal cost, so effort will remain the same.

Although many different combinations of effort and population could have led to the bionomic equilibrium, this discussion demonstrates the problems that are involved. It is, of course, entirely possible that the two systems may never reach a simultaneous equilibrium. This point will be expanded in discussions to follow. As a sidelight, note that, if the initial level of effort is larger than E_0 and if the exit process is very slow, the fish stock may be destroyed. That is, this relatively large amount of effort will bring in catches greater than natural increase until the population is actually fished away.

This dynamic analysis demonstrates that reaching a general bionomic equilibrium can be a long and painful process and that resources devoted to a fishery in the meantime may earn less than a normal return. The observed fact that many fishermen eke out a scanty living may be attributable, then, to the open-access nature of the fishery, combined with the fact that initial high returns may be followed by hesitant and dilatory adjustments in population and in entry or departure.

To make the above analysis more realistic, it should be recalled that prices, costs, and productivity may all change before any bionomic equilibrium can be reached. Moreover, pollution or some other alteration of the environment may affect the population dynamics in such a way that the ultimate position of the equilibrium is altered. Therefore, the fishery on its hopeful way toward equilibrium is constantly subject to shocks. Nonetheless, if it can be established that it is continually moving toward equilibrium, the economist is able to predict the behavior both of individual fishermen and of the fishery as a whole.

Maximum Economic Yield

Put succinctly, proper use of a fish stock requires that resources be utilized to exploit it such that the present value of future net returns is maximized, that is, such that the stream of net incomes that it earns, properly discounted, is a maximum. (A discussion of discounting may be found in chapter 1.) This will guarantee that, if the economy is operating properly elsewhere, the value of production will be maximized. To understand the logic of this statement, let us first analyze the problem in terms of the sustained yield curves in figure 2.3.

If costs and revenues have been correctly measured, the proper amount of effort in a static sense will be E_1 in figure 2.3, where marginal revenue of effort (which is the change in sustained catch brought about by a change in effort, multiplied by the fixed price of fish) just balances the marginal cost of effort. At this point, sustained profit or rent to the fishery (i.e., the difference between revenue and cost) is a maximum.

Consider a fishery operating at E_1. Any increase in effort will decrease sustained annual profits, because costs will increase more than will revenue. Note that to the right of E_1, MC_E is greater than MR_E. Revenues measure what people are willing to pay for the fish, and costs represent the value of the next best use of the inputs necessary to produce the effort used to catch the fish. Therefore, when marginal cost of effort is greater than marginal revenue, society is losing, since the additional fish are being taken at a cost greater than their value to consumers. In other words, when effort is increased, then inputs are being diverted from producing other goods of higher value to society. On the other hand, if effort were to be reduced from E_1, profit would fall, implying that revenues must be falling faster than costs. Therefore, although resources were being released for other production, the resultant goods would have a lower value than the fish that could have been caught.

Thus, in terms of the above, E_1 is the optimal allocation of effort to the fishery, since the value to society of the last unit of fish caught (marginal revenue) just balances the cost of providing it (marginal cost). This is often called the maximum economic yield or MEY point. It is worth emphasizing that what is desirable about this point is not just that the annual profit to the fishery as a whole is maximized, but rather that society's inputs are not being used to exploit the fishery unless using them in the fishery is their highest valued use. This point will be stressed throughout this chapter.

While the above is a good introduction to the basic concept of economic utilization of fisheries, it misses some very important issues because, by focusing on the sustained yield curves, it ignores potential year-to-year changes in stock size. Just as open-access utilization is best thought of as a time pattern of exploitation, the economically efficient output of a fishery is a pattern of exploitation rather than a specific harvest level. This is so because of the potential year-to-year changes in stock size as a result of current harvest and the effect of these changes on the net present value of harvest. The analysis of optimal utilization is more difficult than that of open access but it can be introduced using relatively simple mathematics that can be easily adapted to the above graphics. A more rigorous analysis can be found in Clark (1976) and in Munro (1982), and another graphical analysis is presented in Scott (1955).

Since economic efficiency requires the maximization of the *present value* of harvest and since harvest in one year affects future harvest because of its effect on stock size, an analysis based on sustained yield curves is not adequate. The effect of changing population size must be directly considered. The economic essence of this problem can be described by considering the maximization of the present value of harvest. Recall that annual yield is a function of effort and stock size. It also follows from the analysis of the growth curve and the short-run yield curve in figure 2.2 that stock size next year is a function of effort and stock size this year. That is, stock size this year depends upon stock size last year and how it will change as a result of natural mortality, individual growth and recruitment (which are themselves functions of stock size), and the amount of harvest last year (which is a function of effort last year). Mathematically, this relationship can be expressed as $P_t = P_t$ (E_{t-1}, P_{t-1}), where t indicates the time period.

The net present value of harvest is the sum of discounted net revenues over time. The first two terms of the net present value of harvest equation (which is all we will need at present to make our point) are as follows:

PVprofits =

$$\underbrace{P_F y_t (E_t, P_t) - CE_t}_{\text{profits first year}} + \underbrace{\frac{1}{1 + r} [P_F y_{t+1} (E_{t+1}, P_{t+1} (E_t, P_t)) - CE_{t+1}]}_{\text{discounted profits second year}} \quad (2.1)$$

P_F is the price, and C is the unit cost of effort. The subscripts on y (harvest), E (effort), and P (stock size) represent the year. Because of the relationship between stock size one year and effort and stock size the preceding year, note that profits in year one and year two are both functions of effort in the first year. If the terms for net revenues in other years were included, it could be shown that effort in any period has an effect on harvests, and hence revenues, in all future periods. Using basic calculus, the first-order condition for selecting the optimal amount of effort in the first year can be represented as follows: (For those readers unfamiliar with calculus, it is the economic interpretation of this condition provided below which is important; do not be concerned with the actual derivation.)

$$\frac{\partial \text{PVprofits}}{\partial E_t} = \underbrace{P_F \frac{\partial y_t}{\partial E_t}}_{\substack{\text{marginal} \\ \text{value of} \\ \text{effort}}} - \underbrace{C}_{\substack{\text{marginal} \\ \text{harvest} \\ \text{cost}}} + \underbrace{\frac{1}{1 + r} P_F \frac{\partial y_{t+1}}{\partial P_{t+1}} \frac{\partial P_{t+1}}{\partial y_t} \frac{\partial y_t}{\partial E_t}}_{\substack{\text{marginal} \\ \text{user} \\ \text{cost}}} = 0 \quad (2.2)$$

The interpretation of this expression, taking into account that for mathematical simplicity only two years are considered, can be very useful in explaining many of the principles of optimal utilization. In essence, the equation says that optimal utilization in any period of time will occur at that effort level where the marginal value of harvest is equal to the marginal social cost of providing it. The first two terms are a formalization of the preliminary argument above. The value of extra output must be compared with the marginal harvesting cost. The third term completes this analysis by introducing the concept of the marginal user cost of effort, which is the decreased present value of the future harvest caused by the marginal effort in the first year. By analyzing each of the components of user cost in reverse order, it is possible to obtain a clearer understanding of the economics involved. First, $\partial y_t / \partial E_t$ is the increase in catch this year as a result of an increase in effort this year and $\partial P_{t+1} / \partial y_t$ is the effect on stock next year of a change in harvest this year. Further, $\partial y_{t+1} / \partial P_{t+1}$ is the change in harvest next year as a result of the change in stock size next year. Finally, P_F is current value of a unit of harvest next year and $1/(1 + r)$ is the discount coefficient that changes value next year into present value. The product of these four terms is the present value of the marginal reduction in harvest next year, which results from a marginal increase in effort this year. That is, user cost takes into account that effort this year increases harvest, which decreases stock size, which—all else equal—decreases catch and net revenue next year.

To generalize from this two-period analysis, it follows that user cost should consider the effect of effort on harvest in all future periods. That is, user cost is the present value of decreased future harvests.

In summary, the complete criterion for determining the economically efficient level of effort in any one period involves a comparison of the extra value of harvest and the total social cost of providing it. The latter includes harvesting cost as well as the decrease in the present value of harvests in coming years.

To better perceive the dynamic nature of the optimal utilization of a fishery, assume for the moment that user cost is independent of effort used in the following years so that the graphics can be viewed sequentially. Formally, this means that $\partial y_{t+1} / \partial P_{t+1}$ is the same, regardless of the level of E_{t+1}. Consider figure 2.5, which is similar to figure 2.4. The curve labeled TR is the sustainable revenue curve while R_1 is the short-run revenue curve for the current period when the stock size is equal to P_1. The curve labeled TC represents total harvesting cost while the total social cost curve is the sum of harvesting cost plus user cost. Given the above assumptions, it is now possible to identify the optimal amount of effort for the current period. The optimal level of effort will occur where the difference between short-run total revenue and the total social cost curves is maximized. As drawn, this occurs at a current annual level of effort equal to E_1. Any increases in effort will decrease the present value of harvest in that the increased value of harvest this period will be less than the sum of harvesting costs this period and the decrease in the present value of future harvests.

Note that if effort is held to E_1, the stock size will increase because harvest is less than growth at the existing stock size. This can be seen by noting that growth at the given stock size is equal to catch at the point where the short-run revenue curve intersects the sustained revenue curve (i.e., at E_0), and this is clearly more than harvest at E_1. If the optimal level of effort were greater than E_0, catch would have been greater than growth and the stock size would have decreased.

It follows that the selection of the optimal amount of effort for any given period produces two results. It determines the current amount of harvest as

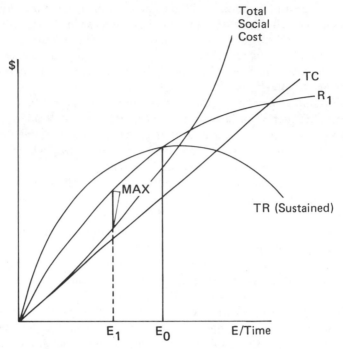

Figure 2.5. *Optimal Annual Level of Effort.*   The optimal level for a given year is where the difference between short-run revenue and total social cost is maximized. In this case catch is less than growth, and so stock size will increase.

well as the size of the fish stock that will be available for harvest next period. Given that new stock size, the above analysis can be repeated to determine the optimal level of effort for the next period. There will be a new short-run revenue curve based on the new stock level. In addition, user cost will likely be different at the new stock size. Given these new curves, the new optimal annual level of effort can be ascertained. This will determine harvest for that period and a new population size for the next period. In some instances stock size will increase while in others it will decrease. All else equal, the higher the user cost, the lower will be the optimal level of effort and the more likely that it will be optimal for the stock size to increase. This only makes sense. With a higher user cost (which is to say that effort this year causes a large decrease in the discounted value of future harvests), it makes sense to invest in the stock rather than harvest it, so that future returns will increase.

It is possible, of course, that a stationary point can be achieved where the optimum yield for a given population size coincides with natural growth. This is depicted in figure 2.6. The optimum annual effort is E_1 because that is where the difference between short-run total revenue and total social cost is maximized. At that point, however, the short-run and sustained revenue

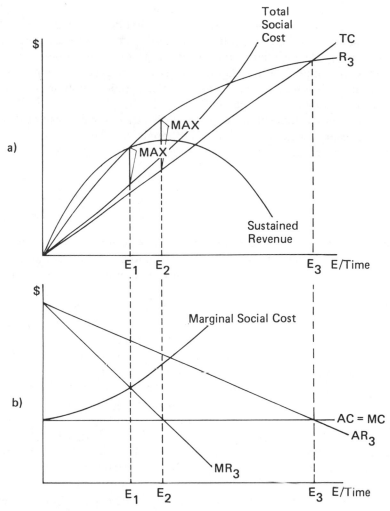

Figure 2.6. *Stationary MEY.*   A stationary MEY point occurs when the difference between annual revenue and total social cost is maximized at a level of effort where catch equals growth. Stock size will not change, and therefore the optimal level of effort will be the same in the next period.

curves intersect, which means that catch equals growth. Thus, population size will not change; hence, the annual curves will remain the same. E_1, therefore, is a stationary optimal level of effort. Note that at this effort level, total pecuniary profits to the fishery are represented by the difference between total revenue and total harvesting cost. In terms of the industry, the user cost turns out to be rent or payment received for optimal utilization through time. This is often called the *scarcity rent*.

In the more realistic case, where user cost in any one year is a function of actual effort in future years, the above sequential analysis does not hold because the user cost cannot be drawn without first determining the effort level for the next year. Therefore, rather than a sequential process, the determination of the optimal exploitation pattern is a simultaneous process. The basic point is the same, however. Optimal harvest can best be thought of as an exploitation time path rather than as a specific static output level. This point will receive more attention below.

Other important aspects of optimal utilization over time can be discussed if the concept is explained in a slightly different way. The complete expression for the present value of harvest can be represented as follows:

Present value =

$$R_0 - C_0 + \frac{R_1 - C_1}{1 + r} + \frac{R_2 - C_2}{(1 + r)^2} + \frac{R_3 - C_3}{(1 + r)^3} + \dots \frac{R_n - C_n}{(1 + r)^n} \qquad (2.3)$$

The subscripts refer to the period of time. For example, R_0 is revenue in the current period while R_2 is revenue in the second period. The time rate of discount is represented by r. (Chapter 1 provides a more complete discussion of present value.)

The level of effort that leads to the maximization of revenues minus costs (i.e., sustainable profits) in every period will not maximize the present value of the returns to the fishery for two basic reasons: (1) the nature of the growth rate of fish stocks, and (2) the difference in value of today's dollar of net revenue as against one sometime in the future, which can be evaluated using the interest rate. To see this, consider two aspects of a fish stock. First, it is a commodity that, when captured and sold, will yield a net revenue. Second, it is a "piece of capital equipment" capable of producing a stream of commodities that can be caught and sold in future periods. It may not be obvious, but both of these uses are directly considered in the sustained yield curve. Paraphrasing from above, this curve shows the level of catch that will be forthcoming from each level of effort after the stock size has adjusted to that level of effort. Therefore, marginal sustainable yield is the *net* effect of the change in harvest due to a change in effort and the change in long-run harvest, due to the change in stock size caused by the change in effort. As the introductory dynamic analysis above shows, however, the sustainable yield curve takes no consideration of the time element involved in the process. The problem of optimal utilization is how to make the best use of the dual utility of the stock over time by taking into account the rate of interest and the growth rate of the stock.

This can be explained in the context of the earlier analysis by using the growth curve and the sustained revenue and cost curves of a fishery, as depicted in figure 2.7. $P*$ is the natural equilibrium population. E_1 is the level of effort that provides the greatest sustained difference between revenue and cost in each period, and P_1 is the equilibrium population for this level of ef-

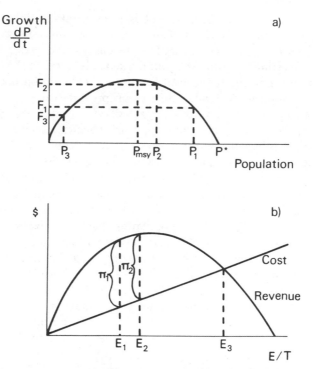

Figure 2.7. *Maximum Economic Yield over Time.* E_1 units of effort applied to a population size of P_1 will produce maximum economic yield in a static sense. It may be beneficial, however, to reduce the population to P_2 and then use E_2 units of effort annually if the net value of an immediate catch of $(P_1 - P_2)$ is greater than the reduction in the present value of future catches by reducing annual profits from π_1 to π_2.

fort. Assume for a moment that the fishery has not been exploited; therefore, the population is P^*. The questions are, how much of the population should be harvested and sold in the current period, and how much should be left to produce fish for future periods? In the sustainable yield analysis, this boils down to, what is the dynamically optimal level of effort to apply to the stock each period? The answer depends upon the relative values of the two uses of the population. When used for current catch, its value equals the net revenue obtained. The value of not harvesting the stock in the current period is the present value of the stream of net revenues thus made possible. This is the reverse of saying that user cost is the decrease in the present value of harvest that results from an extra unit of harvest.

Increases in yearly effort will always result in a once-and-for-all increase in revenue from the sale of that part of the standing stock that is removed as it moves toward its new equilibrium size. But notice that, as yearly effort is increased from zero up to E_1 (which will, in time, cause the stock size to be reduced to P_1), there is also an increase in subsequent sustainable net revenues. Total yearly costs will increase, but up to E_1, total sustainable revenues will increase even more. Increases in effort beyond E_1, however, will result in a decrease in sustainable net revenue. It is obvious, therefore, that if the average cost of harvesting fish from the standing stock is less than the price, then the population should be reduced at least to P_1. (The graph does not give enough information to determine how much present effort is necessary to cause this reduction, but E_1 units of effort will be needed in each succeeding period to hold the stock at that equilibrium size.) Such a reduction in equilibrium population is beneficial in two ways. There is the once-and-for-all gain in harvesting some of the initial population (it is conceivable that, given existing fishing capacity, it may take several years to achieve this reduction, in which case the once-and-for-all gain will be spread over more than one year), and there is an increase in the value of sustained net revenue. (Indeed sustained net revenue is higher at this population than at any other.) Therefore, a reduction in population from P^* to P_1 not only results in current net revenue but also increases potential sustained net revenue in future periods.

But should annual effort be increased beyond E_1? Notice that more intensive current harvesting will again yield a one-time increase in revenues, but it will also decrease sustainable net revenues for future periods. Up to a point, the increase in current net revenue (i.e., the $R_0 - C_0$ in equation 2.3) gained by reducing population will exceed the decrease in present value of the sustained net revenues of the remaining periods (i.e., that amount represented by the remaining part of equation 2.3). In terms of figure 2.7, a reduction in population from P_1 to P_2 (which can be sustained only if effort is increased to E_2) will be beneficial if the net value of $(P_1 - P_2)$ units of fish harvested this period is worth more than the decrease in the present value of net revenues in all subsequent periods caused by the reduction of $(\pi_1 - \pi_2)$ in net revenue in each period. In formal terms, effort should be increased as long as the increase in current revenue compensates for the reduction in the present value of future sustainable revenues. Put differently, the marginal revenue gained from using the population for its first use, providing current catch, should equal the marginal revenue of using it for its second use, a piece of capital equipment to provide fish to be caught in the future.

Assume for the moment that E_2 is the point at which this intertemporal equalization occurs and that growth equals catch so that stock size will not change. This optimum point must be viewed in a dynamic sense, however. Looking at the graph, which can only give a static picture, one might be tempted to suggest a reduction in effort to allow net returns to increase. (Note that a reduction from E_2 to E_1 will cause sustainable profits to increase.) But it must be recalled from earlier discussions of the growth of fish stocks that a decrease in effort will initially decrease catch; it will only increase as the stock size increases. Therefore, in order to obtain the increase in sustainable profits, as indicated on the static graph, sufficient time must be allowed for the stock to reach its new larger equilibrium size, and during that period there will actually be some years when net revenue will fall.

Looking at the problem in reverse, consider the case of an open-access equilibrium that would take place at a level of effort E_3 and an equilibrium population of P_3. At this point too many resources are being allocated to the fishery, and concurrently the population size of the stock is too low. But viewed in a dynamic sense, what is the proper population size and what is the amount of yearly effort that will achieve it? To allow population to grow, harvesting must be cut back; thus revenue in the current period must fall. Economically this will mean a reduction in current net revenue but an increase in the present value of potential future net revenues. In a dynamic analysis, then, population size should be allowed to increase (i.e., yearly effort should be cut back, thus freeing resources for alternative uses) as long as the reduction in current net revenue brought about by the fall in current harvest is more than compensated by the increase in the present value of future harvests at that level of effort. When the net value of the last decrease in current catch is equal to the increase in the present value of future net revenues and stock growth equals harvest, a stationary maximum economic yield level of effort will be obtained.

It may seem paradoxical that, with a positive discount rate, the point yielding the highest sustainable net revenue does not also maximize the present value of the stream of net revenues. The reason for this apparent contradiction is the time required for the fish stock to reach an equilibrium population size. If it were possible to go immediately to a specified size (i.e., if no harvesting were necessary to reduce the population and no reduction in harvesting were necessary to allow it to grow), then the proper stock size would be the one giving the greatest sustainable net revenue. This is because no increase or decrease would occur in current revenue to be balanced off against changes in the present value of potential future net revenue.

A very important factor in determining the actual location of a stationary MEY level of effort in the size of the discount rate. Colin Clark (1973a, 1973b), using a model analogous to the one presented here, has demonstrated that, with a zero discount rate, MEY occurs at a point such as E_1 when sustainable net revenues are maximized. In this case a dollar of future revenue is equal in value to a dollar of present revenue, and so it does not make sense to increase current net revenue at the expense of equal amounts in the future. He also showed that, with an infinite rate of discount, MEY is equivalent to the open-access equilibrium. In this case, future income has no value, and so it makes sense to use as much effort each period as can cover its costs. In the long run, this boils down to operating at open-access equilibrium yield.

Therefore, with a positive discount rate the stationary optimum level of effort, if one exists, is between the level that generates the highest sustainable revenues and the open-access equilibrium level. The precise position depends upon the exact size of the discount rate. Along the same line, this analysis demonstrates that the optimal stock size is somewhere between P_1 and P_3 in figure 2.7. It is interesting to note that this means it is possible that the dynamic optimal stock size may be less than the one that yields the maximum sustainable yield (i.e., less than P_{msy}).

As pointed out above, however, optimum utilization of a fishery may not involve a stationary level of effort. In cases where the stock is relatively slow-growing and the resources used to produce the effort can easily be transferred to other underutilized fisheries or even into nonfishery uses, or when there are economies of scale in the production of effort, the proper intertemporal management policy may consist of "pulse" fishing; that is, the stock should be heavily fished in one period and then fished only lightly or not at all for several periods, because the current large harvest more than compensates for the subsequent reduction in catch. This may be the case in a fish stock where the yearly increment is small relative to the total population size, since it then makes sense to take a large amount every few years rather than a small amount each year. This is especially true if the growth rate increases during extended periods of no harvesting and if cost per unit of fish will decrease with increased harvests taken from a larger stock size.

Also, in other cases the maximization of present value will call for the complete destruction of the fish stock. That is, the value of harvesting the stock until it is depleted, if it is physically possible to do so, is worth more than the value of any sustained catch throughout the future. This case has been examined by Clark (1973a, 1973b), Neher (1974), and Clark and Munro (1978) and can occur under rather specific assumptions concerning yield, when the rate of discount is high relative to the increase in the growth rate of the stock as it increase in size, when the price of fish is high relative to the cost of harvesting the last unit, and when prices are not expected to increase or harvest costs to decrease. To claim that such a policy would provide for optimal use of the stock, however, one would have to argue that the ability to produce fish for man's harvest is its only use. Actually, as a part of the total marine environment, a fish stock provides many services. If the destruction of the stock alters this environment in such a way as to decrease the value of its

Table 2.1. *Present Value of Profit Decision.* The present value of profits will depend upon what policy is used and upon how price varies over time.

	Price remains constant	Price increases
1. No change in the level of effort	$585.71	$633.33
2. Reduction of effort in first year by one-quarter and then adjustments in the second to take advantage of the growth in the stock	$548.80	$796.42

services other than the harvested fish, then the maximization of the present value of the net revenues of the fishery by destruction of the stock will presumably not lead to a proper allocation of resources. All uses of the stock must be considered.

MEY and Changes in Prices or Cost

Before leaving this discussion of MEY, let us now consider intertemporal changes in prices or costs. Besides the discount rate, the main economic determinants of maximum economic yield are the price of fish and the cost of providing the effort to catch them. But both of these are subject to changes from year to year, and as a result maximum economic yield will change also, in a static as well as a dynamic sense. Demand, the measure of what people are willing and able to pay for various amounts of a good, is dependent upon the tastes of the consumers, the prices of related goods, and the total income and income distribution of the economy. If any of these change, demand will change.

For example, when meatless Fridays became a matter of choice rather than of decree, "tastes" changed and the demand for fish diminished (see Bell 1968). However, the rise in the price of meat and the recent medical experiments showing that consuming fish can produce beneficial health effects has increased demand for fish. All such changes affect the size of maximum economic yield. Anything that increases willingness to pay will increase the maximum economic yield, because the extra units of fish will then be worth more than the opportunities foregone to obtain them.

Similarly, improvements in fishing technology and changes in demand for the types of labor and capital used in fisheries will affect the opportunity cost of catching fish. For example, improved fish-finding techniques will lower the cost of landing fish since less gas and other inputs will be used per pound of fish landed. With each decrease in opportunities foregone in obtaining the fish, the maximum economic yield will expand.

These year-to-date changes in economic variables, when combined with the temporal growth of the fish population, can make the problem even more complex. For example, if it is certain that the price of fish will increase next period, it may be wise to cut back on current catch to enable the population to grow to such a level as will increase average and total catch in the period when fish will be more valuable. Whether this is an economically sound decision depends upon the rate of growth of the population and the resultant increase in catch per unit effort, the size of the expected increase in price, and the relative desirability of present over future profit.

Assume that, at current effort levels, the fishery will earn a profit of $300 at this year's prices and that the profit will increase to $350 in the next period due to higher prices; but if effort is reduced by one-quarter this year, current profit will fall to $225, and next year's profit can increase to $600 with appropriate increases in effort. Both of these profits are the results of different costs and different revenues. In the first year, cost is down because effort has decreased, but in the second year it will rise by the extra effort needed to harvest the additional fish. Revenues will fall in the first year due to decreased catch and will be augmented the second year by increased landings and higher prices.

If no long-lasting effects occur in the fishery from either action, then the proper policy is the one yielding the highest present value of profits. If the interest rate is 5 percent, the present value of profits for normal operation is $300 + ($350/1.05) = $633.33. The present value of the alternative policy is $225 + ($600/1.05) = $796.42. Since the policy of curtailing effort has the higher present value of profits, it is superior. What it amounts to is an investment in the population of the fishery. Since the return in future revenue more than makes up for the reduction in this year's profits, the investment is a good one. It should be remembered that this assumes that the resources released from the fishery in the first year can be absorbed immediately into the economy and that extra effort in the second period can easily be obtained.

Such analysis does not assure that this is the *best* policy, however, because only two policy alternatives have been explored. To find the optimum, all relevant possibilities must be considered, and the one having the highest present value of earnings should be selected. Other alternatives could include such policies as no fishing this year followed by extra-heavy fishing next year. To be completely general, the consideration should extend to activities covering as many years as pertinent information can be obtained for price, cost, and population growth.

Also, in most cases it is not possible to be certain about either future prices and costs or about changes in the growth pattern in the fish stock. Therefore, it is necessary to carry the above analysis one step further by considering the relative sizes of the present value of profits of the two policies in the event the predicted price increase does not occur. If effort is not changed and prices do not increase, profit in the second year will remain at $300 and the present value of profits over the two-year period will be $300 + ($300/1.05), or $585.71. Assume that, given a one-quarter reduction this year, with constant prices, the most profit that can be earned in the second year even after adjustments in effort to take advantage of the growth in the stock is $340. This is higher than the $300 it would have been but not as high as the $600 that would have resulted had prices gone up. The present value of profits in this case is $225 + ($340/1.05), or $548.80. All of this information is summarized in table 2.1. The rows represent our possible policies, and the columns, the possible price structures. The figures represent the present value of profits of the various strategies with the specified price outcome.

Looking at this, how does the decisionmaker decide what to do? It is no longer the simple choice between the $633.33 and $796.42, as in the case when the price increase was a certainty. Now it is a choice between the possibility of $585.71 or $633.33 by letting things go as they have been and the possibility of $548.80 and $796.42 by making adjustments in effort. Note that, with changes in effort, the lower present value of profits is lower than when no changes are made, but at the same time the maximum profit is also higher. When there is true uncertainty (i.e., when there is absolutely no information on which of the two prices will prevail), the manager must weigh the potential decrease in profit from changing effort against potential increase. In the event that the profit in the lower left-hand box was extremely low or negative, or, in the other extreme, if the profit in the lower right-hand box is very large relative to the others, the decision might not be too difficult. In the first instance the best policy may be to leave things as they are to insure against the possible large decreases in profits. In the second case, the manager may feel that the gamble for the really large increase in profits is worthwhile and would recommend that effort be modified.

If there are no such extremes, one rule of thumb is to choose that policy that will obtain the highest minimum gain. Using this rule, the best decision would be to make no change in effort because even under the worst conditions profits can be no lower than $585.71.

In case of risk, where there is at least some known or hypothesized probability distribution for the uncertain future events, it is often useful to look at expected values of the various strategies. For example, if forecasters predict that there is a 90 percent chance that prices will not change, then the expected value of the two policies are:

Policy 1   .9($585.71) + .1($633.33), or $590.46
Policy 2   .9($548.80) + .1($796.42), or $573.56

The expected value is the average amount of profits that would be earned if the manager was faced with these different profit possibilities and this set of probabilities for the price increase, and he had the option of undertaking the decision a large number of times. That is, if he undertook policy 1 many times, in 90 percent of the cases he would earn $585.71, and in the other 10 percent a profit of $633.33 would be achieved; the overall average profit would be $590.46. Of course, in actuality, the manager can only make this decision once, and so, if he chooses policy 1 he will make either the larger or the smaller of the two potential profits, not some average of them. Nevertheless, this expected value can be of some use in making his decision.

With these probabilities, note that the expected value of policy 1 is higher. Therefore, since policy 1 maximizes the minimum losses and also has the highest expected value, it appears to be superior. Note, however, that if the probability of price remaining the same fell to 70 percent, the expected values of policies 1 and 2 would become $599.98 and $623.08, respectively. Although policy 2 has a higher expected value of profits, the difference between them is not very large, and a manager might feel hesitant about abandoning policy 1, where his minimum losses are maximized. Now, if the probability of price remaining the same were as low as 20 percent, the expected values of profit would be $623.80 and $746.89. Since the difference between these expected values is so great, policy 2 could now be considered the better choice.

Space does not permit an extended coverage of this type of decision analysis, but with the many risks and uncertainties in both the economic and the biological spheres of fisheries management, it is obvious that it can be a useful tool for decisionmakers. For an enlarged treatment of this subject, see Mishan (1982, part 7). For our purposes the assumption of certainty will enable us to describe the important concepts in a straightforward manner, and so it will be retained throughout.

The conclusion of this entire section is that proper operation of a fishery requires that the sum of the present values of the yearly total returns be maximized. This means that the proper level of catch over time depends upon expected future prices and costs, intertemporal population growth rates, and the rate of interest. In cases where the price of fish is expected to fall drastically, this may call for very heavy fishing in the present even though future outputs will be adversely affected. When the fish stock is extremely slow-growing, or when there are economies of scale in the production of effort, very heavy fishing may be beneficial every five years or so, with little or no harvesting in between. Or if prices and costs are expected to remain relatively constant or to grow at constant rates, the proper output may be an equal amount each year, although with a positive discount rate it will not be the amount that achieves the highest net revenue in each period.

In summary, maximum economic yield of a fishery can be more properly thought of as the optimal stream of yields over time. This stream can consist of a constant amount year after year, or yearly catch may vary widely. To make things more complex, this optimal stream can change over time with changing expectations as to cost, price, and rate of growth of the stock.

Comparison of MEY and Open Access

Using figure 2.6b, it is possible to delineate quite clearly some important distinctions between the optimal and open-access yield at any point in time. Recall that figure 2.6a depicts a stationary state in the optimal utilization of a fishery. The optimal annual harvest is equal to natural stock growth, and so there will be no further changes in stock size. Figure 2.6b contains the short-run average and marginal curves derived from figure 2.6a.

With no controls on entry, the open-access equilibrium level of effort in figure 2.6b will be E_3, where average revenue equals average harvest cost. On the other hand, the optimal annual level of effort, given this stock size, is E_1, where the marginal revenue of effort equals the sum of marginal harvesting cost and marginal user cost. What accounts for this difference in open-access and optimal output levels? Why don't individual producers, who are often motivated by the profit incentive, operate such that present value of profits is maximized? The answer lies in the fact that no one entity owns the fish stock and can prohibit others from using it. Instead, people can use it as they please, and if they make decisions on the basis of individual profits, they will do so as long as their revenues are greater than their costs. Such action results in two types of errors in the way resources are used. First, to the individual, value of output is measured by the average rather than by the marginal revenue curve, and second, the only cost that is considered is harvesting cost rather than the sum of harvesting and user cost. Therefore, there are two kinds of overexploitation under open access (see Henderson and Tugwell [1979]). In the first place, the stock is overutilized in any given period of time. The individual fishermen do not consider the effect that their production will have on the production of all others in the current period. This current period overexploitation can be corrected for by reducing effort from E_3 to E_2 in figure 2.6b. That is, the net effect on fishery output for the fishery as a whole (i.e., the marginal revenue of effort) rather than the revenue per boat (i.e., the average revenue of effort) must be compared with harvest cost. At the same time, however, the stock is being nonoptimally depleted because individual operators do not consider the user cost they are imposing on harvesters in future periods. This future period overexploitation can be corrected by further reducing effort from E_2 to E_1. That is, it is the total effect on the present value of goods and services foregone (i.e., the marginal social cost) rather than just marginal harvesting cost which must be compared with the marginal revenue of effort.

To summarize, the improper allocation of effort to an unregulated fishery results from two factors: (1) the profit or rent that a fishery is capable of earning, and (2) the fact that no one has an exclusive claim to that profit. From the individual fisherman's point of view, his operating decisions are rational, but in the context of a common property resource, they lead to suboptimal results. An uneconomic amount of effort will be applied to the fish stock. As will be shown in the next chapter, the revenue earned by the individual fisherman per unit of effort is equal to the average revenue for the fishery as a whole. Therefore, the average revenue of the fishery is the important consideration for the individual fisherman; he does not stop to weigh marginal revenue for the fishery as a whole. When an additional boat enters the fishery, the revenue of existing boats will fall due to the change in average sustained yield caused by the increase in effort. Marginal revenue of the fishery takes this into account; average revenue does not. But since each boat owner is concerned only with fishery average revenue because this is his return for each unit of effort produced, he is not worrying about the effect his boat will have on the catch and hence on the annual revenue of all boats.

As a final point in this comparison of open access and MEY, it will prove useful to return to the concept of exploitation time paths. Consider figure

2.8a and b. A comparison of intertemporal time harvest paths is presented for two different situations. In both instances it is assumed that an unutilized fish stock is discovered at T_0 and that there is an existing fleet capable of harvesting it. (The case where the fleet must be constructed will be discussed in the next chapter.) The time paths labeled MEY are optimal time paths for the newly discovered fisheries. Optimal annual effort starts out relatively high to take advantage of the large virgin population size but decreases as the stock is thinned out. That is, user cost is quite low at first because of the relatively large stock. It increases as the stock decreases, and hence the optimal amount of effort falls. As drawn here, the fisheries finally obtain a stationary path

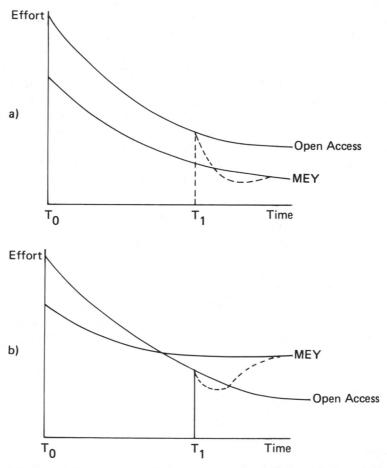

Figure 2.8. *Time Paths of Harvest.* Both open-access and optimal exploitation will involve changes in effort and stock size over time. In this context, fisheries management can be thought of as the proper way to move from the open-access to the optimal path.

where stock growth equals catch, and so stock size and optimum annual effort remain the same. Such a point, which hereafter will be called the stationary MEY point, will always occur with Schaefer growth curves, but it may not with other types of growth. For example, the time paths could oscillate up and down indefinitely. Unless otherwise stated, the analysis in this book will always assume that a stationary MEY will be achieved.

The curves labeled open access represent the annual open-access level of effort that would be produced if the stock were unregulated rather than managed to obtain the maximum present value of harvest. In both instances, the open-access level of effort will be greater than the optimal amount during the early phases of exploitation. The difference is that, in the fishery pictured in figure 8b, open access pushes the stock to such a low level that it can only support a low level of effort and hence after some point the open-access curve is below the MEY curve. This can only occur with a differently shaped sustained yield curve that is explained in chapter 4. See also Southey (1972). The point is, however, that open-access exploitation should also be viewed as a time path, and what is more important, it is a different exploitation time path than the optimal one. Economically speaking, one goal of fisheries management is to correct for this difference (i.e., to change the harvest path from the open-access to the optimal path). If the fishery is regulated from its inception and if economic efficiency is the major goal, then the MEY path is the one that should be used. In most instances, however, regulation will be introduced after the fishery has operated under open access for some time, in which case the problem is truly one of moving from time path to the other. Assume that regulation is to be introduced in both cases at T_1. The dotted lines represent possible ways in which the time path of effort will have to be changed. In both cases there will be a decrease in effort to allow the stock to grow, but effort will gradually increase through time to take advantage of the larger stock. Note that, in the second case, after the initial decrease in effort, the stationary optimal level of effort is greater than the open-access level at which regulation began. This will only happen when the stock is pushed very low under open access, but it can occur.

Before going on, this may be an opportune place to cover one related point. In the past, some fisheries biologists have advocated that the proper amount of effort is that which produces the maximum sustainable yield. Their argument is based on the fact that lower yields represent a waste of the fishery. Sometimes the argument is supplemented by the reprimand that underutilizing a protein source when many of the world's people are starving is an immoral waste, indeed. But this ignores the fact that the yield can be increased only by diverting resources from other production that may have higher value to society (the production of protein on land, for instance, or the production of medical services). So, while maximum sustainable yield may have an appealing ring since it does not take opportunity cost into account, it is not a goal that should be sought after *for its own sake*. Although, from the analysis of figure 2.7, it is possible that an optimal stationary point could occur at maximum sustainable yield.

Comparative Statics

Before going on to analyze open-access exploitation and maximum economic yield in more realistic models, it will prove useful to cover two aspects of the former, using the current model. This section will describe the change that occurs in the open-access equilibrium position of a fishery due to a change in costs, prices, or productivity of gear.

Let us first discuss changes in the costs of inputs used to produce effort. Consider figure 2.9. If C_4 represents the cost curve, then the fishery will not be commercially exploited, since costs will be above revenues at all levels of effort. If, however, the cost curve is C_3, commercial exploitation is possible and E_3 will be the open-access equilibrium level of effort. If for some reason costs fall to C_2, the new equilibrium will be at E_2, because at E_3 revenues will be greater than costs, and so there will be motivation to increase effort to E_2. At this new equilibrium, catch and revenue will have increased, but since total revenue equals total costs the fishermen will be in the same situation as they were previously. Their revenues are just covering costs. If costs were to fall again to C_1, the new equilibrium would be at E_1, but in this case the increase in effort brought about by decreased costs would actually be counter-

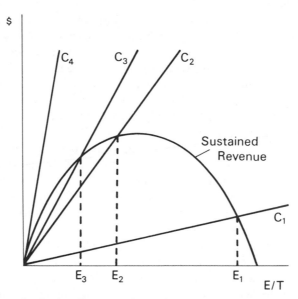

Figure 2.9. *Comparative Statics: Changes in Cost.*   As costs fall, the open-access level of effort will increase, but total revenue will still equal total cost. Not only will production fall in other parts of the economy, but if costs decrease far enough, sustainable yield will fall also.

productive. The increased effort would push the fish population down to such an extent that sustainable yield would fall, as would the total revenue for the fishery due to the decrease in sustainable yield.

It can thus be seen that decreases in the cost of providing fishing effort will only produce transitory gains because any profit they offer will just encourage further entry into the open-access fishery until that profit is eliminated. At the new equilibrium, the individual fishermen will still have costs equal to revenues. Also, in certain cases, depending upon the relative size of price and cost, decreases in cost may actually decrease long-run production from the fishery because of the adverse effect of increased effort on sustained yield.

Changes in productivity such as the introduction of superior nets, better fish-finding gear, and so forth can be analyzed in several different ways, the most simple of which (and the one that is most consistent with the general framework used here) is to consider them as changes in the cost of producing a given amount of effort, where effort is defined, as above, in terms of its effect on the fish stock. In this way, the analysis of technology changes is identical to that of changes in the cost of inputs, as just discussed above. Christy and Scott (1965) present another way that essentially allows for technological changes to redefine effort and as such can be somewhat difficult to utilize. Nevertheless, it is internally consistent and does shed additional light on the subject because of the different point of view it provides. For their analysis, think of effort in terms of a specific physical variable such as days spent fishing. From this point of view, an improvement in technology will increase catching power for each fishing day. That is, each unit of nominal effort is equivalent to a greater amount of effective effort. This can be expressed in terms of our standard diagram, modified only by expressing effort in nominal terms, as a shift of the revenue curve from R to R' in figure 2.10. The curve has been pushed to the left, since each unit of effort is now more effective. For example, it now takes a smaller number of days to catch the maximum sustainable yield, and effort extended for the number of days that formerly were required to catch that level will now reduce the population to such an extent that less will be caught. If the cost curve is C_1, then the equilibrium level of effort will move from E_1 to E_1' as a result of this change. At E_1, with the new revenue curve, costs are greater than revenues, so the number of days will be reduced until E_1' is reached. Note that even though nominal effort is reduced, yield and revenue are the same as they would have been at a level of effort of E_3 before the improvement; therefore, even with reduced nominal effort, the population and the sustained yield have fallen. This is because the smaller amount of nominal effort at E_1' is more effective than the larger amount at E_1. Note, however, that the reduction in costs does allow for an expansion of production in nonfishery output.

For the purpose of comparison, in figure 2.9, where effort is measured in terms of its effect on the stock, this is equivalent to a reduction in the cost

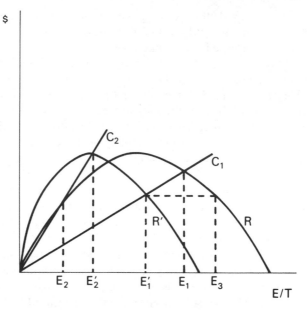

Figure 2.10. *Comparative Statics: Changes in Productivity.*   An increase in productivity will shift the revenue curve from R to R' when effort is measured in nominal terms. The effect of this will depend upon the initial situation. If the fishery was operating beyond maximum sustainable yield, effort, revenue, and yield will fall. If it was operating below MSY, effort, yield, and revenue will increase.

curve from C_2 to C_1. There will be a greater amount of effective effort being applied to the stock at a lower cost and producing a smaller yield and revenue. Whichever way you look at it, however, the individual who is able to continue fishing is not benefited, since costs will equal revenues.

On the other hand, if C_2 in figure 2.10 is the cost curve, the equilibrium will move from E_2 to E_2'. (The difference between these two cost curves is that C_1 crosses both of the revenue curves to the right of their intersection, while C_2 does so to the left.) In this case there will be an expansion of nominal effort, catch, and revenue. The higher level of more effective effort has again decreased the population, but now it is within the range where such a decrease will result in higher sustained yield. Again, in terms of figure 2.9, this is equivalent to a decrease in the cost curve from C_3 to C_2, which obtains a larger amount of effective effort at an increase in cost (resulting from the increase in nominal effort) and which produces an increase in yield and revenue. Utilizing both diagrams, we can conclude that, when an improved technology is introduced in an open-access fishery, it will always result in an increase in effective effort. However, if it is operating beyond maximum sustainable yield (MSY), there will be a decrease in nominal effort and hence a decrease in cost. On the other hand, if the fishery is operating to the left of MSY, there will be an increase in nominal effort and cost.

To summarize, (1) in the long run, improvement in productivity will not affect annual profits to the individual fishermen, although there will be some gains in the transition period, and (2) effort, defined in terms of its effect on the stock, will be increased but nominal effort and catch may increase or decrease depending upon the relationship between cost and revenue.

This slight detour into the difference between nominal effort and effective effort points up a very significant problem in fishery management. When attempting to utilize the theories presented here for management decisions, some physical unit must be used as a proxy for effort. To enable the proper decisions to be made, the physical unit chosen must be closely related to the actual effort placed on the stock, both over time and among different types of fishing vessels. As this discussion demonstrates, the selection of a consistent proxy will be a difficult task that will require continual modification as technology changes. A good example of this can be found in the northwest Atlantic. During the early sixties the amount of effort by nationals of other countries had been increasing significantly while at the same time the average size of their vessels had been growing. Even in cases where officials could determine the number of days they were fishing, it was hard to obtain a good measure of effective total effort. First, how do you compare a day's fishing for the relatively smaller U.S. boats with a day's fishing by larger and larger foreign boats? And, to add to the confusion, it may take new vessels several seasons to adjust to a new area, and so a day fished by a certain vessel in 1962 may have had a different effective effort from a day fished in 1968. These difficulties notwithstanding, bear in mind that, for the remainder of this book, we will, as we have done previously, speak of effort in effective rather than nominal terms.

Consider now the effect of a change in price. In figure 2.11, if price is such that R is the revenue curve, the fishery will not be commercially exploitable at any cost level. An increase in price will shift the revenue curve up, since each level of catch will bring in more revenue, and a price rise that increases revenue to R' will make it worthwhile to fish the stock commercially. Further increases in price will affect the location of the open-access equilibrium. Consider a change in revenue from R' to R''. If C_1 is the cost curve, the open-access equilibrium will move from E_1 to E_1', at which point revenue will have gone up but catch will have fallen, since the fishery is operating to the right of MSY and effort has increased. The decrease in output is more than compensated by the increase in price, however, so the price increase has resulted in more units of effort being expended to catch fewer fish, which are sold for more money. Since costs have gone up by the same amount as revenues, at the new equilibrium the individual fisherman is no better off than previously. If C_2 is the cost curve, the equilibrium will move from E_2 to E_2'. In this case the increase in price stimulates not only an increase in effort and revenue but in catch as well.

In summary, then, price increases, like cost decreases and productivity

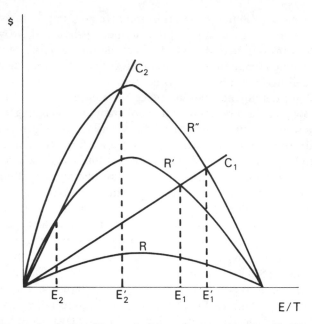

Figure 2.11. *Comparative Statics: Changes in Price.* Increases in price will shift the revenue curve up. If a fishery is operating beyond MSY, an increase in price will increase effort and revenue, but yield will fall. If the fishery is operating below MSY, it will cause effort, revenue, and yield to increase.

improvements, will only provide transitory gains and may even lead to a decrease in catch due to an adverse effect on the fish stock. In all cases, these undesirable results stem from the special nature of production in a fishery in combination with the open-access problem. The increase in profits that these changes provide encourages changes in the level of effort, but it cannot lead to the production of more of the basic capital equipment of the industry—the fish stock—as profits will do in other industries. Instead, the fish stock will be exploited by more fishermen, which will exacerbate the open-access wastes.

Conclusions

This, in a nutshell, is the basic economic analysis of a common-property or open-access fishery. Although the restrictive assumptions prevent analysis of the more subtle issues involved, the basics disclose that an unregulated fishery will use a level of effort differing from the optimal. As we have found, the optimal level is reached when the last unit of yearly effort increases both cost and revenue by the same amount where proper consideration is given to the levels of costs and revenues through time. This level is not achieved in an unregulated fishery for the same reason that the individual fisherman does not benefit from improvements in technology or from cost decreases; that is, entry is open to all who want to join in the great search for fish. The more expanded models that follow will not reach any substantially different results, but by adding greater reality to the model, they will show more vividly the processes involved and will increase the applicability of the conclusions derived.

3

A More Complete Analysis of Fisheries Economics

Introduction

Now that the elements of the analysis have been set out, it is possible to consider other aspects that have previously been ignored. Of the five main sections in this chapter, the first will analyze the operation of the individual fishing unit and how it operates in relation to the fishery as a whole to create the open-access misallocation of resources. In the second section, the assumption of a fixed price of fish is dropped to allow for a complete discussion of maximum economic yield that includes analyses of monopoly profit and consumer surplus. The third section analyzes the fishery as a part of the entire economy in order to get a clearer picture of the potential inefficiencies of unregulated market behavior in open-access fisheries. The fourth section discusses recreational fisheries for the first time and shows that they have open-access problems as well. The final section analyzes the relationship between fisheries management and fisheries development. A brief appendix contains derivations of several of the relationships used in chapters 2 and 3.

A Closer Look at the Individual Fisherman

The purpose of this section is to analyze open-access and maximum economic yield (MEY), taking into account the operations of individual operators. In addition to adding further insight into the reasons why open-access exploitation does not correspond with the economically efficient pattern of utilization, this analysis can provide a more realistic picture of how effort is actually produced and the long- and short-run economic motivations of those who produce it. The main thrust will be to analyze the number of vessels in the fleet and the output level per vessel under various situations. Two types of fisheries, constant cost and increasing cost, will be described. The discussion of open access, in both cases, can best be presented, for the most part, in terms of the sustained yield analysis, but it will be necessary to introduce annual yield curves when discussing MEY. Because of the fixed cost of constructing a fishing boat, the analysis of the optimal harvest time path is rather complicated, and as such initial discussion will compare the open-access and the stationary MEY points. Recall that the latter was defined above as that level of effort at which the optimal time path of effort becomes a straight line. The optimal time pattern to the stationary MEY point will be discussed in a separate section.

Constant Cost Fishery

For simplicity, assume that many identical independent boats are capable of exploiting an unregulated fish stock and that the stock can handle all of them up to reasonable limits. In the context of an open-access fishery, it is useful to think of these individual boats as producers of effort rather than of fish, because no one can control the success of a given unit of effort. Recall from the discussion of figure 2.2b that the long-run catch per unit of effort decreases as total effort is intensified and that this fall is mainly due to the resultant decrease in the fish stock. Under our assumptions, each boat is such a small part of the whole fishery that it cannot control either the total amount of effort being applied or, consequently, its own sustained catch per unit of effort. Rather, these will be determined by the combined independent decisions of all the individual boat operators; if enough of them decide to change their level of effort, then average catch per unit of effort will change. This is analogous to the discussion in chapter 1, where the representative firm in a purely competitive industry has no control over price of output because its sales are so small relative to the total.

The cost curves for the production of effort for the individual boat will be similar to the cost curves discussed in chapter 1, and those for a representative boat in a fishery are as pictured in figure 3.1a. It makes the analysis much simpler to assume that all boats have the same cost curves, and such an assumption detracts nothing from the essence of the argument. For the individual boat, the average cost of producing a unit of effort will at first fall as more units are produced, because of increased efficiency and the wider distribution of the fixed costs. After a while, however, if the boat tries to increase its effort per period, the marginal cost of producing the last unit will increase to such an extent that average cost will begin to increase for various reasons including higher amounts and costs of maintenance due to longer times at sea, etc.

Each boat will act in the manner described in chapter 1 for profit-maximizing firms and will continue to produce effort as long as the return is greater than the cost of producing its last unit. The sustained return per unit

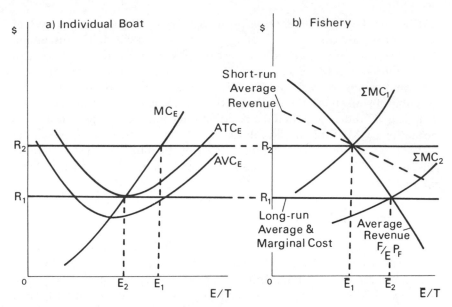

Figure 3.1. *The Fishery and the Individual Boat: Open Access.*   The rate of return per unit of effort is determined by the average productivity of the fishery and the number of boats being used. In open access the number of boats will increase until average revenue falls to the minimum average cost of producing effort *per* boat. This is long-run marginal and average cost. In this case there will be a total of $\bar{E}_2$ units of effort in the fishery. Each boat will produce E_2 units.

of effort is the price of fish multiplied by the average catch per unit of effort. For example, if average catch (which is beyond the control of the independent fisherman) is twelve tons and the price of fish is $10.00 a ton, the fisherman will receive $120.00 for every unit of effort he produces.

For the moment assume that this return equals R_2 in figure 3.1a. In that case the individual boat will produce E_1 units of effort. If it produced less, the cost of producing an extra unit would be less than its return; hence expanded production would be profitable. The reverse would hold if the boat produced more than E_1. Notice that at E_1 the returns per unit of effort are greater than average cost, thus profits are not only a maximum, they are also positive. Even if returns were less than average cost but greater than average variable cost, it would still make sense to produce in the short run—although profits would technically be negative—since total revenues would be greater than total variable costs. For these reasons, the marginal cost of effort above the average variable cost curve is a supply curve of effort for an individual boat. It tells how much effort will be produced by the boat at various levels of return to effort. Likewise, the horizontal summation of these curves for all of the boats in the fishery is the total supply curve of effort to the fishery—for that particular fleet size.

The above demonstrates the profit-maximizing behavior of the individual boat once a return to effort is specified. The next step is to demonstrate how this sustained return is determined. This is analogous to finding the price of output in a purely competitive industry. As discussed in chapter 1, this price is jointly determined by the market demand curve, which is really the average revenue curve, and the market supply curve, which is the sum of supply curves for the individual firms. There are curves that serve a similar purpose in this case. First, the sum of supply curves of effort for individual boats is the supply curve of effort for the fishery as a whole. It tells how much effort will be willingly supplied at various returns to effort, given the number of boats actively engaged in fishing. The curves labeled ΣMC_1 and ΣMC_2 in figure 3.1b are examples.

Second, while there is no such thing as a market or a fisherywide demand curve for effort, the average revenue curve for the fishery described in the discussion of figure 2.3b will serve the same purpose. This curve, also pictured in figure 3.1b, shows how the sustained return per unit of effort changes as total effort is changed and hence shows the effect fisherywide changes in effort will have on return to the individual boat.

When the average revenue curve and the fisherywide supply curve of effort are plotted together, the equilibrium average return to effort is determined by their intersection. At that point, the average revenue per unit of effort is just sufficient to induce the individual boat owner to supply the existing amount of effort. For example, if ΣMC_1 is the industry supply curve, then the equilibrium level of effort for the whole fishery will be $\bar{E}_1$ units. If effort were higher, the average revenue curve would lie below the supply curve; that is, the boats would not earn enough revenue per unit of effort to provide the incentive to keep them producing that amount. Since the reverse would occur below $\bar{E}_1$, that point is an equilibrium. The average return per unit of effort at this point will be R_2, which is actually determined by the independent actions of all operating boats, but because no individual boat can significantly affect the total amount of effort supplied to the fishery, it is equally powerless to affect the size of return per unit of effort. Rather, accepting R_2 as a given, the boat will operate to maximize profit at that level of return.

Let us now turn to the analysis of open-access exploitation in terms of the sustainable curves. To do so, consider figures 3.1a and 3.1b as a unit. The former represents one of many identical boats in the fishery, while the latter, which closely resembles figure 2.3b, represents the fishery as a whole. If ΣMC_1 is the fisherywide supply curve of effort, return per unit of effort is R_2, and so each boat will produce E_1 units of effort, because at that point the return for producing the last unit just equals marginal cost. The total amount of effort for the fishery as a whole will be $\bar{E}_1$. At this point, however, each boat is making higher than normal profits because average revenues are greater than average costs. Therefore, other boats will be motivated to enter the fishery, and the resultant increase in effort will ultimately lower sustained catch per unit of effort. Graphically, this is represented by a shift to the right of the fisherywide supply curve of effort to represent the summation of supply curves of a larger number of boats. It will therefore intersect the average revenue curve for effort at a lower average return. Each boat will react to this lower return by decreasing effort to where return per unit of effort is again equal to marginal cost. The lower return will cause profit per boat to fall even after the adjustment in its level of production. This entry and the simultaneous reduction of effort per boat will continue as long as profits exist. The final equilibrium will occur when the new entry has moved the industry supply curve to ΣMC_2. Return per unit of effort will be lowered to R_1, and so in each boat return will equal marginal cost at E_2, which is at the minimum of its average total cost curve. And so while it will be making a normal return, there will be no excess profit to stimulate entry. Notice that effort produced by each boat has now fallen to E_2, but industry effort has increased to $\bar{E}_2$. At the new equilibrium, a larger number of boats, each producing a smaller amount of effort individually, will be exerting a greater amount in total. Each boat will be producing this effort at the minimum possible cost. Therefore, while the unregulated fishery may be economically inefficient in putting forth too much fishing effort, the amount it does use is produced at the lowest possible cost.

Gould (1972b) has presented a theoretical analysis (the details of which are beyond the scope of this book) demonstrating that, in the case where an open-access resource is exploited utilizing more than one variable input, the above conclusion concerning least cost production of effort does not hold. This has no effect on our results, because in effect the fishery is exploited using only one variable input: effort. Gould's analysis has direct applications, however, when mesh size or other restriction on size at harvest becomes another input in the fishery production function.

$\bar{E}_2$ then is the open-access equilibrium level of effort and in figure 3.1b is analogous to E_3 in figure 2.3b. At both points the average return to effort equals the long-run average cost, which, we found earlier, is the cost of producing effort by adding boats operated at the most efficient level of output. Therefore, the long-run average cost of a constant-cost fishery equals the minimum of the average cost curve of a representative boat. Since long-run average cost is constant, long-run marginal cost is also a constant and is equal to long-run average cost; thus the line tangent to the minimum of the average cost curve of the boat bears the dual label, "long-run average and marginal cost." This curve shows the average and the marginal cost of producing extra effort when more boats can be introduced. In the short run, when time is too short for adding boats, the ΣMC curve for the existing number of boats shows the cost of increasing effort.

The above analysis glosses over the subtleties of the changes in the short-run production function as a result of stock size changes. However, to complete this discussion of open-access utilization, it will be useful to fill in this gap. The dotted curve in figure 3.1b represents the short-run average return curve for the level of fish population that exists at MEY. (It is analogous to the short-run total revenue curves in figure 2.4.) Notice that if the number of boats in the fishery is such that ΣMC_2 is the supply curve of effort, then in the short run, effort will tend to be greater than $\bar{E}_2$. This will mean that catch will be greater than growth and so the short-run revenue curve will shift down. Long-run equilibrium will occur when the curve has shifted down such that it intersects ΣMC_2 at the same place as does the long-run average revenue curve. To go into any greater detail will unduly repeat the analysis of the last chapter carried out in terms of the total curves. It is interesting to note, however, that if in response to short-run economic profits the number of boats increases such that the fisherywide supply curve of effort is below ΣMC_2, the return per unit of effort will be less than average total cost even when the boats are operating at the minimum of the average cost curve. However, if the return is greater than average variable costs, the boats will still remain in the fishery at least for the short run. But the "short run" may be a fairly long time if there are no other productive uses for the vessel and if there are few other employment opportunities for the fisherman, and this may account for the low-income levels of certain fishermen.

The analysis thus far has demonstrated how an individual boat will react to a given return to effort, how the equilibrium return to effort is determined, and how the actions of individual boats will tend to force the fishery to an open-access equilibrium yield where long-run average costs equal average returns. The discussion will now turn to stationary MEY in terms of the individual boat.

Figure 3.2 is similar to 3.1 except that the marginal revenue for effort for the fishery as a whole has been added. Recall from the discussion of figure 2.3b that the marginal revenue of effort is the change in total revenue to the fishery as a whole, resulting from an added unit of effort. In addition, short-run average and marginal revenue curves for a given population size have been included. Also, since the purpose is to discuss MEY, the long-run marginal social cost curve (i.e., the sum of long-run marginal harvest and user costs) has been added to the right-hand side to indicate the long-run impact on both harvesting and user costs from the addition of an extra unit of effort. This same curve was used in the introductory analysis of chapter 2, and it implicitly assumes that boats can enter this particular fishery from other fisheries when it is profitable to do so and can return to fish elsewhere when it is not profitable to remain. When the boats cannot be used in another fishery, the harvesting opportunity costs are different and the analysis must be modified. This case will be discussed below. The marginal social cost curve (MSC) for the vessel has also been added to the left-hand side of the graph to show the marginal user cost at the individual vessel level. This will be explained in more detail below.

In this figure open access will occur at $\bar{E}_2$, where sustainable average revenue equals long-run marginal and average harvesting cost. The open-access fleet will be such that the sum of their marginal harvest cost of effort curves is

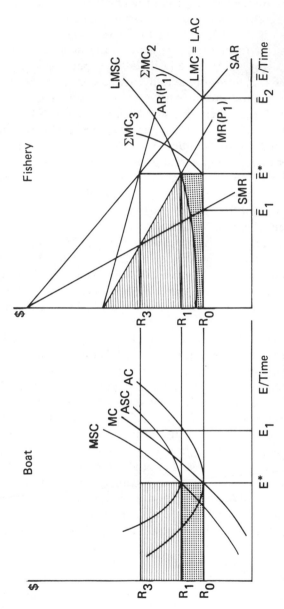

Figure 3.2. *The Fishery and the Individual Boat: MEY.* The optimal total level of effort is $\bar{E}^*$ where marginal size is equal to long-run marginal social cost. Each boat must operate at E^*, the point where the vessel marginal social cost equals the marginal return from the fishery.

equal to ΣMC_2. On the other hand, annual sustainable net revenues are maximized at $\bar{E}_1$ because this is where sustainable MR equals long-run marginal harvesting cost. As pointed out in the previous chapter, the stationary MEY point of effort will be somewhere between these two points. For any stock size, the annual optimum harvest is where short-run marginal revenue equals the social marginal cost of harvest. Fishing level $\bar{E}^*$ is such a point, given a stock size of P_1. This will also be a stationary MEY point if stock growth equals catch such that the population size does not change. Since short-run average revenue for this stock size equals sustained average revenue at $\bar{E}^*$, growth does indeed equal catch, and so E^* is a stationary MEY point.

In terms of this analysis, the fishery can operate in a dynamically optimal way only if fleet size is reduced until the fisherywide supply curve of effort intersects the long-run marginal harvesting cost curve at $\bar{E}^*$. To be precise, the number of boats should be reduced from the open-access level represented by the supply curve ΣMC_2 to a fleet size where the supply curve ΣMC_3 is operative. At this point, if each remaining vessel produces at the minimum of its average cost curve (i.e., at vessel output level E^*), total industry output will be $\bar{E}^*$. The size of the fleet and the operation of each vessel will be such that the optimal amount of effort is produced as efficiently as possible.

In the same way that return per unit of effort is determined by the fishery as a whole, user cost is a function of total industry output and as such can be thought of as constant from the point of view of the individual vessel. The curve labeled MSC on the left side of figure 3.2 represents marginal social cost of effort at the vessel level, given that industry output is $\bar{E}^*$. It is the marginal harvesting cost of effort plus a constant equal to marginal user cost at $\bar{E}^*$. Similarly, the curve labeled ASC is the average social cost of effort for the vessel, taking into account the user cost. Using these curves, it is possible to describe the optimal level of effort in terms of the individual vessel.

Note that at an industry output of $\bar{E}^*$, the marginal revenue of effort is equal to R_1. From the analysis of equation (2.2) in the previous chapter, the optimal amount of effort is obtained where the marginal revenue of effort (which, since price is fixed, represents the value of the marginal output) is equal to the marginal social cost. In figure 3.2a this occurs at vessel output level E^*, where R_1 equals MSC.

While marginal social cost, which is the sum of marginal harvesting and marginal user cost, is used in determining the position of $\bar{E}^*$, note that only harvesting cost is used in the determination of the optimal fleet size. That is, the optimal fleet size is determined by the intersection of the sum of the marginal harvesting cost curves and the long-run marginal harvest cost curve at $\bar{E}^*$. This is because user cost has to do with the foregone present value of future harvests, not with the cost of producing effort in the given period.

The optimal situation then, is $\bar{E}^*$ units of total effort produced by the number of boats that generate ΣMC_3 as the short-run supply curve, with each vessel producing E^* units. At that point, the average harvesting cost per unit of effort is R_0, and the average return is R_3. Therefore, the profit per unit of effort at MEY is R_3 minus R_0, and the total profit for each boat is represented by the shaded area in figure 3.2a. The profits for the boat consist of the annual return or rent to the stock, the hatched area, and the scarcity rent from properly using the stock through time—the dotted area. The sum of these boat profits equals the profit of the fishery and corresponds to the distance between total revenue and total cost at MEY in figure 2.6a. This amount can also be represented by the shaded area in the right-hand side of figure 3.2, which is the difference between total revenue (the area under the $MR_{(P_1)}$ curve out to $\bar{E}^*$) and total harvesting cost (the area under the LMC out to $\bar{E}^*$). The hatched area is the total rent to the stock, and the dotted area is the total scarcity rent. Because of the apparent similarity in the rents per boat and total rents to the fishery, now is a good time to point out again that the scales are different for the boat and the fishery. For example, effort could be measured in units in the former but in thousands in the latter; see chapter 1.

Note, however, that two types of regulation are necessary to keep this position: first, because profits exist, boats will be motivated to enter the fishery; second, because the return per unit of effort at this point is R_3, the boats that remain will want to produce at E_1 rather than E^*. It will be necessary, therefore, to limit both the number of boats that can enter the fishery and the amount of effort each boat can produce. As will be pointed out in chapter 6, this can be done simultaneously by using proper taxes or individual transferable quotas.

Increasing Cost Fisheries

Highliners. In most fisheries, of course, not all boats are equally efficient in producing effort, and so the horizontal long-run harvesting cost of effort curve does not apply. Therefore, it is necessary to modify the previous analysis in order to get a more accurate picture. Cost differences are sometimes due to special skills and knowledge of "highliner" captains and crews. While all vessels can purchase nonlabor inputs at the same cost for any boat, the efficiency with which effort is produced depends upon how many of these inputs have to be combined with labor to produce a given amount of effort. Since there are various degrees of skill, as less skilled labor enters the fishery, the cost of producing extra effort increases because more nonlabor inputs must be used with each unit of labor. Differences in the opportunity cost of labor and vessels in terms of what they could earn if employed elsewhere would also lead to an increasing long-run marginal cost of effort.

In situations such as this, the boat represented in figure 3.2 should be viewed as the marginal or least efficient one operating at any time, but the fisherywide short-run supply curve is still the sum of the marginal cost curves for those boats that are operating. Higher-cost boats will be the first to exit with decreases in returns to effort and the last to enter when the return per unit of effort increases, and so the open-access equilibrium will occur when the last boat to enter the fishery is just covering its costs. This will be where the now upward sloping long-run marginal cost of effort equals the sustained average revenue of effort. At that point, there will be no incentive for other, less efficient boats to enter. Boats operating with costs lower than the marginal boat will be earning more than enough to cover their costs. These points are explained in more detailed below.

The fisherywide long-run marginal cost curve of effort in this case is upward sloping, indicating that even when the marginal boat entering the fishery operates at the minimum of its average cost curve, additional units of effort can be produced only at a higher cost as less efficient boats enter the fishery. The curve labeled LMC in figure 3.3 illustrates such a long-run marginal harvesting cost curve. This figure is similar to the right side of figure 3.2 in other respects. For example, $LMSC$ is the long-run marginal social cost curve of effort. The open-access equilibrium will occur at the intersection of the sustainable average revenue curve, SAR, and the LMC, which in this case

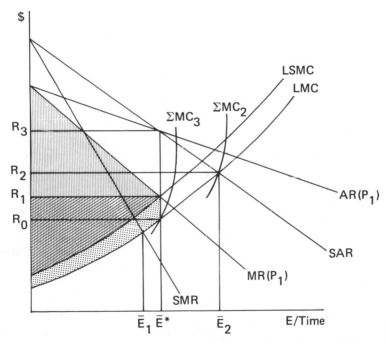

Figure 3.3. *MEY in Increasing-Cost Fisheries: Highliners.* The stationary MEY occurs when growth equals catch at the point where the marginal revenue for the existing stock size equals the long-run marginal social cost for the last (least efficient) boat to operate. All boats will be operating at the same level of marginal social cost, but those with lower average costs will be making highliner profits.

occurs at $\bar{E}_2$, where the return per unit of effort is R_2. The curve labeled ΣMC_2 is the sum of the marginal cost curves for the open-access fleet. All boats will be operating where their MC curve equals R_2. The minimum of the average cost curve for the last vessel will also equal R_2 and it will just break even. However, the average cost at this level of output of all other boats will be lower (by definition of an increasing cost fishery), and they will be earning rents due to the scarcity of their unique labor. Call these *highliner rents*. The more skillful the labor, the lower the actual cost of producing effort and the higher these rents will be.

The stationary MEY point will occur somewhere between $\bar{E}_1$, the point where annual monetary revenues are maximized, and $\bar{E}_2$, the open-access level of effort. In the diagram, such a point occurs at $\bar{E}^*$, the intersection of the short-run marginal revenue curve for stock size P_1—$MR_{(P_1)}$—and the $LMSC$. That this is a stationary point is indicated by the fact that $AR_{(P_1)}$ intersects SAR at this level of effort. In order to achieve this MEY point, the fleet size must be reduced such that the sum of the marginal cost curves is equal to ΣMC_3, and all boats should operate where their individual marginal social cost equal R_1, the marginal revenue of effort at $\bar{E}^*$, because in that way the marginal cost of effort will be the same regardless of which boat produces it and it will be equal to the marginal value of output. At this point, the marginal boat in the optimal fleet will just be covering the social cost of producing effort and will receive no highliner rents. The more efficient boats, however, will more than cover these social costs, and the difference will be highliner rents.

To completely understand the nature of the profits or rents earned at MEY in this case, note that, with the movement from open access, $\bar{E}_2$, to MEY, $\bar{E}^*$, average return per unit of effort has increased (from R_2 to R_3) while the average harvesting cost of effort has decreased due to the removal of the higher-cost boats. In the constant-cost case, only the return increased; cost remained the same. The total shaded area under the marginal revenue of effort for P_1 but above the LMC curve out to $\bar{E}^*$, represents the net returns (i.e., the net increase in the present value of goods and services) from the optimal utilization of the fishery at $\bar{E}^*$. (To review, the area below the marginal revenue equals total revenue, and the area below marginal cost represents total harvesting cost, so the difference equals net gain.) The hatched area represents annual rent to the stock, and the dotted area is the scarcity rent from proper intertemporal use of the stock. These gains are spread among the fleet in proportion to the amount of effort produced. The cross-hatched area represents the highliner rents to the fleet, which are spread according to their relative efficiency of producing effort, with the marginal boat earning none.

Harvesting Congestion.   The marginal harvesting cost curve for the industry as a whole can also be upward sloping in those instances where conges-

tion on the fishing grounds makes it more expensive for any one boat to produce effort. See Smith (1969) and Anderson (1982b). Whereas in the previous
case the industry cost curve increased because the cost curve of each succeeding vessel was higher than that of the previous one, in this case the increase
results because, as each additional boat enters the fishery, the cost curves of
all existing boats shift up. Therefore, the cost of producing each and every
unit of effort (both the marginal unit and all previously produced units) will
increase as additional boats enter the fishery. While such a phenomenon can
occur in the presence of highliner rents, it will be simpler to revert to the
assumption that all boats have identical cost curves.

This situation can be more fully explained with reference to figure 3.4.
The long-run average cost curve for the fishery slopes upward due to the effect
of the marginal boat on all previously operating vessels. For example, if the
fleet is such that E_1 is produced, the minimum of the average cost for all
vessels is at R_0, and the relevant portion of the sum of the marginal cost
curves is ΣMC_1. The part below the LAC is not relevant as a long-run supply
curve.

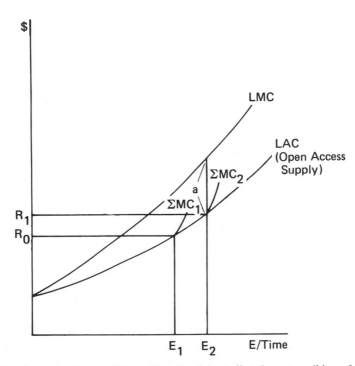

Figure 3.4. *Congestion Costs.* If the actions of each boat affect the cost conditions of all others,
the long-run average cost curve will slope upward because, as more boats enter the fishery, the cost
curves of all boats will shift up.

In order for effort to increase to E_2, an extra boat must enter the fishery. Its operation will increase the real cost of producing effort for all operating boats because of its interference in the production process. Therefore, the sum of the marginal cost curves for the new fleet is represented by ΣMC_2. It is further to the right due to the addition of the extra vessel, but in addition, the lowest relevant point on it is increased because the minimum of the average cost of all vessels has increased. Therefore, the long-run average cost of producing E_2 is R_1.

As will be demonstrated below, in this case it is the LAC curve that is the open-access supply curve. However, the long-run marginal cost curve (see the curve labeled LMC) is required to determine the optimal output level. The distance "a" between the LMC and the LAC at E_2 represents the congestion costs that are imposed on all previously operating boats with the entry of the marginal boat. To be precise, the congestion cost is equal to $n(R_1 - R_0)$ where n is the number of previously operating boats. That is, the congestion cost is the increase in cost imposed on all previously operating vessels. Thus, LMC includes harvesting and congestion costs.

The analysis of open access and MEY in this case is quite similar to the "highliner" case, at least as far as most of the actual graphics are concerned. The important differences are in the explanations of the curves given above and in the nature of the profits at the MEY point. Figure 3.5 is similar to figure 3.3 except that the cost curves from figure 3.4 have been used. The open-access equilibrium occurs at $\bar{E}_2$, at the intersection of the sustained annual average revenue (SAR) and the LAC curves. This is an equilibrium because all boats will just be earning enough to cover their costs including a normal profit, and so there will be no incentive for others to enter the fishery. The return per unit of effort is R_1, and all vessels will be operating where their MC curves and the minimum of their AC curve equal this average return from the fishery. No profits will be earned by any boat.

The stationary MEY point is at $\bar{E}^*$ where the MR for a given population intersects the $LMSC$ curve at the same point that the related AR curve for that population intersects the SAR curve. At this point, the average return has increased to R_3 and the real harvesting costs have decreased to R_0. The move from $\bar{E}_2$ to $\bar{E}^*$ will require a reduction in the fleet such that the short-run supply curve shifts back from ΣMC_2 to ΣMC_3. For optimal vessel operation, each boat must operate where its marginal social cost is equal to R_2, the marginal return per unit of effort at $\bar{E}^*$. This equality will occur at the minimum of their average social and average harvesting cost curves. See figure 3.2.

The net returns from the fishery at the optimal point can be represented by the shaded area in figure 3.5. Again, the hatched and dotted areas represent the annual rent to the stock and the scarcity rent for optimally utilizing it through time, respectively. In this case the crosshatched area represents the gains from correcting for the congestion problem.

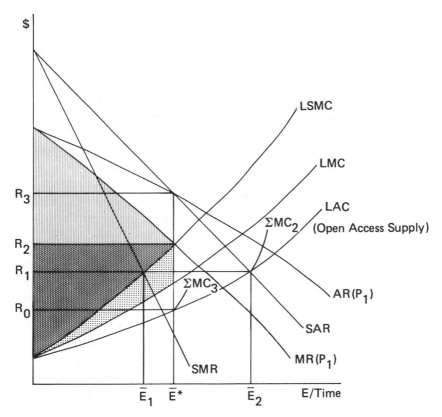

Figure 3.5. *MEY in Increasing-Cost Fisheries: Congestion.*   The stationary MEY occurs when growth equals catch at the point where the marginal revenue for the existing stock equals the long-run marginal social cost of the last unit of effort, including the congestion costs the last boat imposed on all other boats.

There are several differences between these two cases. With congestion, the open-access equilibrium is determined by the long-run average cost curve rather than by the *LMC* curve. In addition, there are no economic profits at open access, whereas highliner rents are earned at open access in the highliner case. Finally, a different kind of rent, a return for controlling congestion, is earned at the MEY point in the congestion case.

Optimal Harvest Time Paths

An important concept in the study of fisheries exploitation is that both open-access and optimal utilization should be viewed dynamically as a harvest time path rather than as a static annual catch level. Granted either time path may reach stationary or equilibrium levels of output where there is only minor year-to-year variation in harvest, as mentioned above, such is normally the case with Schaefer growth curves. In view of this, the above comparison between open-access and stationary optimal harvest points needs to be complemented by a discussion of the optimal time path to a stationary MEY level output. This time path will start at the virgin stock level and with no fleet for a new fishery or from the existing stock size and fleet level for a fishery that has already been exploited under other than optimal conditions. The purpose of this section is to present such a discussion.

The analysis in terms of individual boats is ideal for this analysis because it allows for direct examination of both the amount of fishing effort to use each year and also of the construction and depreciation of vessels. In the discussion of optimal paths depicted in figure 2.8, it was assumed that effort could be added to the fishery independent of the construction of vessels and that it could be reduced with no consideration of other uses for excluded vessels. Where boats can move from fishery to fishery with ease, these assumptions are appropriate and the monotonically increasing or decreasing optimal time paths of effort can make sense. However, when it is necessary to construct new vessels in order to increase the level of effort or when reductions in effort will mean that some vessels will remain idle, the analysis can be different.

Part of this difference has to do with the fixed cost of constructing the vessel. It only makes sense to construct a vessel if the expected returns *over its life* will be enough to cover both construction costs and annual operating costs. The latter are more commonly called the *variable*, as opposed to *fixed*, costs by economists. On the other hand, once a vessel is built, the variable costs are the only relevant costs. For an existing vessel, if annual revenues are expected to be greater than annual operation (variable) costs, it makes sense to continue fishing. The amortization of the construction costs continue whether the boat operates or not, and, as such, should have no influence on the decision to use that vessel to produce effort. Therefore, in certain circumstances, while it may not make sense to build a new boat, it can be quite rational to operate an existing one. The decision to enter a fishery is different from the decision to exit.

The other part of the difference has to do with the opportunity cost of using an existing vessel. When a boat can be used in another fishery, the opportunity cost is the variable operating costs plus the net gain (value of output minus net social costs), which can be earned from using the vessel in the other fishery. Therefore, since the real cost of using an existing vessel is higher when it has other uses, all else equal, it will make sense to continue fishing less often than when there are no other uses. This distinction will be easier to make in the context of the following examples.

Following the work of Clark, Clarke, and Munro (1979), let us analyze optimal harvest paths, taking the difference in entry and exit conditions into consideration. In all cases, the figures are drawn assuming that the fleet is specialized and cannot be used in other fisheries. The alternative situation, however, will be discussed.

Hypothetical optimal time paths of stock size and fleet size are pictured in figure 3.6. While stock and fleet size are measured using different parameters, they are plotted on the same graph for comparative purposes. On an optimal time path, it does not make sense to build a vessel until the time period when it will be utilized. Therefore, fleet size will be used as the measure of effort except where noted.

First, consider a hypothetical fish stock that has been recently discovered and heretofore unexploited. The problem is to determine the optimal way to build up the fleet and to use it to produce effort. Figure 3.6a contains optimal time paths for fleet and stock size that could be appropriate for such a fishery, depending upon the construction costs and time necessary to actually build the boats, annual operation costs, market prices, the size of the initial stock, and the nature of its population dynamics. At time zero, there is a large virgin

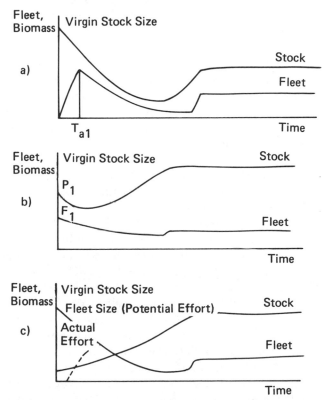

Figure 3.6. *Time Paths of Harvest and Fleet Construction.*   The optimal time path for harvest must take into account other potential uses of vessels. If they have no other uses, it can sometimes be optimal to continue using a larger than optimal fleet for the time it takes the boats to depreciate.

stock but no fleet. From this point the optimal fleet at first grows to a maximum, then decreases, and finally grows again to its stationary optimal size.
Simultaneously, the optimal stock size decreases to a minimum and then increases to its stationary optimum level.

The economic logic behind these curves is as follows. In order to optimally utilize the large initial stock, it can make sense to initially expand the
fleet rapidly so as to obtain those harvests as soon as possible. As the virgin
stock is consumed, this expansion should stop, however. As pictured here,
the relative values of market price and operational harvesting and user costs
are such that it is optimal from point T_{a1} on to halt construction but to continue using existing vessels. It makes sense to use the vessels because the returns are greater than variable harvesting costs and user costs. The decline in
the optimal fleet time path after T_{a1} is explained by the exit of vessels as they
wear out in the order but not at the rate at which they entered. Over this
period, the fleet is large enough to cause stock size to fall, but as the number
of vessels decreases, the pressure on stock diminishes and eventually the population starts to grow again. Once the stock grows to its optimal stationary
size, it is time to start rebuilding the fleet in order to take advantage of the
now higher stock size.

In summary, optimal utilization entails a rapid build up of the fleet followed by a gradual reduction through depreciation. The size of the initial
peak in fleet size will be higher, the larger the initial stock and the shorter the
expected useful operating life of the average vessel. Once the stock has recovered from the effects of allowing the existing fleet to continue to fish, the fleet
must be expanded again. However, the second fleet expansion will never go as
far as the first, the purpose of which was to take advantage of the large virgin
stock.

The above deals with optimal time paths for a fishery that is to be controlled from its inception. The optimal time paths for fisheries that have been
fished under open-access conditions for some period of time are somewhat
different because there is already an existing fleet and the stock size will be
less than its virgin state at the time when optimal utilization begins. In the
initial periods, then, the focus of attention changes from how to build the fleet
to how to use an existing fleet. Two general types of situations can occur.
Figure 3.6b depicts possible optimal time paths in a case where the stock has
been moderately depleted by uncontrolled fishing. Although the existing fleet
is above the optimal stationary size, it makes economic sense to continue using it because annual returns are above variable harvesting and user costs.
However, no new construction should be allowed, and as boats retire from the
fishery they should not be replaced. This harvest pattern will initially cause a
further reduction in the fish stock, but as the fleet begins to decrease through
depreciation, the pressure on the stock will be reduced, and ultimately, when
effort falls such that catch is less than growth, stock size will begin to increase. Once the stock reaches its optimal stationary size, it will then be nec-

essary to begin reinvestment in the fleet. However, the fleet should never again be as high as it was originally.

As another case of optimal utilization of a fishery that has already been fished, consider figure 3.6c. Here the stock is severely depleted by the uncontrolled effort, and there is a relatively large initial fleet size. As pictured here, it is not only necessary to allow the fleet to decrease through depreciation but also, in the initial periods, to restrict effort below that which the fleet is capable of producing. This is indicated by the dotted line for actual effort, which is lower than the potential from the fleet. In this case, even when only considering vessel operating costs and user costs, it does not make sense to use the fleet. In heavily overexploited stocks, this can be explained by a low catch per unit of effort due to the decreased stock size and, in those cases where there is potential for stock recovery, by a higher current user cost. Holding back on effort now, even though the fleet is there, is efficient because of the potential increase in harvests in future periods. In this case, stock size grows monotonically from the start of regulation until it reaches its optimum stationary size while the fleet size is diminished through depreciation. For the first part of the harvesting period, effort will be less than the capacity of the fleet. In fact, as drawn, it is initially equal to zero. However, as the stock size grows, it becomes optimal to use a small amount of the possible effort, and as stock size continues to grow and fleet size diminishes, a point will be reached where it will be optimal to use all of the diminishing fleet. Finally, when the stock size reaches its optimal size, reinvestment in the fleet will be necessary in order to properly utilize the stock.

The difference between the second and third cases has to do with the sizes of the initial fleet and stock relative to their optimums and to the variable costs of harvesting. The lower the variable costs and the higher the initial stock size when optimal utilization begins, the more likely the optimal time paths will be as those pictured in figure 3.6b, as opposed to figure 3.6c.

In all three cases, the reason the fleet must fall below its stationary optimal size in some periods is the necessity of allowing the fish stock to grow. In order to accomplish this, effort will have to be restricted, and it makes no sense to construct vessels in periods when they cannot be used. Looking at it from another way, while it may make sense to use existing vessels until they wear out even if this may cause a temporary further decline in the fish stock, it does make sense to build new vessels and let them sit idle in anticipation of the time when the stock has sufficiently recovered.

The above three cases would be different if the fleet had other uses. Since the alternative to not fishing in that instance is harvesting in another fishery rather than idleness, it makes sense to reduce the fleet by shifting their use instead of merely allowing them to depreciate. Therefore, the fleet reduction will be faster, the stock will not be pushed to as low a level, and the approach to the stationary level will be more direct. In fact, depending on the relative net gains in the two fisheries, it may be optimal to make complete and abrupt shifts. In the first case, if initial returns are high, large numbers of vessels should be brought in immediately to reduce the stock to its stationary optimal size, and the fleet should be immediately reduced to its optimal size once the "thinning" of the stock is completed. In the second two cases, if the returns in the other fishery are high enough, it can be optimal to shift the entire existing fleet to the other use so that the stock can recover as quickly as possible.

These hypothetical optimal time paths cannot be considered blueprints for the optimal utilization of all fisheries because there are many possible variations, depending upon the economic and biological peculiarities of different fisheries. The analysis is useful, however, because it gives a broader perspective on the actual management of fisheries. It shows very clearly that not only is there a difference between optimal and open-access utilization but there is also an appropriate way to change the fishery from one mode of operation to the other.

Conclusion

This analysis of the individual boat and the fishery as a whole is interesting because it allows for a distinction between the sources of increased effort, whether it results from more boats entering the fishery or from each boat producing more effort. In the short run only the latter is possible. For example, if a considerable number of boats were lost at sea, the industry supply curve would shift to the left. The consequent greater return to effort would then cause the remaining boats to fish more intensively. Thereafter, as other boats entered the fishery, the returns would again fall, and each boat would cut back to its old level of production.

These points are ignored in the aggregate model, where the assumption of a constant cost of effort implies that the only variable is the number of boats and that each boat will always operate at the minimum of its average cost curve. In the long run this is a valid assumption, but during periods of entry or exit, the average cost of effort will differ from a straight-line or an increasing average cost curve.

This section has shown how the individual operator reacts in both an open-access and a regulated fishery. It will be well to keep this in mind as we proceed. Most of what follows deals with changes in effort from the standpoint of the whole fishery, but behind that lies the decision-making process of scores of individual boat owners.

The Model with a Variable Price of Fish

Introduction

The restrictive assumption of a fixed price of fish has enabled us to provide a fairly concise description of the operation of an unregulated fishery and the conditions necessary for maximum economic yield. This assumption is valid when the fishery under consideration is such a small part of the total market for fish that its operation will not affect the price. But the law of demand tells us that the selling price of a good will vary inversely with the amount put on the market during a specified period. Therefore, the selling price of fish may change as a fishery that is large relative to the market expands or contracts its effort and, hence, its output. To make our analysis more general, this effect should be considered in a straightforward manner. To do so will be the purpose of this section. Many of the results will be similar to previous sections, but the more general approach will make it possible to consider such details as consumer surplus, monopoly profit, and multiple equilibria.

For purposes of this more general analysis, it is best to change the frame of reference and to consider cost and revenue in terms of fish rather than in terms of effort. Specifically, since the demand curve is an average revenue curve, it is most useful to deal with average revenue and the average cost of fish.

Assume that the downward-sloping curve labeled *Demand* in figure 3.7 is the demand curve facing a particular fishery. It shows the maximum unit price that consumers will pay for various outputs and, as explained before, demonstrates that as the fishery expands output, the market price for its product is driven down. Market price is the average revenue per unit of fish sold.

The backward-bending curve in the figure is the long-run average cost curve in terms of fish for the fishery as a whole. It can be derived directly from the sustained yield curve and the total cost curve for effort, which have been the central part of the earlier analysis. While the complete discussion of the derivation is left to the appendix to this chapter, the logic behind the curve is as follows. Since there are two levels of effort that can catch any sustainable yield (except the maximum), there are two levels of average cost for each of these yields. For instance, the level of catch F_2 can be caught on a sustained basis at costs of $18.00 and $14.00. The lower cost represents a relatively smaller amount of effort working on a large fish population, while the higher one represents a larger amount of effort and a smaller population. It may be useful to conceive of movements along the curve from the origin through the bend and then toward the left-hand corner as representing increases in effort and decreases in population. That is, as effort is added to the fishery, sustainable yield increases, but so does average cost, due to the diminishing marginal catch rate of effort. Once maximum sustained yield is reached, further increases in effort will actually reduce the amount of sustainable catch, and increased total cost of effort and a decreased yield combine to raise average cost. This explains the backward-bending part of the curve: increases in effort will both increase cost and decrease sustainable catch.

The backward-bending average cost curve, directly related to the sustain-

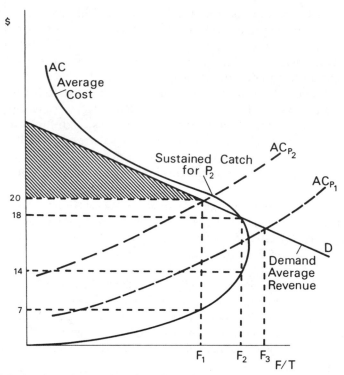

Figure 3.7. *Demand and Average Cost: Open Access.*   The average cost curve for fish bends back on itself because there are two levels of effort that will catch each sustainable yield except the maximum. Open-access equilibrium yield occurs where the demand (average revenue) curve intersects the average cost curve. When this intersection takes place in the backward-bending section of the cost curve, the fishery will be operating beyond maximum sustainable yield.

able yield curve, is the long-run average cost curve for the fishery. Short-run curves also play a part, however. Those labeled AC_{P_2} and AC_{P_1} in figure 3.7 show how average cost per unit of fish varies with output at two different population sizes. The curves have the indicated slopes because of the diminishing average productivity of effort. Each additional unit of effort catches progressively fewer fish, and so, as catch expands, each extra unit of fish caught will require more effort than the previous one. This means that the average cost of fish will increase as the catch gets larger. The cost curve for the population P_2 is higher than the one for P_1 since it takes more effort to get the same catch from a smaller population. These short-run curves will intersect the long-run cost curve at the sustainable yield for the given level of population.

Open-Access Exploitation

Using these curves, let us analyze the operation of an unregulated open-access fishery. The open-access equilibrium occurs where the demand curve intersects the long-run cost curve, because at that point price just equals the average cost of fish. That is, each fisherman will simply be meeting the cost of catching the fish. Consider a fishery that is being exploited for the first time and is producing F_1 units of fish at a cost of \$7.00 per unit. The market price at an output of F_1, as determined by the demand curve, is \$20.00. The resulting profit will encourage an expansion of effort which will continue until sustained yield reaches its maximum and then falls back to F_2. At that point, average cost and price will both reach \$18.00, cancelling any inducement for expansion. If, for some reason, effort is still increased, catch will fall, and the average cost becoming greater than price will lead to a decrease in effort. F_2 then will be the open-access equilibrium yield, and note that this occurs where F_2 units of fish are being taken at the larger of the two possible costs. If the demand curve intersected the average cost curve in its lower half, then the fishery would be obtaining the equilibrium catch at the lower of the two costs but, as should be clear by now, it would still not be operating in an optimal manner.

Again, the process of obtaining an open-access equilibrium yield can be injected very easily, but since this material should be familiar by now, the discussion will be very brief. Given a population of P_1 and, hence, a short-run average cost of AC_{P_1} (figure 3.7), in the short run the fishery will produce F_3 units of fish because that is where price equals short-run average cost. Since the sustained yield for this population is where the short-run curve intersects the long-run curve, catch will be greater than natural increase and the population will fall. If it falls to P_2, then equilibrium output in the next period will fall to F_1. Since this is less than the natural increase for that population level, population will grow. Equilibrium will be reached where the short-run cost curve and the demand curve intersect the long-run cost curve at the same point.

Before leaving this section, it is interesting to note that in figure 3.8a, the demand curve actually intersects the average cost curve at points A, B, and C, thus offering three possible equilibria for the unregulated fishery. Of these, only points A and C are stable in an economic sense. Note that at point B a small increase in effort will decrease catch (the fishery is operating in the downward-sloping part of the sustained yield curve), and revenue will then be greater than cost. Therefore, more boats will be attracted to the fishery, and catch will continue to fall until point C is reached. Similarly, if effort falls from that level at B, catch will increase but costs will exceed revenues, eventually causing an exit of boats, which will continue until point A is reached. At points A and C, however, a small increase or decrease in effort will set in motion a profit situation that will reverse the initial move until equilibrium is again established.

Which of the stable equilibria will prevail at any point in time is hard to predict. For a fishery that expands in a slow and continuous fashion, it is highly likely that the one at point A will hold. However, a big initial surge of

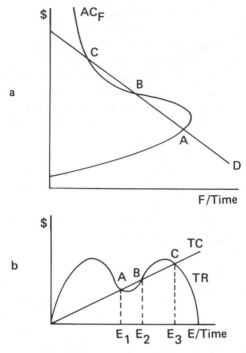

Figure 3.8. *Total Revenue with a Variable Price.*   When price varies with output, the total revenue curve can have this double maxima shape. See figure A.3. This introduces the possibility of
multiple equilibria in an open-access fishery.

entry may affect the fish population to such an extent that point C will be
reached. At that point, although costs are very high because of the small population size, the scarcity of the fish results in a price high enough to cover
costs. Since the boats are all meeting their costs, there is no incentive to reduce effort and population will remain low. Of the two unregulated equilibria, it is obvious that the one at point A is superior in a sustained net revenue
sense because it provides a higher level of output at a lower cost. (See below,
however.)

A clearer description of the possibility of multiple equilibria can be given
by changing the focus of analysis back to effort. When price is a variable,
total revenue and yield will not always change in the same direction. In those
cases the revenue curve will have a double-humped shape, as in figure 3.8b.
The derivation of this double maxima revenue curve is best left to the appendix, but its peculiar shape is due to the fact that at some levels of output the
decrease in price necessary to enable another unit to be sold (which then applies to all previous units sold) will decrease revenue to a greater degree than
the sale of the last unit will add to revenue. (See the discussion of a negative
marginal revenue in chapter 1.) If this point is reached at a level of catch
below maximum sustainable yield, increased effort over a certain range will

increase yield but decrease revenue. After maximum sustained yield is reached, increases in effort will decrease yield but increase revenue. After sustainable yield falls to this critical level of output again, increases in effort will decrease both yield and revenue. (The appendix offers a more complete analysis.)

As drawn, the total cost curve intersects this revenue curve in three places, producing three possible equilibria, analogous to those in figure 3.8a. E_3 has a relatively higher cost than does E_1, but revenues are high enough to compensate for this. The equilibrium at E_2 is not economically stable, because small increases or decreases in effort will both lead to movements away from the equilibrium. For example, if effort were to increase from E_2, revenue would be greater than cost and so more entry would be encouraged. The equilibria at E_1 and E_3, however, are locally stable. In this perspective it is easier to see that a slowly expanding fishery will very probably operate at the equilibrium at E_1, because at any lower levels of effort, profits will encourage entry, and at even a slightly higher point than E_1, losses will cause effort to fall. However, if any reason such as a rapid initial increase in effort causes a point higher than E_2 to be reached, then the equilibrium will settle at E_3.

Maximum Economic Yield

The analysis of maximum economic yield (MEY) is somewhat different here than in the previous case, basically because when price varies with output, marginal revenue is less than price. Figure 3.9 is similar to figure 3.7 except that marginal cost and marginal revenue curves have been added. The marginal revenue curve, it will be recalled from chapter 1, shows the change in revenue produced by a change in the number of fish sold; it is always below the demand curve, because in order to sell more, the price must be lowered. Since this applies to all previous units sold, the increase in revenue will be less than the price of the last unit sold. And since the purpose of the analysis is to analyze MEY, the cost curves will be short-run curves for a given stock size. The curve labeled MC_{P_1} is the marginal harvest cost curve when stock size is P_1; that is, it shows the change in total harvesting cost due to a unit change in the production of fish at this stock size. It has the normal upward-sloping shape due to the diminishing productivity of effort. The MSC_{P_1} curve represents the marginal social cost of producing an extra unit of fish at the given stock size, and it includes marginal user cost as well as marginal harvesting cost. It should be remembered that all of these costs curves are in terms of fish rather than effort, as has previously been the case.

Given this stock size, the optimal production of fish is F^*, the output level at which the social marginal cost curve intersects the demand curve (see point B). This is the maximum economic yield for this period, because at that level of output the price consumers are willing to pay for the last unit of fish exactly equals the social marginal cost of producing the final unit. Therefore,

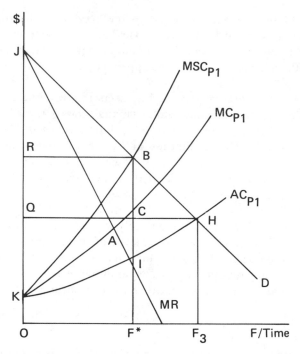

Figure 3.9. *Demand and Average and Marginal Costs of Fish: MEY.*   The optimal output of fish
for any period is where the marginal social cost curve of fish for the existing stock size intersects the
demand curve. Therefore, in this graph an output level of F^* will maximize the current contribution to the present value of the sum of consumer surplus and profits.

from society's point of view, the last unit of fish produced is worth exactly
what it cost to obtain it. The price represents value to the last consumer while
the marginal social cost represents values foregone in terms of the opportunity cost of harvesting and in terms of the present value of future harvest. If
the output of fish were expanded beyond that point, the last unit would cost
more than its market value, so society would be better off if the requisite inputs were transferred to some other use. Similarly, if production were less
than F^*, the last until of fish would cost less than its market price, and production should be increased, since the additional unit of fish would be worth
more to society than the value of alternative goods produced by the same inputs.

The optimal time path for harvest will be obtained if the equivalent of F^*
is produced every period, taking into account the change in stock size from
period to period. A stationary optimum harvest point will occur if the long-
run average cost of fish, as pictured in figure 3.7, intersects the AC curve for
the given stock size at the F^* level of harvest. For example, a stationary point
would obtain if the long-run average cost curve intersected AC_{P_1} in figure 3.9
at point I.

Recall from the above analysis that, when price is a constant, MEY occurs at that intertemporal pattern of output where the present value of profit to the fishery is a maximum. This is not so, however, when price varies with output, because profit is only a partial measure of economic welfare. It reflects what consumers actually do pay but not what they are willing to pay. The proper goal in this more general model is to maximize the present value of the sum of fishery profits and consumer surplus. (For purposes here, profit will be understood to include any highliner rent or producer surplus earned in the production of effort.) As was shown in chapter 1, consumer surplus is the difference between what people are willing to pay for a certain output and the amount they actually do pay in the market place. For example, in figure 3.7, the shaded area represents the consumer surplus when F_1 units of fish are sold, because all consumers pay \$20.00 per unit but some would be willing to pay more. This is evidenced by the fact that, as price is increased, the quantity demanded will decline but it will not fall to zero except at a much higher price.

The logic of why F^* is optimal for the given period has been described in terms of values gained and foregone from producing extra units. It will also be useful to look at it in terms of the sum of consumer surplus and profits. The sum of the annual contribution of consumer surplus and profits at any level of output is always represented by the area below the demand curve and above the marginal cost curve from the vertical axis to a line perpendicular to the horizontal axis at the level of output. For example, at the optimum point, this sum is equal to area $JBCK$. Of that area, JRB is consumer surplus and $RBCK$ is profit. It is easy to see that $RBCK$ is profit because total revenue is equal to RBF^*O and total harvesting cost is equal to the area under the marginal harvesting cost curve out to F^* or $OKCF^*$. In terms of the previous discussion, the profit can be divided into annual rent to the resource, RBK, and the scarcity rent earned for optimal intertemporal use, KBC.

It can be seen that the area above the MC but below the demand curve (i.e., the sum of consumer surplus and profit) is a maximum when final production is at F^*, the MEY. Note, however, that at outputs less than F^*, profits can increase through monopoly pricing although consumer surplus will fall. Similarly, at higher levels of output, profits will be lower but consumer surplus will increase. It is the sum of the two that is maximized at F^*; neither profit nor consumer surplus is at its highest level at that point.

The fact that profit itself is not maximized at the optimum point is important in clarifying the distinction between a model with fixed price and one with variable price. In the former, the optimum point is reached where social marginal cost of effort equals marginal revenue of effort, which is to say that the social marginal cost of fish equals the marginal revenue of fish. But when price is a constant, marginal revenue is always equal to price, and so marginal revenue of fish equaling marginal social cost of fish is equivalent to price of fish equaling marginal cost of fish. When price of fish is a variable, however, marginal revenue is always less than price, so while social marginal cost of effort equaling marginal revenue of effort is still equivalent to marginal cost of fish equaling marginal revenue of fish, it is not the same as social marginal cost of fish equaling price of fish.

One reason for making this distinction is that sometimes it is argued that the proper way to control a fishery is to operate it as a sole owner would. This is true only when the output of the fishery has no effect on price. Otherwise, the sole owner would operate so as to earn monopoly profits but not to maximize the sum of consumer surplus and profits. The constant price model is useful for simplifying much of the analysis, but the goal of maximizing profits, which makes sense in the context of that model, cannot be generalized to the case when price varies with output. For the most part, however, we will continue to use the constant price model.

To summarize, in order to obtain economic efficiency with a variable price of output, a fishery should be operated in each period where the price that consumers are willing to pay for the last unit produced equals the marginal social cost of producing it. This time path of harvest will maximize the present value of the sum of profit to the fishery and consumer surplus.

In addition to allowing for a more complete analysis of optimal yield exploitation by considering consumer surplus, the analysis in terms of a variable price of output can also provide for a more straightforward comparison of the open-access and stationary MEY points. Recall that the stationary MEY point is the level of harvest that occurs when, and if, the optimal time path becomes a straight line. Colin Clark (1976, 159–63) has shown that, for any given interest rate, it is possible to derive a curve showing the optimal stationary harvest level for various price levels. The curve labeled F^* in figure 3.10 is an example. For an infinite discount rate, the optimal stationary harvest curve is equivalent to the long-run average cost-of-fish curve, as represented in this figure by the curve labeled AC_F. With a zero discount rate, the optimal stationary harvest curve is the long-run marginal cost curve of fish. See the curve labeled MC_F. The curve labeled F^* is derived for a finite interest rate in between these two extremes.

The intersection of the demand curve with the F^* curve determines the optimal stationary level of output. If D_1 is the operative demand curve, then open-access equilibrium will occur at F_1 with average harvest cost at point A. The optimal stationary output will occur at F_2 with average harvesting cost at point C. The price at F_2 is at point B, and the distance BC represents the fishery profit per unit of output. In this case, the optimal harvest time path, starting from the open-access point, will eventually result in a decrease in output and in harvesting cost. The reason it is optimal for catch to decrease should be obvious from above; however, the short explanation is that the loss in welfare resulting from the decrease in fish harvest is more than made up for by increases in output elsewhere in the economy as resources are released from the fishing industry.

The analysis is somewhat different if D_2 is the operative demand curve.

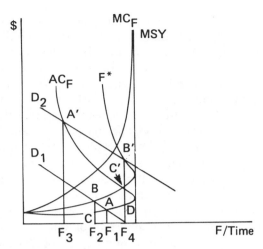

Figure 3.10. *Demand Curves and Stationary MEY.* Stationary MEY can occur such that the operation point is on either the upward sloping or the backward-bending portion of the average cost curve for fish, depending upon the relative position of the demand curve. When it occurs on the backward-bending portion, this means that, although the same output could be harvested at a lower average cost if the stock were allowed to grow, such an increase in stock size would require a reduction in current and near-term harvest that would decrease the net present value of harvests.

In this case the open access occurs at F_3, where average harvest cost is at A' while F_4 is the optimal stationary point. The price at this output level is at B' while the average harvest cost is at C'. The distance $B'C'$ is the per unit level of fishery profit. If a fishery is at the open-access equilibrium, the optimal harvest time path will be from point A' to point C' on the long-run average cost-of-fish curve. This represents a move to larger catches and a larger stock size. Therefore, while the overall trend in output will be upward, there will have to be a decrease in output over some range of the optimal harvest time path in order to allow the stock to grow.

Note that, while the optimal output is harvested at an average cost of C', it is possible to obtain that same level of harvest at the lower cost of D by allowing the stock to grow and then applying a lower level of effort. Because the demand curve intersects the backward-bending portion of the F^* curve, the decrease in the present value of harvest required to allow such an increase in the fish stock will be greater than any savings made possible by the decrease in future harvesting costs. Therefore, as discussed above, the stationary optimal harvest rate can occur at a stock size less than the one that generates maximum sustainable yield (MSY).

The Fishery When Viewed as Part of the Whole Economy

As was pointed out above, MEY is the proper goal, not because the profit to the fishery (in the fixed-price model) reaches a maximum at that point (although in fact it does), but rather because it guarantees that society's resources are being so allocated as to maximize the satisfaction or welfare of its people. Viewed from the other direction, the yield produced in an unregulated fishery is not bad just because the profit from the fishery has been dissipated but because society is not making the best use of all of its resources, including the fishery, to maximize its welfare. To see this point more clearly, it is helpful to use the production possibility (PP) curve and indifference curve analysis introduced in chapter 1 to investigate the operation of a market economy utilizing an open-access fishery. The analysis to follow will be in static terms only because of the nature of the graphical tools, which make it very difficult to introduce the concept of user cost. The purpose of this section is to stress the importance of the nonfishery segments of the economy, and this point can be adequately made in a static analysis.

Recall from chapter 1 that a perfectly functioning market economy will operate so as to reach the highest possible level of welfare, given the PP curve. This section will show that in the case of an open-access fishery the market economy cannot produce these beneficial results, mainly because producers are concerned with average rather than marginal returns to effort.

Assume for simplicity that there are only two goods in the economy, fish (F) and some alternative (G). Since fishermen actually produce effort (E) rather than fish, the economy's productive capacity can be expressed as a PP curve for E and G as pictured in figure 3.11. This curve, representing the combinations of fishing effort and G that the economy can produce in a defined period given the resource stock and the state of technology, is the basis that producers will use in deciding what combination of E and G to produce.

Corresponding to the PP curve for E and G is one for F and G, as pictured in figure 3.11b. The relation between the two curves is discussed in detail in the appendix to this chapter (see figure A.4), but for the moment notice that each level of G produced determines a maximum possible amount of E. When applied to the fishery, this amount results in a specified sustained yield. For example, in the figure, F_1 is the sustained yield from E_1 units of effort per period. The upward-sloping portion of the PP curve for F and G is the result of the downward-sloping segment of the sustained yield curve. In that section sustainable yield increases as resources are transferred out of fishing effort and into G; thus it is possible to have an increase in the production of both F and G. (E_{msy} is the level of effort that obtains the maximum sustainable yield—MSY.)

The slope of the PP curve for F and G is related to the slope of the PP curve for E and G and to the slope of the sustained yield curve. This is because it shows the relationship between a change in G and a change in F, which depends upon the change in E resulting from decreasing the production of G (the slope of the PP curve for E and G) and the change in F resulting from adding this effort to the fishery (the slope of the sustained yield curve). Using Δ to symbolize "change in," this can be expressed mathematically as:

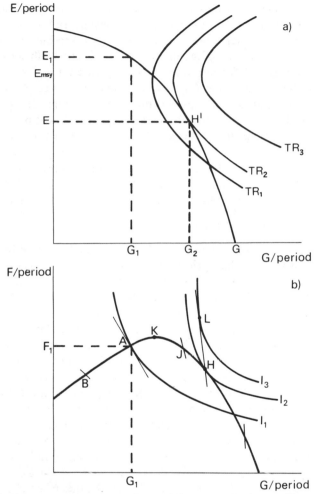

Figure 3.11. *Open Access and MEY in the Total Economy.* Producers will operate on the PP curve for E and G where TR is less than a maximum. This will correspond to a point on the PP curve for F and G where the price ratio is greater (in absolute value) than the slope of the curve. General market equilibrium will occur at that point on the PP curve for F and G where the slope of the price ratio is equal to the slope of the indifference curve at that point (see point A). MEY occurs where the PP curve for F and G touches the highest indifference curve possible (see point H).

$$\frac{\Delta F}{\Delta G} = \frac{\Delta F}{\Delta E} \cdot \frac{\Delta E}{\Delta G} \tag{3.1}$$

The slope of the PP curve for F and G equals the product of the slope of the PP curve for E and G and the slope of the sustained yield curve.

As before, consumers will choose that combination of F and G that maximizes their welfare or satisfaction, given total income and the price ratio associated with a particular production bundle. The economy will reach overall equilibrium when the production bundle that producers find most advantageous to produce is the same one consumers will want to buy, given their income and the relative prices. The remainder of the section will show where on the PP curve for E and G the producers will operate for a given price ratio, the point on the PP curve for F and G to which this corresponds, and the process of reaching an overall equilibrium in the economy. The analysis will correspond to the discussion in chapter 1 except that it will be necessary to consider first the suboptimal behavior of fishermen in an open-access situation.

To do this, let us consider the maximization of total revenue in the economy for a given set of prices in terms of the PP curve for E and G. In this case the formulation for total revenue equivalent to equation 1.1 above is:

$$TR = P_G G + P_F F(E) \qquad (3.2)$$

That is, the total revenue earned by producers equals the sum of the products of outputs multiplied by their prices. Note that the output of fish is a function of the amount of effort produced—$F(E)$ is an expression for the sustainable yield function. Examples of total revenue curves (i.e., curves that show those combinations of E and G where total revenue is maintained at a specified level, given a set of prices; see figure 1.6) using this formulation are pictured in figure 3.11a: TR_3 represents a level of total revenue greater than TR_2, and so forth. Their peculiar shape is related to that of the sustainable yield curve. At levels of effort below E_{msy}, the constant total revenue curve will have its normal negative slope, but, due to the diminishing marginal catch as effort is increased, it will not be a straight line. In this range, as effort goes up, fish production does likewise (although at a decreasing rate), and so total revenue is maintained by reductions in the production of G. At levels of effort above E_{msy}, the curve bends back on itself and becomes positive (indicating that, as E is increased, the production of fish falls), and so the only way total revenue can be maintained is for G to increase. This can be described in a more precise fashion by looking at the slope of the TR curves. Along any TR curve, the changes in G and E are such that total revenue is unchanged. Therefore:

$$P_G \, \Delta G + P_F \cdot \frac{\Delta F}{\Delta E} \cdot \Delta E = 0 \qquad (3.3)$$

Solving for $\Delta E/\Delta G$ (the slope of the TR curve), we obtain:

$$\text{Slope of the TR curve} = -\frac{P_G}{P_F \, (\Delta F/\Delta E)}$$

It can be seen that when $\Delta F/\Delta E$ is positive (i.e., at levels of effort below E_{msy}), the slope will be negative and that the reverse is true when $\Delta F/\Delta E$ is negative.

It is obvious that if the economy is to produce that bundle of outputs where *TR* is a maximum given this specified set of prices, it must produce at point *H'*, where the PP curve for *E* and *G* is just tangent to curve TR_2, the highest-valued curve it can touch. At this point, therefore, the slope of the PP curve is equal to the slope of the *TR* curve, that is,

$$\frac{\Delta E}{\Delta G} = - \frac{P_G}{P_F(\Delta F/\Delta E)} \qquad (3.4)$$

Recall from above that $P_F (\Delta F/\Delta E)$ is equal to the marginal revenue of effort. Therefore, *TR* will be a maximum when the slope of the PP curve for *E* and *G* is equal to the ratio of the price of *G* to the marginal revenue of effort. This is equivalent to the conclusion in chapter 1 that *TR* maximization will occur when the slope of the PP curve is equal to the ratio of prices since, when prices are constant, they are equal to marginal revenue.

If there is open access to the fishery, the economy will not operate at this total revenue maximization point, however. This is because the producers of effort are not concerned with the marginal revenue of effort for the fishery as a whole, but rather, as demonstrated above, they consider the average revenue of the fishery as a whole—that is, $P_F (F/E)$—to be the price of, or return to, effort as far as their production decisions are concerned. Therefore, with open access the economy will operate where the slope of the PP curve for *E* and *G* is equal to the ratio of P_G to $P_F (F/E)$. That is, it will operate where

$$\frac{\Delta E}{\Delta G} = - \frac{P_G}{P_F(F/E)} \qquad (3.5)$$

Since this is different from equation 3.4 (the condition that holds when total revenue is maximized at the given price ratio), an open-access fishery will cause the economy to produce where the value of output is smaller than it can be. To be precise, the open-access fishery will cause the economy to produce too much *E* and not enough *G*.

Let us now translate this into the framework of the PP curve and the price ratio of *F* and *G*. To find the relationship between the slope of this PP curve and the price ratio (i.e., the slope of the price line) at the open-access equilibrium, note that from equation 3.5 at this point

$$- \frac{P_G}{P_F} = \frac{F}{E} \cdot \frac{\Delta E}{\Delta G}$$

As we saw in equation 3.1, the slope of the PP curve for *F* and *G* is

$$\frac{\Delta F}{\Delta G} = \frac{\Delta F}{\Delta E} \cdot \frac{\Delta E}{\Delta G}$$

Since *F/E* is greater than ($\Delta F/\Delta E$ at all levels of effort (see figure 2.2b), then at open-access equilibrium, the slope of the price line is greater in absolute value than the slope of the PP curve for F and G. In general terms, the slope of the price ratio that will cause producers to operate at a certain point on the PP curve for F and G will always be steeper than the slope of the PP curve at that point. Although each price ratio will call forth the production of a specific bundle of F and G, the important thing is that the slope of the price ratio is always steeper than the slope of the PP curve for F and G at that particular point. The short lines through the PP curve for F and G at various points represent the slope of the price line that would call for that production bundle. Their steepness diminishes as G decreases, since, when that occurs, both F/E and $\Delta E/\Delta G$ become smaller. They are always negative even when the slope of the PP curve is positive, because F/E is always positive and $\Delta E/\Delta G$ is always negative.

Using this information, it is possible to describe the location of the open-access equilibrium yield, the MEY, and the process of obtaining the former in an unregulated economy in terms of a simple general equilibrium model where the relative prices are not predetermined. Recall that these price lines are also the budget lines for consumers in the economy who, under any given budget, will desire that bundle of goods which maximizes welfare. What production bundle will provide an equilibrium? It is that one where the slope of the indifference curve through the PP curve just equals the price ratio inducing producers to offer that particular bundle. At that price ratio producers will produce the exact production bundle that consumers will be willing to purchase, given their income and the relative prices. But will the economy reach such an equilibrium? Assume for the moment that the economy is operating at point H. Given the price line that exists at that point as indicated by the short straight line, consumers would want to consume more F and less G than is currently being produced. Specifically, they would like to consume bundle L because that is the highest level of welfare, given the budget line. Therefore, the price of fish would be bid up and the price of G driven down. The price ratio would then become flatter, and producers would be motivated to move toward point A. Given the change in prices, they would find it to their private advantage to increase production of E and to decrease G. Similarly, at a point to the left of A, such as B, the actions of consumers would change prices in the opposite direction to the extent that production would move back toward point A. Therefore, there will be a general tendency for the economy to move to an equilibrium at point A. (All of this assumes away any problem of stock growth and/or exit and entry rates.)

While the equilibrium level of output is at point A, notice that the point on the PP curve that reaches the highest possible indifference curve is H. At this point, the slope of the indifference curve measuring consumers' willingness to trade between F and G is equal to the slope of the PP curve, which represents the opportunity cost of producing F in terms of foregone G. Therefore, their willingness to trade F for G is equal to the opportunity cost of F in terms of G. This is a static MEY.

The relationship between H and H' is as follows. H' is the point on the PP curve for E and G where total revenue is maximized for a given price ratio. It is equivalent to H, the general equilibrium static MEY, only when the price ratio used to construct the total revenue curves is the one that exists at this point. To put it another way, figure 3.11a can be used to describe a static MEY in a partial equilibrium sense when prices are fixed, but figure 3.11b is necessary to describe static MEY when prices are allowed to vary.

Because the open-access equilibrium is not at point H, the free market operation of an open-access fishery will not result in the highest level of welfare possible, given the production potential. The reason for this is that producers care only what their return to effort is and are not concerned with the return to the fishery as a whole.

The goal of fishery regulation in a static sense, then, should be to move the economy from point A to point H. That is, it should strive to cause the movement of productive resources out of the effort industry (i.e., fishing) and into the production of G. As drawn here, such a move would result in a decrease in the amount of fish and an increase in the amount of G produced. Notice, however, that the increase in G more than makes up for the decrease in F. The same thing would happen if the free market equilibrium were at a point such as J. However, if it were at a point such as B, the regulation would result in an increase in both F and G. So, while optimal regulation may increase or decrease the amount of F produced, it will always increase G. By definition of optimal regulation, however, the new production and consumption bundle will always yield higher satisfaction. The subject of regulation will be discussed in more detail in chapter 6.

Maximum sustainable yield is represented by point K. If the market equilibrium is at A, then a movement to MSY will increase welfare but not as much as would a movement to H, which is maximum economic yield. However, if market equilibrium is at point J, then a movement to MSY will actually reduce welfare.

This section has demonstrated that improper allocation of effort is inherent in an open-access fishery. When analysis is in terms of the entire economy, the fact is emphasized that this misallocation affects the production of other goods as well as the production of fish. This very important aspect of fishery economics is often overlooked.

An Analysis of Recreational Fishing

Introduction

The analysis thus far has focused exclusively on the commercial exploitation of fish stocks. However, recreational fishing is often a very large component of total fishing pressure. For example, recreational catch was 30 percent of total marine fish landings (excluding purely industrial species such as menhaden) in the United States in 1980. (Fisheries of the United States 1984). Therefore, for a complete picture of the economic aspects of fisheries utilization, it is necessary to analyze recreational fisheries as well. It will be shown that, while there are some significant differences involved, the open-access problem also exists in recreational fisheries. That is, the open-access level of fishing will not generate the maximum possible gains.

One of the main differences between commercial and recreational fishing as far as this analysis is concerned is the way value is attributed to the fish. In commercial fisheries, the fish are caught directly for their market value. In recreational fishing, the fish are only one part of the recreational fishing experience, and it is this experience per se that is the main focus of attention. Economically speaking, recreational fishing has many of the same attributes as any other good or service in an economy. It is desired by certain consumers, and depending on their tastes, they will be willing to forego other activities or products in order to participate. However, it is not a service that can be purchased in a passive manner. Rather, the consumer must purchase fishing equipment and use time and resources to travel to the fishing site and to engage in fishing. Further, in most instances, the fishing service itself (i.e., the right to engage in fishing) is not purchased because the participant has rights to fish in much the same way that commercial participants do. However, just because recreational fishing is "produced" by individual participants during the recreational experience does not mean that individuals do not value this service in the same way they value an umbrella, a sandwich, or the ability to view a motion picture.

It follows that an individual's demand curve for recreational fishing can be described in very much the same way as can a demand curve for other services. Consider the demand curve labeled II (D_2) in figure 3.12. (The I's stand for the individual, and the meaning of the subscripted D will become clear as the discussion continues.) The number of days fished by the individual is measured on the horizontal axis, while price or average willingness to pay is measured on the vertical axis. The relationship shows that, all else equal (including the individual's tastes and income, the price of complement and substitute goods, and the characteristics of the fishing experience), if the individual were forced to purchase the right to fish by paying a daily fee, he or she would be willing to purchase more recreational fishing days only at lower prices. For example, if the price were P_1, d_0 days would be demanded, but if price were to fall to zero, d_1 days would be demanded. The demand curve can also be interpreted as showing the marginal willingness to pay for various levels of consumption. That is, if d_0 fishing days are consumed, P_1 is the value attached to the last unit. If any of the conditions assumed constant change, the entire demand curve will shift. For example, if the price of fishing equipment were to decrease, the demand curve for fishing days would shift up, for example, from II (D_2) to II (D_1). The distinction between a movement along and a shift in a demand will be important in the analysis below.

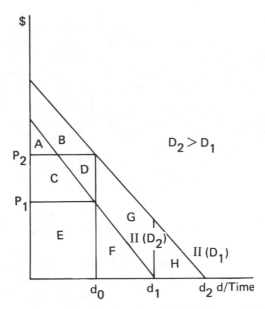

Figure 3.12. *Individual Demand Curve for Recreational Fishing Days.* The individual's demand curve for fishing days will shift to the right if such things as catch per day or average size of fish increase. That is, these changes will increase the number of days purchased at various prices or the value of each day, which is the same thing.

Recall that consumer surplus is the amount individuals would be willing to pay for a certain amount of a good or a service over and above what they have to pay on the market. In terms of figure 3.12, with demand curve $II(D_2)$, if price is P_1, consumer surplus is equal to the areas $A + C$. Note that if price is dropped to zero, consumption increases to d_1 and consumer surplus increases to an amount equal to areas A, C, E, and F. Consumer surplus is an important concept in this analysis because, given that there is no market price per fishing day, it is the full measure of the value of fishing. As will be shown below, it is also the means by which the value added by the fish stock can be ascertained.

This description of a demand curve for recreational fishing for an individual is a fundamental part of understanding the problem of optimal utilization of a recreational fishery. However, to complete the analysis, it is necessary to show how the demand curves for all of the individual participants can be combined to produce the total or market demand curve. A major difficulty in doing so is to specify the relationship between the fishing experience and the stock of fish. How much of the willingness to pay for a recreational fishing day depends upon such things as amount caught and other items related to the fish stock, and how much depends upon other aspects of the experience? One extreme could be that this willingness to pay is strictly related to the market value of the catch. If this were true, management of recreational fishing would be exactly analogous to commercial fishing; it would entail only a comparison of the value of fish captured and the costs of harvesting them. At the other extreme, the amount, size, and edibility of fish caught, the degree of difficulty in landing the fish, etc. would have no effect on the value of a fishing day. If this were the case, there would be no difference between spending a day in a boat or on a pier and catching 10 fish an hour and doing the same thing while catching nothing. More appropriately, there would be no difference between a fishing day with a high probability of catching 10 fish an hour and a fishing day with zero or very low probability of catching anything. Reality is probably somewhere in between. The catch is valuable as a food, a trophy, or because it put up a good fight, and the fishing day has some intrinsic value attached to it as well.

To relate this to the demand curve analysis, recall that the individual demand curve, II (D_2), in figure 3.12 shows the relationship between marginal willingness to pay and the number of recreational fishing days consumed under a given set of economic and biological conditions. If any of the economic conditions change (i.e., if income goes up or if the price of fishing equipment goes down), then in most instances the individual's demand curve for recreational fishing would shift to the right, which is to say that more days would be consumed at every price or the marginal willingness to pay for every fishing day would increase. In the same way, if catch per day or average size of fish caught were to increase, a similar phenomenon would occur. The demand curve would shift to the right. At the zero price, more days would be spent fishing. Or to look at it the other way, the quality of the fishing day would have improved, and therefore the marginal value of each day would have increased.

The interesting point about changes in biological conditions and shifts in the individual's demand curve is that measures of fishing quality are often related to total fishing effort. As aggregate fishing effort increases, the fish stock is normally affected such that catch per day and average size of fish decrease. Therefore, there is a relationship between the aggregate amount of effort applied to a stock and the value each individual obtains from each fishing day. For example, let D_2 represent the aggregate number of fishing days applied to this hypothetical fishery by all individuals. Given this effort, there is an equilibrium-expected catch per day and average fish size, and so the demand curve for the individual will be the curve II (D_2) in figure 3.12. If there are no restrictions on fishing, the individual will consume d_1 fishing days a year, and will obtain a consumer surplus equal to areas $A + C + E + F$. However, if aggregate effort decreased to some lower level, say D_1, these quality measures would improve, and so the willingness to pay for each day fished would increase. This is represented by a shift in the demand curve to II (D_1). Under the same entry conditions, the open-access level of fishing for this individual would increase to d_2, and total consumer surplus would increase by areas $B + D + G + H$. Areas $B + D + G$ represent the increased value of the original d_1 days fished, while area H represents the value associated with extra fishing days.

To summarize, the size and the average catch per day, among other things, are a function of the total fishing effort applied to the stock, and hence, the individual willingness to pay for a fishing day is dependent upon the total effort applied by all recreational fishermen. Therefore, it is impossible to use a straightforward summation of individual demand curves to obtain a market demand curve because total effort is both the item being measured on the horizontal axis for the market demand curve and a shift parameter of the individual demand curves. However, the solution to this problem can be explained in terms of figure 3.13. Let the curve labeled KK_1 be the sum of the individual demand curves when each participant assumes that total effort will be equal to D_1. That is, each individual will assume that average fish size and catch per day are those produced by an aggregate effort of D_1. Each individual, assuming that his or her own fishing effort is small relative to the total effort and hence cannot affect these quality parameters, will take them as given, and individual demand curves will be completely specified. The curve KK_1 is the sum of these individual curves and is a market demand curve assuming a constant quality of fishing. Similarly, the demand

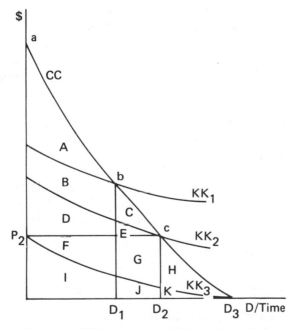

Figure 3.13. *Open Access and MEY in Recreational Fishing.*   Assuming free entry, open-access equilibrium will occur where the operational market demand curve intersects the horizontal axis. MEY occurs at a lower level of effort, where consumer surplus is maximized. Effort should be reduced from the open-access point as long as the losses in consumer surplus due to quantity reduction are less than the increases due to quality improvement.

curve labeled KK_2 is the market demand curve when all individuals assume that total effort is equal to D_2. Note that it is everywhere below KK_1 because individual willingness to pay decreases as the amount of total effort goes up and fishing success for each individual goes down.

There is actually a family of KK curves, one for each possible level of D. The only points on these curves that can have any operational relevance, however, are the places where the actual amount of total effort coincides with the amount used by individuals in formulating their demand curves. These are points b and c for demand curves KK_1 and KK_2, respectively. The demand curve labeled CC is the collection of all the relevant points from all possible KK curves. It is the demand curve that would be observed if it were possible to run an experiment to see how the number of days fished varied with different daily fees for the right to fish. It can be called the operational market demand curve because it shows the actual willingness to pay that will result as users adjust to the changes in fishing success which result from changes in aggregate fishing effort. It should be noted that these curves are analogous to the sustained revenue curves in the analysis of commercial fishing because they are drawn assuming that the stocks have adjusted to each level of effort.

The KK demand curves are important for this analysis because they provide the appropriate measure of consumer surplus. For example, if there are no fishing fees, the aggregate level of effort will equal D_3, and the total consumer surplus at this point is represented by the areas under the curve KK_3, that is, areas I, J, and K, not the entire area under the CC curve. This is because KK_3 shows how individuals would react to different prices if the level of fishing success remained constant; therefore, it is the appropriate curve to use when measuring the maximum people will pay for D_3 units of recreational fishing rather than do without it.

Notice that, if effort is decreased from D_3 to D_2, the consumer surplus, in the absence of user fees, changes from areas I, J, and K to areas D, E, F, G, I, and J because the latter is the area under the KK curve that is associated with D_2 aggregate recreational fishing days. Therefore, whether consumer surplus increases or decreases as the result of the decrease in aggregate effort depends upon the relative sizes of area K and areas D, E, F, and G. That a decrease in effort will not lead to an unambiguous decrease in consumer surplus—as it will for most other market goods and services—is critical to the economic analysis of recreational fisheries.

Open Access and MEY in Recreational Fishing

With open access (i.e., no controls on entry or no daily fishing fees), the equilibrium aggregate effort will be D_3. Marginal willingness to pay is zero, which is to say further days fished will have no value, and so the participation rate will go no higher. As noted above, however, even though the value for the last day is zero, there is still a positive consumer surplus at this point equal to areas I, J, and K. Since fishing success is fixed along any KK curve, this consumer surplus comes exclusively from the diminishing marginal willingness to pay for an increased quantity of constant quality recreation days. That is, it is similar to the consumer surplus for any other good. To understand the nature of the open-access problem in recreational fishing more clearly, consider the gains that can be achieved if aggregate days fished are equal to D_2. Areas D and E represent the "quantity" consumer surplus analogous to areas I, J, and K at D_3 because this area is the difference between the KK curve and the price line that generates effort level D_2. Therefore, areas F, G, I, and J represent a "quality" consumer surplus that is generated by the increased quality of the fishing experience as catch per day, average size, etc., increase with the decrease in aggregate effort. It is this consumer surplus that is dissipated with open access in recreational fishing. It is analogous to the profit or rent to the fish stock that is dissipated in commercial fishing.

For optimization of commercial fishing with a variable price of fish, the goal is to maximize the present value of the sum of producer surplus and consumer surplus. The analogous goal for optimal economic utilization of a recreational fishery is to maximize the present value of the sum of consumer surpluses due to both quantity and quality. In terms of these sustained curves and assuming a zero discount rate, the optimal level of recreational fishing is where the area under the relevant KK curve out to the operational market demand curve is maximized.

While it is not possible to describe the optimum point as the intersection of two curves or the maximum distance between total curves as it is in the graphical analysis of commercial fishing, the process of finding the static optimal level of aggregate effort can be described easily in terms of figure 3.13. For example, consider again the move from D_3, the open-access level of effort to D_2. The loss from such a reduction in effort is equal to area K while the gain is equal to areas $D + E + F + G$. If the gains are greater than the losses, such a reduction in effort is economically rational. Since the number of fishing days is being reduced, there is an overall trade-off between quantity and quality. If the gains due to increased quality exceed the losses from decreased quantity, the reduction makes sense.

Consider now a reduction in effort from D_2 to D_1. In this instance, the loss is equal to areas $E + G + J$, while the gain is equal to area B. In this case it is hard to tell which is greater, but the procedure for determining the optimum level of recreational fishing days should be clear. As long as the gains in consumer surplus in one part of the graph are greater than the cost in terms of lost consumer surplus in the other part of the graph, it makes economic sense to reduce effort.

Perhaps the nature of the problem can be more fully understood by viewing the solution in reverse. Consider a fishery operating at D_1. An increase in effort will increase total consumer surplus by areas $E + G + J$ but reduce it by area B. The former may be called the willingness to pay for the extra fishing days while the latter is the externality cost imposed on the existing fishing days by the increase in fishing activity. The optimizing criterion for recreational fisheries utilization, when viewed in this way, is that the value of the last fishing day should equal its externality cost. If the value of the last day is greater than the externality cost, then effort should be increased. However, if its value is less than the externality cost, the provision of an extra fishing day is not economically optimal. At the optimal point, the sum of quantity and quality consumer surplus is maximized.

For ease of exposition, this analysis has been in terms of sustained curves and under the assumption of a zero discount rate; hence, it has not provided an explicit analysis of user cost, which certainly applies here as well. The externality cost should also include the present value of the decrease in consumer surplus in future periods. The main point of the discussion has been to show that recreational use will result in suboptimal utilization just as does commercial use. This has been accomplished in terms of a somewhat limited analysis; a complete discussion may be found in McConnell and Sutinen (1979).

Economic Analysis of Fisheries Development

While most of the highly valued stocks of fish in the world are actively fished, there are still some that are unutilized or have very low exploitation rates. For example, there is considerable room for expansion in some fisheries off Alaska, and many coastal developing nations have acquired control of valuable stocks with the creation of exclusive economic zones. As such, fisheries development is of interest to many nations. And, although it may not be apparent at the surface, the subject is closely related to fisheries management.

A fundamental conclusion of the analysis thus far is that the open-access harvest pattern of a fishery over time will be different from the MEY harvest pattern; therefore, government intervention to control the level of fishing can provide the potential for a net increase in the value of goods and services if management costs are less than potential gains. (The final chapters will discuss this latter point in greater detail.) On the other hand, a fundamental proposition of economic development theory is that, when there are barriers to the development of particular industries, government policies and programs can sometimes remove these barriers such that the industry is able to operate successfully independent of further government intervention. Taking these two points and applying them to fisheries development, it follows that economic development policies for fisheries should include the provision for a change in the impetus of government intervention from that of an accelerator during the process of removing barriers to that of a brake once the fishery is established. In the real world, however, it has frequently been the case that exclusive attention has been focused on breaking the barriers, and it is forgotten that, once moving, an open-access fishery will, by its very nature, become overextended. The purpose of this section is to discuss some of the reasons that fisheries development programs may be justified but more importantly to explain their ramifications in terms of the analysis of this book.

Economic Justifications for Fisheries Development

A biologically viable fish stock is only one part of a well-functioning fishing industry. It must be possible to harvest, process, and distribute the fish products such that the participants earn a reasonable return and, at the same time, consumers obtain an acceptable product at a price that is comparable to similar goods. In short, there must be an economically viable market. It should be obvious, therefore, that many possible obstructions can prevent the development or improvement of a fishing industry even in the presence of a productive fish stock. For example, there may be a problem with consumer acceptance of the ultimate product. Protein content is important, but taste, texture, appearance, and smell can also be vital in appealing to buyers. Sometimes these attributes are less important than familiarity, habit, and cultural or religious restrictions. On the other hand, if consumer income and hence the demand for fish is low, the fact that they desire the fish does not mean they will be able to pay for it. These principles apply for fish destined for industrial use as well as that bound for the dinner table. If people do not buy a certain fish, for whatever reason, the fact that a viable stock is available for exploitation is of very little economic consequence.

Another impediment to develop is imperfect distribution channels. Fish is highly perishable, and market size depends, among other things, upon how well a suitable product can be distributed. Market channels can fail to develop for many reasons. In some instances there is a lack of roads or trucks; in others it may be a scarcity of final retail outlets; in still others there may be inadequate postharvest preservation technologies. On other occasions, there may be no entrepreneur willing to take on the role of middleman between the fisherman and the final consumer. There is often a "chicken and egg" problem. Individuals are unwilling to set up marketing channels unless they can be assured of a reasonably large and steady supply, but fishermen are hesitant to build a fleet that could provide such a supply until they are assured of a steady market. Since it is very difficult for one group to commit to a course of action independently, fishery development is hindered. In still other instances, the size of the country prevents the development of a viable industry. Some fish products, such as fish meal, have such a low unit value that large-scale production is necessary to earn a reasonable return. If the country's demand for these products, including existing export potential, is small relative to the scale of operation necessary for profitability, an industry will not develop.

Viable fisheries may also fail to develop if existing harvesting and processing technologies are such that costs are high, relative to the prices of substitute products. The problem may be complicated by the lack of access to capital markets, which prevents the introduction of new technology, or by a restricted market size, which would make the introduction of the new large-scale technology unprofitable. A further complication is the lack of trained workers familiar with and willing to use the new technologies.

A related problem is the lack of port and harbor facilities, which are necessary for a viable fishing industry. When the types of structures needed are modest, fisherman cooperatives may be formed in order to construct them. Restricted access to capital markets or the lack of managerial talent may prevent it from occurring, though. In other cases, the facilities that would be the most appropriate would be far too expensive to be constructed by cooperatives. The problem is much more complex when the facilities needed for fisheries development are part of large and diversified harbor and port requirements.

In some instances, a lack of access to the market for loans can prevent a fishery from developing. For example, banks may be hesitant to make loans to fishermen in small villages in dispersed areas because of a lack of familiarity with their working and repayment habits or the lack of opportunities to collect loan payments easily. This may be so even if the loans would allow for the development of a productive small fishery that, besides being a useful contribution to the economy, could easily provide enough income to repay the loans.

In summary, anything that affects the price at which fishermen can sell their output or the cost of harvesting, processing, and distributing their catch will have an effect on the viability of the fisheries sector. When there are artificial or relatively easily removed impediments that prevent revenues from covering costs, the fishery may not be appropriately utilized. Further, if the impediments can be removed at a cost that is low, relative to the gains to be derived, it makes sense to correct for this improper utilization. It is important to realize that such problems can occur in developed as well as developing nations. In the United States, squid and groundfish off Alaska are good examples of underdeveloped fisheries. If it can be shown that such barriers can be removed at a cost lower than potential increases for net value of fishing output, then an appropriate development project makes good economic sense.

The Paradox of Fisheries Development with Open Access

Even in those cases where there are potential net benefits from fisheries development, it does not follow that these gains will actually be achieved. The paradox of fisheries development in open-access fisheries is that, unless appropriate measures are taken, the end result of development will be an overutilization of the fish stock and an overexpansion of the resources used to exploit it. It will be shown below that proper consideration of the open-access problem is necessary to achieve all potential gains from development projects. If open access is not curtailed, some of the gains will be lost, and in some cases there may even be net losses.

Consider the case of a fisheries development project to lower the cost of producing fishing effort, say, by the introduction of more cost-effective vessels. For ease of exposition, we will use the variable price model. If AC_1 in figure 3.14 is the existing average cost curve, cost will be above the demand curve at all levels of output, and there will be no commercial fishery prior to the development project. Assume that the technological improvement program can decrease cost such that AC_2 becomes the relevant average cost curve. If there are no constraints on entry, open-access equilibrium will occur at F_2 at a price of P_2. Annual net gains to the economy in terms of the increase in the value of goods and services produced will equal the sum of consumer surplus and producer surplus. However, since under open access fishermen enter until the rent due to the fishery is dissipated, it follows that producer surplus is zero at this point (assume that there are no highliner rents), and so the annual net economic gain is only consumer surplus, which is area A. Even

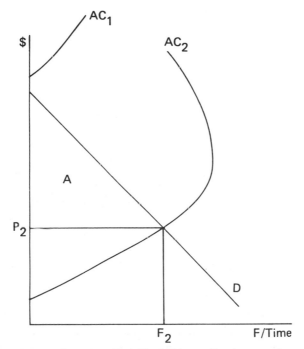

Figure 3.14. *Development Gains from Unutilized Fishery.*   Development of an unutilized fishery, in the absence of regulation, will normally lead to consumer surplus gains, but total potential efficiency gains will not be obtained because the sum of consumer surplus and profit will not be maximized.

under open access, it is possible to have a positive gain from fisheries development. With the opening of the fishery, consumers are able to purchase fish products with a higher value than the goods foregone to obtain them. Due to the overexploitation caused by open access, however, some of the potential benefits of opening the fishery have been lost. Specifically, the loss is the difference in the present values of the optimal harvest time path and the open-access time path.

There are certain instances, however, when cost reduction innovations can result in losses. Consider figure 3.15. If a development project decreases cost from AC_1 to AC_2, open-access equilibrium will shift from F_1 to F_2. This decrease in output results because the fishery is operating in the backward-bending portion of the AC curve and the cost decrease actually reduces open-access catch. As a result, sustainable consumer surplus will fall by an amount equal to areas $B + C + D$. Areas $C + D$ represent the loss due to the decrease in output while area B represents the loss due to a higher price for the remaining output. Of course, if the fishery were to be operated efficiently, the

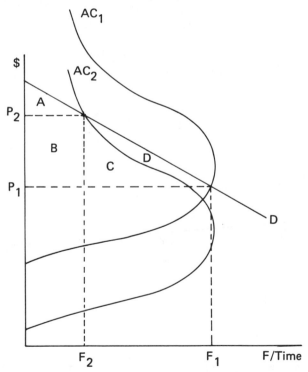

Figure 3.15. *Development Gains from Operating Fisheries.* In the absence of regulation, not only will some potential gains be wasted, cost reducing developing projects can actually lead to losses if the increased open-access activity drives the stocks to low levels.

decrease in cost provided by the project would allow for more output at lower costs.

To be precise, the true gains to society would have to be measured in terms of the change in the present value of output, taking into account the process by which the fishery adjusts to the new open-access equilibrium. The thrust of the argument remains the same, however; unless there are significant increases in consumer surplus early in the development process when costs first fall but before the stock has been driven to low levels, those development programs ultimately resulting in decreases in consumer surplus can cause the present value of production in the fishery to fall.

The above demonstrates that, while some fisheries development programs can yield positive economic benefits, there can actually be net losses in those instances where sufficient extra pressure is put on the stock such that catch falls. However, in either of the above cases, the gains from development can be increased by controlling the fishery such that it operates at the MEY harvest path rather than the open-access path.

The purpose of this discussion has been to show the importance of relating fisheries development and fisheries management. It is useful to note that doing so can solve a problem that has constantly troubled fisheries managers. By building appropriate management controls into newly developing fisheries, they will not become overcapitalized, and regulators will not be faced with the difficult task of restricting access to the stock after the fleet has become too large. Developing management programs in fisheries where the stocks are already heavily exploited by an existing fleet is a much more difficult problem.

It is true, however, that fisheries development activities are often focused on artisanal or small-scale fisheries, where management can be quite difficult. First, there is often little information on the economics or biology of the fishery, and hence it is not possible to correctly specify optimal utilization levels. In addition, enforcement can be very difficult because of the widely dispersed fleet and the high cost of surveillance. Nonetheless, there is a potential for increasing the gains from development projects by combining them with management. Since the presumed goal of these projects is to increase the welfare of individuals working in these types of fisheries, the possibility of introducing management should not be ignored.

In summary, part or all of the potential net benefits of fisheries development projects can be dissipated if there is open access to the fishery. However, if the fishery is properly regulated, all of the potential gains can be achieved.

Final Remarks

I feel the importance of stressing again the context in which these theoretical descriptions of a fishery should be viewed. If we had perfect (or at least very good) information on the biological and economic parameters involved, and if resources were easily transferable from one use to another within the economy, then the conclusions derived thus far could be used in a straightforward manner in regulating fisheries. Unfortunately, not all this information is available, and what we do have is very difficult and expensive to obtain. Also many institutional and "people" problems prevent rapid movements of resources from one use to another. This does not mean that the lessons learned from economic analysis are of no use; rather, they set objectives to be sought in the formulation of policies.

For instance, any call for reduction in effort on certain fisheries should include analysis of the optimal time over which to make this reduction, to minimize the economic and personal costs of this transfer. Also, while it may be that proper operation of a given fishery implies different levels of catch each year, the cost and uncertainties of deciding those varied levels may dictate that the best policy is to set a middle-of-the-road yield and change it only at five-year intervals. Indeed, the need for a stable policy is one of the chief justifications of looking at the (generally) incomplete static formulation, since dynamic optimization is much more complex.

Economic analysis as a tool should be used to the fullest extent possible in any given circumstances. If other tools of fishery regulation such as biological and political analysis are unworkable, and if economic, biological, and political data are incomplete, then economic analysis cannot be expected to yield its fullest results. But it still can, and should be, put to the best use possible in the structuring of fishery policy.

Appendix

This appendix describes the derivation of several important functional relationships in fishery economics. The geometric method used allows relationships between certain parameters to be condensed into a single relationship between those parameters that are of particular concern. Although the four separate graphs in each diagram may at first cause some confusion, especially since some are plotted in unfamiliar ways, the method can show the interrelationships that exist.

The Sustained Yield Curve

The sustained yield curve can be derived from relationships between growth rate and size of biomass and between level of effort and the equilibrium biomass. The former is pictured in section 1 of figure A.1, where increases in population are measured leftward, while the latter is plotted in section 4 with increases in population measured downward. This is the population equilibrium curve. The sustained yield curve, which is the long-run relationship between effort and catch, can be derived in section 2 from

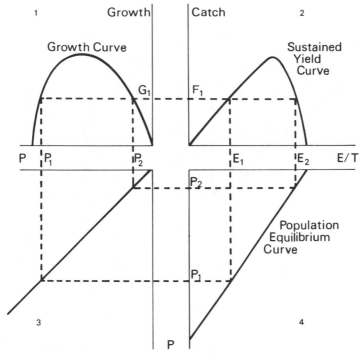

Figure A.1. *The Derivation of the Sustained Yield Curve.*   Any point on the sustained yield curve can be determined in the following manner. Pick a level of effort and, using the population equilibrium curve, determine the equilibrium level of population. Associated with this level of population is a natural growth rate. The sustainable yield at the chosen level of effort will equal this growth rate.

information contained in the other sections. For example, at fishing effort E_1, the population will achieve an equilibrium at P_1. At that level, growth will equal G_1; therefore, the sustained yield at E_1 will be a catch of F_1 that is equal to G_1. Note that E_2 units of effort will cause the population to fall to P_2, but P_2 also has a growth of G_2; therefore, sustained yield at E_2 also equals F_1. By similar process, every point on the sustained yield curve can be derived. Looked at as a unit, figure A.1 shows that, as effort goes up, population will decrease. Ultimately, this decrease causes sustained yield to fall.

The Cost Curve for Fish

The determinants of cost per fish are the relationships between sustained yield and effort and between effort and total cost. The former is plotted in section 4 of figure A.2 with an increase in effort measured downward, and the latter is in section 1 with increases in effort measured leftward. The total cost curve in terms of fish can be derived in section 2. From it the average and marginal cost curves in terms of fish can be derived. To derive the cost curve,

THE ECONOMICS OF FISHERIES MANAGEMENT

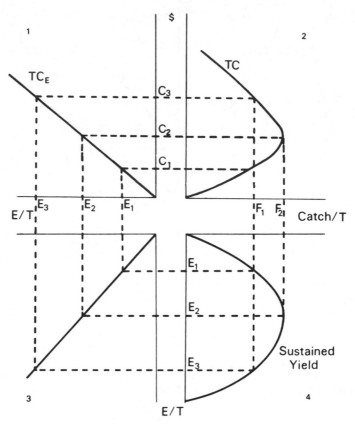

Figure A.2. *The Derivation of the Total Cost Curve.*   The two levels of cost associated with any level of sustainable yield (except MSY) can be determined in the following manner. Pick a level of sustainable yield and, using the sustainable yield curve, find the two levels of effort that will harvest it. Associated with each of these levels of effort is a total cost. These are the two total costs for the chosen amount of effort.

note that both E_1 and E_2 units of effort will obtain a sustained yield of F_1 but that the latter will result in a higher cost per fish. The cost for each level of sustainable catch can be found by ascertaining the level of effort necessary to catch it and then finding the costs involved.

The Double Maxima Revenue Curve

The relationship between effort and total revenue depends upon the relationships between effort and catch and between catch and revenue. An upside-down version of the former is presented in section 4 of figure A.3, and the latter is in section 1, with increases in catch being measured leftward. Total revenue at first increases as catch goes up, but eventually decreases and will ultimately fall to zero. The logic behind this is the relationship between a change in catch or quantity sold and the change in the selling price. Econo-

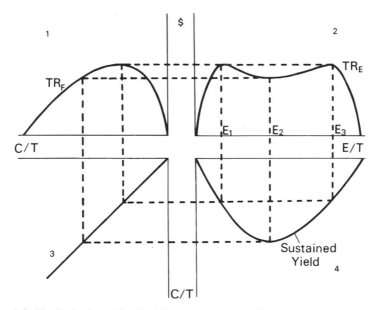

Figure A.3. *The Derivation of the Total Revenue of Effort.* The level of revenue associated with any level of effort can be determined in the following manner. Pick a level of effort and, using the sustainable yield curve, determine the level of sustained yield it will produce. Then using the total revenue of fish curve, which is derived from the demand curve, determine the amount of revenue this amount of fish will earn. This is the revenue associated with the chosen amount of effort. Notice that if MSY is larger than the amount of fish that will earn the maximum revenue, the total revenue curve for effort will have two maxima.

mists call this relationship the elasticity of demand. Initially, as a greater quantity is sold, the price will fall, but the larger sales will more than make up for lower price. Eventually, however, the price decrease that affects all units sold will exert a stronger influence on total revenue than will the increased output, and total revenue will fall.

Whenever the amount of catch that earns the maximum revenue possible is less than the maximum sustainable yield, the revenue curve in terms of effort will have two maxima, as derived in section 2 in the normal manner. Pick a level of E and, tracing it down to section 4, determine the amount of catch it will produce. Then, tracing over to section 1, determine the revenue this catch will earn. The result is one point on the effort and total revenue curve. Note that, as effort is increased to E_1, both catch and total revenue increase, but from E_1 to E_2, although catch goes up, total revenue will fall. Increases in effort from E_2 to E_3 will result in decreases in catch, but these will cause total revenue to increase. Finally, increases beyond E_3 will also lead to a decrease in catch, but in this instance total revenue will also fall.

The Production Possibility Curve for Fish and Another Good

The PP curve for fish and another good (G) depends upon the PP curve for effort and G and upon the sustained yield curve. The former is pictured in

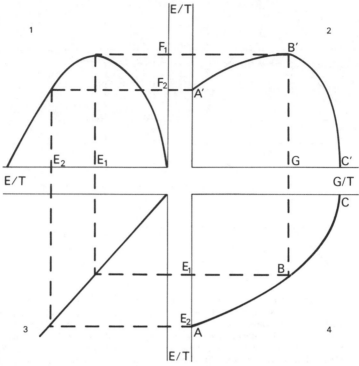

Figure A.4. *The Derivation of the Production Possibility Curve for* F *and* G. The production possibility curve for *F* and *G* can be determined in the following manner. Pick a level of *G* and, using the PP curve for *E* and *G*, determine the maximum amount of effort that can be produced in combination with it. Then, using the sustainable yield curve, find the amount of fish this amount of effort will obtain annually. This is the amount of fish that can be produced in combination with the chosen amount of *G*. Notice that, if the maximum amount of effort the economy can produce is greater than the amount that will obtain maximum sustainable yield, the PP curve for *F* and *G* will have a positively sloped section.

section 4 of figure A.4 in an upside-down version, and the latter is in section 1, with increases in effort measured leftward.

When all of the economy's resources are being used to produce effort, it will operate at point A in section 4, producing E_2 units of effort. Tracing over into section 1, it can be shown that this amount of effort will produce F_2 units of fish; therefore, the economy will operate at A' in section 2. As the output bundle in section 4 changes from A to B, the amount of G will increase, while the production of E will fall. However, over this range of the sustained yield curve, the decreases in effort result in increases in catch, and so the PP curve in section 2 from A' to B' will be upward sloping. Further decreases in the production of effort will allow for G to increase but will cause F to decrease, and the PP curve for F and G will slope downward from B' to C'.

4

Refinements of the Analysis

Introduction

The previous chapter has mainly outlined the basic aspects of fishery economics. Accordingly, the assumptions behind much of the analysis have been quite restrictive, to keep everything as straightforward as possible. This chapter will introduce assumptions both more realistic and more complex, in order to add verisimilitude to the model. The first two sections deal with different assumptions concerning the population dynamics of exploited fish stocks. In the first the Schaefer model is explained in more detail while the second discusses the dynamic pool model. The possibility of fishery management goals other than economic maximization is the subject of the third section. The fourth expands analysis of the production possibility curve to include the case of more than one country exploiting the same fishery. A brief introduction to more complex dynamic models of fishery exploitation is followed by a section on the share system of crew remuneration.

In all that follows the caveat put forth in chapter 2 concerning the stochastic nature of the growth of stocks of fish applies, and perhaps even more strongly. The exact relationship between the growth of related stocks is a good case in point. Nevertheless, the general forms put forth are very useful for our purposes.

An Expansion of the Schaefer Model

The biological basis for the analysis thus far has been the Schaefer sustained yield model, which combines the effects of recruitment, individual growth, and natural and fishing mortality into one simple function. For the most part, only the most simple version of this approach has been used so as to more clearly achieve the goal of enunciating the important economic concepts of fisheries utilization. The purpose of this and the following section is to delve a little deeper into the intricacies of fisheries population dynamics. Based on the analyses thus far, those with economics training could come away with a very naive view of the problems of fishery management, while biologists may have difficulty seeing how the economic principles can apply in more realistic situations. While there will be no attempt to present a detailed analysis of fisheries population dynamics, the discussion will attempt to give a more realistic view of the biological complexities of exploited stocks while at the same time explaining the two types of models commonly used in fisheries management. This section will focus on expanding the Schaefer analysis so as to give a better picture of year-to-year stock adjustments. In the next section, aspects of the dynamic pool model, where growth, recruitment, and natural and fishing mortality can be treated independently, will be described.

Review of the Sustained Yield Curve

Before we begin a consideration of different assumptions related to the shape of the sustained yield curve, let us review briefly its underpinnings, as discussed in chapter 2. The catch or yield of a fishery during any period depends upon both the level of effort applied and the existing population size. The stock size in turn depends upon its natural growth rate and the rate of catch. The former, it will be recalled, is the net result of recruitment, individual growth, and natural mortality. Since the latter is a function of effort, population size is also thereby related to the amount of effort being applied to the fish stock. Given the ecological parameters and a specified level of effort, the population will reach an equilibrium size when the rate of growth equals the catch. A change in the level of effort will ultimately lead to a change in the equilibrium population size. This relationship between effort and equilibrium population is the population equilibrium curve pictured in figure 2.1b. The sustainable yield curve indicates the relationship between catch and effort, given that the stock has achieved an equilibrium for a particular level of effort. Each point on this curve corresponds to a specific combination of effort and stock size on the population equilibrium curve.

Obviously, the shape of the sustained yield curve is highly dependent upon the shape of the population equilibrium curve. As drawn in figure 2.1b, the latter shows that equilibrium population size monotonically decreases as effort increases. Catch will eventually always be larger than growth, thus equilibrium population will fall to zero. This inverse relationship between effort and equilibrium population size has been used in most studies of fisheries economics. Review for a moment the graphical derivation of this curve, as described in chapter 2. Figure 2.1 contains a growth curve and four curves representing the relationship between population size and catch, each for a different level of effort. The higher the curve the larger is the specified level of effort. It was shown that the equilibrium population size for a given level of effort occurs where the growth curve and the particular catch curve intersect. At that point catch will equal net natural increase, and population size will not change. Notice that, as effort is increased (that is, as the catch curves are shifted up), the equilibrium population size falls; this is so because the catch curves are drawn in such a way that (1) they intersect the growth curve only once and always from below, and (2) eventually one lies entirely above it.

It is possible that these two conditions will not always hold. If not, the shapes of the population equilibrium and the sustained yield curves will be changed. The next two parts of this section will discuss the resultant new curves and how they affect the conclusions derived so far.

An Asymptotic Population Equilibrium Curve

The increase in catch due to an increase in the level of effort is measured by the vertical displacement of the catch curves in figure 2.1a. The size of these displacements can affect the shape of the population equilibrium curve. If, as effort increases, the amount of extra catch becomes smaller and smaller, the population equilibrium curve may become asymptotic to the horizontal axis. In terms of figure 2.1, if the catch curves draw closer together at higher levels of effort and rise above the growth curve only at extreme levels of effort, then the change in equilibrium population will become smaller and smaller as the level of effort increases, and population will reach zero only at very great levels of effort. The population equilibrium curve and the sustained yield curve that will result are pictured in figures 4.1a and 4.1b, respectively. The diminishing effect of effort means that destruction of the population is virtually impossible; the fishery can sustain a great amount of effort, but the yield will be very low. This type of yield curve is probably applicable to elusive species, such as cod.

A Forward-bending Population Equilibrium Curve

The basis for another type of population equilibrium curve is illustrated in figure 4.2, parts a and b, where the catch curves for specified levels of effort are drawn in such a way that they intersect the growth curve in two places. Figure 4.2b uses a different type of growth curve to cover a case where growth is negative below some minimum population size; for these sizes the stock will not be viable. If for some reason the stock is reduced below this critical level, the net effect of recruitment, individual growth, and mortality is negative and so the size will actually decrease. This type of growth curve, which has been discussed in the literature by Schaefer, would make multiple intersections necessary, but they are possible for both types of curves. Throughout the discussion, parts a and b of figure 4.2 can be used interchangeably.

As the curves are drawn in both diagrams, E_1 units of effort will correspond to two equilibrium population sizes, P_5 and P_1, because the catch

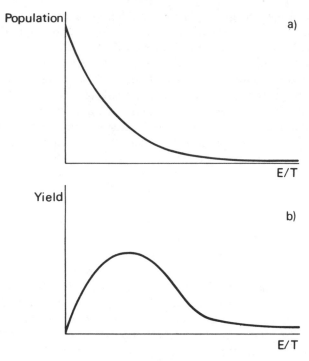

Figure 4.1. *The Asymptotic Population Equilibrium Curve.*   If increases in effort have an increasingly diminishing effect on catch, the population equilibrium curve and the sustained yield curve will become asymptotic to the horizontal axis. This means that it will be virtually impossible to destroy the fish stock.

curve f_{E1}, intersects the growth curve at both these points. Therefore, growth equals catch at two different population sizes when effort is E_1. However, although both P_1 and P_5 are equilibrium populations for E_1, only the latter is stable. For population sizes greater than P_5 catch is greater than growth, while for populations less than this, growth is greater than catch. Therefore, any move away from equilibrium at P_5 will set in motion a move to restore it, since above P_5 net growth is negative and below it net growth is positive. On the other hand, if the population for some reason were to increase slightly from P_1, growth would be greater than catch, and the population would increase to P_5, whereas a slight decrease from P_1 would result in a catch greater than growth, and population would fall to zero. As will be shown later, when economic considerations are included, it is possible to demonstrate that a stable equilibrium may occur at P_1.

Notice that if effort is increased to E_2 in either diagram, two equilibrium populations will again appear—at P_4 and P_2. The larger of these will be smaller than the maximum equilibrium size produced at the previous effort level, E_1. Vice versa, the smaller one will surpass the lesser of the two at E_1. In terms of the graph, P_4 is less than P_5, but P_2 is greater than P_1. Note that P_4

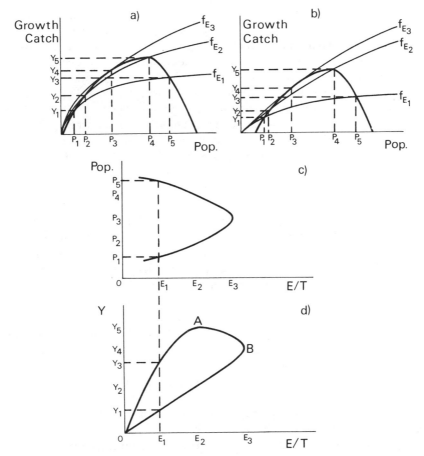

Figure 4.2. *The Forward-bending Population Equilibrium Curve.* If the catch curves for each level of effort intersect the growth curve in two places, there will be two equilibrium population sizes associated with each level of effort. This will result in a forward-bending population equilibrium curve and a forward-bending sustained yield curve, as pictured in parts c and d, respectively. This means that after some point, a decrease in population will have to be matched by a decrease in effort in order to maintain a biological equilibrium.

occurs where the growth rate is a maximum. If effort is increased further to E_3, only one equilibrium will result—at P_3—because the catch curve for E_3 is just tangent to the growth curve. For still higher levels of effort, the catch curves will lie entirely above the growth curve, and so the equilibrium population will be zero.

The population equilibrium curve derived from either of these cases is pictured in figure 4.2c. This curve should not be misinterpreted as intended to show how population size will change with differing levels of effort. The correct interpretation is that the curve shows the level of effort that will produce a catch equal to the growth rate at various population sizes. Alternatively, it shows the equilibrium population size (or sizes) that will correspond to various levels of effort. The positively sloped section means that, at lower populations, a decrease in population size must be matched by a decrease in effort to assure that the new population is an equilibrium. It does not mean that an increase in effort will increase the equilibrium population size; an increase in effort at a given equilibrium population will obviously decrease the population, because catch will become larger than growth. For example, at P_1 in parts a and b of figure 4.2, notice that an increase in effort from E_1 to E_2 will cause population to fall, since catch will be greater than growth. However, at P_2, which is a larger population, growth will equal catch.

Given this population equilibrium curve, sustained yield will be represented by the forward-bending curve pictured in figure 4.2d. The reader may find it useful to construct this curve, using a diagram similar to figure A.1. There are two sustainable yields for every level of effort less than E_3—one for each equilibrium population size that corresponds to it. E_3 has only one equilibrium population and thus only one sustainable yield. For levels of effort greater than E_3, the equilibrium population is zero (or, to be mathematically precise, it does not exist); therefore, sustainable yield is zero. Segment OAB of the curve, which corresponds to the negatively sloped portion of the population equilibrium curve, is subject to the same interpretation as is the sustained yield curve used in the last chapter. Call this the "normal" portion of the curve. For the range of population sizes for which it is relevant, it shows how sustained yield will vary with changes in the level of effort. Segment BO (call it the forward-bending portion) must be interpreted differently, however. For its relevant range of populations (the range over which the population equilibrium curve is positively sloped), an increase in effort will not mean an increase in sustained yield. Rather, it means that an increased level of effort will be consistent with a higher sustained yield but that population must be increased to obtain it. That is, if population is allowed to increase, a larger amount of effort applied to that larger population will produce a greater sustainable yield.

Although it is an extreme case, it is likely that the California sardine has this type of yield curve, and it is now being operated on the forward-bending portion at a very low level of effort. During the heyday of this fishery the population was driven very low, and now it can sustain only a small number of vessels.

As discussed earlier, the shape and position of the sustained yield curve depend jointly upon the characteristics of population growth and of fishing mortality or catch. The former is a function of population size, and the latter a function of effort and population size. Whether the yield curve will attain a forward-bending portion is determined by the effects of any change in population size on sustainable yield and on actual catch. At any level of effort, when a change in population will change sustainable yield by a greater amount than it will change catch, *then for that level of population*, the yield curve will be forward bending. This can be seen graphically in figure 4.2, parts a and b. When effort is E_1, the slope of the growth curve is greater than the slope of the catch curve at P_1. Therefore, a positive change in population will increase sustained yield by a greater amount than it will increase catch. This combination of effort and population size is in the forward-bending portion of the yield curve. At a population of P_5, however, the slope of the growth curve is less than the slope of the catch curve. Therefore, a positive change in population size will increase sustained yield by a smaller amount than it will increase catch, and the combination of E_1 and P_5 will be in the normal portion of the yield curve (see the dotted lines in parts c and d of Figure 4.2).

To clarify the point, let us consider in more detail the effect of a change in effort on both portions of the new sustainable yield curve, using the sustained yield curve and the short-run yield curves for various levels of population. The dotted curves in figure 4.3 are yield curves for fixed levels of population. The higher the curve, the higher is the population. As explained earlier, these curves intersect the sustained yield curve at that level of effort where catch equals growth for the specified level of population. Note that, in the normal portion of the sustainable yield curve, a decrease in population must be matched with an increase in effort in order to maintain a sustainable yield. On the other hand, in the forward-bending portion, a decrease in population

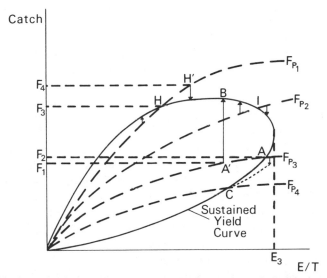

Figure 4.3. *The Forward-bending Sustained Yield Curve.*   In the top half of the forward-bending sustained yield curve, an increase or a decrease in effort will eventually result in a new biological equilibrium at another point on the same part of the curve. However, due to differences in the effects of population and effort on growth and catch, in the lower half of this curve a decrease in effort will result in a new equilibrium on the top half of the curve, and an increase in effort will result in destruction of the fish stock.

must be matched with a decrease in effort to permit the maintenance of a sustainable yield.

At an equilibrium point such as H, which is to the left of maximum sustainable yield, an increase in effort, say to H', will, in the short run, lead to an increase in catch such that it will be greater than growth (catch will equal F_4, but growth for population P_1 equals F_3). The population will fall, causing the catch curve to fall in the direction of the arrow at H', and this decrease will lower the catch rate until eventually it will again equal growth. In this range of population sizes, a decrease in population actually increases sustainable yield. Therefore, the combination of greater effort and a smaller but more productive population leads to higher sustained yield. The opposite occurs when effort is slackened. Catch then decreases in the short run, which makes it less than growth, and so population size will increase, leading to a higher catch rate until it eventually again equals growth. The increased stock has a smaller growth rate and thus lower sustained yield.

At point I, to the right of MSY, similar results will follow increases or decreases in effort. The only difference is that within this range of populations, a decrease in population will correspondingly decrease the growth rate; thus, an increase in effort will decrease sustained yield, and vice versa.

Assume the fishery is operating in the forward-bending portion of the sustained yield curve at point A with an equilibrium population size of P_3. A decrease in effort to point A' will decrease catch in the short run. Stock size will increase, since growth will now be greater than catch (catch will equal F_1, but growth will equal F_2). If the level of effort remains constant, population will continue to grow until a new equilibrium is reached at point B in the normal portion of the curve. As population size grows, both the growth rate (which is sustainable yield) and actual catch rate will increase. Since the catch rate will increase faster, it will eventually come into equality with the growth rate and at this point a new sustainable yield will be established. The movement from point A' to point B is analogous to a movement from, say, P_2 to P_5 if effort is E_1 (see either figure 4.2a or 4.2b).

On the other hand, because an increase in effort from an equilibrium at point A will cause short-run catch to become greater than growth, population size will decrease and both the catch rate and the growth rate will consequently fall. The rate of catch will always be larger than the rate of growth, so population will continue to fall until it is eventually destroyed. Once the population is decreased, the only way a sustained yield can be obtained again is to reduce effort below its original level. For example, a new equilibrium is possible at point C (see dotted line from A to C).

To generalize the foregoing, any point on that part of a short-run yield curve below the forward-bending portion of the sustained yield curve represents a combination of effort and population where catch is greater than growth and where, if effort is held constant, population will eventually be destroyed. Any point on that part of a short-run yield curve above the forward-bending portion but below the normal portion (i.e., that lies in the area proscribed by the sustainable yield curve) represents a combination of effort and population where growth is greater than catch and where, if effort is held constant, the population will grow until the normal portion of the curve is reached. Finally, any point on that part of a short-run yield curve above the normal portion of the sustainable yield curve represents a combination of effort and population where catch is greater than growth and where, if effort is held constant, the population will fall until the normal part of the curve is reached. A point above the normal part of the curve differs from one below the forward-bending part for this reason: at the former point, the decrease in population will make it so difficult to harvest fish that the catch will eventually fall to the level of growth and the population decline will cease. At the latter point, the decrease in population will not exert so strong an effect, and catch will always be greater than growth. It should be pointed out that, if any level of effort greater than E_3 is maintained, the population will eventually be destroyed.

Even though no stable population equilibrium can exist in the forward-bending portion of the sustained yield curve in figure 4.3, the area is still of interest in a study of commercial fisheries. Recall that final equilibrium in an open-access commercial fishery (call it a bioeconomic equilibrium) must comprise both an economic and a biological equilibrium. That is, (1) there is no incentive to increase or decrease the level of effort, and (2) the population size will not change. In certain instances, conditions leading to an economic equilibrium can counter the instability of the biological equilibrium to such a degree as to stabilize the bioeconomic equilibrium in the forward-bending section.

The following example will demonstrate this. For simplicity, the price of fish will be assumed to be a constant; otherwise, the shape of the revenue curve corresponding to a forward-bending sustained yield curve is very difficult to handle. With a constant price for fish, the revenue curve will have the same general shape as the yield curve. A stable bioeconomic equilibrium in the forward-bending portion of the sustained yield curve is then *possible* if: (1) the cost curve intersects the sustained revenue curve in this section from above, (2) an increase in stock size will increase the catch per period for any level of effort, and (3) each short-run yield curve (that is, the yield curve for a fixed population) is monotonically increasing.

This case is illustrated in figure 4.4. As before, the sustained revenue curve and the short-run revenue curves can be thought of as a monetized version of their respective yield curves. The constant price means that a unit of fish equals a specified amount of dollars. Bioeconomic equilibrium will occur at point B because revenue there equals cost, and catch equals growth. In effect, the fishery is operating on the short-run revenue curve through point B. But will an equilibrium at this point ever be reached? Assume that population is P_1. In that case, the short-run equilibrium is at point A. The sustained

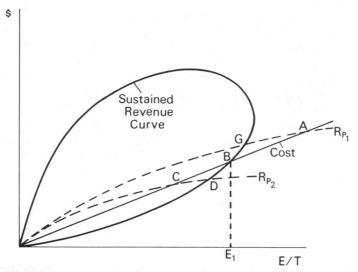

Figure 4.4. *Equilibria in the Lower Half of the Forward-bending Sustained Revenue Curve: I.* If the cost curve intersects the lower half of the forward-bending sustained revenue curve from above and the short-run revenue curves are as drawn, economic incentives will change the level of effort in such a way that it *may* compensate for biological instability, and hence a stable bioeconomic equilibrium in this portion of the curve may be possible.

yield for that population is at point G; therefore, catch is greater than sustained yield, and population will fall. In fact, if effort were to remain constant, population would fall to zero. The decline in population will, however, lower revenues since the short-run yield curves will fall. Therefore, effort will tend to decrease. This will reduce catch, thus dampening the decrease in population. There will be a tendency for this process to continue until the short-run revenue curve has fallen such that it passes through point B and for effort to fall to E_1. Similarly, at a population of P_2, the short-run equilibrium is at point C, while sustained yield is at point D. Catch is less than sustained yield, so population will grow. Such growth will encourage an expansion of effort, which will check the increase in population. The short-run revenue curve will tend to shift up until it intersects point B, and effort will increase to E_1. Whether an actual equilibrium is reached cannot be stated a priori, but a stable equilibrium is indeed possible if the relative rates of change of effort and of population size are appropriate. Other relative rates will lead to extinction or oscillation around E_1 (see Clark 1976, chaps. 2 and 6).

Figure 4.5 illustrates the case where the cost curve intersects the forward-bending portion of the sustained revenue curve from below, thus precluding any stable equilibrium. In this case, with a population of P_1, the short-run equilibrium will be at point A. The sustained yield at this population is at point G, so growth is greater than catch. This will lead to an increase in population that, by shifting the short-run yield curve upward, will encourage more

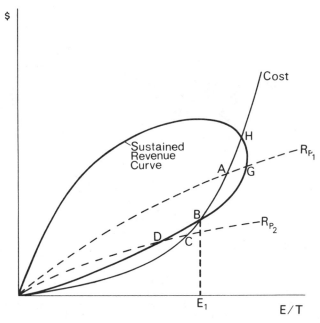

Figure 4.5. *Equilibria in the Lower Half of the Forward-bending Sustained Revenue Curve: II.*
If the cost curve intersects the lower half of the forward-bending sustained revenue curve from below and the short-run revenue curves are as drawn, economic incentives will change the level of effort in such a way that a stable bioeconomic equilibrium in this portion of the curve is impossible.

effort to enter. The fishery will move toward an equilibrium at point H. If
population were P_2, the short-run equilibrium at point C would result in a
decrease in population, because at P_2 sustainable yield is at point D. As population falls, the short-run yield curve will fall and the amount of effort will
decrease. Since the cost curve is below the sustained revenue curve in this
region, the new short-run equilibrium will again lead to a reduction in population. This alternate process will continue until the population is eventually
destroyed. Therefore, it is evident that no stable bionomic equilibrium is possible in the forward-bending portion of the sustained yield curve depicted in
figure 4.5. It has now been demonstrated that a forward-bending yield curve
is feasible and that under certain conditions a stable bionomic equilibrium
can exist in the forward-bending part of it despite the instability of the biological equilibrium there. This adds a new dimension to the model. For one
thing, as Southey (1972) has pointed out, regulation will not always entail a
long-run decrease in effort. Consider figure 4.6. Point A is open-access equilibrium yield, and point B, which has a higher level of effort, is the static
maximum economic yield. If point A is a stable equilibrium in an unregulated
fishery, then regulation for MEY would call for a movement from point A
toward point B, which would necessitate an initial decrease in the level of

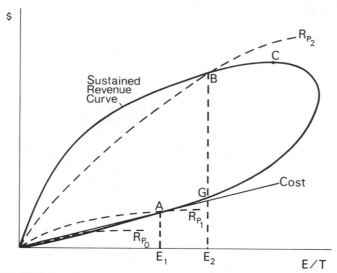

Figure 4.6. *Equilibria in the Lower Half of the Forward-bending Sustained Revenue Curve: III.*
If a stable equilibrium is possible at point A, the open-access equilibrium will occur at E_1 units of
effort. Maximum economic yield occurs at a higher level of effort but with a larger fish stock. This
means that, after an initial period to allow the population to grow, MEY will actually call for an increase in effort. Notice that, if the population falls to P_0 or lower, the fishery will be economically
nonviable because revenue will be less than cost at all levels of effort.

effort to allow the population to increase from P_1 toward P_2, but would ultimately call for an increase in effort from E_1 to E_2. The MEY will occur somewhere between point A and point B on the sustained revenue curve. Exactly
where it will occur will depend upon the discount rate and the rate of growth
of the stock. In any event, proper regulation will actually call for an increase
in the level of effort in the long run. So rather than shifting resources away
from the fishery, optimal regulation may do the opposite. As before, the problem is to find the optimal population size and level of effort and the proper
rate of achieving them. Should effort be cut to zero to allow a rapid increase,
or should it be decreased gradually to permit a slower increase in population?
Either decision would entail giving up fish production now for increased production in the future. Which choice is better depends upon people's taste for
goods now versus goods in the future, as discussed in chapter 2.

As figure 4.5 demonstrated, a forward-bending yield curve admits the
possibility of the biological extinction of a commercial fishery in a straightforward fashion. In such a case, if the population falls to a low enough level, it
will yet support a level of effort adequate to harvest more than the natural
growth. Even though effort will be falling, it will not be falling fast enough. If
the cost curve lies entirely below the forward-bending portion of a sustained
revenue curve, then the unregulated fishery is destined for biological extinction, no matter what the population size, because the short-run yield curve
will always intersect the cost curve at a point where catch is greater than

growth. If the blue whale fishery were not regulated, it might be in just this situation.

A more common occurrence is the economic destruction of a fishery in such a way that, although the population remains viable, it can support little or no effort. The haddock fishery in the northwest Atlantic is often dangerously close to this situation. This can be caused by overfishing, by a rapid increase in the cost of effort, or by a decrease in the price of fish. In figure 4.6 this is demonstrated by a population equal to P_0. In the short run, revenue would be less than cost for all levels of effort; thus effort would tend to fall to zero and economic destruction would have been effected. Under our assumptions, the population would now increase, and eventually the fishery would start up again. How long the fishery would have been "destroyed" would depend upon the growth rate of the population and the promptness with which effort could be reapplied. In some cases, however, once a population is diminished, its ecological niche is filled by another species that blocks its restoration. In that case the fishery will remain economically destroyed, barring some favorable change in demand or in fishery technology.

To clarify this, compare the equilibrium at point A in figure 4.6 with the position of an overexploited fishery having a yield curve as depicted in figure 4.1b. In the latter case, a relatively large amount of effort produces a small sustainable yield. The forward-bending yield curve, on the other hand, demonstrates that an overexploited fishery may operate with a comparatively smaller amount of effort, producing a small sustainable yield. Therefore, an overexploited fishery will result in a small population and a low catch, but the effort necessary to harvest the sustainable yield may be either large or small.

Although the discussion has so far assumed a constant price of fish, the forward-bending yield curve can be introduced into the more general model of a variable price with comparatively little difficulty by expanding the analysis in chapter 3 to take into account the effect the differently shaped yield curve will have on the shape of the average cost curve in terms of fish. This can be done using the method described in the appendix to chapter 3. There will be no significant changes in the result that have not already been discussed here or in chapters 2 and 3.

Aspects of the Dynamic Pool Model

As mentioned above, the difference between Schaefer and dynamic pool models is that the latter gives independent attention to the growth of individual fish, recruitment, and natural and fishing mortality. While a rigorous analysis of the details of this model are beyond the scope of this book, some of the important concepts will be explained such that they can be integrated into the economic and biological analysis already presented. Those readers wishing a more detailed analysis are referred to Clark (1976, chaps. 7 and 8), Gulland (1974, chap. 4), Hannesson (1978, chap. 8), and Waugh (1984, chap. 3). The analysis here will focus primarily on recruitment and individual growth.

Regenerative Species: The Relationship between Stock and Recruitment

In salmon species, recruitment is the primary factor influencing the size of the yearly stock. Because salmon die during or after the trip to the spawning grounds, there is no carry-over of individuals to the next periods. Therefore, the number of individuals available to breed is more important in determining population size in the next period than is the growth of existing individuals. The purpose of this section is to analyze this growth pattern more closely and to compare it with the more general model. While the resulting sustained yield curve is essentially the same, it is interesting to study its different basis.

The size of a salmon population in any one period—measured in numbers of individuals, not in weight as above—is a function of the number of spawners from the previous period. (Different species have different reproductive patterns. Some salmon spawn in one-year cycles while others remain at sea for several years before returning to spawn. This analysis will assume an annual spawn.) This number, called escapement, can for our purposes be considered to be equal to the original stock (i.e., recruits) minus the catch by man. (This ignores natural mortality, but the essence of the argument is the same.) A reproduction function for regenerative species is plotted in figure 4.7a. At low levels, increases in escapement result in increases in the stock size for the next period, but at higher levels the opposite is true because of overcrowding on the spawning beds and other density-dependent effects. The distance between the curve and the dotted line drawn through the origin at a 45-degree angle represents the amount of fish harvestable at any population while yet allowing an escapement sufficient to produce that population in the next period. For example, if stock size is P_m, then if catch is equal to the arrow labeled C_2, escapement equals the distance between the 45-degree line and the horizontal axis. By construction, this level of escapement, Esc_4, is the amount necessary to exactly reproduce a population of P_m.

P_e in the figure is the equilibrium population if there is no exploitation by man, because only at that point will escapement of the entire stock serve to reproduce the same population size. At stock sizes lower than P_e, breeding by the entire stock will lead to greater numbers in the next period. Above P_e, a breeding stock of that size will lead to a decrease in numbers for the next interval. Note that, as the curves are drawn, the equilibrium population is less than P_m, the maximum population (P_e will equal P_m if the 45-degree line intersects the escapement function in the latter's positively sloped portion). P_1 is the population size that yields the highest catch while still allowing an escapement sufficient to produce an identical population. Another important fact is that, for populations larger than P_e, there are two levels of escapement

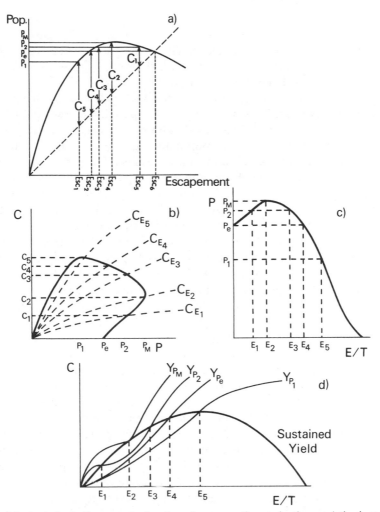

Figure 4.7. *Analysis of a Regenerative Species.*   In regenerative species the population in any one period depends upon the escapement in the previous period. Utilizing the escapement curve in figure 4.7a, it is possible to construct the allowable catch curve in figure 4.7b. This can be used in the normal fashion to construct the population equilibrium curve pictured in figure 4.7c. The sustained yield curve in figure 4.7d can be constructed from the above two curves in the manner described in figure A.1. The analysis using this curve is essentially the same as in other cases except that an increase in effort can sometimes actually lead to an increase in equilibrium population size.

that will return the same population. For example, both Esc_2 and Esc_6 will return a population of P_e.

In the previous analysis, the growth curve was used to define the sustainable yield and to derive a population equilibrium curve. Through the use of the latter, together with the growth curve, we were then able to construct a sustained yield curve. Now, in the present case of the salmon stock, a curve that is analogous to the growth curve must be obtained in order to derive the population equilibrium and the sustainable yield curve. The curve we are looking for—call it the "allowable catch curve"—must show sustainable yields for various populations. An example is shown in figure 4.7b, and it can be derived from 4.7a. For example, at P_1 a level of catch of C_5 will be sustainable because if leaves an escapement of Esc_1, which will produce a population of P_1 all over again. Similarly, for every level of population less than P_e, one sustainable level of catch will equal the difference between the escapement function and the 45-degree line. At populations greater than P_e, two sustainable catch levels are possible. For example, consider P_2. Here, catches of C_3 and C_1 allow for escapement of Esc_3 and Esc_5, respectively, both of which will reproduce a population equal to P_2. Similarly, any other population in this range will have two levels of allowable catch because there are two levels of escapement that will produce them. By plotting the combinations of population and catch, an allowable catch curve similar to the one in figure 4.7b can be derived. Note that for populations less than P_e there is only one level of allowable catch, but for populations above P_e, there are two. Note also that the maximum allowable catch occurs at a population size of P_1.

Joining catch curves for specified levels of effort (i.e., C_{E_1}, C_{E_2}, etc.) with the allowable catch curve, it is possible to construct a population equilibrium curve in the same manner as in figure 2.1, where the growth curve was used with the catch curves. An example of this population equilibrium curve is pictured in figure 4.7c. For example, a level of effort of E_1 in figure 4.7b will result in an equilibrium population of P_2, because only at that level will the actual catch equal the allowable catch. Similarly, E_2 will yield an equilibrium population of P_m, whereas E_3 will indicate a population of P_2. Note that, as effort is increased from zero to E_2, the equilibrium population size actually increases. This happens because the more intensive effort reduces escapement, and over this range such a reduction is beneficial to population for the next period. Increases in effort beyond E_2 will have a different effect, however, because further decreases in escapement will reduce future populations (see figure 4.7a).

Although this curve—call it the "upward-rising population equilibrium curve"—does have a positively sloped portion, it differs substantially from the forward-bending one described in the last section. For one thing, the latter presented a range over which each level of effort could correspond to more than one equilibrium level of population. In this case, over some range each population size is an equilibrium population for two levels of effort and hence is capable of yielding two different amounts of sustainable or allowable catch for that stock size. This peculiarity leads to variations in interpretation. As stressed earlier, the positively sloped portion of the forward-bending curve does not mean that an increase in effort will increase equilibrium population but rather that, if population is increased, an equilibrium can be sustained at a higher level of effort. In the upward-rising population equilibrium curve, the positively sloped portion can be thus interpreted, however. True, an increase in effort will increase catch, thus reducing escapement, but in this range of population sizes a decrease in escapement leads to a larger stock in the next period. In terms of figure 4.7a, the positive portion corresponds to reductions in escapement from Esc_6 to Esc_4, where we see that increases in effort actually increase the population size.

Before moving on, it should be noted that if the catch curves intersect the allowable catch curve more than once, it is then also possible to have a forward-bending portion of the population equilibrium curve. This has been adequately covered in the preceding section, and details are unnecessary here.

The sustained yield curve for regenerative species, as pictured in figure 4.7d, can be derived from 4.7b and 4.7c and is, surprisingly enough, of the normal shape. For all practical purposes, then, the entire analysis developed previously applies directly in this case as well. (The interested reader may satisfy himself that the curves have the same shape by using the method described in figure A.1.) The short-term yield curves intersect differently with the sustained yield curves, however. For stock sizes having *only* one level of allowable catch (i.e., those less than P_e), the yield curves intersect the sustained yield curve only once and from below. This is the way that all short-run catch curves used thus far have been pictured. Curves Y_{P_1} and Y_{P_e} in figure 4.7d are examples; see also the short-run catch curves in figure 2.2a. For population sizes having two allowable catches, the yield curve will intersect twice, first from above and second from below (see Y_{P_2}). As population increases, the first intersection moves to a higher level of effort and the second to a lower one. The yield curve for P_m does not intersect the sustained yield curve at all but, rather, is tangent at one point. All the above intersections and the one tangency occur at those levels of effort that produce the allowable catch(es) for various levels of population.

The above leads to a slight change in the dynamic analysis in the portion of the sustained yield curve to the left of E_2. For example, assume that an equilibrium is reached at E_2 with population equal to P_m. Note that a decrease in effort to E_1 will initially reduce catch along the Y_{P_m} curve. For the given stock size, actual catch is now less than allowable catch (it was equal at the equilibrium before the decrease in effort), and so escapement increases. In this size range, however, an increase in escapement will decrease stock size and cause the short-run yield curve to fall. This trend will continue until Y_{P2} is reached, at which point actual catch will again be equal to allowable catch. The analysis of this section is different; a decrease in effort will cause population size to fall, and vice versa, but nonetheless the general results are the same (changes in effort will cause the population to change in such a way that the short-run yield curve will eventually intersect the sustained yield curve at the new level of effort).

A sustained curve such as this offers the intriguing possibility that regulation may actually lead to a lower equilibrium size for population. This would be the case if the cost curve were such that an unregulated fishery would exert effort at a level of E_2, whereas E_1 would produce static maximum economic yield. Regulation would then call for a decrease in population from P_m to P_2.

As a final point, note that if the escapement function in figure 4.7 intersects the 45-degree line to the left of maximum population, then (while the method of constructing the allowable catch curve does not change) the curve will have the same shape as the growth curve. In such a case the standard analysis derived earlier applies completely: the population equilibrium curve will not be upward rising, and the short-run yield curves will intersect the sustained yield curve only in the normal fashion.

Shrimp Fisheries: No-Stock Recruitment Relationship

As opposed to salmon stocks, the population size of shrimp stocks in any one year depends chiefly upon certain ecological conditions during critical phases of its life cycle and bears little relation to population size in the previous year. Therefore, no population equilibrium curve is feasible for these stocks because population size has little or no relation to the level of effort. Each period will produce a specific stock size exogenously determined as far as management is concerned. Associated with these populations are the normal short-run yield and revenue curves.

Given the shape of these curves, the standard short-run analysis applies. An unregulated fishery will expand production during the year to the point where short-run costs equal revenues. Because there is no relationship between effort and stock size in future years, there is no user cost. The optimum point for any year, therefore, is the place where the difference between the annual revenue and annual harvesting costs is maximized, and this point will shift from year to year with changes in the population size. If the size of the yearly population is subject to wide fluctuations, and if the entry and especially the exit of effort are slow, then the problem of overcapacity in an unregulated fishery is compounded. This independence of population size from the level of effort precludes any long-run equilibrium position. Good years (i.e., large stock sizes) will lead to high capacity; if they are followed by a long period of bad years, then large amounts of capital and large numbers of men may remain tied up in a fishery where they are earning smaller than normal profits.

Long-term regulation is more difficult in this case for the same reasons. The maximum economic yield output level may vary from year to year, but unless effort is highly mobile, it does not make sense to restrict effort in a bad year unless the revenue earned is less than variable costs, such as fuel. Similarly, in especially good years, boats should not be brought into the fishery except on a short-term basis. A proper goal would be to maintain enough capacity to harvest at a minimum cost the maximum economic yield for the "average" year while at the same time making provision for short-term increases or decreases in effort.

General Stock Recruitment Relationships

Salmon and shrimp stocks are the two extremes as far as stock recruitment relationships are concerned. In the former there is a strong relationship that has been shown to be statistically significant. See Ricker (1975) and Cushing (1977b). In the latter it appears that there is no relationship. In most other marine species the relationships are not that clear. In fact, a stock recruitment relationship has been determined with any degree of accuracy for only a minority of stocks. One of the reasons for this is the population dynamics of each particular species. Salmon, which produce only a few thousand eggs per female, tend to have a clearly defined curve that reaches a peak and then falls off. See figure 4.7a. Marine flatfish, such as flounder, which produce hundreds of thousands of eggs per female, tend to have flat curves with high amounts of variation but which show little proportionality except at very small population levels. Figure 4.8 presents an example. See Gulland (1974, 101).

By observation, it is clear that, except at low population levels, there must be other factors besides stock size that can explain recruitment. Part of the explanation is that the number of eggs is often not the binding constraint on survival. The ocean environment is harsh, and one of the attributes of stocks that have survived is the large number of eggs per female. Therefore, even with a small number of spawning females, there are more than enough eggs, relative to the expected amounts of habitat, food supplies, natural mortality, and predation. The variation in recruitment pictured in figure 4.8 is more likely due to changes in these factors than in changes in stock size.

For those stocks for which stock recruitment curves are relevant, there are two important implications for management. The first is the range over which the positive relationship between stock and recruitment holds. With the curve in figure 4.8, there is little fear that heavy exploitation will have a significant effect on recruitment. Large amounts of effort can still affect long-run catch level by harvesting fish before they have a chance to grow, and so there will still be a user cost associated with current harvests, but the survival of the stock will not be in danger. If the curve increases at a less steep angle, then the effect of effort on stock size and recruitment will be more important.

The second issue is the variability around the curve. The higher the variability, the less confidence there can be that a change in stock size will affect recruitment in the next few years. Expected recruitment may fall with a decrease in stock size, but on the other hand it may actually increase if the stock decrease is matched by a fortuitous improvement in environmental conditions

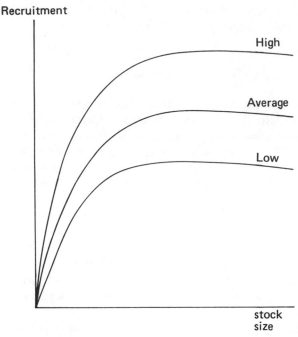

Figure 4.8. *Stock Recruitment Relationships.*   Certain species, such as marine flatfish, show little proportionality between stock and recruitment except at small stock sizes. However, there can be significant variability between the high and low levels of recruitment at any one stock size, depending upon other natural phenomena.

affecting survival of eggs and postlarvae. Similarly, increases in stock size may not necessarily be matched by an increase in recruitment.

The Eumetric Yield Curve: Consideration of Individual Growth

Because of the specific characteristics of certain fisheries, the gear to be used can be just as important a variable as fishing effort in determining an optimal management policy. This is the case where the fishery presents distinctive year classes; where the fishing method can select the size at which fish are subject to capture; where the population fished is distributed in such a way that the gear actually contacts a range of sizes, including those above a critical minimum size; and where the level of effort does not affect recruitment significantly. Gear selectivity is any consideration that affects the size or age of capture. Throughout this discussion, mesh size in a net fishery will be used as the typical example. If, as effort changes, proper adjustments are made in the size of fish taken, then greater effort need never result in decreased sustained yield. This selection of the proper combination of effort and gear selectivity is called *eumetric fishing*. The sustainable yield curve that results is pictured in figure 4.9c.

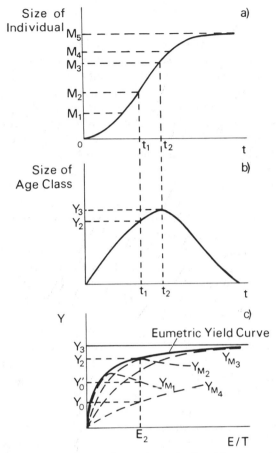

Figure 4.9. *The Eumetric Yield Curve.* In certain species, by taking account of the change in the size of the individual and of the number of individuals, it is possible to pick a mesh size for each level of effort where sustained yield will be maximized. In this way, sustained yield need never decrease with increases in effort. As effort is increased, the appropriate mesh size approaches the size of the individual fish when the biomass of each year class is a maximum. This biomass is the maximum catch possible, but effort must approach infinity to obtain it.

The logic behind eumetric fishing is as follows. Over time, the individual fish in each year class increases in weight according to a sigmoid growth curve. (Assume for the moment that the number in each year class is a constant.) The individuals will initially grow rapidly, then more slowly until they reach an average maximum size, as graphed in figure 4.9a. At the same time, however, the number in the class is decreased by disease, old age, and other mortality factors. The total weight of a year class at any point in time is determined by the relative strengths of these two factors. At early ages, the rapid growth of individuals outweighs the low death rate, and the total weight of the year class will increase. Eventually, however, the weight loss due to mortality excccds the gain by individual growth, and total weight of the year class will fall. At some intermediate point, that total will have reached a maximum. The growth function of the year class is pictured in figure 4.9b, with a time scale identical to that of figure 4.9a. For example, at time t_1 the average size of the individual fish is M_2, and the total weight of the year class is Y_2.

Given the relationship between individual growth and year-class growth, the maximum possible yield from a specific year class will depend upon the mesh size. In terms of figure 4.9, parts a and b, if the gear is set in such a way that fish smaller than M_3 are allowed to escape, sustainable catch can conceivably reach as high as Y_3, since the fish will be allowed to grow to the proper size; just how much of that potential will be caught then depends upon the level of effort. If the minimum mesh size is set at M_2, the maximum possible catch is Y_2. Thus, an increase in minimum size from M_2 to M_3 allows the fish to grow until the heavier individual size more than compensates for decreases in total weight due to mortality.

This same information can be displayed as a series of sustained yield curves, one for each minimum fish size, as shown for four sizes in figure 4.9c. Each of the curves relates effort per period of time to sustained yield for a given mesh size; Y_{M1} represents the yield curve if the mesh size frees fish smaller than M_1 in size, and so forth. (The sizes correspond to those in figure 4.9a so that M_2 is greater than M_1.) These curves are drawn to reflect empirical work by Beverton and Holt (1957), which has shown that, as the minimum fish size is increased toward that which yields the largest possible year-class size, two things occur: first, the maximum possible sustained yield increases, although it is achieved at a higher level of effort; and second, the downward-sloping segments of these curves gradually disappear.

The eumetric yield curve is the envelope curve of the set of sustained yield curves for minimum fish size of M_3 or less. In effect, it is the result of optimum combinations of gear selectivity and fishing effort. For example, at fishing effort E_2, the proper choice is to reject fish smaller than M_2, because mesh of that size will yield maximum catch at the given level of effort. If the mesh size were at M_1, at a level of effort of E_2, increasing it to M_2 would, in the long run, increase sustainable yield from Y_0' to Y_2. In the short run, catch would fall because more fish would be released by the gear; but as the population size and age distribution adjusted to the change in mesh size, catch at that level of effort would increase. A further increase in minimum size to M_4, however, would decrease sustained yield to Y_0. Similarly, at every other level of effort there is a particular minimum fish size where sustained yield will be a maximum.

The open-access operation of a fishery for which the eumetric yield curve is applicable can be described using figure 4.10. With no control on effort or the size at first capture, individual vessels continue to enter the fishery as long as it is profitable to do so. Further, they will set the mesh size in their nets for the smallest fish that is acceptable to the market. This can be called the *open-*

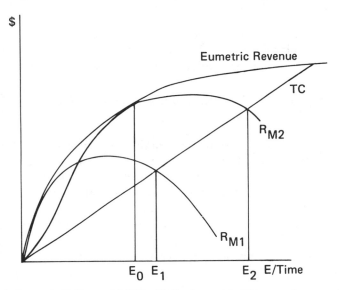

Figure 4.10. *Eumetric Fishing and MEY.*   Optimal eumetric fishing requires a combination of size selection and level of effort such that the proper amount of fish will be harvested at the proper size.

access mesh size. Using a smaller size would only increase costs because of the necessity of sorting the catch and discarding nonmarketable fish. On the other hand, a larger mesh size would allow potentially marketable fish to escape. Figure 4.10 contains revenue curves for the eumetric yield curve and for the sustainable yield curves for two mesh sizes, M_1 and M_2. If M_1 is the open-access mesh size, the open-access equilibrium will occur at E_1.

Assuming for the moment a zero discount rate, a stationary MEY point will occur at the level of effort where the distance between the eumetric revenue curve and the total cost curve is a maximum. As indicated in the graph, this will occur at E_0 units of effort and a mesh size equal to M_2. This will involve two specific controls. For example, if the minimum mesh size is stipulated to be M_2, the revenue curve will change from R_{M1} to R_{M2}, but with no control on effort, the open-access equilibrium will change from E_1 to E_2. Alternatively, if the mesh size is not controlled but effort is reduced from E_1 to E_0, all potential gains will not be realized because revenue will be earned according to R_{M1}, not the eumetric revenue curve.

Because it takes time for the stock to adjust to changes in mesh size and hence for the eumetric revenue curve to be reached, E_0 is not the optimal level of effort with a postive discount rate. Although a straightforward analytical solution of the optimal combination of effort and mesh size is difficult if not impossible to obtain (see Clark 1976, 285), it is possible to derive practical estimates using numerical optimization techniques (see Waugh 1984, chap. 6). Given the complexity of the analysis, there will be no attempt to discuss the dynamic optimum combination of effort and mesh in any detail here. However, with the cost and eumetric revenue curves in figure 4.10, optimal utilization would involve a level of effort less than E_0 and a mesh size smaller than M_2, with the operational point below the eumetric revenue curve.

Combined Analysis: Considerations of Stock Recruitment and Individual Growth

In cases where the mesh size is not optimally adjusted to the level of effort, the reduction in yield is sometimes called *growth over fishing* because the fish are harvested before growing to an optimum size. Alternatively, when fishing effort is so high that the stock is pushed into the range where recruitment falls drastically, the long-term reduction in harvest is called *recruitment overfishing*. While both result in a loss of potential catch, the latter may have significant effects on the ability of the stock to survive.

As indicated in the previous subsection, the eumetric yield curve is constructed assuming constant recruitment. With a recruitment curve similar to those pictured in figure 4.8, recruitment is in fact constant over a wide range of stock sizes. However, if effort were large enough to significantly reduce stock size, recruitment would fall. In that case, the eumetric yield curve would no longer apply. Although what fish remain would be harvested at the optimal size, there would be a lower overall catch because of the reduction in long-term stock size.

The eumetric yield curve obviously does not hold in a straightforward manner when recruitment is highly variable either, but some of the principles apply. The problem is to take appropriate consideration of the strengths of various year classes so that proper advantage can be taken of both individual growth and the size and life expectancy of the various year classes. The optimal mesh size will probably not change from year to year. However, the optimal amount of effort will vary with the strengths of the year class passing through the stock. If there is little recruitment for several years, effort and catch must be small to avoid economic waste as well as the possibility of recruitment overfishing. However, with very big year classes, catch can be much higher. Viewing the optimal harvest problem in this light places the role of the sustainable yield function in its proper perspective. Where there is variable recruitment, sustained yield may be useful for long-range planning, but it will be less valuable in determining the optimal harvest for a single year. However, if research biologists can estimate the strengths of incoming year classes, appropriate harvest strategies can be determined (see Anderson 1986).

One type of harvest strategy that has received some attention is the concept of *pulse fishing*. The stock is allowed to grow unaffected by fishing mortality until it reaches a certain size, and then it is fished rather heavily over a short period of time. After another interval that allows the stock to grow, it is cropped again. See Clark (1976, 273) and Hannesson (1975). In certain instances, this will obtain higher yields and higher net present value than will a sustained level of harvest. One problem with this type of policy is utilization of the fleet during the time the stock is allowed to grow. It is more likely that pulse fishing will be optimal when there are several stocks over which the fleet can be rotated. Before the age of extended fisheries jurisdiction, distant-water fishing nations such as Russia and Japan often found this strategy to be optimal. They could fish stocks in one area of the world and move on to other areas while the stocks recovered.

Is There a Maximum Social Yield?

The main emphasis to this point has been on maximum economic yield as the proper goal for fishery management. MEY will guarantee that the net contribution of the fishery to the economy is maximized. It is a logical goal, and its exact location can theoretically be pinpointed. However, society may choose to sacrifice some economic efficiency for the sake of other important goals. The purpose of this section is to describe some of the other possible goals and to show how they can be related to the model.

Some of the multiple other goals that society may wish to use in fisheries management include (1) income redistribution, (2) maintenance of a balance of payments equilibrium, (3) reduction in structural unemployment, and (4) provision of recreational activities. This list is not complete, and certainly these goals do not concern fisheries exclusively. Rather, they are basic responsibilities of government in most nations of the world today. Depending upon how each of these goals is perceived, they can complement or conflict with each other and other governmental activities. For example, some apparently desirable changes in income redistribution may have a harmful effect on the balance of payments if there is a relative increase in the incomes of individuals with a tendency to purchase imported goods. Also, construction of freeways through certain areas of our cities may help a large portion of the population by decreasing their travel time, but it may also force lower-income families out of their homes. Likewise, attempts to give structurally unemployed workers jobs in a fishery can affect total productivity in the economy by necessitating a transfer of variable inputs such as fuel, maintenance services, and so forth to the fishery from other segments of the economy where their value in use is higher than the value of the extra fish obtained. When such conflicts exist, the problem of just what the trade-off between the two competing goals should be must be solved. Fishery management is but one of many tools available to government in the effort to advance the overall welfare of society, and the proper goal for it should be derived in this context.

Let us consider these other objectives in somewhat greater detail. Shifting resources from a fishery to other uses—which, as discussed in the next chapter, is the proper goal of fishery regulation—can result in many types of income redistribution. Those allowed to remain will enjoy an increase in profits because of the increase in catch per unit of effort, but those who must move will be deprived of this benefit and, in fact, their incomes will probably fall. Their nonmoney income may also suffer if they find the new job less enjoyable. Consumers of fish may lose because of a smaller supply and a higher price. Consumers of certain other goods may benefit because of an increased supply and decreased price, but this means that the original producers of those goods may suffer a fall in profits. These varied redistributions of income can include shifts among income classes, among geographical regions of the country, and among economic sectors of industry. Assuming that the costs of regulation are relatively small, the movement from unregulated equilibrium to maximum economic yield will always result in a net increase in the value of goods produced, but the market may fail to distribute the gains in what is considered an equitable fashion. In fact, some people or some areas may suffer absolute losses. A country implementing a conscious policy to redistribute income should make sure that the net effects of fisheries managment do not prove counterproductive. More positively, it may want to design management goals with certain carefully assessed redistributive criteria in mind.

There are two ways to deal with unfavorable income redistributions resulting from fisheries management. One is to correct them by transfer payments; the other is to change the policy. Those arguing for the former contend that maximum economic yield provides the largest net output of the fishery and that everyone can benefit from a relatively simple transfer of gains. Changing to a goal other than MEY decreases the net gain from the fishery, so any improvement in distribution comes at the expense of that potential. Those recommending a change in policy say that, although transfers are fine in theory, they are oftentimes not politically feasible. For example, the electorate would be expected to favor a plan that allowed certain fishermen to exploit a fishery beyond MEY rather than one that paid the men for not fishing or that subsidized them in another endeavor.

The basic logic of the first argument cannot be denied. It makes sense to make the pie as big as possible before cutting it up. On the other hand, some real problems interfere with setting up certain types of transfer programs. Which method is more advantageous can ultimately be decided only on a fishery-by-fishery basis.

Another possible national goal is that of keeping the balance of payments in equilibrium. Fisheries can enter into this in two ways. Countries having a deficit in balance of payments may decide to use the fishery (1) to produce goods for export, or (2) for import substitution. Many of the developing countries are in the former position; needing to import goods to forward their industrial growth, they pay for these with fish. The United States is in the latter position; currently sending more money abroad than other countries are willing to spend here, we are buying a multitude of goods, including fishery products. Any increase in home production of fish would help curtail this outflow of cash. A country facing a sizable balance-of-payments problem may therefore deem it desirable to operate its fishery beyond MEY.

A third among the possible national goals mentioned above is the reduction of structural unemployment. Some areas of the country suffer perpetually high levels of unemployment, usually where the labor force is comparatively unskilled and where the main industries have diminished for some reason. Lacking skills, the workers have little hope of finding work elsewhere, and the area itself does not attract new industry. A fishery accessible to such an area would have a comparatively high level of employment *even at MEY* because of the low opportunity cost of labor, but administrative decisionmakers might yet choose to operate beyond that point to provide more jobs. In some cases, regulations might even prohibit entry to would-be fishermen from other areas where employment is more abundant.

The problem of structural unemployment should not be confused with the difficulty of transferring resources from the fishery to other uses in the economy. The latter can be handled by adjusting the speed with which the fishery is shifted to MEY, not by allowing another goal to be substituted for it. This problem will be dealt with in greater detail in chapter 6.

For any one, or any combination, of the above reasons, a country may choose to operate at some level other than MEY, which may then be called the maximum social yield (MScY). Is there any basis for selecting one point as an MScY? Many dimensions are involved, and no suitable common denominator can provide a ready answer. The proper process for selection may require comparison of discrete levels of efforts as to their effect on the distribution of income, the balance of payments, and so on. The one that appears to score the best should be chosen as the MScY. It is obvious that such a process will yield different results, depending upon who makes the decisions.

Another approach is to use MEY as a starting point, moving from it only when gains are felt to be worth the loss in efficiency. This can be demonstrated in terms of MEY using the profit function in figure 4.11, which plots present value of returns to the fishery as a function of effort. As will be recalled, at stationary MEY the present value of returns to the fishery is at a maximum; therefore, in the graph it is at E_1. If effort is allowed to increase to E_2, returns will fall to PVR_1, and this reduction is the loss in welfare to the country, measured in terms of diminished value of production. Greater effort may increase revenue, but it will also increase costs—the value of things foregone to produce the fish. Therefore, when returns fall, the value of the increase in fish is more than canceled by the decrease in the production of other goods.

Assume that if a country increases its effort from E_1 to E_2 it will produce enough extra fish so that their export will eliminate the deficit in the balance of payments. Or, to use another example, suppose that moving from E_1 to E_2 will eliminate structural unemployment. The decrease in the total value of

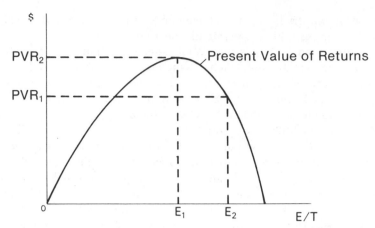

Figure 4.11. *Location of Maximum Social Yield.* E_1 is the level of effort that obtains maximum economic yield. A move to E_2 to achieve a stated goal (i.e., to reduce a balance of payments deficit) should be undertaken only if the achievement of the goal is worth more than the loss of the present value of returns ($PVR_2 - PVR_1$) and if there is no less expensive way of obtaining it.

production caused by the shift, measured by the distance between PVR_2 and PVR_1 can be thought of as the price paid to obtain the goal. Only if it is felt that this decrease in value of production is less important than the improvement in social welfare to be gained from removal of the deficit or reduction of structural unemployment, should E_2 be chosen as the MScY. Even then it should not be chosen unless it can be shown that the desired goal cannot be reached in any other way at a smaller loss in welfare.

Another way a country may look at the problem is to decide the maximum reduction in welfare that will be allowed in the process of attaining other goals. For example (in figure 4.11), a limit may be set that returns can fall no lower than PVR_1; then effort cannot be expanded beyond E_2.

Whether effort is allowed to expand and the gain is compared with measured loss or whether a predetermined maximum loss sets the bound for expansion, this type of analysis provides something substantial for the policy makers in their work. Reduction of structural unemployment and improvement in the distribution of income can be admirable goals, but a given level of effort cannot be called an MScY simply because it approaches those goals to some extent. Nor is the level of effort that puts the most unemployed people back to work necessarily the best choice. Before any policy can be defended as the definitive MScY, one has to ask, "What is being given up in the process of attaining this much good?" While it may be wise, or simply politically expedient, to use a yardstick other than MEY as a goal for fisheries management, movements away from that objective should be made only with caution—and with a carefully balanced set of scales.

International Exploitation of a Fishery

The economics of the exploitation of a fish stock by more than one country is complicated by the probability of varied demand and cost structures. If a unit of fish is valued differently in each country, which measure should be used in deciding whether one more fish should be caught? Similarly, which valuation of the cost of goods foregone is to be used? The far greater problem, however, is the basically noneconomic question of how the wealth of the fishery is to be distributed. No universal answer as to the best distribution is possible, but economic analysis can be used to describe a rational procedure for determining an equitable arrangement. The purpose of this section will be to discuss this procedure and to describe the conditions that must hold for an international maximum economic yield. To keep the analysis simple, only a one-period MEY will be considered, although the general principles discussed earlier concerning dynamic MEY will also apply here.

This discussion is relevant to many cases including that of the United States and Canada, where fish stocks migrate between their fishing zones such that both can harvest them, although it does not deal specifically with the myriad of problems concerning entry of other countries with or without the consent of those already there; that is possible in fishing areas beyond the economic zones of coastal nations. Although the analysis can be completely general, we will, for ease of exposition, assume that two countries, country X and country Y, enjoy exclusive access to a fishery. To free the analysis from emotional considerations, also assume that they are relatively similar in life-style, military might, economic development, and proximity to the fishery and that no barriers against international trade or any political motivations prevent free and open cooperation. These admittedly restrictive assumptions allow for a discussion of the main economic concepts of international fisheries management. These concepts are valid even in cases where such assumptions do not hold, although the chances of their being used are small.

Under the assumption of two good economies, and given their respective productive capacities, each country has a production possibility curve (PP curve) for effort (E) and for the other good (G) identical to those discussed in chapter 3 (see figure 3.11a). Their PP curves for fish (F) and G will be interdependent, however. The shape and position of X's PP curve for F and G will depend upon the amount of effort country Y is using on the fishery. The more Y uses, the lower will be catch per unit of effort even before X begins to fish, and hence, the lower will be X's ultimate production of fish for every level of G produced. Two possible PP curves for country X—PP_{EY1} and PP_{EY2}—are depicted in figure 4.12a. These curves represent the amount of fish that can be caught for each level of G produced, given the amount of fishing the other country is doing; PP_{EY2} is for a higher level of effort in Y. Note that this curve

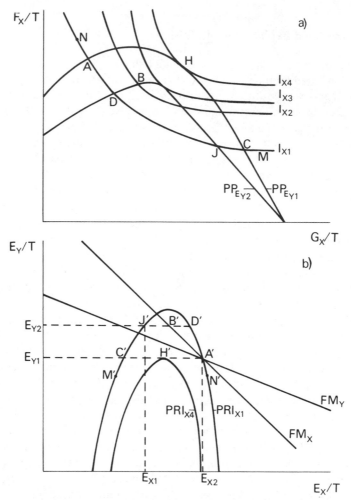

Figure 4.12. *International Open-Access Equilibrium and Potential Gains.* FM_x shows the equilibrium open-access level of effort in country X for each level of effort in country Y. FM_y has the same meaning for country Y with respect to country X. The intersection of these curves determines international open-access equilibrium level of effort in each country. PRI_{x1} shows the various combinations of effort in each country that will obtain a level of consumer welfare in country X equal to that at the international open-access equilibrium. At any combination inside that curve, country X will receive an increase in consumer welfare.

has a lower maximum sustained yield and that it is reached at a higher level of production of G. This is because it takes less effort in X to take MSY when effort in Y is increased. The vertical distance between the curves represents the decrease in fish caught in country X at each level of G when effort in country Y is increased from E_{Y1} to E_{Y2}.

The equilibrium production point and, hence, the level of welfare in each country is thus related to the amount of effort produced in the other. For example, if Y is producing E_{Y1} units of effort, then country X could be in equilibrium at a point such as A in figure 4.12a (refer to the analysis of figure 3.11). At that point it is operating on social indifference curve I_{X1}. However, if Y were to increase its effort to E_{Y2}, then X would shift to PP_{EY2}. While it is not always the case, it appears likely that the new equilibrium on that curve would be at a point where a larger amount of G is produced. When Y increased its effort, it lowered the catch and thereby the revenue per unit of effort. Profit-maximizing producers in X would now shift to the production of G. For purposes of this simple model, then, an increase in effort in Y can be expected to lead to a decrease in the amount of effort that X will produce, as depicted by the reaction curve FM_X in figure 4.12b. Each point in the diagram represents a combination of effort from the two countries, while each point on the FM_X curve shows the open-access production of effort in X for specified levels of effort produced in Y. Points A' and B' are analogous to points A and B in figure 4.12a.

It should be pointed out that, if the fishery is unable to reach an equilibrium position because of the particular combination of growth rate of the stock and exit and entry rate of boats, then country X will not operate on this curve. For purposes of discussion let us ignore that technicality.

The same sort of reasoning applies to the amount of E produced in Y. The greater the effort produced by X, the lower will be the equilibrium level in Y; this relationship is pictured as FM_Y. These two curves describe the amount of effort that one country will want to produce, given a specified production of effort in the other country. The intersection of the two reaction curves sets the international equilibrium. Each country will be producing the profit-maximizing amount of effort, given the level produced in the other. As long as the FM_X curve intersects the FM_Y curve from above, the equilibrium will be stable. For example, if for some reason the two countries were operating so that point J' represents the combination of international effort, country Y would want to reduce its level of effort to reach the FM_Y curve, and X would want to increase its effort to the FM_X curve. This would result in a general movement to point A. (The interested reader may demonstrate for himself that at any other point both countries will want to change their level of effort toward the equilibrium.) This international open-access equilibrium is the combination of effort from the two countries that will be forthcoming in the absence of regulation. At this point the countries have in effect divided up the fishery by the rule of capture. Country X has earned the "right" to use E_{X2} units of effort on the fishery, and country Y to use E_{Y1}. However, these very tenuous rights cannot be bought or sold, and if they are not exercised at all times, the other country will step in and appropriate at least a portion of them.

It is implicitly assumed that at point A' both countries are devoting all resources not used in the production of effort to the efficient production of G. Therefore, this point, as well as all others in the diagram, can be thought of as a specific distribution of the property rights to the fishery and a specific allocation of resources among the production of E and G.

As an interesting sidelight, notice that, when Y produces E_{Y1} units of effort, the static MEY for country X is located at point H. That is, it would be worthwhile to regulate a decrease in effort, thus allowing for an increase in the production of G. However, this reduction in effort will cause Y to increase effort; as a result, X's PP curve will fall, causing a movement to a lower social indifference curve. It is entirely possible that the decrease in X's welfare caused by the increase in effort in Y will outweigh the benefits from X's own reduction in effort. The point here is that unilateral regulation must take into account possible changes in effort by the other country and the way in which these changes will affect local welfare.

To return to the main argument, in our discussions of a national fishery the movement from the unregulated equilibrium to MEY was a reallocation of resources such that the value of the country's output increased. In terms of figure 4.12a, the reallocation allowed the country to reach the highest social indifference curve possible, given the PP curve. Maximum economic yield in an international fishery is not as easy to pin down, but movements toward it can be looked at in the same manner. They are reallocations of the resources of the two countries, either individually or in concert, such that one or both of them can reach a higher social indifference curve without forcing the other to a lower one. When no more reallocations of that sort are possible, static maximum economic yield has been reached for the internationally exploited fishery.

Three conceptually separate but mutually *interdependent* criteria, two of which are central to our analysis, must be met in reaching that point where no further beneficial reallocations are possible. They are (1) no changes in the combination of allowable fishing effort can be made without causing a decline in welfare for one of the two countries; (2) no further mutual gains are attainable from trades in effort or in fishing rights; and (3) no further mutual gains can result from trade in any of the other goods. The first criterion determines what the optimal yield of the fishery should be and how the rights to it should be distributed; the second insures that the optimal yield will be caught at the least expense; and the third guarantees a proper distribution of the final goods. Let us now turn to a discussion of each of these in turn, beginning with the combination of allowable fishing effort. Throughout the discussion it should be remembered that, while each of these criteria are being discussed individually, they are interdependent.

Earlier, the ability to use the open-access equilibrium levels of effort was referred to as a tenuous property right. If this right, which can be viewed as the allowable level of effort, can be made more secure, then negotiations can lead to each country's agreeing to put forth a level of effort quite different from that determined by the rule of capture. Mutual gains can result from this rational approach to management. Up to a point, if either of the countries reduces its level of effort and transfers resources to the production of G, both will gain. A graphical description of this in terms of country X can be seen in figure 4.12a. Changes in the amount of effort allowed to Y will alter the shape and position of X's PP curve. Changes in the amount allowed to X will result in a movement to a different point on the same PP curve. Changes in both will move the PP curve and the production point. Any of these moves will cause X to operate on a different social indifference curve or, in some special cases, on a different point on the same indifference curve. The curve PRI_{x1} (property-right indifference curve) in figure 4.12b represents that set of property right distributions that will place country X at the same level of welfare as at point A', the open-access equilibrium. This welfare level is represented by social indifference curve I_{x1} in figure 4.12a. Points N', A', D', J', C', and M', on PRI_{x1}, are analogous to points N, A, D, J, C, and M on I_{x1}. For example, since they are on the same PP curve, X can move from point A to point C merely by switching resources from producing effort to producing G, and its level of welfare will remain the same. A movement from A to any other point on I_{x1}, however, requires a change in effort in both countries. Movements to D and J require reductions in E_x and an increase in E_y. A movement to N requires an increase in E_x and a decrease in E_y. A movement to M will also require a decrease in E_y but in combination with a decrease in E_x. In general, any point to the left of A requires an increase in E_x while points to the right require the opposite, and any point below PP_{Ey1} requires an increase in E_y while any point above it requires the opposite.

To summarize, any point on the PRI_{x1} curve represents a combination of effort in both countries (i.e., a distribution of international property rights) that, if the other resources are used efficiently in the production of G, will allow country X to retain the same level of welfare as at the open-access equilibrium. The fluctuation in welfare that occurs when X changes its level of effort is exactly offset by that resulting from the change of effort in country Y. The shift of effort in country X directly affects its own welfare by altering the production bundle. Changes in effort in country Y *indirectly* influence the welfare of X by affecting the productivity of its effort. When effort increases in country Y, the catch per unit of effort decreases in country X.

Any point inside the PRI_{x1} curve in figure 4.12b represents an international property right distribution where country X will be better off than at open-access equilibrium. At any of those points, the value of the production bundle in X will be higher than at point A. At these points a net increase in welfare is brought about by the cumulative effects of the changes in effort in both countries. Note that there are some combinations that yield an improvement where X decreases its effort and Y increases its level. Actually, there is a series of these property-right indifference curves, each analogous to a social indifference curve in figure 4.12a. For example, PRI_{x4} is the set of international property-right distributions that will lead country X to operate on indifference curve I_{x4}. Each point on I_{x4} is analogous to a point on PRI_{x4}. Just as a move from a point on I_{x1} to one on I_{x4} means an improvement in the welfare of X, so does a move from PRI_{x1} to PRI_{x4}. In general, movements in a downward direction in figure 4.12b result in an increase in welfare for country X.

Although the discussion has been in terms of country X, the analysis of the relationship between Y's welfare and the international property-right distribution is identical. The curve labeled PRI_{y1} in figure 4.13 is the set of international combinations of effort where Y will enjoy the same level of welfare as at A'. The area between that curve and the vertical axis represents those combinations that would increase the welfare of Y. PRI_{y6} is just another property-right indifference curve for Y. In this case, movements in a leftward direction result in improved welfare for country Y; thus points on PRI_{y6} are more desirable than those on PRI_{y1}.

It is now possible to delineate an area, representing distributions of rights to the fishery, in which both countries are better off than at open-access equilibrium. Indicated in the figure by hatch marks, it is the common ground of the areas inside the PRI_{x1} and the PRI_{y1} curves. This mean that, if both countries could agree to change their allowable level of effort to such a degree that they would move from A' to some point in the hatched area, and if they would transfer any of the resources thus released into the production of G, they

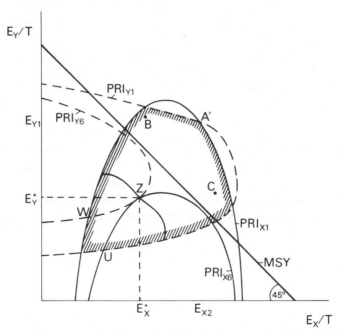

Figure 4.13. *Potential International Gains.*   Any point in the area indicated by the hatch marks represents a combination of effort in each country where both will receive an increase in consumer welfare. One condition for an international MEY is that a point in this area be reached where neither country can increase its welfare without decreasing the welfare of the other.

could both improve their welfare. The new production bundle in each country would have a higher value than did the old.

It is interesting to note, however, that this area contains distributions where one country has a lower allowable level of effort and the other has a higher one than at point A'. For example, at point B, Y is allowed a greater effort and X a lesser; the opposite is true at point C. Yet, at these points both countries are made better off. The logic behind this is very similar to that of the sidelight discussed above. Since both countries are producing too much effort at point A', up to a point either one can transfer effort to the production of other goods and still be better off, even if the other country does increase fishing effort.

This analysis can be carried one step further. Unless the movement from A' is to a point where the PRI curves of the two countries are tangent, then further mutually advantageous moves are possible. For example, assume that both countries agree to change their level of effort to such a degree that W is achieved. At that point, country X will show no improvement in welfare, but Y will move to PRI_{y6}. Because the PRI curves are not tangent, further jointly useful moves are possible. For example, any point in the area bounded by PRI_{x1} and PRI_{y6} would be on a higher PRI curve for both. The countries will suffer needless reductions in welfare if they do not take advantage of this. The same type of reasoning applies at point U, where both countries stand to gain from appropriate changes in effort.

At a point such as Z, where the curves are tangent, no further moves can result in mutual benefit. At any other point one or both of the countries will move to a lower property-right indifference curve. The line through Z represents all points in the delineated area where there is tangency between the PRI curves. If any point on that line can be agreed upon as the distribution of property rights, any shift away from the line will decrease the welfare of one of the countries.

This, then, may be called the optimal yield and distribution line. Each point on it represents two things: a specific yield and a specific distribution of the wealth of the fishery. For example, at point Z the yield is that taken by E_x^* units of effort from X plus E_y^* units from country Y. Of that amount, country X will receive a fraction equal to $E_x^*/(E_x^* + E_y^*)$, and the remainder will go to Y. The value of these catches to each country is the difference between what their citizens are willing to pay for them and the cost of obtaining them. Alternatively, the distribution can be thought of in terms of fishing rights: X has the right to apply E_x^* units of effort, and Y to apply E_x^* units. The value of these rights depends upon the average catch per unit effort (a function of the total number of rights), the price of fish, and the cost of effort. This value, which will be called rent, will be explained in more detail shortly.

An important point to be made now is that these rights are defined as a part of the wealth of the fishery. That is, each country has the right to apply a certain effort to the fish stock each period, secure in the knowledge that the other country will also be operating within accepted limits. Under these conditions, the effort will yield a specified average annual catch; therefore, these rights can be measured in terms of the average quantity of fish caught. The value of the rights is the worth of the fish minus the cost of obtaining them.

We shall soon see that in some cases a country can benefit more from these rights either by leasing them out or by hiring effort from other countries to harvest the fish. Therefore, it is in each country's interest that the rights should be defined in terms of the wealth of the fishery rather than in terms of the "right to go fishing." The latter would imply that, in order to obtain any of the wealth, the country would have to take the fish with locally produced effort.

To return to the main argument, once a point such as Z on the optimal yield and distribution line has been reached, any change in the rights to the fishery will mean that at least one country loses (this, of course, assumes that the other two criteria mentioned above are met at the same time). This is comparable to an MEY in a nationally managed fishery, where any change in the amount of fish caught will decrease the country's welfare. However, a particular optimum yield and distribution point cannot be equated with international MEY unless the catch is being taken at the lowest possible cost. This aspect will be discussed later.

Disregarding the cost element for a moment, it is interesting to note that more than one catch level can be called optimal in the international case. This is true because the wealth from the fishery affects demand. It will be recalled from chapter 1 that the demand for any good depends upon income, tastes, and prices of other goods. The wealth of the fishery adds to income, and its distribution will have some impact on the demand for goods in both countries. In the national case, since the income earned by the fishery always remains within the country, it can alter only one set of demand conditions. In the international case, each of the many ways the fishery can be divided among the two countries will result in a specified set of international demand conditions. Since they determine the relative valuation of F and G, each set will produce a different point where the last unit of fish caught is worth the cost of catching it in terms of G foregone.

Let's review the significance of this analysis. It shows that if both countries are willing and able to negotiate the amount of effort they will apply to the fishery, each country can increase its welfare over that at the international open-access equilibrium. A move to any point inside the delineated area will improve the outcome for both, yet further mutual gains can be arranged if the PRI curves are not tangent at that point. Therefore, free and open negotiations could result in the countries' operating somewhere on the optimal yield and distribution line, but it is impossible to predict in advance just what point on that line will be reached. That will depend upon the bargaining strengths and skills of the two countries and, to some degree, upon the number and type of changes made before the line is reached. With regard to the latter, notice that, if at first the countries agreed to move from A' to U (which would mean that Y lacked a very good negotiator since he did not improve its welfare at all), then the final point chosen would have to lie on or to the right of Z on the MEY line. Otherwise, country X would suffer a decrease in welfare. It is also impossible to choose one point on the curve as superior to any other unless one is willing to make value judgments regarding the distribution of wealth.

These negotiations should be thought of as mutually beneficial redistributions of the rights to the fishery or changes in the allowable levels of effort. They entail internal reallocations of resources within each country but no physical exchange between them. The end result is the selection of the proper amount of catch. Any change in the allowable levels of effort from those agreed upon will be harmful to at least one of the countries.

The second criterion for an international MEY is that no further mutual gains from trades in effort or fishing rights be possible. This condition guarantees that the optimal yield will be taken at the lowest possible cost, and the resultant saving will permit increased production of other goods, which can be distributed in such a way that both gain.

That is, economically speaking, fishing rights should not be viewed as an obligation to take the fish with local effort or even to take the fish at all. If both countries are willing to engage in trade—either in fishing rights or in fishing effort—and if they can do so within the bounds of the agreements determining the rights, both can benefit.

Neither country is reaching the highest possible level of welfare unless the effort to land the optimal catch is produced at lowest cost. This means that a country's right to use a specified amount of effort does not necessarily imply the home production of that effort. For example, if, after the negotiations are complete, it proves more expensive to produce effort in country X (i.e., X is operating on its PP curve for G and E so that the cost of E in terms of G foregone is higher than in country Y), then both countries can benefit if X pays Y to produce some of its effort. This will result in an increase in the production of E in Y and a reduction in X. From the discussion of the PP curve in chapter 1, it will be recalled that, as more of any good is produced, its opportunity cost rises. Therefore, these arrangements will, if carried far enough, equalize the opportunity cost of effort in both countries, and at that point the cost of producing the allotted amount of effort will be minimized.

Such transactions will involve both reallocations of resources within the countries and physical exchanges between them, but they will not result in any net increase in effort. Any increase in one country must be matched by a decrease in the other, for that is the nature of the trade. Such trades can take place in either of two ways: first, country X can buy (hire) units of effort from country Y; second, Y can lease fishing rights from X. In the latter case, X retains the property rights acquired in the negotiation process, but allows Y to share in them for a price. Both methods can be described in more detail by use of a numerical example in our simple two-good model, expressing costs and prices in terms of G rather than introducing complex currency evaluations. The reader will find it useful to refer to table 4.1 as we discuss these alternative arrangements. Assume that at the optimal yield the total amount of effort is such that catch per unit of effort is $5F/E$. Also assume that the international price of fish is $4G/F$. That is, the price for one unit of fish is four units of G. Therefore, the value of the catch per unit effort in terms of G is $20G/E$. This is summarized in rows 1 through 3 of table 4.1.

Let the cost of producing one unit of effort per period in terms of G in

Table 4.1. *Analysis of Trade in Effort and Rights to Fish.* Given the value of catch per unit of effort and the relative cost of producing it in the two countries, potential mutual gains from trade exist. If country X buys one unit of effort from country Y at a price of $7G/1E$, both countries will show a net increase equal in value to $2G$. The same results will occur if country Y buys a right to use one unit of effort from country X at a price of $13G/1E$.

	Country X	Country Y
Catch per unit effort	$\dfrac{5F}{E}$	
International price of F in terms of G	$\dfrac{4G}{F}$	
Value of catch per unit effort	$\dfrac{5F}{E}\cdot\dfrac{4G}{F}=\dfrac{20G}{E}$	
Cost of effort in terms of G	$\dfrac{9G}{E}$	$\dfrac{5G}{E}$
Rent of property right $P_F\cdot\dfrac{F}{E}-P_E$	$\dfrac{20G}{E}-\dfrac{9G}{1E}=\dfrac{11G}{E}$	$\dfrac{20G}{E}-\dfrac{5G}{E}=\dfrac{15G}{E}$
Analysis of trade in effort at price of $\dfrac{7G}{1E}$	Buys 1 unit of effort from Y: Cost $=-7G$ Cuts back on production of effort by 1 unit: Saving $=\ 9G$ Net Gain to $X=\ 2G$	Increases production of effort by 1 unit: Cost $=-5G$ Sells it to X: Revenue $=\ 7G$ Net Gain to $Y=\ 2G$
Analysis of trade in property rights at price of $\dfrac{13G}{1E}$	Sells right to use 1 unit of effort: Revenue $=+13G$ Forced to reduce effort by 1 unit: Value of catch falls by $-20G$ But production of G can increase by $+9G$ Net gain to $X=\ 2G$	Buys right to use 1 unit of effort: Cost $=-13G$ Must increase production of effort by 1 unit: Cost $=-5G$ But value of catch increases by $+20G$ Net gain to $Y=\ 2G$

countries X and Y be $9G/E$ and $5G/E$, respectively. This means that at their existing levels of output Y is more efficient in the production of effort since it must sacrifice four fewer units of G to obtain a unit of E. (The cost of effort will change in each country as output levels change, but for simplicity assume that they remain constant.)

It is now possible to determine the annual value of the right to apply one unit of effort to the fishery. This amount, which can be called the rent of the property right, is the difference between the value of the catch per unit of effort per period and the annual cost of producing a unit of effort. It is obvious that, under the given conditions, the rent will be different in each country because of the variant costs of producing effort. As rows 4 and 5 of table 4.1 show, the annual rents of the property right in countries X and Y are $11G/E$ and $15G/E$, respectively.

It is now possible to analyze the two types of trade. Consider, first, trade in effort. Since Y can produce effort more efficiently than can X, both can gain if X buys effort from Y at a price somewhere between the two internal prices. Consider the case where the price is $7G/E$. In that case if X buys one unit per period, it must give up seven units of G. But, since X can use only a specific amount of effort, if it buys one unit from Y, it must reduce its own production accordingly and thus will free enough resources to increase the production of G by nine units per period. Therefore, X will enjoy a net gain from the trade of two units of G per period while producing the same harvest of fish as before. Only the production location of one unit of effort will have changed.

If Y is to sell one unit of effort to X, it must sacrifice five units of G per period; however, it receives seven units of G when the effort is traded. This is a net gain to Y of two units of G per period. Although its production of effort is increased, its local fish harvest remains the same because the increased effort was exported.

The above demonstrates that trade in effort can be beneficial to both countries; since each has the same quantity of fish but more G, each has attained a higher level of welfare. Note that the sum of the net gains matches the divergence in production costs in the two countries. The price used in the example was exactly halfway between those costs, and so each country received an equal gain in G. At higher prices the gain to Y would increase, while X would benefit from lower prices. It is important to realize, however, that as long as the price is between $9G/E$ and $5G/E$, both countries will realize a positive net gain.

Let us now consider trade in the property rights to fish. Since the rent earned from the right to use one unit of effort is higher in country Y than in X, both countries can gain if Y leases property rights from X at a price somewhere between the two internal values. Consider a case where the lease price is $13G/E$ per period. By leasing the right to use one unit of effort, X will earn $13G$ per period. However, it will be forced to reduce its own production of effort by one unit because it has surrendered the right to do that much fishing. The value of its catch will therefore fall by $20G$, but this will release resources sufficient to produce nine extra units of G per period, or a net increase of two G per period in the value of its goods available. Its fishery production will be lower, but the increase in the production of G when added to the G that it earns in the trade will be more valuable. In effect, X has traded some of the wealth obtained from international negotiation for the fishery in favor of other goods that it values more than the fish.

Country Y, on the other hand, will have to give 13 units of G per period to obtain the right to use the effort. It must then increase its production of effort by one unit, which means that production of G will fall by five units. As a result of the new effort, the value of the fish catch will increase by $20G$, giving Y a net gain equal in value to two G. Y will have less G because it is exporting some and its production has decreased, but the value of the increase in catch will more than make up for this.

As in the earlier example, the total combined gain is four units of G, the actual distribution of which depends upon the exchange price. The higher the price, the larger is the gain to X, whereas Y will benefit from lower prices. Gains to both are indicated, however, as long as the price is between $11G/E$ and $15G/E$.

Any difference, then, between two countries in the cost of producing effort or in the rent earned by the right to produce a unit of effort, implies the possibility of mutual gains from trade in effort or in fishing rights. But regardless of the type, if such trades are expanded, production of E in Y will increase where that in X will fall. Therefore, the cost of effort in terms of G will fall in X and increase in Y. When the cost is the same in both countries, no further mutually advantageous trades are possible.

It should be noted that the previous discussions apply here also with regard to the difficulty of moving resources from one use to another and the problems of the internal distribution of gains. In the present context, the reallocations are due to trade rather than to fishery regulation, but the same time lags are involved. Again, some sectors of the economy may receive most of the gains while others may even suffer a net loss. Also, this presentation is strictly in terms of economic management goals, ignoring possible social goals. When making applications of this model, these factors should be kept in mind.

We come now to the third criterion for an international MEY, namely, that no further mutual gains be attainable from trade in final goods (F and G). Since this question is only indirectly related to a discussion of international fishery management, it is enough to say here that, even if the optimal quantity of fish is being taken at the lowest cost possible, both countries can still be made better off by engaging in trade if their internal relative prices differ. A demonstration of this would be similar to the analysis in table 4.1. This type of trading will guarantee that the fish will be consumed by those who place the highest value on it, regardless of which country has the right to catch it or in whose boats it was actually caught. A country having the right to catch fish, and able to do so efficiently, may yet rationally prefer to trade the catch for other types of goods.

By way of summary, MEY prevails in an international fishery when an optimal quantity of fish is being taken at the lowest possible cost and when free trade occurs between the countries. A number of yields can be called optimal, each related to a specific distribution of the fishing rights. A point of optimal yield and distribution has been reached when any change in the amount of yield or in its distribution will decrease the welfare of at least one country. Open negotiations between the countries can lead to such a result. Which of the alternative arrangements is finally chosen will depend to a large degree upon the respective skills of the negotiators. The lowest harvesting cost possible can be achieved by trades in either fishing effort or fishing rights. If the cost of producing effort differs between the two countries, such trade will allow the optimal amount of catch to be taken at the lowest possible cost, and the resultant savings can be so distributed that both countries gain. For such trades to be feasible, the rights granted in the negotiation process must be fully negotiable, that is, they must be rights to the wealth inherent in the fishery and not merely rights to fish. A country having a relatively low demand for fish and a relatively high cost of producing effort can then simply trade its fishing rights (its share of the wealth) for goods that it values more than the fish. Free trade will allow mutually beneficial reallocations of final products. Unfortunately, all this does not imply that countries will automatically work together to ensure an MEY; it simply lists the interdependent criteria that must be met if they are to reach such an ideal accommodation.

Although each of the criteria for an international maximum economic yield has been discussed separately, they are interdependent. For example, trade in the final goods will determine the international price of F in terms of G. This price, it will be recalled, is a factor in determining the rent from a right to use a unit of effort. Also, the relative rents in the two countries will determine the magnitude and direction of trade in rights. Again, since gains from trade in effort, rights, or final goods end up as income, they in turn affect demand conditions for each of the others.

A few more sidelights on this subject are in order. First, although the concept of maximum sustainable yield has not been used in this discussion, it is easily introduced. MSY is caught by a specific amount of effort; thus it is obtained in an international fishery whenever the sum of the countries' efforts reaches that level. Graphically, this can be represented by the straight line MSY in figure 4.13. Since the line intersects the horizontal axis at an angle of 45 degrees, each point on it will represent a combination of international effort where the sum is a constant.

As drawn here, the MSY line lies to the southwest of point A', which means that open-access equilibrium will be at a point beyond MSY. Those points on the MSY line that lie within the delineated area represent a distribution of the MSY where both countries will be better off than at A'. It is possible that the MSY line may lie to the northeast of the delineated area for mutual gains. In that case a movement from A' to the MSY line would result in a decrease in welfare for both.

It should be stressed again that this entire analysis has been static; however, the same general conclusions apply in a dynamic model. The only difference is the fact that, when making their trades to the optimal yield and distribution line, the countries must consider production levels in future periods, the rate of discount, and the rate at which fishery output will change as effort is changed.

Finally, the beginning point for negotiations on changes in the level of allowable effort has been placed at A', where the free market reaction curves intersect simply because that is where the unregulated fishery would operate, given that an equilibrium is possible. If for any reason another initial point is used, the remainder of the analysis would not differ; negotiations could still result in mutually beneficial changes in allowable effort. As one example, a point other than A' might be chosen if the "world order" were to decide on some normative grounds that one country deserved more rights to the fishery than did another. In such a case, however, the composition of the international MEY would almost certainly change.

Introduction to Formal Dynamic Analysis

A good deal of work in fisheries economics has been devoted to developing formal dynamic models of open-access commercial fisheries. See Berck (1981), Cheng and Lin (1981), Fullenbaum et al. (1971), Fullenbaum (1972), Leung and Wang (1976), Plourde (1971), Quirk and Smith (1970), Smith (1968, 1969, 1971, 1972), and Wang and Cheng (1978). They attempt to describe the process of how population size and the level of effort change through time and the conditions that must be met to achieve an open-access equilibrium. Since these models involve considerable and rather difficult mathematics, it would be beyond the scope of this book to analyze them in detail. Rather, a brief verbal description of the model will be followed by a geometric interpretation, which, although not as rigorous as the mathematics, does convey the essence of the models. It also ties the dynamic analysis to our earlier discussion.

It will be recalled that bioeconomic equilibrium in an exploited fishery implies a simultaneous biological and economic equilibrium. Biological equilibrium occurs when the increase in population size per period exactly equals the catch per period, so that population size is static. Since population increase is a function of population size and catch is a function of population size and effort, the net population change in an exploited fishery can be expressed as a function of population size and effort. Biological equilibrium will occur at those combinations of P and E where that function is equal to zero, that is, at those combinations where growth equals catch:

$$\frac{dP}{dt} = f(P,E) = 0 \tag{4.1}$$

Economic equilibrium occurs when all producers are earning enough revenue to cover costs and still make a normal profit. At that point, no one will leave the fishery because each is earning as much profit as he could elsewhere. At the same time, there will be no incentive to enter because no one could increase his profits by so doing. Effort will increase when revenue sufficiently exceeds costs to attract new producers, and it will decrease when revenue falls far enough below costs that producers are driven out. The rate at which effort will enter or leave the fishery will, more than likely, be directly related to the absolute difference between revenue and cost. The greater the positive difference, the higher will be the rate of increase in effort, and conversely, the greater the negative difference, the higher will be the rate of decrease.

Revenue depends on catch, which is a function of population size and effort. Cost is a function of effort. Therefore, since the rate of change of effort is a function of revenue and cost, it can also be expressed as a function of population size and effort. Economic equilibrium will occur at those combinations of P and E where that function is equal to zero, that is, at those combinations where revenue equals cost:

$$\frac{dE}{dt} = g(P,E) = 0 \tag{4.2}$$

Those combinations of P and E that are solutions to the set of simultaneous differential equations 4.1 and 4.2 will yield a bioeconomic equilibrium, at which points neither effort nor population will change. The interested reader may want to refer to the above cited references for examples of some of the mathematical forms that the equations can take, and also to an appropriate mathematics book for a description of the methods of solving differential equations and of determining the stability of the solutions. For present purposes a geometric interpretation must suffice.

Equation 4.1 is simply a mathematical representation of the population equilibrium curves discussed above. The curve labeled *PEC* in figure 4.14a is an example of the forward-bending population equilibrium curve. It is the locus of combinations of P and E where population will be in equilibrium. To put it another way, it is a line connecting all the combinations of P and E where catch will equal growth. The arrows in the diagram indicate the direction in which population will change at other combinations of P and E. Remember that each combination represents a specific catch rate and a specific natural increase rate. Everywhere inside the area bounded by the curve, population will increase at each level of effort, because at those combinations

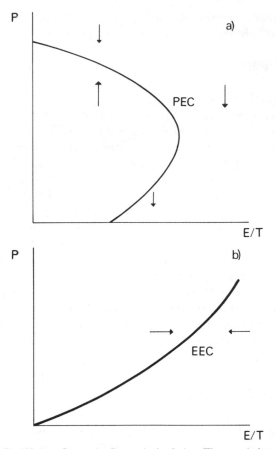

Figure 4.14. *The Equilibrium Curves for Dynamic Analysis.*   The population equilibrium curve in part a is the collection of those combinations of effort and population where there is an equilibrium population size. At any point outside the curve, catch is greater than growth, and so population will fall. At any point inside the curve, the opposite is true and population will increase. The economic equilibrium curve in part b is the collection of combinations of effort and population where there is an equilibrium level of effort. At any point to the left of the curve, revenue is greater than cost and so effort will increase. At any point to the right, the opposite is true and so effort will fall.

catch is less than natural increase. Everywhere outside this area, population will decrease at each level of effort, because at those combinations catch is greater than natural increase.

Equation 4.2 is plotted in figure 4.14b. This, the economic equilibrium curve, has not been formally examined in our earlier analysis. It follows directly from our earlier discussion, however. Recall that, as stock size increases, the short-run revenue curve is shifted out. Therefore, higher stock sizes will result in higher short-run equilibrium levels of effort. In other words, the larger the population size, the higher the level of effort that can be supported.

Every point on the economic equilibrium curve represents a combination of effort and population that produces an equilibrium level of effort. The arrows in the diagram represent the direction in which effort will change at other combinations of P and E. To the left of the curve, effort will tend to increase at every level of population, because in that section revenues will be greater than costs. The opposite holds true for the area to the right of the curve: effort is too high at every level of population; hence, revenues will be below costs and effort will fall.

These two curves can be used to describe the equilibrium point and the process of moving toward one. Recall that the population equilibrium curve (PEC) is the collection of those combinations of P and E where net population growth is zero, and that the economic equilibrium curve (EEC) is the collection of combinations of P and E where the change in effort is zero. The point of intersection of these curves represents that combination of P and E where both net population growth and change in effort reach zero. This is a bioeconomic equilibrium point. The number, location, and stability of the bioeconomic equilibria depend upon the intersection of the two curves and the relative changes in P and E at nonintersection points. Consider the intersection of EEC_1 and PEC_1 in figure 4.15. At those levels of effort and population the change in each will be zero, and this constitutes a bioeconomic equilibrium. Will the fishery ever reach this point? To answer that, it must be determined how fast and in what direction E and P will be changing at other points. The direction of these changes will depend upon the location of the point relative to the EEC and PEC curves, as explained above. The solid arrows indicate these directions for various sections of the diagram (ignore for a moment the dotted arrows). For example, point B is to the left of the EEC and outside the PEC. Therefore, if the fishery is operating at that point, effort will increase, population will decrease, and the point of operation for the fishery will move in a southeasterly direction. The exact angle of movement will depend upon the relative changes in P and E.

Let us consider a few hypothetical cases of movement to an open-access equilibrium. Assume that EEC_1 and PEC_1 are the relevant curves and that the fishery is operating at that combination of P and E represented by point B. The curved solid line from B to the equilibrium at A represents a possible time path for the fishery. No matter what sector the operation point occupies, the general direction of the change in P and E will be toward the equilibrium. For example, at first the direction of change is in a southeasterly direction; effort will increase and population will decrease. As soon as the time path crosses the EEC curve, the direction of change shifts to a southwesterly direction; population and effort will both be decreasing. This type of activity will continue until point A is reached.

It is possible that open-access exploitation may result in the extinction of

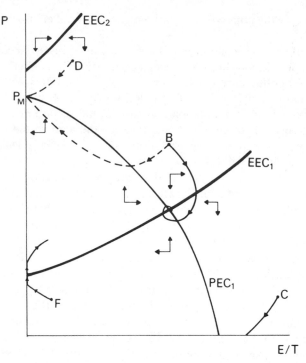

Figure 4.15. *Dynamic Analysis: I.*   With EEC_1 and PEC_1, a stable equilibrium is possible at their intersection. However, from point C the rate of population decline may be so fast relative to the decrease in effort that the population may be destroyed. Also, from point F the economic viability of the fishery may be destroyed. With EEC_2 the fishery is not economically viable.

the population. For example, if the fishery is at point C and the exit of effort is slow, relative to the decrease in population, the time path as indicated could result in its destruction. Temporary economic extinction is represented by the time path from point F, whereby effort falls so fast relative to the increase of population that it actually reaches zero. Population then begins to grow until its size again justifies fishing effort. The precise shape of the time path will depend upon the exact formulation of equations 4.1 and 4.2.

If the EEC curve were to move to EEC_2 because of a decrease in price or an increase in cost, the fishery would not be exploited at all. If the economic equilibrium curve were so situated, the cost of effort and the price of fish would decree a shutdown of all boats at all relevant population levels. Only if population were above its average biological maximum due to a temporary ecological phenomenon could a positive level of effort be rational. If the fishery continues operating, due either to misinformation or to its former profitability, the dynamic process described above will reduce effort to zero and will permit the population to achieve its natural equilibrium size. For example, the dotted curves from points B and D represent possible time paths to a point of zero effort for two such cases. The direction of the changes in effort and population will depend on the location of the point relative to the EEC and the PEC curves. The dotted arrows indicate these directions for PEC_1 and EEC_2.

Figure 4.16 represents the opposite of nonexploitation. In this case, the fishery will inevitably be fished to extinction. The shape and position of the two equilibrium curves are such that the time path will always lead to the origin, indicating only one equilibrium point at zero units of effort and a zero level of population. Any point within the PEC curve will result in an increase in effort and population until the fishery is operating outside of the curve; once there, effort may fluctuate around the EEC curve, but population will always fall until it reaches zero.

Figure 4.17 depicts a case having more than one possible equilibrium. The arrows indicate the general direction of change of stock size and effort for different areas of the diagram. They are constructed using the directions shown in figure 4.14, parts a and b.

In cases like this, the geometric analysis is not straightforward. The equilibrium at point A is similar to that in figure 4.15. The directional arrows indicate that points near the equilibrium will tend to cause changes in population and effort such that point A will be achieved, but this is not the case for the equilibria at B and C. For example, the time path from point D, which is quite close to the equilibrium at point B, ultimately leads to an equilibrium at

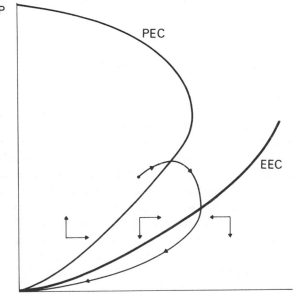

Figure 4.16. *Dynamic Analysis: II.*   With these equilibrium curves, the fishery is doomed to biological extinction because the industry remains viable even as the population continues to fall.

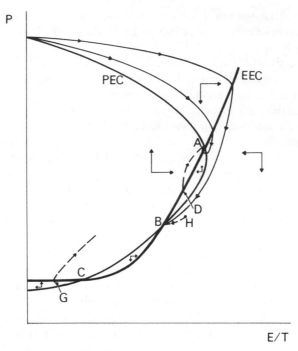

Figure 4.17. *Dynamic Analysis: III.* These equilibrium curves demonstrate the possibility of multiple equilibria. Whether any of them will ever be achieved depends upon the relative rates of change in effort and population size.

point A. Similarly, point G is close to C, but the time path from it will initially proceed in the opposite direction. After it crosses the PEC, it can head for points A and B as well as C.

It should be pointed out that there are many possible time paths. Some points near an equilibrium will have time paths leading back to it, while others have paths that move away. Therefore, the situation of the actual bioeconomic equilibrium will depend upon the relative rates of change of E and P, as demonstrated in figure 4.17. Let the time path begin where population is the biological maximum and effort is zero. The lower of the two time paths emanating from that point represents the case where the relative changes in P and E are such that A will be the equilibrium. The higher path, representing a relatively larger entry rate of effort, will result in equilibrium at point B. It is also possible that a time path may never cross an equilibrium point. In this case, the fishery will be subject to continual fluctuations in the level of effort and the size of the fish stock.

Whether a particular equilibrium is stable or not depends upon the size of the random move from it and the relative rates of change. For example, as the curves are drawn, a move from the equilibrium at point B to point D will result in a new equilibrium at point A. A movement from B to point H, however, will result in a reestablishment of equilibrium at B. The movement to D represents an increase in effort and population, at which point further growth will occur and, initially, effort will fall. That is, catch will be less than net natural increase, and revenues will be less than costs. As population grows, revenues will increase until they ultimately exceed costs, and effort will begin to expand. This process will shift both effort and population away from point B. In contrast, the movement from point B to point H also represents an increase in both effort and population, but while costs will still be greater than revenues, catch will now be greater than natural increase. Therefore, both effort and population will fall and, as the curve is drawn here, the equilibrium becomes reestablished at point B.

In summary, the formal dynamic model employs a set of two differential equations specifying the rates of change of effort and of population, explicitly treating the changes in both, and showing their interrelationships. The geometric interpretation of these equations is not entirely new. The population equilibrium curve has been used extensively before, although in a somewhat different context. With geometry as a tool, it is possible to describe equilibria, the possibility of stability, and cases of nonexploitation, of temporary economic extinction, and of biological extinction. All but the first involve the use of time paths that show the direction and rate of change of both P and E with time. The shape and position of a time path from any point must depend upon the exact make-up of equations 4.1 and 4.2, and only the general direction can be ascertained from the geometric model. Nevertheless, this approach is useful for describing the essence of the dynamics of an exploited fishery.

The Share System of Crew Remuneration

The share or lay system of remuneration whereby the crew, in one of almost an infinite number of ways, receives a percentage of the net proceeds of harvest has been a fundamental part of almost all fisheries throughout the world for centuries. There can be enormous differences concerning which costs are paid "off the top" and which are paid out of the owner's share as well as in the actual share rates used. In addition, in some systems the crew receives a fixed wage as well as a share of net proceeds. In spite of these surface differences, the basic mechanics and the economic repercussions of most are fairly general and can be explained quite briefly. While space does not allow a detailed discussion of all such systems, a basic understanding of how they work is important to comprehend fully open-access utilization and also will be useful in the discussions of regulation that follow. The purpose of this section, therefore, is to explain why this peculiar system of employee compensation has developed, how the share rate is determined, and the effect share rates can have on the distribution of fishery rents between boat owners and crews.

Why a Share System?

While there have been a number of explanations for the existence of the share system—see Zoeteweij (1956) and Sutinen (1979)—the most likely are (1) risk sharing, (2) incentives for hard work and careful handling of catches, and (3) the encouragement of cost minimization in the production of effort. Each of these will be discussed in turn.

The commercial operation of a fishing vessel is a risky venture, indeed. Contrary to the above discussion about average annual catch per unit of effort, catch per trip for any vessel can be highly variable. Bad weather can make it difficult to set and retrieve the gear or may cause the fish to move such that they are not susceptible to the gear. The returns for such trips can be quite low. At the other extreme, catches on particular trips can be many times the average, which will result in very high profits. The variability of profits can be especially high because, for the most part, costs do not vary with the amount of catch but are fairly well fixed on a trip-by-trip basis. Therefore, while trip costs, including vessel depreciation, remain the same, revenue can vary significantly.

The share system allows for both the low returns of bad trips and the high returns of good trips to be shared between the boat owner and the crew. Sharing the bad times is especially important as far as investment in vessels is concerned. If boat owners had to pay a fixed wage per trip even when catches were low, expected returns would be lower than if crew payments were based on the size of the catch. Hence, the tendency to invest in a boat would be decreased. While there has been some discussion concerning the exact net benefits of this method of sharing the risks of variable catches, Sutinen (1979) has shown that, under a wide range of circumstances, a share system—as opposed to a wage system—will increase the number of fishermen employed and crew incomes as well as total output from the fishery.

The second explanation for the prevalence of the share system is the incentive it offers to workers. The amount of catch and the quality of catch from a particular trip is related to the crew's willingness to fish (particularly in rough weather or for long periods of time, once a good stock has been located), to search for higher-valued species, and to properly maintain the catch once it is on board. Work on a commercial boat is definitely not a "9-to-5" operation and to do the job right requires long hours of very strenuous and very difficult work. It is also work that cannot be easily monitored. But to the extent that crew members can see that properly operating the vessel and handling the catch will directly increase their incomes, they will be motivated to do so. The share system offers just such motivation.

The final explanation for the share system is its beneficial effect on the utilization of costly inputs. Since, in most cases, it is the net proceeds that are shared, there is a strong incentive to decrease the costs of the shared inputs.

For example, if fuel is considered a shared expense, crew members will have an incentive to run the vessel at a speed that uses less fuel and to compare the gains of shifting fishing positions with the cost of moving to another location. However, if fuel expense is not shared, there is no incentive to economize on its use, and the cost of producing effort will be higher than need be. For more detail, see Anderson (1982e).

Determination of the Share Rate

The formal analysis of the determination of the share rate involves some rather complicated algebra and, as such, will be left to an appendix. The discussion here will focus on a simple graphical analysis. A more complete analysis can be found in Anderson (1982e) and in Griffin, Lacewell, and Nichols (1976). To review what is to come, the share rate is determined by implicit or explicit bargaining between crew members and boat owners, and it is a function of the opportunity cost of labor, the size of any fixed wages, and the annual fixed cost of operating the vessel. A fixed wage is a trip minimum that is sometimes used to provide encouragement for potential crew members to join a vessel. Under such a system, the crew members' total earnings will be the fixed amount plus their share of net proceeds.

Given the price of fish, the productivity of the fish stock, the cost of non-labor inputs, including the average annual fixed cost of the vessel, and any fixed wage to labor, the equilibrium number of vessels that owners will will-ingly use in the fishery will depend upon the share rate. For example, assume that there is no fixed wage meaning that total income to the crew is their share of the net proceeds. Let S, which can take on any value between zero and one, represent the share rate to the crew. The share rate is the specified percentage of the net proceeds (total trip receipts minus trip expenses) that is distributed to crew members. For example, if the sale of the catch from one fishing trip generated $5,000, and fuel, oil, food, ice, bait, and unloading costs total $3,000, net proceeds would be $2,000. Further, if the share rate were 60 per-cent, the crew would have $1,200 for the trip to divide among themselves. (All else equal, therefore, crew members would want the crew size to be as small as possible as long as it could perform the work effectively and safely.) The boat owner (who can also act as a crew member and hence receive a crew share as well) will receive $800 to cover fixed costs such as depreciation, wharfage fees, and a normal return on the investment in the boat and gear.

If S equals one then all net proceeds go to the crew. In this situation, no boat would be willing to operate since there would be no returns to cover fixed costs. At a share rate of zero, however, all net proceeds would go to the boat owner, and the equilibrium number of vessels that owners would be willing to use would be that which produces a gross vessel return equal to the total non-labor (fuel, oil, etc.) costs. Recall that, as the number of vessels in a fishery increases, catch per unit of effort falls. In this analysis, the share rate determines how much of the net proceeds goes to boat owners and hence how many boats can be supported before catch per unit of effort and net returns to boat owners no longer cover nonlabor costs. Specifically, the lower the share rate, the larger will be the size of the fleet that is willing to operate because the return to owners will be higher. This relationship is captured by the curve labeled *BEC* in figure 4.18. The share rate is on the vertical axis, and effort in terms of identical boats is on the horizontal axis. The *BEC* stands for the boat equilibrium curve because this curve shows the equilibrium number of boats that owners will be willing to put into the fishery at various share rates.

With a fixed wage rate added to the share system, the boat equilibrium curve would shift to the left. In the presence of such a wage, the same share rate would produce lower net revenues, and hence the fish stock would be capable of supporting only a smaller number of boats. A mathematical derivation of the *BEC* and a proof that it is downward sloping and will shift to the left as the wage rate increases can be found in the appendix.

From the other side of the market, the curve labeled *CEC* shows the equilibrium number of vessels that crew members would be willing to operate, given a share rate. Although there are a number of factors that determine the willingness of individuals to work on fishing vessels, the relationship between their opportunity cost in terms of potential earnings from other types of employment and the returns earned in fishing is very important. All else equal

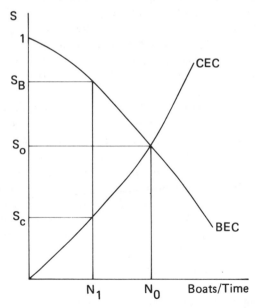

Figure 4.18. *Determining the Equilibrium Share Rate.* The boat equilibrium curve (*BEC*) shows how many boats will willingly be provided at various share rates. Similarly, the crew equilibrium curve (*CEC*) shows how many boats can find crews at various share rates. Their intersection, which always occurs at the open-access fleet size, determines the equilibrium share rate.

(i.e., skill levels, tastes, present location), if the returns earned in fishing are higher than the returns earned for comparable work on land, individuals will prefer to fish. In terms of this analysis, as long as the share rate is such that the net returns per unit of labor are higher than what they earn elsewhere, individuals will continue to shift into employment in fishing. The movement into fishing will cease when the catch per unit of effort falls such that, given the share rate, the returns to fishing are equal to their opportunity costs.

If S is equal to zero, crew members will receive none of the net proceeds, and hence they will not be willing to fish. However, as the share rate increases, the percentage of the net proceeds going to crews increases, and hence the larger will be the number that can fish and still have proceeds to the crew cover their opportunity cost. Therefore, the higher the share rate, the larger the number of boats that can be supported.

In the case of the CEC, the addition of a fixed wage will shift the curve to the right. Given such a wage, the same share rate will now generate a larger total return to labor, and hence the opportunity costs of more workers can be covered.

Since the BEC shows the equilibrium amount of vessels willingly provided at each share rate and the CEC shows the number of vessels that labor will willingly crew for each share rate, their intersection will determine the equilibrium or natural share rate. In the graph, the equilibrium share rate is labeled S_0. Above S_0, the number of boats willing to work is less than is necessary to offer positions to all those individuals desiring to work. However, those crew members who are able to obtain positions will be earning incomes higher than their opportunity costs. For example, at share rate S_B, only N_1 vessels would be willing to work. However, from the CEC curve, it can be seen that enough workers would be willing to crew N_1 vessels at a share rate as low as S_C. Therefore, labor must be earning more than its opportunity cost at a share rate of S_B. At S_B, however, other workers will be willing to crew boats in order to capture some of these rents. The only way they can actually find work is to agree to work for a lower share rate. There will, therefore, be a tendency for the share rate to be bid down.

Alternatively, if the share rate is below S_0, the number of boats that can be crewed is less than the number boat owners will wish to use. Those boat owners who are able to obtain crews will be earning rents, however. At a share rate of S_C, boat owners will only be able to find crews for N_1 vessels; however, from the BEC they will be willing to pay a share rate as high as S_B with this many boats. At S_C they will be earning revenues in excess of all their fixed costs. Since operating owners will be earning rents, others will desire to enter the fishery, but the only way they will be able to obtain crews will be to offer a higher share rate. Therefore, there will be a tendency for the share rate to increase. Only at S_0 will the desires of owners and crews be compatible, and so the share rate will tend to settle there. At this point, the number of vessels is N_0.

It is demonstrated in the appendix that the fleet size equivalent to N_0 is the one where all the rents are dissipated and profits are zero. This is a fundamental result of fisheries economics and should come as no surprise. Also, as demonstrated in the appendix, the natural share rate can be expressed as follows:

$$S_0 = \frac{e(C_1 - \theta)}{eC_1 + K}$$

In the above, e represents the amount of effort used per vessel, C_1 represents the opportunity cost of the labor used to produce one unit of effort, θ represents the fixed wage, if any, for the amount of labor used to produce one unit of effort, and K is the annual fixed cost of each boat. It can be seen, therefore, that the natural share rate is a function of those costs that are not shared. When θ is equal to zero, the natural share rate is the ratio of the opportunity cost of labor per boat to the sum of the opportunity cost of labor and the annual fixed opportunity cost per boat. Such a share rate is necessary because, at open access, the net revenues must be shared such that both owners and crew members cover their opportunity costs. With a fixed wage rate, the numerator of the ratio decreases such that it is only that portion of the opportunity cost of labor not covered by the fixed wage.

From the expression, it is easy to see that S_0 will increase with increases in the opportunity cost of labor, C_1, but will decrease with increases in the fixed wage rate, θ, and in the annual fixed cost of operating the vessel, K.

From this expression, it should also not come as any surprise that there are a multitude of share rates throughout various fisheries in the world. Even without a fixed wage component, differences in share rates can be explained by differences in opportunity costs of capital and labor. With fixed wages there is an infinite number of combinations of wage and share rates. However, in all instances the basic result is the same. The share system will be such that the size of share rate and the fixed wage rate as well as the determination of which costs are to be shared (i.e., which costs will be subtracted from gross revenues to obtain net proceeds) will be such that both crew members and boat owners are at least earning their opportunity costs.

Share Rates and the Distribution of Rents

It has been emphasized above that the rents dissipated through open access can be captured through proper fishery regulation. The existing share rate will be relevant in this regard because it will determine how these rents will be divided between crew and boat owners. For example, assume that by some means the fleet size is reduced from N_0 to N_1. At that fleet size, S_B is the highest share rate boat owners can afford to pay and still remain in business. Similarly, S_C is the lowest share rate that labor will accept for crewing this number of vessels. If the share rate remains at S_0, the rents will be distributed between the two groups, and the percentage to each group will depend upon the relative sizes of S_B, S_0, and S_C. The closer S_0 is to S_B, the more will be received by crews, and vice versa the closer S_0 is to S_C. The interrelationship between regulation, the share rate, and the distribution of rents, if any, will be discussed in more detail in chapter 6.

Appendix

The purpose of this appendix is to explain the analysis of the share system more rigorously and to prove some of the points made in the text. Because of the nature of the share system, it is necessary to modify the traditional model by introducing vessels and the level of vessel output. Let:

$y(Ne)$ = the sustainable yield function for the exploited fish stock.
N = the number of vessels operating in the fishery.
e = the annual amount of effort produced by each boat that is assumed to be constant.
P = the constant price of fish.
C_1 = the opportunity cost of labor used to produce one unit of effort, a constant.
C_2 = opportunity costs of nonlabor inputs used to produce one unit of effort, a constant.
C_3 = opportunity costs of nonlabor inputs used to produce the on-board processing and handling services associated with one unit of output, a constant.
K = the annual fixed cost of each boat, including a normal return.
S = the share of net proceeds paid to the crew.
$[(P - C_3)y - NeC_2]$ = annual net proceeds for the entire fleet.

The equilibrium for owners will occur where total profits to boats are zero. This can be expressed as follows:

$$\pi_B = (1 - S)\,[(P - C_3)y - NeC_2] - Ne\theta - NK = 0$$

The first term is the net revenue share to the owners while the second two are the fixed labor and capital costs, respectively. The boat must cover these costs with its share of the net proceeds, or it will lose money. Fleet size equilibrium occurs when π_B is zero because all boats will just be covering their entire costs. Positive profits will encourage boats to enter the fishery while negative profits will do the opposite. Solving the above for S will provide an expression for the boat equilibrium curve used in the text:

$$S_B = \frac{(P - C_3)y/N - eC_2 - (K + e\theta)}{(P - C_3)y/N - eC_2}$$

Similarly, the equilibrium for workers is where total returns to labor from fishing are equal to opportunity costs:

$$\pi_C = S[(P - C_3)y - NeC_2] + Ne\theta - NeC_1 = 0$$

The first two terms are net revenue share to labor and fixed wage earnings, whie the third is the opportunity cost of labor. If the first two are greater than NeC_1, then labor will be earning more than its opportunity cost, and there will be entry into the fishing labor force. Only when π_C equals zero will there be a stable labor force. The crew equilibrium curve can be expressed as:

$$S_C = \frac{(C_1 - \theta)e}{(P - C_3)y/N - eC_2}$$

The natural share rate occurs where $S_B = S_C$. Equating these two expressions and simplifying obtains

$$(P - C_3)y/N - e(C_1 + C_2) - K = 0$$

Therefore, the equilibrium will occur when returns per boat equal total costs per boat, which is to say, when all of the rents have been dissipated. This is the open-access equilibrium condition.

The equation for the natural share rate can be obtained by solving the above for y/N and substituting it into either S_B or S_C. The result is

$$S_0 = \frac{(C_1 - \theta)e}{eC_1 + K}$$

5

Beyond the Independent Single Species Model

Introduction

For the most part, the analysis thus far has been in terms of a single fleet of identical vessels, which harvests fish from a biologically independent stock. These simplifying assumptions have been very useful in demonstrating the basic principles of fisheries economics. While these concepts apply to more complex fisheries, the model from which they are derived is much too simple to provide a reasonable understanding of the open-access exploitation and management problems of real-world fisheries. The purpose of this chapter is to expand the model so as to more closely describe the biological and technical intricacies existing in most fisheries. It will not be possible, however, to describe all of the possible nuances that can occur. Rather, six basic types will be described. They are general enough that most of the world's fisheries can be classified as one or some combination of them.

Fisheries can be distinguished according to the number and type of fleets, the number and type of stocks, and the relationships between and among both. The six types to be discussed below are: one fleet that simultaneously harvests multiple related stocks, one fleet that divides its efforts between more than one independent stock, one fleet that harvests different stocks at different times of the year, two fleets each focusing on one stock but which have incidental catch of the stock that is the primary interest of the other, two fleets each focusing on separate stocks that are biologically interrelated, and two fleets that focus on the same stock.

Whatever the nature of the fishery, however, open-access utilization will result in an economically suboptimal harvest time path. Similarly, the economically efficient harvest time path that maximizes the net present value of harvest will be obtained if, in each time period, the marginal value of harvest equals the sum of marginal harvest and marginal user costs. The peculiarities of open-access and optimal utilization will be described for each fishery type.

However, as important as these considerations are, they will be only a small part of the substantive material in the chapter, because they should be quite familiar by now and because they are fairly similar from case to case. The emphasis will be on the nature of the different types of fisheries and the direct and indirect relationships between their economic and biological components.

One Fleet, Multiple Joint-Stock Fishery

In some fisheries, the gear comes into contact with stocks of different species, and a mixed catch results. Although the number of species caught in these instances can be quite high, we will only consider the case where it is equal to two. Each unit of effort obviously affects both stocks; hence, the bioeconomic analysis of both the open-access and the optimally regulated fishery becomes more complex. This is primarily because more than one price must now be considered and because the varied populations may react differently to the fishing effort. Also, the stocks may be in competition for the same food, or there may be a predator-prey relationship between them.

Consider first a very simple case where the fishery consists of a group of boats with nondiscriminatory gear harvesting fish from two independent species; call them A and B. (We will consider several types of interdependencies among the species below.) The quantity caught of either type of fish depends upon the effort used and the size of the respective populations. Each species will have a normal population equilibrium curve, as pictured in a hypothetical example in figure 5.1a. Since the two populations are independent, the curves are derived in the same manner described in the discussion of figure 2.1b in chapter 2. The curves can be interpreted as follows. In the absence of predation by man, species A will have a natural population equilibrium size of P_3. Similarly, the natural equilibrium size of species B will be P_1. As effort is expanded, greater catches result in both species, so a new equilibrium will be reached at a lower population size. Note that, as the curves are drawn here, when effort reaches E_2, the stock size of species B will be zero but that of species A will be P_2. Effort will have to get as high as E_4 before the population of species A will be destroyed.

Each species will have a sustainable yield derivable in the normal manner (see figure 5.1b). The total sustainable yield from this fishery is the sum of those from both species. For example, with effort at E_1 the equilibrium yield of species A will be Y_1, while at the same time that level of effort will also be harvesting Y_2 units of species B. Therefore, the total sustainable yield at this level of effort comprises those two quantities, and the revenue earned will depend upon the relative prices of the two species.

The fishery will reach maximum sustainable yield at that point where the sum of the individual sustainable yields is a maximum. In a multispecies fishery an attempt to operate at MSY makes even less sense than in fisheries of a

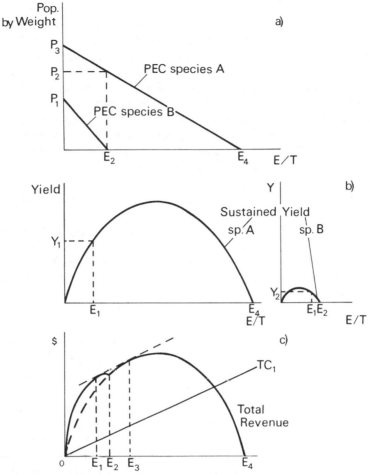

Figure 5.1. *One Fleet, Two Stocks.* In these fisheries there is a population equilibrium and a sustained yield curve for each species. The sustained revenue curve is a monetized version of the sum of the two yield curves. Its exact shape depends upon the shapes of the yield curves and the price of each species. The open-access equilibrium yield and the maximum economic yield are determined in the normal fashion. Both may lead to the extinction of the smaller stock.

single species, because such a goal does not take into account the relative market values of the two species. The revenue earned at any level of effort depends upon the size of each type of catch and their relative prices. It is possible, therefore, that a small catch consisting primarily of the more valuable species will earn more revenue than would a larger catch with different components.

A sustainable total revenue curve for the fishery, plotted in figure 5.1c, is the vertical summation of the revenue curve of each of the two independent species. Its form depends upon the shapes of the individual yield curves and

the relative prices of the two types of fish. The distance between the total
revenue curve and the dotted line (the latter representing the total revenue for
species A up to E_1) shows the revenue earned from species B over this range.
Beyond E_2, species B is destroyed; thus, total revenue arises entirely from the
catch of species A.

As discussed earlier, the open-access bionomic equilibrium of the fishery
lies at that level of effort where total sustainable revenue equals total cost;
and achieving this equilibrium may prove to be such a long and tedious process as never to be attained in an open-access fishery. The process may be even
more complicated in a multispecies fishery. Bearing this in mind, let us further investigate conditions at the open-access equilibrium, assuming such exists. If TC_1 is the total cost curve, the open-access fishery will operate at a
level of effort greater than E_2, and species B will be eliminated. However, if
the relative price-cost structure is such that the cost curve intersects the revenue curve to the left of E_2, the open-access fishery will utilize both species.

The peculiar shape of the total revenue curve adds an interesting aspect
to the analysis of stationary maximum economic yield. Note that the existing
cost curve presents two levels of effort, E_1 and E_3, where the difference between revenue and cost is a maximum. From E_1 to E_2 net revenue falls, but it
then rises to another maximum at E_3. If the cost curve were higher than TC_1,
the stationary MEY could occur at a point to the left of E_1; were it lower,
MEY would lie to the right of E_3. This means that, if the fishery started out as
a high-cost operation but achieved lower costs, stationary MEY would increase. If costs then continued to decrease, stationary MEY would take a
jump to E_3 and thereafter expand gradually as cost conditions improved.

To insure the economically optimal utilization of this fishery, the harvest
time plan must be selected such that in each period the value of the marginal
harvest (which can consist of both types of fish) is equal to the marginal harvesting cost and the marginal user cost in terms of the effect on the present
value of harvest from both stocks. The stationary equilibrium point, if one
exists, will be somewhere between the level of effort that generates maximum
annual net revenue and the open-access level, depending on the discount rate.

Before concluding the discussion of this case, two further points should
be raised. First, if a cost curve above TC_1 still intersects the revenue curve to
the right of E_2, the open-access equilibrium yield will dictate that only species
A survives, although at the stationary MEY it may be that both species should
be utilized. If species B is actually biologically destroyed (and not just reduced so low that it cannot support a commercial fishery), then no amount of
regulation will bring it back and the open-access fishery will have destroyed a
resource that would have been of value to society. Such a stock can be saved
only by optimal regulation of the entire fishery from its inception.

Note also that, if the cost curve is less than TC_1, the stationary MEY of
the fishery will call for the destruction of species B, *provided* the entire value
of this stock is captured in the revenue curve, for in that case its extinction will

be so offset by the greater value of the catch from species A as to increase total net revenue. If, however, the stock of species B has additional uses in sports fishing or as a food for other valuable marine life, then the impact of its destruction on these other uses must be taken into consideration. For a more detailed analysis of this complex issue, the reader is referred to the literature on the economics of endangered species—Bishop (1978), Brown and Goldstein (1984), and Miller and Menz (1979).

Let us now consider different examples of these fisheries where the populations of the stocks are interdependent. In the first two cases the stocks are mutually competitive; in the third, a predator-prey relationship exists.

When two species of fish are competing for food or for some other limiting factor in a certain ecosystem, then—assuming this competition does not destroy both of them—either they will reach a point of coexistence where both achieve a viable natural equilibrium population size, or one will eventually erode the ability of the other to maintain a viable population. Each of these situations is analyzed below.

The case of a hypothetical fishery exploiting a pair of stocks that have reached a stable coexistence, with no fishing by man, is pictured in figure 5.2. The population equilibrium curves show that, prior to exploitation by man, species B had the larger of the two stable populations. Note that, as effort is exerted and expanded the equilibrium population size of this species decreases in the normal fashion. However, in this hypothetical case the size of species A actually increases, because, despite its exploitation by man, its competitive position is now improved by the decrease in population of species B. This growth will continue until effort reaches E_1, the level at which the population of species B is destroyed. The stable coexistence of the natural equilibrium has been upset by fishing. At that point species A will have reached a size of P_3, and any further increases in effort will serve to decrease its equilibrium population size. (It is also possible, however, that the smaller of the two populations will decrease as effort expands, thus allowing the other to become even larger, or that both will decrease because the effect of exploitation on species A is greater than the reduced competition from species B.)

The sustainable yield curves of the two species are pictured in figure 5.2b. Note the abrupt change in the curve for species A at E_1. Up to that point, the yield has increased rapidly due to the concurrent growth in its equilibrium population size; beyond E_1, the yield curve attains the standard shape that results from the normal reaction between population and effort. The sustainable yield curve of species B shows the standard shape throughout because no abrupt changes alter its population equilibrium curve.

A total revenue curve for the fishery as a whole is pictured in figure 5.2c; again it is the vertical sum of the revenues earned from both species. As drawn, it is identical to that for independent species shown above, although other shapes are possible, depending upon the shapes of the yield curves of the two species.

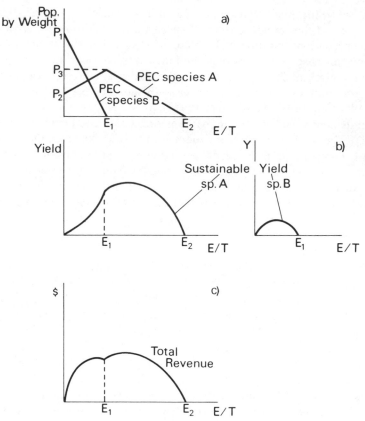

Figure 5.2. *One Fleet, Two Stocks with Competitive Coexistence.* If the two species are in competition for some factor in the environment, but they both have a viable population with no fishing
by man, increased effort may actually increase the population size of one stock as its competitive
position is strengthened by the decrease in population size of the other stock. This will result in
peculiarly shaped yield curves.

The case of a fishery exploiting two interdependent species that have a
competitive-exclusion natural equilibrium is pictured in figure 5.3. With no
exploitation by man, species B will be pushed to very low levels. As effort is
expanded from zero to E_1, the equilibrium population size of species A will
decrease in the normal manner until it reaches P_2. At that point the other
species has a new lease on competitive life, and its population will grow as
increases in effort up to E_2 continue to whittle down the number of species A.
Here again, species B gains more from its improved competitive position than
it loses by way of the more intensive fishing. Note also that the equilibrium
population size of species A drops at a faster rate as species B becomes viable,
because it now has to contend not only with the increased exploitation by man
but also with increased competition. At E_2 species A is destroyed and species

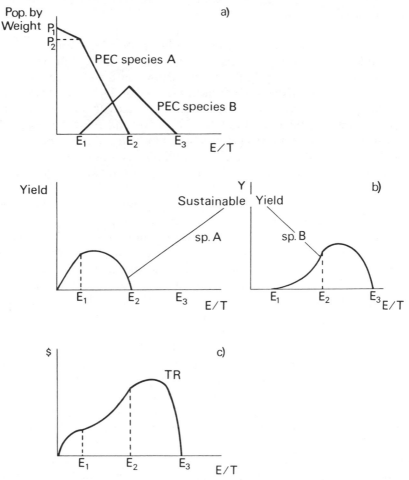

Figure 5.3. *One Fleet, Two Stocks with Competitive Exclusion.* If both species are in competition for some factor of the environment and only one secures a viable population with no fishing, the other may become viable as effort reduces the population size of its competitors. This will result in peculiarly shaped yield curves.

B reaches its maximum size, after which increases in effort will cause its population to decrease in the normal manner.

In summary, at low levels of effort resultant changes in the natural system serve to reduce the stronger of the two species. At slightly higher levels of effort, both species are viable, and over this range of effort one increases while the other decreases. Finally, at higher levels of effort the natural equilibrium is altered to the extent that the exclusion is reversed and the originally dominant species does not survive.

The sustainable yield curves for these species are pictured in figure 5.3b.

Note that at E_1 sustainable yield from species B is finally greater than zero. Also, this level of effort produces an abrupt change in the shape of the sustainable yield curve of species A due to the increased competition. At E_2 the sustainable yield of species A becomes zero, and the shape of the yield curve of species B changes abruptly, due to the removal of the other species.

A total revenue curve for this fishery, pictured in figure 5.3c, is drawn on the assumption that species B commands a substantially higher price than species A. Like all the other total revenue curves, its exact shape depends upon the nature of the two yield curves (i.e., in which section of the curve the "bend" due to the change in the other population is located, etc.) and upon relative prices. If the prices were closer together, the total revenue curve would be more like those already discussed.

If the two species exploited bear a predator-prey relationship, the analysis is much the same. Without fishing by man, the species will reach a natural biological equilibrium. As fishing begins, the equilibrium population size of the predator species will always decline, but that of the prey may increase if it gains more from the reduction of its natural enemies than it loses to the nets of the fishermen. Graphical analysis of the case where both species are reduced by fishing resembles that in figure 5.1. The case where the prey actually increases in population is very similar to figure 5.2, with species B as the predator.

The revenue curves of fisheries having these three types of interdependent species—competitively coexistent, competitively exclusionary, and predator-prey—are similar to those of fisheries with independent species; thus the economic analysis is similar also, and the main conclusions derived earlier through the use of figure 5.1 apply equally to this consideration of interdependent species. Open-access fishing may or may not destroy the smaller of the two populations, depending upon the relative sizes of revenue and cost. Also, the optimal regulation of the fishery may call for the destruction of one population *if* the total value of the fish stock is represented in the revenue curve. The other conclusions hold as well.

Before leaving this section, however, it should be pointed out that the models used were not very complex. It was assumed that nonselective fishing gear excluded the possibility of using different methods on the different species. It was also implicitly assumed that intertemporal changes in effort within a season would not affect the type of fish captured. In addition, the interdependencies were considered to be all-or-nothing affairs: for example, in the case of competitive coexistence, the population of species A would continue to grow as long as that of species B decreased. It is possible that, over some ranges, increases in effort will decrease both populations. But the purpose of the discussion was not to provide a casebook for every possible situation that can occur. Rather it was to explain the nature of the issues and the new problems that can arise and to provide an introduction to their solution and a framework for studying more complex fisheries. The importance of population dynamics and ecological relationships should be evident. While the basic principles of the economics of fisheries utilization are fairly straightforward, this and the discussions in the remainder of this chapter should make it very clear that their application can often be quite complex.

One Fleet, Multiple Independent-Stock Fishery

In this type of fishery the fleet also exploits more than one stock, but the fishing activities for each are mutually exclusive. Instead of each unit of effort yielding a specified combination of the various stocks at any given time, effort can be directed exclusively at any one of a number of stocks. The simplest example is where more than one independent stock of the same species is harvested by the same group of fishermen. This type was identified by Gordon (1954) in his early works and has received more detailed treatment by Huppert (1979) and Anderson (1982d).

Assume that there are two distinct fishing grounds, each with its sustainable yield curve, and that one of the grounds is more productive than the other. For simplicity assume also that the marginal cost of supplying effort is constant and is the same in both areas. The average and marginal revenue curves for these grounds are pictured in figure 5.4. The graphs are identical to that in figure 2.3, but in this case the fishery must be represented by two

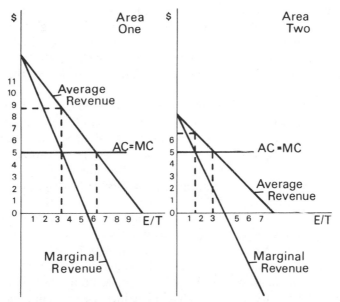

Figure 5.4. *One Fleet, Two Fishing Grounds.*   To achieve a maximum economic yield in a fishery with two grounds, effort should be expanded in each area until marginal revenue of effort is equal to its marginal cost. The fact that average revenue in the two areas may be different at this point is of no importance from a total fishery point of view.

diagrams because of the independence of the two fishing grounds. Note that the variation in productivity implies that equal amounts of effort will earn different amounts of revenue in the two grounds: two units of effort in the first area will earn about $10.50, while the same effort in the second will earn only $6.00.

An open-access fishery would operate in such a way that about 6.2 units of effort would be applied in Area One and 3 units of effort would be applied in Area Two. At these levels, each unit of effort would be earning just enough revenue to cover costs. It has already been explained that this would waste resources, since marginal revenue would be less than marginal cost on both grounds. In this case, however, the waste has an added dimension in that a reallocation of effort among the grounds will increase both catch and revenue. Note that, at the open-access equilibrium points, the marginal revenue in Area One is actually negative, whereas in Area Two it is $2.00. This means that the last unit of effort used in Area One actually decreased the catch and so lessened total revenue. On the other hand, the last unit of effort in Area Two increased the catch enough to augment the revenue. The marginal revenue curve also indicates that if effort were increased in Area Two, the marginal revenue, although diminished, would still be positive. In sum, it is evident that, although it would not affect total cost, a unit of effort removed from Area One and put to use in Area Two would increase both total production and total revenue. Reduction of effort in Area One will actually increase catch there, while the addition of effort in the other area will also increase its yield. The same general result would follow even if the marginal revenue in Area One were positive but less than $2.00. In that case, the shifting of effort from Area One to Area Two would lead to a net increase in catch and revenue, since the increase in Area Two would more than compensate for the decrease in Area One.

To make the analysis of optimal utilization as simple as possible, assume for the moment that there is a zero discount rate so that the stationary MEY point is where the annual revenues from the whole fishery are maximized. This will occur where the marginal revenue of effort in both areas equals the marginal cost of effort. This would be 3.2 and 1.6 units of effort in Areas One and Two, respectively. Note that at these points the average revenue (and hence the average catch) differs between the two areas. At first this may appear paradoxical, but the important criterion is that at those levels of output the marginal revenues equal marginal costs. The averages of cost and revenue are not the relevant point of comparison in this regard. As long as the marginal revenues are equal to each other and to marginal costs, the fishery is being exploited in an optimal manner. Since the last unit of effort is producing the same marginal return in each area, no increase in production is possible from interarea switches; moreover, the value of the marginal catch in each area equals the marginal cost of producing effort. Therefore, resources are being used to produce only enough effort to return a value equal to the cost of those resources. In more general terms, the optimal harvest time path is achieved by allocating effort to the various grounds such that the value of the marginal catch in each is equal to the sum of marginal harvesting and user cost in each.

The distinctive aspect of this type of fishery is that both the open-access and the optimal harvest time path must be described in two dimensions: the size of the fleet and the allocation of effort to the various fishing grounds. This, of course, means that there is another aspect to fisheries regulation. To achieve full optimality, not only will it be necessary to reduce fleet size, but it will also be necessary to control where boats actually fish. If only fleet size is controlled, the remaining boats will spread themselves across the grounds according to the average rather than marginal returns. As a result, all of the potential gains from correcting open access will not be obtained.

Multipurpose Fleet, Seasonally Fished Stocks

In this case there is also a single fleet harvesting two stocks, but instead of dividing up and each part focusing on one stock, the entire fleet exploits both species. The structural difference is that the stocks are available during different parts of the year. The Alaskan fleet that harvests groundfish part of the year and crab during the remainder is an excellent example. In these fisheries it is also necessary to consider both the size of the fleet and the allocation of effort to the two stocks. The latter is especially important when the stocks differ in their ability to sustain harvest pressure.

To analyze the problems of a multipurpose fleet fishery, consider a fleet that can exploit two species, S_1 and S_2, which are available at completely different times of the year. (If there are overlaps in the harvest periods, some of the problems of the previous case are introduced.) Let T_1 and T_2 be the number of days that species S_1 and S_2, respectively, are available for harvest. Further, let t_1 and t_2 be the actual number of days fished per boat during each season.

Let up first discuss the open-access utilization in terms of the sustained average yield and revenue curves. Because the fixed cost of a vessel must be spread over the harvest of both stocks, a simple analysis of total revenues and total costs is not quite as useful. Rather, it is necessary to slightly modify the normal analysis by comparing the average annual returns, net of variable harvesting costs, from both fisheries with the annual fixed cost of maintaining a vessel. The latter includes amortization and such items as dock rental space, insurance, annual maintenance costs, etc. A vessel will remain in the fishery if the sum of the net returns from both fisheries is greater than or equal to the annual fixed costs of maintaining the boat.

The daily average net return for operating in either season is the difference between the value of the harvest and daily harvesting costs. The former is the product of market price and daily catch per unit of effort. Assuming that market price and daily harvesting costs are fixed, the net daily return in either season will be determined by the daily catch per unit of effort, which is a function of the total effort exerted on the stock. Total effort in either season will depend upon the number of boats in the fleet and the number of days fished by each boat. Assuming that all boats act in the same way, this information can be useful in explaining vessel and fleet behavior. See figure 5.5. The daily net sustained return per boat for each season is plotted against the number of days fished that season by each vessel. The curves labeled ANR_1 (N_1) and ANR_2 (N_1) show how average daily net sustained returns decrease with increased days fished on each stock for stocks 1 and 2, respectively, when fleet size is N_1. The lower curves represent the same relationships when the fleet size is expanded to N_2.

Note that, with a fleet size of N_1, the daily return for the two stocks will be r_{11} and r_{21}, respectively, when all boats fish on all available days during both seasons. Further, when the fleet is increased to N_2, daily net return falls to r_{12} on stock 2 if all boats fish T_1 days. However, at that fleet size, stock 2 cannot sustain all of the potential effort, and sustained net daily revenue will be negative if all vessels fish T_2 days during season 2.

In the short run, it makes sense to operate on any given day as long as the net returns are positive or zero (remember average costs include a normal profit, so a net return of zero means that all opportunity costs are being met). Therefore, the ANR curves can be used to determine the equilibrium number of days fished per boat for each species. If the ANR curve intersects the line representing the maximum possible days fished for their season, all boats will fish for the entire season and will be earning more than enough to cover variable harvesting costs. If the ANR curve intersects the horizontal axis to the

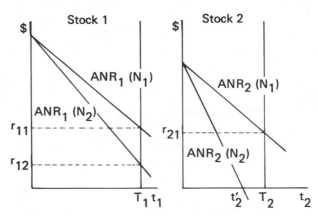

Figure 5.5. *Multipurpose Fleet, Seasonally Fished Stocks: Open Access Boats.* The vessel average net revenue per day (*ANR*) is related to the number of vessels in the fleet and number of days each one fishes. Boats will continue fishing in each season as long as *ANR* is positive, and open-access equilibrium will occur when the earnings over variable costs in both seasons equal vessel fixed cost.

left of the T line, that intersection point is the largest number of days fished per boat that the stock can handle and still cover variable harvesting costs. In these instances, vessel operators will not use all of the available fishing days.

The basics of individual vessel behavior can be explained using this information. There will be a family of ANR curves, one for each different fleet size, and each will show the net daily return per vessel, assuming all vessels operate in the same way. As N increases, the curves will rotate around the intersection point on the vertical axis. As drawn here, when fleet size is equal to N_1, the available fishing season will be binding for both species and so, t_1 will equal T_1 and t_2 will equal T_2. However, as the fleet size increases, the curves rotate down, and eventually one and/or both of the constraints will become nonbinding. For these fleet sizes there will be idle capacity during the affected season in that vessels will not be fishing on every available day. For example, with a fleet size of N_2, the equilibrium number of days fished during the season for stock 2 will be t_2'.

Vessel operation can be described in somewhat more detail in figure 5.6a. This diagram demonstrates how each vessel will operate at different fleet sizes. We will discuss below what the actual fleet size under open access will be. Fleet size is plotted on the horizontal axis, and the days fished for both stocks are plotted on the vertical axis with t_1 being measured in a positive direction from the lower horizontal axis and t_2 being measured in a negative direction from the upper horizontal axis. For low levels of N both t_1 and t_2 will be at their maximum allowable level. However, as the fleet size expands and the ANR curves in figure 5.5 rotate down, first one and then the other will fall below the maximum possible amounts. As depicted here, all vessels will be operating at full capacity until fleet size equals N_3, at which time there will be "idle capacity" during the season for species 2. Similarly, with fleet sizes beyond N_5, there will be idle capacity during the season for species 1 as well. The hatched area represents the idle capacity for each individual vessel.

Using information from figure 5.6a to determine average boat revenue, it is possible to describe the open-access fleet size. The AR_{oa} curve in figure 5.6b shows how the equilibrium average annual return per boat net of harvesting costs will vary with fleet size. Revenue will be determined, in part, by the open-access distribution of effort described in figure 5.6a. That is, the AR_{oa} curve shows the average annual sustained net revenue per vessel for all fleet sizes, given the equilibrium number of days fished per vessel and the average daily net revenue for each stock that is obtained with each fleet size. (See below.) The curve labeled I represents the fixed annual maintenance cost of the representative boat. The open-access equilibrium will occur at a fleet size of N_4, where average annual net revenue per vessel is equal to annual capital costs.

As drawn here, at the open-access equilibrium, there will be idle capacity in the season for species 2. This is a distinct possibility in multipurpose fleets with nonoverlapping seasons. Let us consider this in more detail. In order for

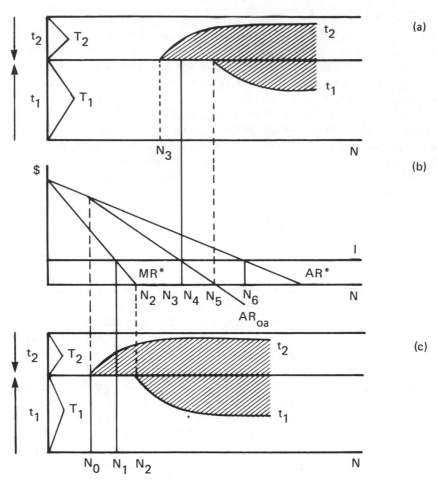

Figure 5.6. *Multipurpose Fleet, Seasonally Fished Stocks: Fishery MEY.*   Average revenue per boat under open access (AR_{ao}) and optimal conditions ($AR*$) can be determined from the vessel effort distribution diagrams in parts a and c, respectively. It is then possible to describe fleet size and vessel operating conditions in both situations.

a vessel to break even, the sum of the net returns from each season must be enough to cover the annual fixed costs. Depending upon the nature of the population dynamics for each stock, this can happen in two ways. First, if N_1 in figure 5.5 is the open-access equilibrium, all boats will work to full capacity in both seasons, and the average daily net variable return for the two species will be r_{11} and r_{21}, respectively. This will be an equilibrium fleet size if $T_1r_{11} + T_2r_{21} = I$, that is, if earnings over and above variable costs are just enough to cover the annual capital costs but no more. Boats will have no tendency to enter the fishery, but at the same time there will be no incentive for exit either. However, if returns are greater than I, there will be entry into the fishery.

On the other hand, if N_2 is an open-access equilibrium, then if the entire fleet worked to full capacity during the first season, the net return will be equal to r_{12}. The *ANR* curve for species 2 intersects the horizontal axis, indicating that the net return for fishing in this season will fall to zero at a level of effort when all existing boats are not fishing the full season. This can still be an equilibrium fleet size, however, if $T_1 r_{12} = I$, that is, if the fishery for species 1 is profitable enough to support the fleet by itself. In such a case, however, once the fleet is operating, it will make sense to fish during the season for species 2 as long as variable costs (including a normal profit) are being covered. Just how much effort will be applied to the second stock under open access is hard to determine. In figure 5.5, as long as the amount of effort per boat allocated to species 2 is less than t_2', there will be some positive net returns over variable costs. But since at its equilibrium size the fleet has the potential to exert T_2 units of effort during the season, under open access there will probably be something approaching pulse fishing for species 2. All vessels will fish until the long-run return becomes negative, and then many or all will cease. As a result of the decreased effort, the stock will rebuild and the net return will increase to levels that will encourage fishing, and the cycle will start over. With a homogeneous fleet, it is very difficult to picture any other pattern of individual firm behavior that makes sense. If it appears profitable for one vessel to fish, it will appear profitable for all to fish. All boats acting in concert will reduce the returns during this season such that it will be profitable to none.

The analysis of optimal fleet and vessel behavior is fairly easy to explain if we adopt the expedient of assuming a zero discount rate so that the stationary MEY point is where annual revenues, net of both variable harvesting costs and fixed annual costs, are maximized. Just as in the one-fleet, multiple independent-stock fishery, the stationary MEY point can be distinguished by the number of vessels and the way they are used on the two stocks. For a given fleet size, the open-access number of days fished on both stocks is determined by the average net daily revenue. See figure 5.5. However, as in all of the analysis above, the optimal number of days fished for each stock is determined by the marginal net daily revenue. While the former is calculated with average catch per unit of effort, the latter uses marginal catch per unit of effort. To be specific, marginal net daily revenue is the value of the extra harvest minus the daily harvesting cost. From an economic-optimizing point of view, it makes sense to continue operating a boat as long as the net value of the marginal day is positive or at least equal to zero.

The difference between open access and MEY for any fleet size is demonstrated in figure 5.7. The *MNR* curve for a given fleet is below the associated *ANR* curve for the same reason that the MR_E curve is below the AR_E curve in the standard diagram. The *MNR* curve takes into account the effect on total fishery yield if all boats in the fleet increase effort by one unit, while the *ANR*

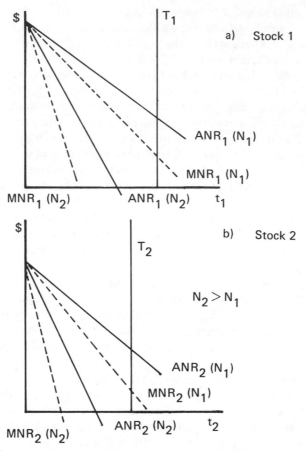

Figure 5.7. *Multipurpose Fleet, Seasonally Fished Stocks: Boat MEY.* The vessel marginal net revenue per day fished curve takes into account the effects of effort by each boat on the catch levels of all others. These curves can be used to determine the optimal vessel level of effort in each season.

curve just takes into account the average catch per vessel with increases in days fished by all vessels.

The optimal number of days fished for each stock will be T_1 and T_2 if the respective *MNR* curves are positive at those levels of effort. As long as the marginal net revenue per day is positive, it makes sense to fish as many days as possible. In those instances where the *MNR* curve intersects the horizontal axis, the optimal number of days fished is represented by the point of intersection. While there may be more days on which it is possible to fish, it does not make economic sense to do so if that will push marginal net daily returns below zero.

It can be seen, therefore, that at lower fleet sizes the optimal amounts of t_1 and t_2 at MEY will be equal to that produced under open-access conditions because both the ANR and the MNR intersect the seasonal constraint line at a positive return. As the fleet expands, however, a point will be reached where the optimal level of t_1 and t_2 will be less than that supplied under open access. The optimal number of days fished during each season as a function of fleet size is plotted in figure 5.6c. The difference between open-access and MEY seasonal vessel behavior at various fleet sizes can be seen by comparing figures 5.6a and 5.6c. For example, if fleet size is N_1, it is optimal to have idle capacity during S_2 even though all the boats would be used during open access. Using this information on optimal vessel behavior at various fleet sizes, it is possible to determine what the optimal fleet size should be.

The average revenue per boat derived from the optimal utilization pattern is plotted as AR^* in figure 5.6b. AR^* will be higher than AR_{oa} from the point at which the optimal seasonal fishing pattern is different from the open-access pattern (i.e., at fleet size N_0), because, at each fleet level, the efficiency of vessel use is improved. Specifically, the overutilization of stock 2 at fleet sizes between N_0 and N_2, and of both stocks at fleets larger than N_2, is prevented.

The curve labeled MR^* is the annual marginal net revenue curve that is associated with the AR^* curve. Annual net revenues for the fishery as a whole are maximized at the fleet size where the MR^* curve intersects the I curve *if* the fleet is used in the appropriate manner with respect to both stocks. Optimal fleet size is N_1, and the optimal vessel behavior can be determined from figure 5.6c. As drawn here, the optimal fleet will have idle capacity during the season for species 2. The main condition for MEY is that the value of the extra output to the fleet as a whole caused by entry of the marginal boat be equal to the opportunity cost of that boat. The fact that there is idle capacity for part of one of the seasons does not indicate a waste of resources. Marginal benefits are at least equal to marginal costs and if the vessels expand effort beyond the designated amount during the slack season, there would actually be a decrease in the value of output. In other cost and revenue situations, the optimal fleet may be fully utilized in both seasons. In such instances, the fleet needs the earnings above variable harvesting costs from both fisheries in order to cover its fixed costs.

Actually, the stationary MEY fleet level will be somewhere between N_1 and N_4, depending on the discount rate, and the optimal fleet use will have to be determined taking into account marginal user cost in each season, but the essence of this argument should be clear.

There is one interesting point from the above that is worth emphasizing. First, note that gains are possible merely by changing vessel behavior, even if there is no control on effort. At fleet size N_4, average return can be increased from the AR_{oa} curve to the AR^* curve by reducing the number of days fished per boat in each season. Compare again figures 5.6a and 5.6c. Further gains are possible if the fleet is reduced and appropriate changes are made in seasonal fishing behavior. The converse of this is that, if fleet size is restricted without placing limits on seasonal fishing behavior, the full potential gains will not be achieved.

Two Fleets, Biological Interdependence

This fishery type is characterized by two fleets pursuing stocks that are biologically interrelated. As before, the stocks can have a competitive or a predator-prey relationship with each other. In either case, effort in one fishery will produce an interfishery indirect effect on the performance of the other. For example, when the two stocks are environmentally competitive, an increase in effort in one fishery can actually benefit the other. An increase in effort by one fleet will tend to reduce the size of its stock, which will improve the competitive position of the stock exploited by the other fishery. Over some ranges of effort, this can actually lead to an indirect increase in the stock and hence the productive potential of that fishery.

If there is a predator-prey relationship between the stocks, the indirect fishery effect will be positive or negative, depending on which stock the fishery exploits. An increase in effort on the predator stock will lower natural mortality on the prey stock and hence will tend to improve the productive potential of the fishery exploiting it. On the other hand, an increase in effort on the prey stock will reduce the food available to the predator stock, which will be detrimental to the other fishery. In general terms, this means that the sustained yield curve in either fishery is a function of the amount of effort in the other fishery. For example, with competitive stocks, an increase in effort in either fishery will tend to shift up the sustained yield curve of the other, whereas an increase in effort on a prey stock will tend to reduce the sustained yield curve of the fishery for the predator stock.

These indirect effects are important considerations in the determination of the open access and the optimal utilization of these stocks. Let us turn first to open-access utilization. To set the stage, recall that in an independent fishery, open-access equilibrium occurs where total sustained revenue equals total cost. Because it is a sustained revenue, catch equals natural growth and stock size will not change. Further, since revenues equal cost, there will be no profits to attract new vessels. This has been called a bioeconomic equilibrium because of the simultaneous equilibrium in both components of the fishery. The conditions for open-access equilibrium for either of the interdependent fisheries are the same. However, to have a true equilibrium, they must hold in both fisheries at the same time. This can get somewhat complex, however, because the open-access equilibrium position in either fishery depends upon the amount of effort produced in the other, due to the interrelationship between effort in one and the sustained yield curve in the other.

The explanation of this general open-access equilibrium and the process of obtaining it can be discussed in more detail with reference to figure 5.8. Assume that there are two fisheries, fishery 1 and fishery 2, the stocks of

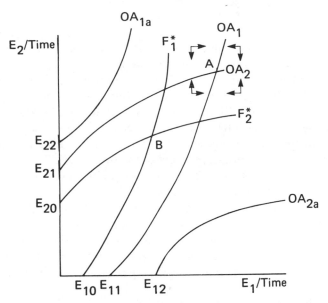

Figure 5.8. *Two Fleets, Biological Interdependence.* The open-access curves for the two fisheries, *OA* and *OA₂*, show the open-access level of effort in one fishery for a given level of effort in the other. Their intersection determines the interdependent open-access point. The optimal curves, F_1^* and F_2^*, determine in an analogous way the interdependent MEY point.

which have a competitive biological interrelationship. Let E_1 and E_2 represent the amount of effort exerted on these fisheries, respectively. In the figure, the levels of effort in the two fisheries are plotted on the two axes. As such, each point in the graph represents a combination of effort from the two fisheries. The curve labeled OA_2 is the open-access equilibrium curve for fishery 2; it shows the open-access amount of effort that will be produced in fishery 2 for various levels of effort in fishery 1, given existing prices and harvesting costs. That is, it shows the effort combinations where revenue and cost are equal in fishery 2. As drawn, the open-access level of effort in fishery 2 increases with increases in E_1. The OA_2 curve has a positive slope because of the nature of the interfishery indirect effect with biological interdependence. As E_1 is increased, the stock it exploits (S_1) is driven down, which will tend to increase the stock of the other fishery (S_2). This shifts up the sustained yield curve for fishery 2, making it intersect the cost curve at a higher level of effort. Therefore, the open-access equilibrium point in fishery 2 shifts out. The interfishery indirect effect probably diminishes as S_1 is pushed to low levels, and so the OA_2 curve is positive with a decreasing slope.

The exact position of the curve depends upon the biological and economic parameters. An increase in the cost of providing effort will shift the curve toward the horizontal axis; an increase in the market price of fish or in the growth rate will shift it up, etc.

At any combination of effort above the OA_2 curve, revenue in fishery 2 will be less than cost, and so effort will tend to decrease. This can be easily demonstrated by noting that, at any point on the OA_2 curve, profit in fishery 2 is zero. Points above the curve represent an increase in E_2 for any level of E_1, which is analogous to an increase in effort from the open-access equilibrium in figure 2.3. Revenues fall below costs, and there will be a tendency for vessels to leave the fishery. By the same token, at any combination of effort below the curve, revenues will be greater than cost, and so effort will increase. The arrows in the diagram indicate the direction in which E_2 will likely change at various combinations of effort in the two fisheries.

The curve labeled OA_1 is the open-access equilibrium curve for fishery 1 and is subject to an identical interpretation. It shows the open-access equilibrium level of effort in fishery 1 for various levels of effort in fishery 2, given existing market conditions. At any combination of effort to the left of the curve, revenue will be greater than cost and so effort in fishery 1 will increase while the opposite is true for combinations to the right of the curve. Again the arrows indicate the likely direction of change in E_1 at various places in the diagram.

Since each curve represents the open-access level of effort in one fishery for various levels in the other, the intersection of the curves at point A represents a simultaneous open-access equilibrium of both. Only at this combination of effort will revenue equal cost in both fisheries, given the level of effort in the other.

Because of the indicated direction of change in the level of effort in both fisheries at points other than the equilibrium (see arrows), there is reason to believe that this will be a stable equilibrium. The movement toward an equilibrium depends upon the rate and direction of change in both the population size and the level of effort in both fisheries. With certain relative rates of change, a bioeconomic equilibrium will actually occur. With other relative rates, continual oscillation in the levels of effort and stock sizes will occur, and with still others a population can fall so fast that it will be physically destroyed or reduced to a level where commercial exploitation is no longer feasible. In summary, while the intersection of the two curves can describe the location of the joint open-access equilibrium, further study of the biological and economic factors is necessary to ascertain if it will ever be reached. See the discussion in the last section of chapter 4.

Consider the following situations where the biological and economic parameters are such that the open-access equilibrium curves are in different relative positions. If the open-access curve for fishery 2 shifts to OA_{2a} in figure 5.8, the equilibrium will occur on the horizontal axis at E_{11}. Fishery 2 will not produce any effort unless fishery 1 is operating at a level greater than E_{12}, but since the latter will produce only E_{11} units of effort when fishery 2 is not operating, under open-access conditions fishery 2 will not be commercially active. If OA_{1a} and OA_2 are the equilibrium curves, the situation is reversed and only fishery 2 will be commercially active at a level of effort equal to E_{21}. Finally, if OA_{1a} and OA_{2a} are the curves, neither fishery will operate; they both need a positive level of effort in the other fishery before their stock is strong enough such that revenues will cover costs, and therefore neither will initiate operations. There is, of course, nothing special about the case where one or both of the fisheries are not commercially active; it merely means that no commercial market exists even though there is a viable population.

Although the analysis of open access where the two stocks have a predator-prey relationship is similar, there are some fundamental differences and more possible general equilibrium positions. As such, it is worthwhile to discuss this situation briefly.

Let S_1 be the predator stock and S_2 be the prey. The slope of the open-access equilibrium curves will be as pictured in figure 5.9. The slope of the open-access curve for the fishery exploiting the prey stock will be positive as before, but the curve for the fishery on the predator stock will have a negative slope, relative to the E_1 axis. An increase in E_2 will decrease the prey stock, which in the long run will mean a decrease in the open-access equilibrium level of E_1. To be specific, an increase in E_2 will decrease the sustained yield curve for S_1, which will cause the sustained revenue curve to intersect the cost curve at a lower level of effort. It is possible that there will be no open-access equilibrium curve for the predator stock, at least not in the positive quadrant. This would be the case where, even when E_2 is zero and the prey stock is as

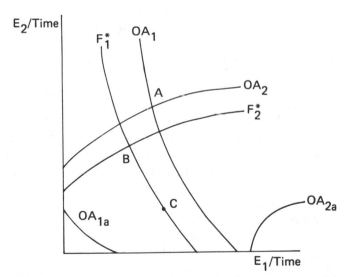

Figure 5.9. *Two Fleets, Biological Interdependence: Predator-Prey Stocks.* The OA and the F^* curves for the fishery that focus on the predator stock (fishery 1) will be negatively sloped because increases in effort in fishery 2 will decrease the food supply for its stock. The analysis of open access and MEY is the same, however.

large as possible, the predator stock is not commercially exploitable (i.e., costs are less than revenues for all levels of effort).

Let us now consider possible equilibrium positions. If OA_1 and OA_2 are the open-access equilibrium curves, the equilibrium will occur at their intersection, and both fisheries will be commercially active. The opposite extreme would occur if there were no curve for fishery 1, for the reasons explained above, and OA_{2a} were the curve for fishery 2; neither fishery would be capable of sustaining any level of effort under the existing market conditions. If OA_{2a} and OA_1 are the curves, only fishery 1 will be commercially active, but if OA_{1a} and OA_2 are the curves, only fishery 2 will be active. The two situations appear similar, but they occur for different reasons. In the first instance (i.e., OA_1 and OA_{2a}), under open access E_1 will not get high enough (i.e., P_1 will not be pushed low enough) to allow the prey stock to become commercially profitable. In order to make it so, E_1 would have to be increased. On the other hand, with OA_{1a} and OA_2, the open-access level of E_2 is so high (i.e., the stock of Pa_2 is so low) that the predator fishery is no longer profitable. In order to make it so, E_2 would have to be decreased. In other words, in the first case the exploitation of the predator is not high enough to allow for commercial exploitation of the prey stock, and in the second the open-access exploitation of the prey stock will reduce it to such a low population size that the fishery for the predator stock will be commercially destroyed although it will still be biologically viable.

To summarize the open-access analysis, using graphical techniques it is possible to show where an equilibrium will be. The path to that equilibrium will depend upon the interrelated reaction speeds of the fleets and the stocks. At this equilibrium, it is possible to have none, one, or both of the fisheries commercially active.

Let us turn now to the problem of optimal utilization. In an independent fishery, the optimizing rule for maximizing the present value of harvest is that, in any given period, effort should be increased as long as the value of additional harvest is greater than the sum of marginal harvesting cost and marginal user cost. The latter cost is the change in the present value of future harvests. When fisheries are interrelated, it is no longer possible to talk about optimal utilization of each fishery. Optimization must be a simultaneous process, taking account of the interrelationship between the fisheries. To be specific, the goal should be to maximize the present value of the sum of their harvests. The optimizing rule for each fishery is that in any period effort should be expanded as long as the value of harvest in that fishery is greater than harvest costs, any decrease in the present harvest in the other fishery due to the biological interrelationships, and the user cost in terms of the change in the present value of future harvest from both fisheries.

The curves labeled F_1^* and F_2^* in figures 5.8 and 5.9 are analogous to the OA curves in that they show the stationary optimal level of effort in one fishery for a given level of effort in the other. The shape and position of the F^*

curves are related to the biological and economic parameters of the two fisheries as well as to the discount rate. For purposes of discussion, assume that the F^* curves are for the same conditions that generate curves OA_1 and OA_2 and an open-access equilibrium at point A. If the discount rate is infinite, the F^* curves will be the same as the OA curves. With a positive discount rate, the F^* curve will be inside the companion OA curve. The actual distance between the two curves depends upon the size of the discount rate. The lower the discount rate, the further toward the respective axes the F^* curve will be.

The intersection of these F^* curves represents the stationary optimal joint combination of effort for the two fisheries. With competitive stocks the OA curves are shaped such that the optimum combination at point B will always contain less of both types of effort. See figure 5.8. On the other hand, if there is a predator-prey relationship, this is not necessarily the case. As drawn in figure 5.9, the F^* curves do in fact intersect such that there is a smaller amount of both types of effort, but if the F_2^* curve were lower it could intersect at point C on the F_1^*, indicating that the optimal combination of effort would require an increase in effort in fishery 1. The reasoning behind this possibility is that it may be necessary to push down the predator stock so that the prey stock could increase and produce more.

In both instances it is possible that optimal utilization may involve utilization of only one of the fisheries. For example, in figure 5.8 if the F_1^* curve were to intersect the vertical axis above the F_2^* curve, then optimal E_1 should be zero and optimal E_2 should be E_{20}. Such a situation could arise if S_1 were quite low and could only be increased by high levels of E_2, but given the returns in fishery 2 and any potential gains in fishery 1, it does not make sense to increase E_2 that much.

A similar situation could occur in figure 5.9 if the F_2^* curve intersected the horizontal axis to the right of F_1^*. Here the optimal amount of E_2 would be zero. Such a situation could occur if the predator stock were relatively more valuable and the returns to the prey stock were higher if used as a food supply to the other fishery.

Two Fleets, Technological Interdependence

Fisheries are technologically interdependent if the gear of either affects the man-made mortality of the stock exploited by the other. Consider two fisheries, fishery 1 and fishery 2, and assume that, while each fishery directs its effort at a particular stock, it also obtains incidental catch from the other stock in the process of fishing. That is, fleet 1 directs its effort at stock 1 but catches fish from stock 2 as well. Similarly, fleet 2 directs at stock 2 but obtains some catch from stock 1.

Because of this technological interrelationship, the size of both stocks is a function of the level of effort in both fisheries. These fisheries may be said to have an interfishery direct effect. A change in the level of effort in one fishery will, through mortality, have a direct effect on the equilibrium population size of the stock at which the other directs its effort. (Recall that in the previous case there was an indirect effect between the fisheries through the biological interrelationships of the population.) Here again, the sustained yield from both stocks will be a function of the level of effort in both fisheries. However, since these yields will be divided between the fleets, the sustainable revenue curve analysis is not directly applicable in this case. Nonetheless, it is still possible to make a straightforward analysis of open-access and optimal utilization of the two fisheries.

The revenue in each fishery will be the sum of the market returns from the directed and incidental catches. However, since the sustained yield from either stock is a function of the effort from both fleets, the actual returns generated for any level of effort in one fishery will depend upon the amount of fishing effort in the other fishery.

To make this explicit, the sustained profit equations for the two fisheries can be represented as follows,

$$\text{Profit}_1 = P_1 Y_{11} (E_1, E_2) + P_2 Y_{21} (E_1, E_2) - C_1 E_1 \qquad \text{(fishery 1)}$$

$$\text{Profit}_2 = P_2 Y_{22} (E_1, E_2) + P_1 Y_{12} (E_1, E_2) - C_2 E_2 \qquad \text{(fishery 2)}$$

where the P's and C's represent the prices for the fish of, and the cost of effort directed at, the indicated stocks. The y_{ij} terms represent the sustained catch of ith stock by the jth fishery. When i and j are the same it is a directed catch, and where they are different it is an incidental catch.

Here again, the open-access equilibrium level of effort in one fishery depends upon the level of effort in the other. The open-access equilibrium curves showing the equilibrium amount of effort that will be produced in one fishery for a given level of effort in the other are plotted in figure 5.10. Because of the interfishery direct effect, the open-access amount of effort in each fishery will fall as the level of effort increases in the other. As effort in one fishery goes up, the sustained yield for both direct and incidental catch obtained by the other fishery will go down, causing its open-access level of effort to fall. The shape and position of the OA curves will depend upon the biological and economic parameters of the two fisheries. Increases in the cost of effort will shift the curves in, while price increases or improvements in the natural productivity of the stock will shift them out.

At the intersection of these two curves, both fisheries will be in an open-access equilibrium for the given level of effort in the other, and so a simultaneous open-access equilibrium will exist. If no intersection exists in the positive quadrant, then only one or neither of the fisheries will be commercially active. This can be demonstrated using figure 5.10. The case where neither fishery will be active will occur when neither of the open-access curves is present in the positive quadrant, that is, when the returns are so low relative to costs that effort in both fisheries will be zero, regardless of the level of effort in the other.

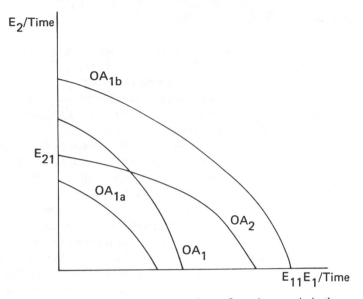

Figure 5.10. *Two Fleets, Technological Interdependence: Open Access.* As in the case of biological interdependence, open-access equilibrium may involve exclusive operation of one or the other of the fleets, or both fleets may operate simultaneously, depending upon the intersection of the *OA* curves.

If OA_1 and OA_2 are the relevant curves, a simultaneous open-access equilibrium at their intersection is possible. If OA_{1a} and OA_2 are the curves, the equilibrium will be on the vertical axis at E_{21}. The open-access equilibrium level of effort in fishery 2 will have such a high incidental catch for stock 1 that fishery 1 will not be commercially profitable. The opposite will occur when OA_{1b} and OA_2 are the curves. The equilibrium will occur on the horizontal axis at E_{11}. The open-access equilibrium level of effort in fishery 1 will obtain such a high incidental catch from stock 2 that fishery 2 will be rendered commercially unprofitable. When the open-access situation is such that only one fleet is operating, this analysis degenerates to the one fleet, multiple joint-stock fishery case, and as mentioned above, it is possible that one of the stocks can be destroyed as a by-product of heavy fishing for the other.

Again, because of the interdependence of the two stocks, optimal exploitation must be a simultaneous process where these interdependencies are given direct consideration. As with the previous case, it is necessary to select the level of effort in both fisheries, taking into account the direct interfishery effects. In any period of time, effort should be expanded in both fisheries as long as the value of the direct and incidental harvest is greater than harvesting costs, any decrease in current direct and incidental harvest by the other fleet, and the user cost in terms of foregone present value of harvest from both fisheries.

The relationships between the optimal stationary equilibrium effort in both fisheries for a given level of effort in the other are plotted as the $F*$ curves in figure 5.11, along with the open-access equilibrium curves. As drawn, the open-access equilibrium, if one is possible, will occur at point A while the stationary optimal joint-effort combination is at point B. Note that, at the optimum point, there is a smaller amount of both E_1 and E_2, but this need not be the case. If the F_2* curve were higher, the optimal combination of effort would contain a larger amount of E_2 than would the open access. In fact, if the F_2* curve shifted up such that it was above the F_1* curve, optimal exploitation would call for the ultimate removal of the first fleet and an increase in the second, as compared with open access. The same sort of thing could hold true for fishery 1 if the F_1* curve were to shift to the right.

To summarize the results of the previous two sections, note first that, when analyzing biologically or technologically interdependent fisheries, it is necessary to think in terms of combinations of effort from the two fisheries. There is an open-access combination, and an optimal combination and effort from one or both of the fleets can be zero in either of these combinations. Also, the move to the optimal combination may, in some cases, involve an increase in one of the types of effort. To be precise, there is an optimal way to change from the open-access to the optimal combination, and many of the points raised in the analyses of single species fisheries with respect to this change apply here as well. To be frank, however, as Clark (1976) has pointed

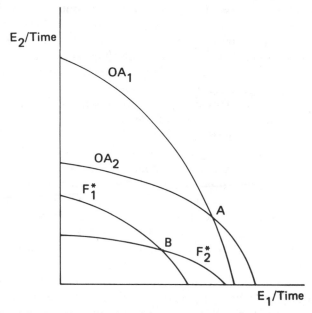

Figure 5.11. *Two Fleets, Technological Interdependence: MEY.* As in the case of biological interdependence, the MEY point may require a decrease in both fleets or an increase in one and a decrease in the other, depending on the shapes and positions of the *OA* and the *F** curves.

out, the technical solution to discovering the exact nature of this path may well be impossible. Nonetheless, the basic points apply and can be helpful in obtaining heuristic solutions that can be quite useful, given the availability and reliability of the required fisheries data.

Two Fleets, One Stock

It is often the case that different types of fleets will exploit the same stock. For example, gill-netters from one port could compete with trawlers from another port. Another example that is receiving more and more attention is recreational fishermen competing with a commercial fleet for the same stock of fish. Because both fleets or groups are working on the same stock, the operation of one will have a direct effect on the other. An increase in effort by one group can have repercussions on stock size, and this will affect the yield of the other group. The analysis of this case is very similar to the previous one, but because it exists so often it will be useful to discuss it separately. For ease of exposition, the discussion will be in terms of joint harvest by a commercial fleet and recreationalists. Figure 5.12 is similar to figures 5.10 and 5.11 ex-

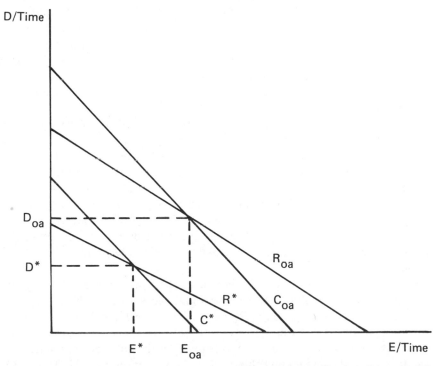

Figure 5.12. *Two Fleets, One Stock.*   Joint commercial-recreational utilization of the same fish stock can be described in terms of open-access and optimal utilization curves that are analogous to those used in the analyses of biologically and technologically interdependent stocks.

cept that E on the horizontal axis represents a commercial fishing effort while D on the vertical axis represents recreational fishing days.

The curve labeled C_{oa}, in figure 5.12 shows the amounts of E that will provide an equilibrium in the commercial fishery for various levels of effort in the recreational fishery. Similarly, the R_{oa} curve shows the amount of D that will provide an equilibrium in the recreational fishery for various levels of effort in the commercial fishery. The intersection of the two curves represents a general equilibrium point for both fisheries because the amount of effort in both fisheries at this point is in equilibrium combination with the amount in the other. As the curves are drawn, the equilibrium combination at E_{oa} and D_{oa} gives a positive amount of effort in both fisheries. It is possible, however, that these two curves may not intersect in the positive quadrant. If the C_{oa} curve is below the R_{oa} curve, the equilibrium will occur at the vertical intercept of the R_{oa} curve, and there will be no commercial fishery. Similarly, an equilibrium could occur at the horizontal intercept of the C_{oa} curve where there is no recreational fishing at open access. The former would occur if the relative returns to commercial fishing were so high that E is high enough to push the stock down such that recreational fishing would yield no benefits. The latter would occur in the opposite case.

The open-access combination of commercial and recreational fishing will not be optimal as far as economic efficiency is concerned, however, for the very reasons described in the single sector models above. In addition, the open-access point will be suboptimal because of the negative effects the commercial and recreational sectors are imposing on each other. The economically optimal point occurs where the sum of the values generated in both sectors is maximized.

Optimal utilization in the commercial fleet requires that E be expanded in any period as long as the value of extra commercial harvest is greater than the sum of marginal harvesting cost, the change in the current value generated in the recreational fishery, and the marginal user cost. Simultaneously, recreational fishing should be allowed to increase as long as the value of the last day is greater than the sum of the decrease in the current value of other recreational fishing days, plus any change in the value of commercial harvest and marginal user cost. In both cases, marginal user cost represents the change in the present value of the sum of commercial returns and recreational value.

The curves labeled C^* and R^* in figure 5.12 represent the stationary optimum level of effort in one fishery for a given level in the other. They will always lay inside the C_{oa} and the R_{oa} curves, respectively, and each one shows the optimal amount of one type of effort given a specified amount of the other. The intersection of the two curves provides the optimal combination of recreational and commercial fishing effort. This is represented as D^* and E^* in the figure. Note that, as pictured, the optimal combination contains less of both types of effort than does the open-access equilibrium. Again, this will not always be the case. For example, if the $R*$ curve were shifted up, it would be possible to achieve an intersection with the $C*$ curve at a level of D higher than D_{oa}. In this case, the optimal regulation of the combined fishery would call for a reduction in commercial fishing but would allow for an increase in recreational fishing. Note also that, if the $R*$ curve were shifted higher, it could intersect the $C*$ curve in the second quadrant. In that instance, the optimal combination would occur at the intersection of the $R*$ curve and the vertical axis, and optimality would require that commercial fishing be eliminated. Of course, the reverse could be true if the $C*$ curve were to shift up. In addition, the optimal point could occur where it is only optimal to have exclusive commercial or recreational fishing.

6

Regulation

Introduction

The discussion thus far has centered on why an open-access fishery will not operate in an optimal way and how a fishery managed to achieve economic efficiency should operate. An important conclusion of the discussion of the latter is that the concept of optimal use is multidimensional. In the first place, optimal fishery operation is a time pattern of harvest that more than likely involves changes in annual catch and effort, at least initially. Further, optimal utilization at any point in time must specify the size of total catch, the size of individual fish being harvested, the size and composition of the fleet, and details of vessel operation levels and spatial and temporal deployment on different stocks. All this is necessary to insure that the correct amount of fish is being caught at the proper size, at the proper time, and at the lowest possible cost.

Optimal fisheries regulation, in terms of this discussion, can be viewed as that combination of government policies and programs which causes a change in vessel and fleet operations from the open-access to the optimal time pattern of utilization. In addition to addressing the multidimensional aspects of optimal fisheries utilization as far as it is reasonable to do so, a proper regulation regime should also have the following characteristics:

1. It should encourage innovation and research into new fishing methods.
2. It should be flexible enough to allow for proper reaction to changes in economic and biological conditions.
3. It should have the support of the majority of the fishermen involved.
4. It must also take full cognizance of the costs of negotiations, research, and enforcement necessary to undertake the program; if these costs are not less than the benefits to be gained from regulating, the program cannot be justified.
5. Finally, its effects on the distribution of wealth and on other manage-

ment objectives such as maintaining employment, improving the balance of trade, etc., must be acceptable.

Changing the vessel and fleet operations from the open-access to the MEY time path can be viewed as a reallocation of resources in the economy, as described in chapter 1. It generally involves a net movement from the fishery to other productive uses in the economy. The difficulties of reallocating resources in a complicated modern economy are compounded when the resources include the services of human beings with different skills and, just as important, with different motivations concerning types and locations of work. Also, since sociological factors are just as vital as economic ones in determining the proper assimilation rate, the period over which a regulation program is instituted is important. Therefore, proper regulation must do more than strive for an optimal level of effort; it must also find the proper time path for moving toward it. The exact timing will depend largely upon the speed with which released resources can be smoothly assimilated into other parts of the economy and upon the rate of growth of the fish stock.

The purpose of this chapter is to evaluate the various types of fishery regulatory techniques as to their appropriate use in an optimal management plan. The primary focus will be on economic efficiency attributes, although other objectives of management will be addressed as well. The first section, which comprises the major part of the chapter, will describe the efficiency effects of the various techniques, given that they can be suitably instituted, and it will be shown that while some regulations directly or indirectly cause economic inefficiency in harvest and are often biologically ineffective as well, others have neither of these weaknesses. The second section briefly describes how the share system of remuneration can be affected by regulation. The third section expands the analysis in the first by considering the economic efficiency effects of actually implementing regulation programs, and it is shown that the range of useful techniques is broader than might be expected from the previous analysis. Following this, a suggested process for developing fishery management policy is presented. The final section is an introduction to the problems of international management.

Although this is a very long chapter covering many issues, it is possible to summarize a main concept that will be reinforced throughout, and it will be useful to anticipate the discussion by presenting it here. There is no one optimal management technique that applies equally well in all situations. The correct choice depends upon the biological, economic, and institutional peculiarities of the particular fishery involved.

Economic Analysis of Regulatory Techniques

Types of Techniques

The object of regulation is to cause the fishery to change from the open-access harvest time pattern to a more desirable pattern. (While we have nor-

mally referred to the MEY harvest time path as a desirable objective of regulation, others may elect to move toward another path. The economic analysis
that follows, however, applies, no matter what time path is chosen as a goal.)
The open-access pattern is determined by the individual decisions of private
fishermen, each operating such that profits are maximized. Accordingly, the
harvest pattern can be modified by changing the profitability of various components of the individual fisherman's operation. It will be recalled that catch
per boat depends upon the catch per unit of effort, which is a function of
aggregate effort and the amount of effort produced by the boat. For purposes
here, however, it is important to realize that fishing effort is produced by
combining various inputs. Therefore, the profit function for a typical boat
can be expressed as follows:

$$\text{Boat Profit} = P_F \text{FE} (m, f_1, f_2, \ldots f_n) - \sum_{i=1}^{n} w_i f_i \qquad (6.1)$$

where

P_F $\qquad$ = price of fish
F $\qquad$ = catch per unit effort
E $\qquad$ = vessel effort
m $\qquad$ = mesh size
f_i $\qquad$ = inputs, $i = 1$ to n
w_i $\qquad$ = cost of input, i

Total revenue depends upon the price of fish and the amount of fish caught.
As far as the boat is concerned, the latter is determined by the level of vessel
effort, which is a function of the mesh size and the type and quantity of the
various inputs used. Total cost will be a function of the amounts and prices of
the inputs. The profit-maximizing vessel operator will choose that combination of inputs which maximizes profits. This involves choosing both the
proper level of output and the combination of inputs which will produce that
output at the lowest possible cost. The effect of mesh size on output should be
obvious by now, and it can also affect costs. For example, mesh size may
affect the drag on the vessel and hence fuel consumption.

This analysis stresses the point that effort can be produced in any number
of ways. Effort is a function of the size, power, and type of boat, the type of
gear, the temporal and spatial distribution of fishing, the crew size, and the
special skills of the captain or the crew. Depending on the relative prices of
these various inputs, cost to the boat will be minimized by using different
combinations. For example, if the price of gasoline is very high, the cost-effective input combination will likely involve fishing longer hours near shore
with a larger crew rather than fishing long distances from port. These aspects
of effort production are important because regulation can affect the type of

inputs and the way they can be used, which can obviously have an effect on the efficiency of producing effort and ultimately on the efficiency of harvest.

To return to the main argument, changes in fishing behavior can be achieved by changing the way in which operators are allowed to pursue profits. In fact, although there are many ways to classify regulatory techniques, one useful way is to divide them according to which parts of the profit equation they affect—the prices or the quantities. Prices received for selling fish or paid for inputs can be affected by user taxes and subsidies. Taxes will decrease profits, thereby having a tendency to decrease effort, while subsidies will do the reverse. On the other hand, the harvest level or the quantity of all or some of the inputs can be controlled. This is, in fact, what traditional fisheries regulations have attempted to do. Gear restrictions affect the type and amount of inputs employed, while area and time closures affect the way inputs can be used. License limitation programs restrict the number of vessels or fishermen allowed to operate. Total quotas for the fishery as a whole have an indirect effect on input usage because individual fishermen realize that their total catch can be limited by the combined behavior of the entire fleet. They will, therefore, be motivated to obtain their harvest as quickly as possible in order to ensure a profitable year before the total quota is reached. This extra speed will entail a change in fishing behavior and hence a change in the types of inputs employed and the way they are used. Mesh or hook size restrictions can affect the size of fish captured, which can have both short- and long-term effects on profits through changes in total harvest and revenues if price varies with the size of fish. Further, if mesh size restrictions can affect the drag of the net, those regulations can also affect profits through the cost of operating the vessel.

Another regulation that affects the quantity part of the profit equation is the individual quota system. Under this program, those vessels allowed to fish are permitted a specified harvest each year. In order to maximize profits, the boat owner must plan operations such that the fixed amount can be harvested as cheaply as possible.

Of the above regulations, only taxes, license limitation programs, and individual quotas have the potential truly to limit access to the fishery. As such, they are frequently classified as *limited-entry techniques*. For lack of a better word, the others can be called *open-access techniques.*

In the subsections to follow, each of these regulation types will be described and analyzed in more detail. Before doing so, however, it will be useful to discuss briefly some of the realities of management in the real world.

Most management programs in the past have consisted of regulations restricting the ability to produce effort of at least part of the participants in the fishery. The regulations have normally been imposed for one of two reasons: to save the fish stock from destruction or to protect the economic position of certain groups in the fishery. In neither case were the complete economic ramifications considered. Prohibiting the use of efficient techniques can, at least in the short run, prevent the destruction of the fishery since catches are decreased. It can also protect the earning power of those fishermen tied to old, inefficient means of fishing. It will not, however, guarantee that the proper amount of fish will be taken at the minimum cost to society.

Most fishery regulations are passed only at the insistence of those in the industry, especially the fishermen. Although the whole economy will benefit from proper management, the gain to the average noninvolved citizen is neither evident enough nor large enough to induce his active support in the political arena. Obviously, fishermen whose incomes are at stake will be highly motivated to push for laws favorable to them and will never argue for regulations that may exclude them from the fishery. This is especially true since, once they leave, some of the economic rent of the fishery may accrue to the survivors. On the whole, they will oppose regulations that restrict effort (unless, of course, it is the effort of others that is affected) while supporting some controls if they see that the fish stock may otherwise be destroyed. Even then they will favor only those types that still permit them free access to the fishery, such as gear restrictions or closed seasons. As will be shown later, such measures offer no effective long-run solution; at best, they help the fish stock by temporarily cutting down total effort in such a way that the fishermen's proportionate chances of catching fish are unchanged.

Where fishermen with different types of gear work the same stock, each group (like any other special-interest group in a modern economy) can be expected to propose regulations beneficial to its earning potential. Users of any given type of gear will try to prevent the introduction of more efficient or more diversified gear that will cut down the catch available to them. Customarily, their argument for restrictions will be in terms of saving the fishery; they will say that more powerful gear will destroy the fish stock. Properly regulated, the disputed gear may or may not destroy the fishery; all it will do for sure is lower the income of certain groups of fishermen. Granted, these aspects of income distribution are an important element in regulation and will be discussed in detail below.

Because the individual in an open-access fishery can see potential benefits only from such regulations as will conserve the stock without hurting his relative position or as will place him in a favored position, he will have reason to oppose any other. Given the institutional procedures for getting regulations approved, it is not surprising that only open-access regulations have been the historical norm.

Regulations That Affect the Size of Fish Caught

Regulations of this type may be justified on two grounds. First, it may prevent the ultimate destruction of the fishery by restricting effort at times when the stock is particularly vulnerable. Second, it may be an essential part of a program to obtain an MEY by providing the possibility of increases in catch at a later time or of eumetric fishing, the latter of which, as explained in the last chapter, is the proper combination of gear selectivity and total effort. The main types of regulation that fall into this classification are prohibitions of fishing in nursery areas (usually referred to as area closures), seasonal closures, size limits, and required selectivity of gear.

If, in fact, the fish do congregate in a specific area at certain critical periods in their life cycles, or if they are particularly susceptible to catch during certain times of the year, then curtailment of effort in these areas or at these times may be necessary. It should be noted, however, that if the fish are in the same area at the same time every year, the two types of regulation are effectively the same thing. Other types of regulations that restrict the total amount of effort may serve just as well, however. Whether, in fact, closures are necessary to protect the stock is essentially a question that should be answered by solid biological evidence before such measures are imposed. Their ostensible goal of "saving the stock" may cloak the real purpose of benefiting a certain group in the fishery.

There are two sides to the question of restricting the size of fish caught in order to increase the catch in later periods. First, will the particular regulation actually reduce the present catch? Second, will the increased future value of the catch justify the immediate reduction? To answer the first part, area and seasonal closures will, again, be effective only if the stock exhibits a distinct spatial or temporal distribution. If these fish are generally available in many areas during most parts of the year and if the cost of effort is not sensitive to place or to the length or the timing of the season, these restrictions will change the location or the time of catch but not the total amount.

Size limits will be effective only if the fish can be returned to the water safely or if their size can be determined before capture, as in whaling. Unless this is the case, mortality may not be reduced; true, only fish above a certain size will actually be sold, but smaller ones will be uselessly killed. Not only does this waste the fish; it also increases cost due to the sorting and disposal of the undersized fish while doing nothing to protect the stock.

It should be pointed out, however, that size limits may have positive long-run benefits because fishermen will be motivated by self-interest to plan their fishing in order to reduce the catch of sublegal fish. Their costs of sorting may be lower if they fish at those times or in those areas where fewer small fish are caught or if they develop new techniques that will selectively harvest the larger fish.

Regulation on the size of fish to be taken also faces some limitations. It works fairly well in trawl fisheries but only over a range of sizes. In long-line fisheries, the size of fish caught can be influenced by the size of the hook, but the relationship is not exact. When a purse seine is used, it is almost impossible to regulate the size at capture. Regulation by size is even more troublesome in multispecies fisheries, where the same gear harvests more than one type of fish. A mesh large enough to allow one species to grow to optimal size may permit practically all of another species to escape permanently. A smaller mesh, on the other hand, will reduce or even destroy the stock of the first species while allowing a reasonable catch in the second. Proper utilization of such fisheries will require regulation more complex than by size alone.

The only economic justification for regulating the size of fish caught is the hope of insuring a larger future value of catch. For this hope to be realistic, the stock must meet certain requirements. First, those fish protected by the regulations must be susceptible to the gear at a later time with a fairly high probability of catch. Second, the individual growth rate must usually be large relative to the natural mortality rate, so that the future value of the catch will compensate for the extra time allotted. Only if the present value of the expected future catch exceeds the value of the possible immediate catch can these regulations be justified. Under no other circumstances would society benefit by foregoing fishing today in expectation of a larger catch in the future.

Catch can become more valuable over time for several reasons. First, the total weight may be greater. Second, larger-sized fish may have a higher market price per unit. If both of these conditions hold, then value will surely go up in the future; it is possible, too, that an increase in unit value can even make up for a decrease in the total weight. It should be remembered, however, that a simple rise in the value of future catches is not enough; the increase must be sufficient to compensate for the extra waiting time to consumption. The same basic argument applies to gear restrictions for eumetric fishing. The increase in the value of future catches must overbalance the decrease in present catch, requisite to allowing the fish to grow.

The effect of size regulation on costs of capture must also be considered, to insure that the net value of future catch will be adequately increased. For example, prohibition of fishing in a nursery area may mean that the fish must be taken when they are spread out over a larger area, so even though the actual catch is larger, it may be much more expensive to harvest. Gear regulations may affect direct costs, for example, as a beneficial side effect: a larger mesh size may reduce the drag, thus saving fuel costs.

Even with due consideration of all these factors, however, the use of size regulation exclusively will not ordinarily lead to a proper use of the fishery. For example, if restrictions on gear selectivity do increase the net value of catch at the existing level of activity, the increased profit position will attract more effort. As a result, at least some of the potential rents can be lost in increased costs. Therefore, size regulations will produce their greatest advantage if used in combination with other controls that limit total fishing pressure.

In summary, an optimal fishery management plan may include regulations restricting the size of fish at first capture if this method seems best adapted to save the stock from actual destruction or if it can provide a sufficiently large increase in the value of future catches. Even with such justification, however, the exclusive use of such controls is highly unlikely to produce the proper harvest of fish at minimum cost.

Closed Seasons, Closed Areas, Size Limitation, and Quotas

The effects of closed seasons, closed areas, and, to some extent, size limitation are very closely related. In fact, if the various year-classes within the fish stock grow and migrate in a similar way each year, the methods are analytically indistinguishable. Prohibition of fishing in a particular area, for instance, effectively prohibits fishing during certain times of the year and for certain size fish. To review briefly, if the major portion of the population is available at all times of the year and in many different areas, these regulations will simply cause effort to be expanded in other places and at other times at higher cost. Therefore, only in limited cases will they be effective in changing the average size at which fish are harvested or in reducing the total amount of effort. As mentioned earlier, regulation of the size of fish at harvest can be justified only in specific instances in which the stock is particularly vulnerable and there is no better way to protect them, or in which putting off catch now will sufficiently increase the value of future catches.

In many ways, quotas act in the same way (at least in the short run) as seasonal and area closures, since the timing or length of such restriction is usually based on the amount of fish the regulatory agency thinks should be harvested during a given period. In their effect, closures are simply an indirect way of setting a quota.

As was stated above, fishermen will choose that combination of inputs which minimizes the cost of producing any given level of effort per period. And in the long run, competition among fishermen in an open-access fishery will force each to operate at that level of output where average cost is a minimum (see the section on the individual fisherman in chapter 3). The fishery-wide total cost curves in this book are based on minimum costs thus determined: for example, consider the total cost curve labeled TC_1 in the upper left-hand quadrant of figure 6.1. It shows that if E_1 units of effort are produced each period, the minimum cost of doing so is C_1. Similarly, the minimum cost of producing E_2 units per period is C_2. Recall that the time dimension is very important and that producing E_1 units of effort in a shorter period will normally entail a greater cost than C_1.

Bearing these fundamentals of cost derivation in mind, let us consider how these types of regulations will affect the cost of producing effort and, consequently, the operation of the fishery. The discussion will be in terms of the diagrams in figure 6.1a. As before, the revenue curves are drawn assuming a constant price for fish. (In both cases, TC_1 is the cost curve of the unregulated fishery; in case I it intersects the total revenue curve where its slope is positive, while in case II the intersection is where the slope is negative. Most

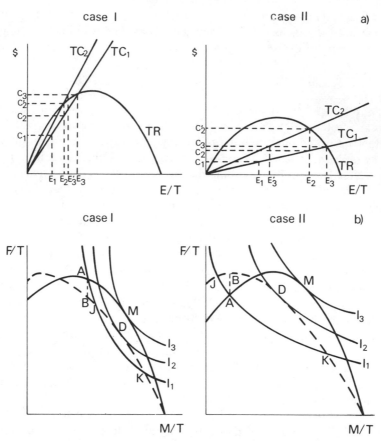

Figure 6.1. *Regulation by Inefficiency.* Forced inefficiencies will reduce the open-access level of effort by increasing unit costs. Inefficiencies will shift the economy to the dotted production possibility curve pictured in both parts of figure 6.1b. While it is possible that this may result in an increase in welfare from the open-access equilibrium, this is not always the case. Also, it will always prevent the economy from achieving maximum potential consumer satisfaction, given productive constraints.

of the analysis involves case I, but the analysis of case II is similar. The latter will enter the discussion explicitly only when there are significant variances, but the interested reader should have no trouble in making the appropriate comparisons along the way.) The open-access equilibrium level of effort will be E_3 units of effort per period. At this point costs for the fishery are C_3. Assume that MEY occurs at E_1.

Let us consider first restrictions on time and area fished. Both will cause the cost of producing effort, where effort is defined in terms of the effect on the stock, to go up because of the constraints that are put on the way inputs can be used. Put very simply, time restrictions limit the duration of use of capital equipment (i.e., the boat), which means that it must be used more

intensively during that period and/or in combination with more variable inputs (i.e., men, nets, winches, etc.) in order to produce effort beyond the
point where the time limit becomes binding. Therefore, beyond that point,
the average cost of producing effort must increase, which means that the average cost curve for the individual fisherman will shift upward. Assuming that a
time limit does in fact cut down on the time that would ordinarily be spent
fishing, this means that the total cost curve for the fishery as a whole (which
represents the minimum point on the average cost curve on the representative
boat) will be shifted up. Similarly, to the extent that area closures force fishermen to use more costly methods to effect the same amount of effort on the
fish stock by forcing them to fish on less productive grounds, the cost curves
for the individual fishermen and the fishery as a whole will also shift up. For
purposes of discussion, assume that TC_2 is the total cost curve for the fishery
with certain time restrictions. This means that the cost of producing E_2 units
in the shorter time period or in other areas has increased from C_2 to C_2'. The
new equilibrium point for the fishery will occur where the new total cost curve
intersects the total revenue curve (i.e., at E_2). Note that, as the curves are
drawn here, the end result is a net reduction in effort and a decrease in catch,
revenue, and cost. Effort is reduced, but only through the indirect effect of its
greater total cost. Note that case II shows an increase in catch, revenue, and
cost at the lower equilibrium level of effort. In both cases, however, at the new
equilibrium, effort is being produced at a cost higher than necessary. Note
also that, in order to force the fishery to operate at E_1—the level of effort that
achieves a steady state MEY—it will be necessary to implement further restrictions to push the cost curve up so that it intersects the revenue curve at
E_1. Even if this were accomplished, however, it could in no way be considered
a maximum economic yield, because although effort is at its proper level, it is
not being produced as efficiently as possible.

　　Let us now turn to quotas, which are regulations prohibiting further fishing once a specified catch has been taken. In terms of figure 6.1a, the proper
quota would prohibit further fishing after effort has reached E_1 per period,
because at that point the proper amounts have been taken. The potential
profit at that point will encourage each fisherman to increase his fishing
power so that he can bring in a larger individual share of the catch before the
overall quota is reached. To do this, each must organize his activities to produce effort faster, which will lead to an increase in average cost. This race
against time will continue until the total cost of producing the effort necessary
to catch the quota equals the total revenue at that point. Referring to the
diagram, fishermen will keep striving to decrease the time it takes to produce
a unit of effort, which will, at the same time, increase their costs, until the
total cost curve intersects the total revenue curve at E_1. Although the proper
catch is taken in each period, the cost of doing so is definitely not a minimum.
It should also be noted that the allotted catch is achieved faster than it would
have been in the absence of a quota.

Other important economic consequences arise from these types of regulation. First is the problem of what happens to the men and equipment excluded from fishing. As long as they remain idle, society is losing part of its productive capacity. If the sustained yield of the fishery has been sufficiently increased by the decrease in effort, a partial gain may result even in this case. But if the released labor and gear can be shifted to some underutilized fishery, or into an entirely different segment of the economy, a net gain will be realized in the form of an increase in production. Some gains may also be found in the performance of preventive maintenance that would otherwise have gone undone. Of course, if the effort is transferred into a fishery already suffering from overexploitation, then regulation in the first fishery may be counterproductive overall. A vital consideration in setting up any regulatory program must always be the weighing of such relative gains and losses to determine whether a net benefit will result.

An economic consequence of closures is their long-run effect of expanding effort into other fishing areas or into other parts of the year at an increase in cost. Comparably, quotas will decrease the length of the fishing season, also at an increase in cost. Three closely related inefficiencies result from this. First, some peculiar things may happen at the level of the individual boat. For example, if a boat is on the fishing grounds and the captain knows that he does not have time to get into port, unload his catch, and return before the season is closed or the quota is reached, he will be motivated to cut down on the ice or even to deck-load the fish to accommodate more on board. This will probably make many fish unsalable, but as long as the total usable harvest has increased, the boat will show higher revenue. By this reasoning, more fish than normal will be taken during the period (even taking into account the increased fishing power), but the quality will be low for at least part of the catch.

The processing and marketing sectors of the fishing industry will also experience some direct effects. This is especially true in the long run, because as fishermen adjust their effort to the shortened season or to getting "their share" of the quota, the actual time spent fishing each year will become progressively shorter. Either the quota will be obtained more quickly or the regulation agency will find it necessary to cut the fishing season even more drastically to protect the fish from increasingly powerful gear. A good example of the latter is the Pacific halibut fishery, where the season has been reduced to a few weeks in certain years.

This means that the fish must also be processed on a tighter schedule. If, prior to regulation, the fishery was operating beyond maximum sustainable yield, a still greater number of fish may now be landed during the shorter period, putting a further burden on the processing plants, which will have to be large enough to handle such peak flows. And, unless they can adapt to serve other fisheries at other times, these plants will remain idle for the rest of the year. The regulation will thus have tied up money in underutilized plants.

Consumption may also be adversely affected, since fresh fish will now be available for a shorter time. Costs will go up because more of the fish will have to be frozen or otherwise preserved and stored for off-season use. And if such costs are very high, the fish may be sold immediately into less valuable uses such as pet food or meal.

This is not to say that peak-load processing of particular items is always economically inconsistent or is even uncommon. Many agricultural products must be handled in this way because of the short harvest season. Also, in fisheries such as the Pacific salmon, the effort must be concentrated in times and places where the fish congregate. Nevertheless, the artificial creation of peak-processing periods, or their further reduction in cases where they already exist, is of dubious value. A better procedure would be to regulate the fishery so that it may operate over a longer time, providing steadier employment for the fishermen and extended input for smaller processing plants.

Finally, such regulations may directly affect the geographical extension of the fishery or of port location. The competitive race for fish will encourage fishermen to stay closer to the port even though productivity per unit of effort may be higher on more remote grounds. This would be a rational decision from the individual fisherman's point of view, if running time to the more remote grounds precluded many trips in a short season. His concern is with net revenue—not with the average catch while fishing. If the season or the quota dictates that the extra running time will not be compensated by increased catch, then the end result of the regulation may be overfishing on nearby grounds and little or no fishing on distant grounds.

On the other hand, if the distant grounds are highly productive, an incentive exists to create fishing ports closer to them. The original port was presumably chosen because it had other economic advantages that made up for the long running time. For example, it may have been closer to supplies of labor and other materials needed for processing or to the marketing distribution system. But if the prize is valuable enough, competing fishermen may now find it worthwhile to set up a higher-cost port closer to the better fishing ground. This will entail the construction of facilities in the new port and the enforced idleness of those at the original one—a clear waste of resources. It will also mean that the less productive grounds will now be underutilized. Another possibility in this same situation would be literally to bring the port to the boats on the fishing grounds in the form of collector ships. Again, if such ships were not used before the quota or closure regulations were instituted, it seems logical to assume that only the restrictions made their use practical and that the original landing method was the more efficient. An open-access fishery "sins" not by forcing individual units to act in an uneconomical manner but merely by encouraging too many small units to participate, so that the fishery as a whole is operating inefficiently. A regulation system, however, can coerce fishermen to use methods that are truly inefficient, because they are the most profitable under the imposed constraints.

It should be pointed out that some of the detrimental side effects of seasonal and area closures and of quotas can be ameliorated by proper modifications. For example, setting a quota applicable to each specific fishing ground or subjecting each to a different open season could, to some extent, make up for the misallocation of effort among grounds. The latter method would also lengthen the overall fishing season and thus lead to better use of processing facilities. But every good has its price. Adjustments of this kind would require more information about the various grounds, and enforcement would also be more costly because of the need to treat each ground separately. It should also be taken into account that these modifications, to be properly effective, will have to be a part of the original regulation package. If they are added at a later time, they may be of little value; once the larger processing factory is in place, the new port has been built, or the collecting ships are in use, any move to displace them will be an overall economic loss unless the facilities have productive uses in other sectors of the economy.

Modifications of seasonal and area closure can be of real advantage, however, in the management of multispecies fisheries. If the proportions of different species caught vary from area to area, or from season to season in the same area, proper regulation can insure the most valuable combination of species in the final catch.

Gear Restrictions

Gear restrictions limit the type, amount, or usage of fishing equipment. Sometimes they involve outright bans while in other cases they only limit the size or amount of gear. An example of the former is a ban on fish traps or gill nets, while prohibitions on boats over 100 tons is an example of the latter.

If these regulations are to be effective, they must ban or limit activities in which fishermen would have otherwise engaged. Economically, this means that certain cost-effective ways of operating are proscribed, and so the cost of producing effort will go up. Therefore, just as with area and time closures, gear restrictions will shift the industry total cost curve in figure 6.1 up. As such, it will reduce the open-access equilibrium level of effort.

There is another aspect to this problem that should be discussed. Given time to adjust, fishermen can often find technological improvements to get around the restrictions. This means that the cost curve will again fall, and effort will expand. Therefore, in order to keep effort at specified levels, further restrictions will have to be implemented. Fishery control can thereby become a race between the fisherman to get around artificial inefficiencies and the regulator to impose further inefficiencies, with nobody having a chance to be a clear winner.

Because gear restrictions are a clear restriction on the efficiency of production, it will prove useful to discuss the economic implications of such regulation in more detail. Recall that the economic rationale for regulation is that the open-access fishery, by allocating too many resources to the fishery, reduces the total potential value of production in the economy. Regulations, therefore, should do more than just cut back effort; they should aid, or at least make possible, transfers of excess resources to other uses. How does the imposition of inefficiency through gear restriction measure up against this criterion? To answer this, let us look more carefully at the hypothetical fisheries pictured in figure 6.1. Figure 6.1a describes two fisheries, but only in terms of catch and effort. In figure 6.1b the diagrams of the production possibility curve and indifference curves, as explained in detail in chapter 3, set forth the same general analysis, taking into account other types of production as well. The solid PP curve in both cases is the normal production possibility curve; the dotted PP curve represents the possible production bundles with gear restrictions. In this case, the actual amount of effort that can be produced at every production level of the other good (M) is reduced. Therefore, the amount of fish harvested at every level will fall, except at very low levels of M (i.e., high levels of E) where, because the fishery is operating beyond maximum sustainable yield, less effort will actually catch more fish.

Let us first consider case I, where the open-access equilibrium is to the left of maximum sustained yield. In terms of figure 6.1a, a regulated inefficiency will shift the cost curve up from TC_1 to TC_2, causing a decrease in the open-access equilibrium level of effort from E_3 to E_2 and in this case, a decrease in total yield. Notice that, although the unit cost of producing effort has gone up, the total cost of producing effort has decreased from C_3 to C_2'. Since at the new intersection total revenue is still equal to total cost, the decrease in the market value of the catch is equal to the decrease in costs. And remembering the concept of opportunity cost, this means that the decrease in the production of fish is just matched by an increase of equal value in the production of other goods in the economy. What can be said about a regulation policy that reduces the value of the catch but also reduces the total cost of producing effort by an equal amount? Given the information at hand, it can only be stated that the amount of fish caught could be obtained at a lower cost if the restrictions were removed; that is, it would be possible to reduce costs to C_2 at this level of effort. In other words, producing the same level of effort without the inefficiencies could result in an increase in the value of the total production bundle of the economy. To answer the question in any more detail requires a study of the economywide effects of such regulations. This can be done using the production possibility curve for case I.

Assume that the open-access equilibrium equivalent to E_3 units of effort occurs at point A. At that point returns to fishermen equal their marginal costs, and so they have no incentive to bid resources away from other uses in the economy to produce more effort. As pointed out in chapter 3, this will not occur at M, that point on the PP curve where the social welfare of the economy is maximized.

The regulated inefficiencies shift the economy to the dotted PP curve.

Whether in fact the regulation will be beneficial overall depends upon how far the PP curve is shifted and exactly where on the new curve the economy will operate. If the new PP curve is located everywhere beneath I_1, the indifference curve through point A, then under all circumstances the regulations will be harmful because they will force the economy to operate on a lower social indifference curve. As drawn here, the new PP curve intersects I_1, and so potential gains are possible. If the economy operates somewhere to the right of point J but to the left of point K, the resultant level of social welfare will be higher than before the regulation. How is it possible for inefficiencies to improve the welfare of society? Recall that, under open access, the economy was using too many resources on the fishery. If the inefficiencies increase relative costs in such a way that less effort is produced, it is possible that the increased production of other goods may more than compensate for the lowered production of fish. It should be stressed, however, that this is still a second-best situation. The economy may show an increase in social welfare, but the inefficiencies will preclude its ever reaching point M, where social welfare is the maximum possible, given its resources.

Can anything be said about where on the new PP curve the economy will operate? Only that it depends upon how (1) the relative costs and (2) the relative desires for the two goods have changed, as a result of the new regulations. We can discover the essence of this by examining the two diagrams for case I, even though they are not strictly comparable; figure 6.1a is a partial equilibrium analysis in that it assumes all prices to remain constant throughout, while figure 6.1b as a general equilibrium analysis allows the prices and outputs of both goods to vary. Nevertheless, a careful comparison of the two diagrams can shed more light on the problem. Note that the diagram for the fishery itself shows that, after the inefficiencies are imposed, the industry spending the same amount as before (i.e., C_3) will now produce only E_3' units of effort. That is, the same foregone opportunities have resulted in less production of effort because the components of effort cannot be combined in the most efficient manner. However, given the existing demand structure and hence price level, revenue will be less than cost at this point; therefore, the production of effort will be reduced still further to E_2, where revenues equal costs. The consequence is a net decrease in the total cost of producing effort, which will allow for an increase in production of the other goods.

In terms of the diagram for the economy as a whole, the move from point A to point B is analogous to a move from E_3 to E_3'. It shows the amount of fish that can be obtained under the restrictions if the amount of M remains unchanged. (This is equivalent to total cost in the fishing industry remaining constant.) At this point, note that the opportunity cost of F relative to M will have gone up because of the forced inefficiencies. Now if demand conditions do not change significantly, it is logical to assume that the conclusion drawn from figure 6.1a—that the fishery will be losing money at this point—is valid here also. (Demand conditions will change because inefficiencies have decreased the income of the economy, which is an important determinant of demand.) If the fishing industry is suffering losses at point B, the point of operation of the economy will move to the right along the dotted PP curve because resources released from the fishing industry will be used to increase the production of M. Whether the economy will show a net gain in welfare from the regulations depends upon how far that move is. If it is such that the new equilibrium is to the right of point J, then there will be a net gain, because the economy will be operating on a higher social welfare indifference curve than at the preregulation situation. That is, as these curves are drawn here, at the new market valuations of the two goods, the value of the increased productions of the other good is greater than the decreased production of fish.

But is such a move likely? Note that at point B the ratio of F to M in the consumer's market basket will be lower than at the old equilibrium at point A, which would indicate that relative demands will more than likely be shifting in favor of F. This will change the relative prices to favor F, thus improving the relative profitability of fishing and tending to counteract any move toward point J. In fact, if the change in relative demands is strong enough, it will more than compensate for the increase in relative costs for F. In this instance the fishing industry will be making profits at point B, indicating that the equilibrium point will be to the left of that point. Therefore, while there is the possibility of improving welfare when operating to the left of MSY by imposing inefficiencies, it appears unlikely that this would ever occur unless it also results in a change in relative demands toward M.

Let us briefly examine case II, where the fishery is operating in the downward-sloping portion of the sustainable yield curve both before and after the regulations. Here the inefficiencies will cause the new equilibrium level of effort to fall from E_3 to E_2, at which point the market value of total yield and the total cost of producing effort have gone up by an equal amount. Total cost will increase from C_3 to C_2'. From the partial equilibrium point of view, are these regulations worthwhile? Since more fish are now obtained, the value of which is just equal to their opportunity cost, there is no gain. The increased production of fish is matched by a decrease, equal in value, of some other good. Again, it is obvious that the same catch could have been obtained at a lower cost by efficient harvesting (i.e., cost at E_2 could be reduced from C_2' to C_2). Clearly, then, even if catch were to remain the same, efficient harvesting techniques would yield higher gains.

To assess gains to the whole society, consider case II in figure 6.1b. If A is the original equilibrium point, there will be a net gain if the new equilibrium is above I_1, the social welfare curve through point A. Where will the new equilibrium occur? Again, the answer depends on relative changes in costs and demands, and comparison of the two graphs for case II will shed some light on the question. If the fishery keeps its total costs at the same level after the regulations are instituted, effort will fall from E_3 to E_3'. At this point revenues are greater than cost, and production will tend to expand to E_2, where the two are equal. That is, more resources will be put into the production of effort and less into the production of the other good. In terms of the diagram for the economy as a whole, keeping total costs constant is equivalent to a move from point A to point B. This is clearly an improvement for the economy. The cost (i.e., the amount of M given up) is unchanged, but the harvest of fish increases, and the economy is thus operating on a higher social welfare curve than at the preregulation point. Note, however, that it has not yet reached the highest point, given the existing production possibility curve.

Because of changes in the relative prices and costs for the two goods, point B more than likely will not be an equilibrium point. If there is no significant change, however, the fishery will be making a profit at this point and so will expand production of effort. This will result in a movement to the left of point B, because resources will be shifted out of the production of M and into the production of E. Since the fishery is operating in the downward-sloping portion of the sustained yield curve, such a move decreases the amount of fish caught as well as the amount of M produced, and so welfare will fall. In fact, if the equilibrium point were to be to the left of point J, there would be a lower level of welfare than at the preregulation point. Such a drastic result appears unlikely, however, because the increased ratio of F to M will change relative demands to favor M. This will tend to counteract any shift to the left from point B.

The above analysis has been in terms of a constant-cost fishery, where all boats in the fishery operate in the same way. The analysis is somewhat different in an increasing-cost fishery in that potential gains may be possible even if there are no changes elsewhere in the economy, as is required in the constant-cost fishery. See Anderson (1985b). This can be demonstrated in the fixed price of a fish model using figure 6.2, which is analogous to figure 3.3 above.

Let LMC_0 represent the long-run marginal cost curve of a highliner fishery, taking into account the increased costs of the additional vessels that enter the fleet; see chapter 3. It is the supply curve of effort for the fishery. The open-access equilibrium is at E_1, where the return per unit of effort, R_1, is equal to the minimum of the average cost of the marginal vessel. There is no incentive for other (less efficient) vessels to enter, but all intramarginal vessels will be earning rents.

A gear restriction policy that is imposed on all boats will increase their cost curves. Therefore, the supply curve of the fishery will shift up as well. Assume that such a policy is implemented, and as a result the effort supply curve shifts to LMC_1. This policy will initially result in the exit of the marginal boats that are made unprofitable. Some or all of them may return, however, if the increase in return per unit of effort due to the initial decrease in fishing pressure (i.e., from R_1 to R_2) is enough to compensate for this. These changes are subsumed in the construction of the two supply curves. The new equilibrium will occur at E_2'. Note, however, that in the short run (before the catch per unit of effort and hence average return to fishing has increased, due to the

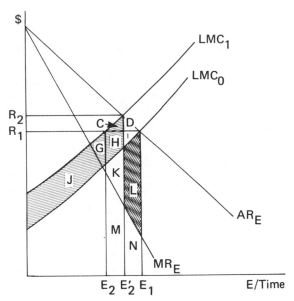

Figure 6.2. *Gear Restrictions in Increasing-Cost Fisheries.* In the short run, gear restrictions will reduce effort to E_2 for a reduction of open-access wastes equal to areas K and L. Inefficiencies, however, will cause costs to increase by areas $J + G$. In the long run, the fishery will expand to E_2', which will generate open-access wastes of $K + H + C$. Whether the net effect will be positive or negative depends upon the characteristics of the particular fishery.

increased productivity of the stock as a result of the decreased effort), industry output will fall to E_2. The argument for the failure of gear restrictions is that any potential gains from effort reduction are dissipated through cost increases. While some dissipation will occur, it is possible that there may be net positive economic efficiency benefits. This can be demonstrated by analyzing the effects of such a program in a sequential manner. In the short run, effort is reduced from E_1 to E_2, which by itself has positive net benefits because it corrects for some of the open-access overexploitation. Costs are reduced by an amount equal to areas $K + L + M + N$ (i.e., the area under the marginal cost curve), while the value of output only falls by an amount equal to areas $M + N$ (the area under the marginal revenue curve). The gain from this is equal to areas $K + L$. However, even in the short run this benefit does not come free as there is an increase in the cost of producing the E_2 units of effort equal to areas $J + G$, the area between the open-access and the restricted supply curves over this range. If area $K + L$ is greater than $J + G$, there will be net short-run gains.

In the long run, as the catch per unit effort increases as a result of the reduced fishing, effort will expand to E_2'. This increase is a clear dissipation of benefits because the value of output which results (area M) is less than the marginal cost of producing it (areas $M + K + H + C$).

The overall net effect of these gains and losses is indicated in the figure.

The gain is the hatched area L, which is the net increase in value that results from reducing effort in the open-access fishery. The loss is the crosshatched area $J + G + H + C$, which is the increased cost of producing the remaining amount of effort. Depending on the relative size of the two areas, the net effect can be positive, negative, or zero. It should be pointed out, however, that even where gains exist, they are not as high as they could be without the inefficiencies.

The actual gain from the regulation will be the present value of gains and losses over its expected life span including the short-run adjustment period, where the gains are more likely to be positive.

It should be noted that, since the analysis has been in terms of the fixed-price model in the positive sloped portion of the yield curve, possible important changes in consumer surplus have been ignored. Obviously in real-world applications this should be considered, but the conclusions derived here still apply. Gear restrictions can sometimes produce net gains in increasing-cost fisheries, but they will not yield maximum gains.

To summarize, it is indeed possible that regulated inefficiencies *may* lead to a net increase in the social welfare of the economy. This will be the case if the regulation adequately counters losses to the economy which formerly resulted from nonoptimal expenditure of resources in the fishery. But of course this does not always happen, although, as the above shows, it is more likely when the fishery is operating beyond MSY. The net outcome depends on how debilitating the inefficiencies actually are and upon the reaction of the overall economy, that is, upon how far the PP curve shifts and where on that curve the new equilibrium settles. In neither case, however, is the economy operating at its best. Further gains in welfare will accrue if proper regulations remove the inefficiencies. In short, even though imposed inefficiencies may on occasion render a net benefit in social welfare, greater gains are always possible by other methods.

Still other effects of regulated inefficiencies must be considered. First, they can inhibit research activity in devising more efficient methods of harvesting fish. A progressive industry should always be searching for ways to increase real productivity, but private interests will have little incentive to invest scarce research funds if there is a good chance that any newly discovered technique will be unusable.

This brings us to the question of how fast improvements in methods should be introduced. This problem is faced by every industry, but in the case of fisheries the common-property aspect adds a special dimension. In other industries the rate at which new technologies are introduced depends upon the costs of the necessary new capital equipment, the scrap value of the old equipment, and estimates of the future revenues and costs of the old and the new methods. New firms normally have a better reason to install the latest technologies, while established ones rationally choose to wear out existing equipment before modernizing, so long as they can still cover their variable costs of production and so long as the new producers are not able to undersell them on the basis of new technology.

Individual firms in a fishery face a much more difficult situation, however. Since no one owns the fish stock, a race to catch the fish may deny any participant the option of waiting until his old gear wears out. If he delays investing in new equipment, other fishermen using newer techniques may gain a relative or an absolute advantage over him. This means that perfectly good equipment is abandoned much earlier than necessary, constituting a waste of resources from an economic point of view. If the equipment cannot be put to alternative use, it should continue in service as long as the returns are greater than variable costs.

Because of this incentive for open-access fisheries to adopt new technologies too rapidly, there is some justification for restricting the introduction of new methods—but only long enough to allow existing equipment to wear out. Any permanent or long-term ban prevents maximum output and discourages innovations. As will be pointed out later, a program to limit entry will go a long way toward reducing this technology problem. Since each participant will be guaranteed a portion of the catch regardless of his method, it will obviously be to his advantage to keep using his old gear if it is earning enough to cover its variable costs. Only when he sees that increased profits can offset the costs of the new equipment will he have reason to introduce the new technique.

Gear restrictions may also have a proper role to play in cases of interdependent fisheries. The prohibition of certain equipment or certain methods that are very effective in the harvest of one species may be justified if they are particularly damaging to another. The proper gear should be chosen in a broad context, since restrictions on the output of one fishery or of one species in a fishery may produce a net increase in the value of total catch.

In summary, while gear restrictions for the purpose of restricting total effort may in special cases actually lead to an increase in total welfare, they are always a second-best alternative for this objective. Further gains in welfare are possible by way of other regulatory methods. In addition, gear restrictions tend to discourage efforts to increase productivity. However, this type of regulation can be a valuable part of a program designed to slow down the turnover rate of fishing equipment or to discriminate among stocks in multispecies or interdependent fisheries.

License Limitation Programs

As the name implies, license limitation programs attempt to control harvesting pressure by restricting access to the stock by issuing a limited number of licenses or permits to fish. (The problem of who does and does not get a license is obviously a very important question. Since it is also an issue with individual transferable quotas, it will be treated in a separate subsection to follow.) Although the licenses may be defined in terms of an individual or some particular piece of gear (i.e., a fishing weir), they are most commonly denominated in terms of vessels. And because different vessels can exert different amounts of fishing pressure, a license is normally assigned to a specified type of vessel in terms of displacement, length, and gear.

In many ways license limitation programs are very similar to gear restrictions because it is the ultimate type of "gear" (i.e., the broadly defined vessel) that is restricted. However, it is the generality of the definition of a vessel which sets it apart, and it is most often classified as a limited-entry technique.

Regardless of how it is classified, outright restrictions on the number of fishing units will also result in increased cost, but as an indirect result of the fishermen's reactions rather than as a direct result of the control. In the short run, effort is reduced simply because it is not possible to produce as much per period with the existing vessels. However, since this is only a partial control, fishermen still utilizing the normal profit-maximizing behavior will react differently in the long run. As the productivity of the stock increases because of the reduction in total effort, the average return per unit of effort will increase. Therefore, each fisherman will find it profitable to expand production of effort until marginal cost is equal to the now higher return (see figure 3.1). This means that each boat will be operating beyond the minimum of its average cost curve, and so the cost of producing the total effort will be higher than indicated by TC_1 in the figures. In the long run this increased productivity may also encourage fishermen to modify their boats so as to be able to produce more effort per period. This will of course increase costs even more, and although they could not have afforded to do so with open access, it will be profitable, given the restrictions on effort and the increased averaged return that results.

The net economic effect of such behavior can be discussed in detail using the fixed-price model as pictured in figure 6.3, which is based on figure 3.1. The curve labeled $\bar{S}$ is the long-run supply curve of a constant-cost fishery under open access when there is no regulation program in place and hence no control on fleet size. It is located at the minimum of the long-run average cost curve for the representative vessel in the fishery. The open-access equilibrium will occur at $\bar{E}_1$ with each boat operating at E_1. The short-run supply curve for the open-access fleet is the sum of their marginal cost curves above the long-run average cost curves. This is represented by ΣMC_1. This curve shows how effort will change in the short run with increases in return per unit of effort. Note that total cost for a given fleet can be measured using the $\bar{S}$ curve out to the fleet supply curve and the latter curve from that point on. The first part is the long-run cost of operating each boat in the fleet at the optimum level of output (i.e., at the minimum of the long-run average cost curve). The second part is the cost of expanding effort by increasing the output of each boat rather than by increasing the fleet.

A license limitation program, if it is to be effective, will allocate fewer

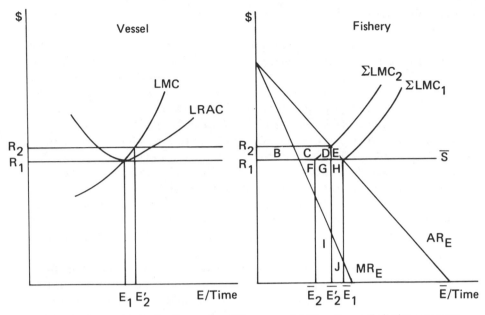

Figure 6.3. *License Limitation Programs.* Like gear restrictions, license limitation programs can produce net gains, even though there may be some inefficiency losses if the expansion in effort by the restricted number of boats (i.e., from E_2 to E_2') is not that large.

licenses than vessels in the open-access fleet. A license program, which will actually constrain effort, can be depicted by a decrease in the short-run (i.e., fixed-fleet size) effort supply curve, such as from ΣLMC_1 to ΣLMC_2 in the figure. It is the sum of the MC curves of the reduced number of firms. This is to be distinguished from the analysis of gear restrictions, where the change in the supply curve was the result of an increase in the costs of all firms and the possible exit of some high-cost firms.

With such a license program, the regulated equilibrium will first shift back to $\bar{E}_2$, but as the benefits of control are manifested in increased returns per unit of effort, the final equilibrium will occur at $\bar{E}_2'$, with each of the remaining vessels operating at E_2'. It is this vessel operational level beyond the minimum of the average cost curve which causes the inefficiency in license limitation programs.

However, an inefficiency does not mean that net gains are not possible. As with gear restrictions, the initial effect of the license limitation program will be to reduce total effort, in this case to $\bar{E}_2$, which will result in a gain equal to areas $G + H$, the difference between the cost savings from vessel reduction $(G + H + I + J)$ and the value of the output lost $(I + J)$. As opposed to the gear restriction case, there are no short-term losses in terms of increased costs. The reduction in effort is due to an actual removal of boats rather than to a reduction in output by each vessel in response to artificially imposed increases in costs.

As the fishery responds to the reduced harvesting pressure and resultant increased catch per unit of effort, the final equilibrium will occur at $\bar{E}_2'$. The dissipation that occurs as a result of this increase in effort is equal to areas $D + G$, the difference between the increase in cost ($I + G + D$) and the smaller increase in value of output (I). The net effect of the license program is therefore the difference between areas H and D. The former is the net increase in output in the economy as a result of reduction in effort, while the latter is the cost of expanding effort from $\bar{E}_2$ to $\bar{E}_2'$ with the fixed fleet size.

In the case of a constant-cost fishery, this will always be positive. Note that, under open-access conditions, all rents to the fishery are dissipated. However, with the license program, rent to the boats equals areas $B + C$, the difference between total revenues to the fishery when producing $\bar{E}_2'$ units of output at a return of R_2 and the total cost of producing $\bar{E}_2'$, as measured in the manner noted above.

Since there were no rents before but there were postive rents after, it follows that the program generates net benefits. Therefore, area H must be larger than area D. The only time all of the gains from fleet reduction can be dissipated is when the fleet supply curve is perfectly elastic and hence corresponds to the long-run open entry supply curve. This, of course, has to do with the substitutability of other inputs for the restricted input—the boat. As long as other inputs are not perfectly substitutable for the vessel in terms of producing effort, the restricted supply curve in a constant-cost fishery will not be horizontal, and hence there will be potential gains, although second-best gains, from license limitation programs. The points raised above in the summary of the section on gear restrictions about the present value of gains and about consumer surplus changes apply here as well.

Although it will not be presented here, the analysis of license limitation programs in increasing-cost fisheries is similar. In some instances, license programs can also produce net gains in these types of fisheries. They will not always produce gains over open access, however, as they will in constant-cost fisheries, because of the potential negative effect on open-access highliner rents. See Anderson (1985b) for more details.

In summary, license limitation programs curtail harvesting pressure by restricting the number of units, usually vessels, that can exploit a particular stock. These programs will indirectly lead to increases in the cost of producing effort because individuals are motivated to increase output from the limited fleet. This extra production can also have an effect on the biological efficacy of the control. If it is quite easy to expand output from the existing fleet, the overall long-run control on fishing pressure will not be effective, and hence there may be a need for further restrictions in the number of licenses. While there can be gains from such programs, this is not always the case, and they should be instituted only after it can be shown that positive gains are possible.

Individual Transferable Quotas

The use of individual transferable quotas, one of the regulatory techniques classified as limited entry, has the potential to correct for open-access wastes without causing inefficiencies in the production of effort. (See the following section for a discussion of the distributional issues involved.) Sometimes they are known as stock certificates, fishermen shares, or quantitative rights, but in all cases the basic notion is to assign a particular amount of catch to specific entities. In essence, parts of a total quota are assigned to individuals to correct for the inefficiencies caused by the race for fish that would otherwise occur. The amount of the individual quota can be a specified number of physical units, but in those fisheries where stock size can vary significantly from year to year, it is often better to define it in terms of a fixed percentage of annually determined allowable catch. For example, in the first instance, an operator would be allowed to harvest, say, 200 tons per year, while in the second he or she would have the right to harvest, say, 15 percent of the yearly allowable catch. See Anderson (1986) for an economic approach to determining the yearly allowable catch in fisheries with fluctuating stocks.

The advantage of individual transferable quotas is that owners are motivated to harvest their allowable catch as efficiently as possible because they reap the financial benefits from such frugality. This is the opposite signal afforded by total quota programs, where fishermen are motivated to expand their capacity so as to catch as much of the quota as possible. With total quota programs, catching fish in an otherwise inefficient way is preferable to not catching it at all so long as the costs are still less than the revenues. To fully take advantage of the motivations for efficiency, individual quotas have to be transferable. That is, the owner must have the right to sell or rent this allowable catch. This will be discussed in detail below.

The economic advantages of the individual transferable quota can be described in terms of a simple example. Since operating decisions are made at the individual firms rather than at the industry level, the analysis must focus on the firm. Figure 6.4 contains the average cost curve of a representative vessel in a hypothetical fishery that has been the left-hand side of our vessel fishery analysis above. For ease of discussion, it will be assumed that effort can be measured in terms of standardized fishing days. Assume for the moment that a specified total quota for the fishery has been determined and partitioned out to individuals in 100-ton amounts. That is, each vessel operating at the start of the program is given the right to harvest 100 tons per year. In order for this to be a binding regulation, the average harvest per boat be-

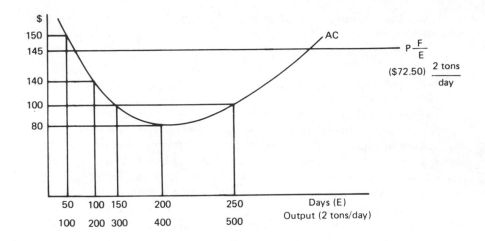

Output	50 days 100 tons	100 days 200 tons	150 days 300 tons	200 days 400 tons	210 days 420 tons	250 days 500 tons
Average Cost Per Day	150	140	100	80	82	100
Total Cost Of Fishing	7,500	14,000	15,000	16,000	17,220	25,000
Cost Per Ton	75.00	70.00	50.00	40.00	41.00	50.00
Revenue Per Ton	72.50	72.50	72.50	72.50	72.50	72.50
Profit Per Ton	-2.50	2.50	22.50	32.50	31.50	22.50
Total Profit	-250.00	500.00	6,750.00	13,000.00	13,230.00	11,250.00

Figure 6.4. *Individual Quotas.* The gains from transferability of individual quotas is based upon the decreasing average cost of effort. If two boats are each producing 100 tons by operating 50 days, their average cost per ton is $75. By combining efforts and producing 200 tons on one boat operating 100 days, the average cost per ton falls to $70.

fore regulation must be greater than 100 tons, and it is assumed that this is the case.

Given the overall total quota, there will be a fixed catch per unit of effort for the fishery as a whole. In the deterministic model used above, if total catch is fixed, the amount of effort necessary to obtain it is known and hence catch per unit of effort will be determined. Assume that, when the fishery is in equilibrium at this level of effort, the average catch per day per vessel is two tons. Also assume that the market price of fish is $72.50 per ton, which means that the return per unit of effort (i.e., return per fishing day) is $145. The individual boat owner can do nothing to change this gross return. As long as average catch and the price of fish remain the same, this is the gross earnings the boat will receive for producing a fishing day. Depending upon how the boat is operated, however, the cost per day can vary, and it will be to the boat owner's advantage to keep this as low as possible.

Given the average catch of two tons per day and the 100-ton individual quota, each vessel will be allowed to fish 50 days per year. According to figure 6.4 and the accompanying table, at this operational level, the average cost per day fished is $150, which means that total annual fishing costs will be $7,500. Dividing this by 100 tons, it can be seen that cost per ton is $75. Since the revenue per ton is $72.50, it is obvious that at this output level, the vessels will not cover their costs. Indeed, they will suffer losses of $250 per year.

The benefits of transferability can be clearly demonstrated in this case. Note, as the number of days fished per year increases, average cost per day for the boat will decrease. This produces the possibility of profitable cooperative arrangements or for the mutually advantageous sale or rental of the individual transferable quotas. For example, if two fishermen agree to harvest their total of 200 tons per year using only one boat, both can then make a profit. Operating one vessel for 100 days, instead of two vessels for 50 days each, will still yield 200 tons of fish but average cost per day falls to $140, which means that the total cost of fishing is $14,000. For the one boat, output has doubled but cost has less than doubled, and so the cost per ton decreases from $75 to $70. Therefore, rather than losing $2.50 per ton, the boat is making $2.50 a ton. Under the cooperative agreement, each fisherman is making $250 a year rather than losing money.

In addition, there is a potential for further gains. If the two fishermen can entice others to join with them, up to a point all can benefit. Note that if another fisherman joins with them, it will take 150 days to catch the 300 tons the three of them are permitted, but the average cost decreases such that the cost per ton becomes $50. This means that profit per ton will be $22.50. The maximum profit per ton will be generated if four individuals pool their shares and operate one vessel for 200 days, where average cost per day fished is $80. This translates into a cost per ton of fish of $40, leaving a profit per ton of $32.50. It will not make sense to allow another fisherman to join them because average cost for producing effort increases, and hence profits per individual fisherman would fall.

Note that the profit per vessel could increase if the boat were to fish 210 days and catch 420 tons; however, profit per ton would decrease. Remember from above that the profit-maximizing point is where the marginal cost of effort (not shown in the figure) intersects the revenue per day fished, which in cases such as this will always occur at an output beyond the minimum of the average cost curve. But operators with individual transferable quotas are not concerned with profit per boat. Since each has the right to a specific tonnage, they want to maximize the profit per ton. Notice, however, that as long as profit per ton is increasing, cost per ton is falling. Therefore, the regulation is sending the right signals because firms are motivated to maximize profits per ton, and in so doing they achieve the socially beneficial effect of minimizing the cost of producing a given ton of fish.

The same benefits can accrue if the shares can be sold or rented. Since there may be instances when cooperative behavior is not possible, it is thus necessary to allow transferability to have the potential for gains in all cases. The possibility of gains from transferability can be explained as follows. Profit per ton when a vessel is operating 200 days and producing 400 tons is $32.50. Therefore, an enterprising vessel owner, who only has the right to harvest 100 tons, would be motivated to find three other fishermen, who, when they produce their 100 tons, lose $2.50 per ton, and offer to buy their rights to produce. For example, if he pays them $15 per ton per year for the right to use their individual quotas, these fishermen will earn $1,500 per year for sitting on shore instead of losing $250 if they fish. If they can sell their boats or even if their fixed expenses are less than $1,500, they may well be enticed to agree to the offer. The enterprising fisherman will benefit as well because his cost for producing his 100 tons will decrease, and in addition, he will make $32.50 per ton on the rights he has purchased while only paying $15 per ton to obtain them. Before the arrangement the individual who bought rights was losing $250 a year. He now has total revenues of $29,000 (400 tons at $72.50) and total harvesting costs of $16,000 (400 tons at $40) plus payments to the other fishermen of $4,500 (300 tons at $15). This will leave him an annual profit of $8,500. Both he and the fishermen who sell their individual quotas for the year will be better off as a result of the sale.

Note that the total profit to sellers and the buyer is $13,000, which is the profit for 200 days fished. The distribution of the profits will depend upon the transfer price of the individual quotas. The higher the price, the lower the share of gains to the one who continues to fish. In general, the maximum price will be the maximum profit per ton, which in this case is $32.50. It will be useful to anticipate the analysis to follow by noting that tax programs with a $32.50 per ton tax will be technically identical to the individual quota-transfer program. The only difference will be that the profits will be collected by the government.

In summary, the behavior of profit-seeking individuals will be such that fishermen will try to produce effort as efficiently as possible, given their scale of operation. Further, if the quotas are transferable, owners will also have an incentive to either form cooperatives or to buy and sell the annual individual quotas such that the remaining boats will be producing at the minimum of their average cost curves. If any boat is not operating at this point, its profit can be potentially increased by buying or selling individual quotas. In those cases where the fishery is composed of different types of boats, those with lower costs will be able to pay more to obtain rights to fish, and hence not only will boats operate as efficiently as possible, but only the most efficient vessels will continue to fish. As a sidelight, note that under this policy producers will be motivated to find new technologies that will lower the real cost of producing effort.

Taxes

A tax program changes the level of effort in a fishery by directly changing the profitability of fishing. However, since a properly instituted tax program will not cause inefficiencies in the production of effort, it is quite different from other programs that do affect financial returns to fishermen. The following discussion will compare the effects of taxes on effort, on components of effort (such as boats), and on fish. It will be shown that only taxes on effort or fish can produce economically efficient reductions in effort. Other strengths and weaknesses of tax programs will be described, and an equation for optimal taxes on effort and fish will be derived.

For purposes of this discussion, assume again for simplicity that the market price for fish and the long-run fisherywide unit cost of effort are constant. The analysis will be in terms of the hypothetical fishery in figure 6.5. Figure 6.5a contains the total revenue and cost curves for the fishery, and figure 6.5c the average and marginal curves as well as the fisherywide supply curves of effort (see ΣMC_1, etc.), each of which is the sum of the marginal cost curves of all the boats in the fishery at any one time. The solid curves in figure 6.5b represent the average and marginal cost curves of a representative boat with no taxes. The dotted curves will be explained below. (Parts b and c of figure 6.5 are identical to the diagrams in figure 3.1.) Effort for the fishery as a whole has been labeled $\bar{E}$ and that for the individual fisherman as E.

The open-access equilibrium will be at $\bar{E}_1$ where total revenue equals total cost or, put another way, where average revenue equals fisherywide average cost prior to taxes (i.e., AC_1). At this equilibrium the individual boat operator will produce E^* units of effort per period, where his average costs are a minimum. He will operate there because at that point his return per unit of effort, as determined by the fishery as a whole, is equal to his marginal cost of producing effort. At this point, then, a determinate number of boats in the fishery will each be producing E^* units of effort per period, resulting in a total of $\bar{E}_1$. The curve labeled ΣMC_1—the sum of the marginal cost curves for these boats—shows how total effort will change in the short run in response to changes in average return.

Given the initial open-access equilibrium, let us investigate the effect of taxes on the operation of the fishery. The discussion will be general at this point. A discussion of the theoretically optimal taxes will follow.

A constant unit tax on effort will cause a proportional increase in the total cost of producing effort in the fishery as a whole and will increase the average and the marginal cost of producing effort on the part of the individual boat. In terms of figure 6.5a, the normal total cost curve for the fishery is TC_1, and TC_t is the total cost curve in the presence of the tax. The difference between

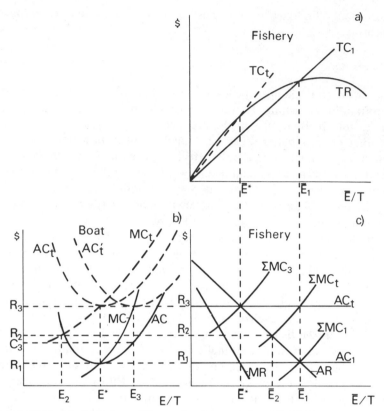

Figure 6.5. *Effects of a Unit Tax on Effort.*   A unit tax on effort will shift the cost curves up. The proper tax will raise costs so that, when the fishery as a whole operates where average revenue equals tax-adjusted long-run average and marginal cost, it is actually operating where fishery marginal revenue equals long-run marginal cost. Because of different effects on the average cost curves of the individual boat, a unit tax on boats cannot produce these desirable results.

the two is the total amount of taxes paid. Similarly, AC_t and MC_t in figure 6.5b are the new average and marginal cost curves for each boat. (Ignore for a moment the curve labeled AC'_t.) The difference between the old and the new marginal cost curves is the amount of the unit tax. With the shift of the curves of the individual boat, the fisherywide average cost curve shifts to AC_t, and the short-run supply curve of effort shifts to ΣMC_t. The vertical distance between both ΣMC_1 and ΣMC_t, and AC_1 and AC_t, is also equal to the amount of the tax.

   The actual resource cost of producing effort has not changed, however. The same number of inputs is still used to produce them, the only difference being that the fishermen must pay a tax on each unit produced. As far as the rest of the economy is concerned, the cost of producing effort is still represented by the original cost curves. But since profit-maximizing boat operators must pay the tax, they will use the new cost curves in determining the amount of effort they desire to produce.

This tax will change the equilibrium level of effort in the fishery to $\bar{E}^*$, and the reduction in effort results from a decrease in the number of efficiently operating boats. The process of moving to the new equilibrium can be traced in figure 6.5, parts b and c. The immediate effects of the tax will be a shift in the fisherywide equilibrium to $\bar{E}_2$, where the new fisherywide supply curve of effort intersects the average-revenue-per-unit-of-effort curve. At this point, the return per unit of effort is R_2. This amount of effort will be produced by the same number of boats each producing E_2 units of effort, the point where the marginal cost of effort including the tax equals R_2. However, since average revenues are less than average costs at this point, some boats will leave the fishery, thereby increasing the catch per unit of effort for those that remain. Graphically, this is represented by a shift in the fisherywide supply curve to the left, raising the return per unit of effort. As a result, each remaining boat will increase its effort. A new equilibrium is reached when enough boats have left, so that the fisherywide supply curve of effort shifts to ΣMC_3. At this point, each boat will be producing E^* units of effort and will be covering all of its costs including the taxes. The actual average cost of producing the effort, however, will be R_1, the minimum possible average cost, and the total effort in the fishery will be $\bar{E}^*$.

A tax on effort has thus reduced the total produced by forcing some vessels out of the fishery while insuring that those remaining are still using the most favorable methods to produce effort. Assuming that the resources forced out of the fishery are put to constructive uses in other parts of the economy, the goal of fishery regulation has been met. The current catch is harvested in the most efficient manner, and excess resources are released for other uses.

Note that at this regulated equilibrium the tax captures all of the rent from the fishery. On the other hand, remember that in the case of an open-access fishery rent was lost because efficient individual producers were racing for profits, and in fisheries regulated by the other techniques previously described the rent was lost because fishermen were forced to use inefficient methods. (To put the latter distinction another way, the only reason that individual fishermen can stay in business when forced to use inefficient methods is that the fishery is capable of earning a rent no one entity in the fishery can keep to himself.) When taxes are imposed, the rent is claimed by the government, and remaining individual fishermen must use efficient methods of production.

It is important to stress, however, that the tax should be on overall effort. A tax that affects only one of its components will be less effective, because fishermen will rely more heavily on the other nontaxed components, and, as a result, the average cost of effort will increase. Consider, for example, a tax on boats. Such a tax would not affect the marginal cost of producing effort because it will not change operating costs; it does affect fixed costs, however, and thereby changes average costs.

Assume that the tax shifts the average cost for the representative boat to AC_t', the minimum point of which is also at AC_t. As mentioned before, the MC_1 will still be the marginal cost curve. Each boat that continues to produce E^* units of effort will suffer a loss because average costs with taxes are greater than average revenues. Therefore, some boats will leave, causing the fishery-wide supply curve of effort to shift to the left until enough have exited for the curve to reach ΣMC_3. At that point each boat will just cover its costs (including taxes) by producing E_3 units of effort. The total production for the fishery will be $\bar{E}^*$ units. However, this tax is not correct, because the cost of producing this effort is too high.

Recall that, with a tax on effort, $\bar{E}^*$ total units were produced with each boat producing E^* units. Since in this case the same amount of total effort is produced even though each boat is contributing more, there must obviously be fewer boats in the fishery. Each will be operating at the minimum average cost including tax, but note that the average cost of actually producing the effort (i.e., cost net of tax) is C_3, which is greater than the minimum of the pretax average cost curve.

Thus, each remaining boat will be producing a larger amount of effort at a higher average cost than would have been necessary under an optimal tax program. Additionally, in the long run such a tax may encourage fishermen to build bigger boats. Assuming that the fishery was originally using boats of the optimal size, such a move will cause a further increase in the cost of producing effort.

Let us consider the effects of a tax on fish in terms of the fishery in figure 6.6, which reaches an open-access equilibrium with $\bar{E}_1$ total units of effort and with each boat producing E^* units. A per-unit tax on fish will lower the average revenue curve by the amount of the tax and the total revenue curve by the total amount of tax collected at each level of effort. That is, before the tax, average revenue equaled the price of fish times the average catch per unit of effort ($P_F F/E$); with the tax it equals the difference between the price and the per-unit tax times the average catch per unit of effort, or $(P_F - t_F)F/E$. Similarly, total revenue, which formerly was price times total fish caught, now equals price-minus-tax times the total fish caught. The dotted curve labeled TR_t in figure 6.6a is the total revenue curve facing the fishery in the presence of the tax. The difference between the two total revenue curves represents the total amount of tax collected; that is, at any level of effort the actual proceeds from the sale of the fish are shown by the curve labeled TR, but the income to fishermen is shown by TR_t. The dotted curve labeled AR_t is the average revenue curve with the tax.

Under this tax, the fishery will reach a regulated equilibrium where the tax-adjusted total revenue curve intersects the total cost curve at $\bar{E}^*$. This

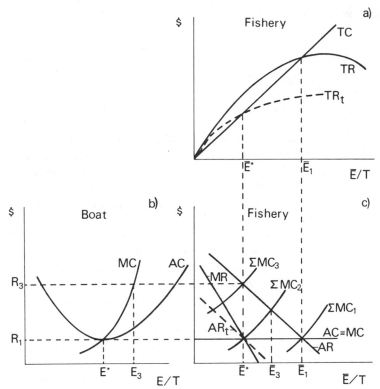

Figure 6.6. *Effect of a Unit Tax on Fish.* A unit tax on fish will lower the revenue curves. Total revenue becomes total receipts minus total taxes, and average revenue becomes average receipts minus the unit tax. The optimal tax is the one that causes the fishery to operate at maximum economic yield. Notice that, if the tax is such that TR_t and AR_t become the new revenue curves, individual fishermen, by operating where tax-adjusted fisherywide average revenue equals the minimum average cost of producing effort per boat (i.e., where it is equal to long-run marginal and average cost), are actually producing where fishery marginal revenue equals long-run marginal cost.

reduction results from a decrease in the number of boats in the fishery, which can be demonstrated by examining parts b and c of figure 6.6. Note that, if the fishery stays at its original level of effort after the taxes are introduced, the average return after taxes per unit of effort will be negative and each boat in the fishery will initially be losing money. All will try to cut back their production of effort to equate their return (which is the average return of the fishery as a whole) and marginal costs, and some will be forced to give up fishing entirely. As they do, the fisherywide supply curve of effort will shift to the left, causing average revenue per unit of effort to increase. Individual boats will continue to suffer losses until enough boats have left to bring the net average return after taxes equal to average cost, which will occur when the fisherywide supply curve has shifted to ΣMC_2. Therefore, at the new equilibrium a smaller number of boats will each be producing at the minimum of their average cost curves. From a business point of view, the revenues have gone down due to the tax, but the actual cost of production will remain the same. At the equilibrium point the actual average cost of producing is R_1, which is equal to their return net of taxes. Because effort has now been reduced in an efficient manner, labor and equipment have been released to increment production in other parts of the economy.

The short-run fishery supply curve, ΣMC_2, is analogous to the curve ΣMC_3 in figure 6.5c, which for convenience is reproduced here. They both represent the same number of boats; ΣMC_3 is higher because of the tax on effort. This means that the effects of a proper tax on fish are identical to those of a proper tax on effort. The same number of boats will be producing the same amount of effort at the same cost in terms of resources.

In summary, a tax on each boat can be set in such a way as to result in any specified amount of fishing effort but not at the lowest possible average cost of production. As the use of a boat becomes relatively more expensive, fishermen will try to substitute other components of fishing effort. They may stay out longer, increase the size of their nets, or, in the long run, increase the actual size of the boat. The end result will be fewer than optimal boats in the fishery, each producing beyond the point of minimum average cost.

As far as taxes in general are concerned, either a tax on fish or a tax on effort (but not one of the components of effort) can lead to the correct catch at the lowest possible cost. But some practical problems arise in the implementation of taxes. For one thing, a regulation program should be flexible enough to permit easy adjustment to fluctuating market and environmental factors. A change in the price of fish, in the cost of producing effort, or in the growth rate of the stock will affect the location of maximum economic yield and require corresponding changes in the regulatory tax. Two problems are apparent. First, it may be very difficult to get the changes approved; second, even after such tax changes are made institutionally, fishermen need time to adjust properly to them. Therefore, any need for a change in the tax may be separated by a long time lag from its beneficial results.

Another problem is that a uniform tax will not work on fisheries that have several fishing grounds with varying degrees of productivity. The proper tax must be set so the return to effort after tax is equal to the long-run marginal cost of producing it, but since the return to effort will be different in each of the areas, special tax will be necessary for each one. Enforcement of such a complex tax schedule would be difficult, as it would also be in the cases of multispecies or interdependent fisheries. The setting of tax levels would have to take these complications into account.

Finally, a tax program would encounter understandable opposition from the fishermen themselves. Given the fact that no regulatory measures have much hope of being instituted without their support, it is unlikely that taxes will ever become a popular regulatory technique.

In summary, taxes offer great potential for the proper regulation of fisheries, but serious problems stand in their way. Like all other regulatory techniques, their actual usefulness will depend upon the exact circumstances existing in a particular fishery.

In the above analysis, it was shown that, regardless of the type or size of a tax, the effect on the fishery will be the same—a reduction in output. As far as practical policy is concerned, however, the major problem is to obtain the correct tax. If the tax is set below the optimum size, there will be some gross economic efficiency gains, but there will still be some open-access waste because effort is not reduced enough. If the tax is set too high, there will be too much reduction in output and some of the potential gains from fishery utilization will be lost. Depending upon the exact size of the tax, these losses from excessive reductions in effort can be higher than the open-access waste from overexploitation, and as a result, the tax program will cause absolute losses to the economy. Of course, the same can be said for overextending any type of regulation.

It can be seen, therefore, that the problem of determining the optimal tax size is critical. Given the above discussion of the problems of using taxes and of the complexity of the optimal tax itself, the practical application of the discussion to follow may be of only academic interest. However, it will be useful for the insights the interpretation of the optimal tax provides on the nature of optimal utilization.

It will be recalled from the discussion in chapter 2 that the optimal utilization point for any given stock size is the place where the value of the marginal harvest is equal to the sum of the marginal cost of marginal effort and user cost.

For this analysis it will be useful to look into the concept of user cost in more detail. An expression for marginal user cost in terms of a two-period model analogous to the one in chapter 2 is:

$$\text{marginal user cost} = \frac{1}{1 + r} \, P_F \frac{\partial y_2}{\partial P_2} \frac{\partial P_2}{\partial y_1} \frac{\partial y_1}{\partial E_1} \tag{6.1}$$

The marginal user cost is the decrease in the present value of future harvests resulting from current harvest. Reading the expression in reverse order, this can be made more explicit. An increase in effort will increase catch this year; an increase in catch this year will decrease stock size next year; a decrease in stock next year will decrease catch next year, which will decrease the present value of harvest next year by the discounted unit price of harvest. The negative of the first four terms can be thought of as the value of a unit of catch left in the water. If an extra fish is left in the water (i.e., not harvested), the stock size next period will be different than it would have been, which, all else equal, means a change in the present value of future harvest. In general terms, of course, both marginal user cost and the value of a unit of catch left in the water must consider the effect of changes in all relevant future harvests. For simplicity, label this value of a unit of fish in the water as λ.

With this substitution, the condition for an optimal utilization can be expressed as:

$$P_F \frac{\partial y_1}{\partial E_1} - C - \lambda \frac{\partial y_1}{\partial E_1} = 0$$

or

$$(P_F - \lambda) \frac{\partial y_1}{\partial E_1} - C = 0 \tag{6.2}$$

Given the meaning of λ, the interpretation of the optimizing condition is that the net value of the marginal unit of harvest (where net value is the difference between the price of fish as a consumer good and the value of fish when left in the water) should be equal to the marginal cost of the effort to catch it.

On the other hand, the open-access point occurs where average revenue equals the constant unit cost of effort:

$$P_F \frac{y_1}{E_1} - C_1 = 0 \tag{6.3}$$

The optimal tax on effort is the one that will force producers to use equation 6.2 rather than equation 6.3 as their operative decision rule. An expression for this tax can be obtained from the following:

$$P_F \frac{y_1}{E_1} - C - t_E = (P_F - \lambda) \frac{\partial y_1}{\partial E_1} - C \tag{6.4}$$

The left-hand side is the open-access condition with a tax on effort, while the right-hand side is the necessary condition for achieving MEY. Solving for t_E obtains:

$$t_E = P_F \left(\frac{y_1}{E_1} - \frac{\partial y_1}{\partial E_1} \right) + \lambda \frac{\partial y_1}{\partial E_1} \tag{6.5}$$

Recall from chapter 2 that there are two types of overexploitation errors in an open-access fishery. In the first place, the stock is overutilized in any given period of time because individual fishermen do not consider the effect their production has on the production of all others in the current period. Further, the stock is nonoptimally depleted because individual operators do not consider the user cost they are imposing on harvesters in future periods. The two parts of this tax address each of these problems. The first part is the difference between average and marginal revenues for the fishery as a whole. The interpretation of this is really quite straigthforward. Profit-maximizing individual operators compare only their private returns to effort (which is the average return per unit of effort for the fishery as a whole) with their marginal cost of effort. They ignore the effect their effort has on the revenue of other boats in the fishery—which is to say that they ignore the marginal revenue of the fishery as a whole. As a result of this part of the tax, the fisherman—while trying to maximize profits given the tax— will be forced to take into account the difference between average and marginal yield, which was previously ignored. The tax will force the operator to compare the marginal revenue of effort for the fishery as a whole with marginal cost of producing it when making private output decisions. The second part of the tax is the marginal user cost per unit of effort (i.e., the value of a unit of fish in the water times the change in catch due to a change in effort), and hence will force the fishermen to consider this aspect of overexploitation as well.

The size of the above tax varies with total effort because average and marginal revenues vary with the level of effort. Such a variable tax would be quite difficult to administer, but the same results can be obtained by using a constant tax equal to the above evaluated at the stationary MEY level of effort.

The optimal tax on fish, which will make equation 6.3 equivalent to equation 6.2, can be derived from the following expression:

$$(P_F - t_f)\frac{y_1}{E_1} - C = (P_F - \lambda)\frac{\partial y_1}{\partial E_1} - C \tag{6.6}$$

The solution is:

$$t_f = P_F - \left[(P_F - \lambda)\frac{\partial y_1}{\partial E_1}\right]\Bigg/\frac{y_1}{E_1} \tag{6.7}$$

Evaluating this at the optimal output level where, from 6.2,

$$P_F = \lambda + \frac{C}{\partial y_1/\partial E_1} \tag{6.2'}$$

the optimal tax on fish can be expressed as:

$$t_f = \left(\frac{C}{\frac{\partial y_1}{\partial E_1}} - \frac{C}{\frac{y_1}{E_1}}\right) + \lambda$$

The terms in the parentheses will be recognized as the marginal and the average cost of fish, that is:

$$t_f = (MC_F - AC_F) + \lambda$$

The optimal tax on fish is the difference between the marginal and the average cost of fish (because in open access fishermen only consider the latter), which corrects for the overuse in the current period plus the value of a unit of fish in the water, which corrects for the nonoptimal depletion of the stock.

Distribution Issues with Licenses and Individual Transferable Quotas

The analysis in the previous two sections has demonstrated the potential economic gains that are possible with license programs and especially with individual transferable quotas. However, both differ sharply from other regulations in that individuals are directly forced out of the fishery. With gear restrictions, total quotas, etc., the fishermen who leave the fishery do so of their own volition because they cannot make a profit under the regulatory constraints. But under licensing and individual transferable quotas, some fishermen are allowed to continue their trade while others are excluded; therefore, distribution is part and parcel of the regulation. As such, it is imperative that the distribution aspects are considered carefully. Granting the property rights inherent in the licenses or individual transferable quotas is important for the potential economic efficiency improvements they can induce, but it is also important for the distribution of the gains made possible by these improvements.

To examine the implications of various distributional schemes, it may be useful to start with an illustration not related to a fishery. In the early history of the western United States, land was a form of common property to which settlers could stake claims pursuant to certain rules. This normally meant that if they lived on certain sections long enough and made proper improvements, the land was theirs. Essentially, they obtained it by the rule of capture and thereafter could use it as they pleased; they could farm it, commercialize it, or, after a certain period, sell it. Once the land became private property, its status changed. Where once it had been open for anyone to use or misuse, it now offered motivation for the owner to protect and to use properly to his best advantage.

The classic example of such a land distribution scheme was the Oklahoma land rush. All candidates for homesteads were told to meet at a given site on the Oklahoma border from which, on signal, they were free to enter the territory to look for the land they wanted; if they obeyed certain rules, the land they claimed would in due time become their property. Their title to the land was essentially won by a race. This is one way to divide up potentially valuable income-earning natural resources. One further point should be remembered: the American Indians who lived on the land were probably not too pleased about the plan for redistribution. Even if they had been allowed to join the "race," why should they want to compete for something they felt was already theirs?

The regulation of a fishery by granting property rights raises the identical sort of problems. Both systems of distribution will, on the whole, result in proper utilization of the resource, but both must face the problem of how to make an equitable distribution. The situation is further complicated when some groups are already using the resource under the existing institutional framework—and it need hardly be stressed that for most fisheries any licensing program will involve a redistribution rather than an original distribution. Whether the fishermen already on the grounds are companies or individuals, they are earning a certain amount of income from fishing, and they have made investments in capital equipment and life-styles based on the assumption that they will continue. Historically, the operation of most fisheries in this country and around the world makes this a logical assumption, and regulatory measures that may forbid or reduce the extent to which a man can fish are, in effect, a change of rules in the middle of the game. Such regulation will result in a once-and-for-all redistribution of wealth in the course of which those forced out will lose and those remaining will gain. It should be noted that, with relatively small regulatory costs, the potential gains from changing from the open-access equilibrium to a maximum economic yield are greater than the potential losses; thus, the gainers theoretically could compensate the losers and still enjoy a net benefit for themselves. Unfortunately, it is extremely difficult to include provisions for such compensation in a distribution program.

Licenses can be distributed in a variety of ways, each having a specific impact on the operation of the fishery. One method would be a grandfather system by which licenses would be granted to those already in the fishery. Apart from establishing just who belongs in this category, a more difficult problem would be the need for additional regulation, in most cases, to cause a permanent decrease in the amount of effort. Although a grandfather system would keep others from entering the fishery, it would fail to cut back on effort. One way to correct this would be to make each license nontransferable and to retract it as the holder retires until the proper number remain outstanding, at which time all licenses would become transferable.

The inequity of such a plan is that the wealth of the fishery is thus distributed according to the longevity of the original group. Perhaps a better way, then, to protect the original participants is by implementing a government buy-back plan. By this modification of the grandfather system, the licenses would be freely transferable, and the government could buy the proper number at a predetermined rate to attain the optimal number. Rational licenses, able to capture some of the wealth of the fishery in the form of payment for their licenses would not sell unless the purchase price approximated the discounted value of the stream of net income they could earn by continued fishing. This measure would go up as more fishermen sold out, so those who held out longest would obtain the most benefits.

The money to buy back the licenses would presumably come from general government funds, in which case fishermen, especially the holdouts, would be subsidized by the rest of the economy. The fishermen who remained would be benefited in two ways: the net value of their catches would improve as total effort is reduced while at the same time the value of their licenses would increase. This may offer some justification for taxing them to raise money for the buy-back program. Increased returns from the fishery would in this way be used to compensate the fishermen that choose to leave and, although the remaining fishermen would be footing the bill, it should be recalled that they paid nothing for the original license.

An additional advantage of making the licenses freely transferable is the encouragement to younger men to enter the fishery. No one is forbidden to become a fisherman; he only needs the desire and enough money to buy a piece of the production capacity, as is the case in most other industries.

Another means of distribution would be to offer fishing licenses for sale at auction. No special prerogative would have to be offered those already in the activity, although their existing equipment, skill, and preparation would put them in a favored position to use the license. Under a system of auction, the licenses could be either permanent or valid for only a specified time. In either case, the number sold could be immediately restricted to the proper total, or a larger number could be sold with the intent of buying back or eliminating some of them through time. The selling of a greater number than the optimum would ease the problem of transferring resources to other uses in the economy, since fewer fishermen would be required to make adjustments to leaving the fishery under pressure of time.

This plan would put most of the rent from the fishery into the public coffers. The actual price for a license would depend upon the number offered: the fewer available, the higher the potential profit for those who fish and the more they would bid for the license, basing their maximum bid on their anticipated increase in net revenue due to the increased catch per unit of effort. This amount would equal the average value of the rent of the fishery per unit of effort when the proper number of licenses were auctioned. Therefore, the total revenue from selling the optimal number of licenses would approach the maximum economic rent from the fishery.

One technical point should be considered: if the licenses are not permanent, they should extend long enough to enable fishermen to use the most efficient equipment. The holder of a one-year license, unsure whether he would be able to renew it, would be highly unlikely to invest in capital equipment that may take many years to amortize.

The options for the distribution of individual transferable quotas are basically the same as for licenses. Under a grandfathering system, all active participants in the fleet at a given point in time or over a specified period of time can be given a share of the total allowable catch. Obviously, if there is to be a decrease in fishing pressure, everyone will receive less than he would have caught under open access. The share to each participant is also a question of distributional equity. It can be based on percentages of individual historical catches over previous seasons or in relationship to the value of capital equipment a person owns, or it could be some combination of both. Special policies will be necessary to consider vessels under construction at the time of program initiation.

As long as the quotas are transferable, and the allowable catch is less than it would be under open access, the problems encountered with a grandfathering system with licensing do not occur. Total catch will be reduced and after the cooperative activity has been arranged or the buying and selling of quota rights has taken place, the catch will be harvested as efficiently as possible. On the other hand, if the individual quotas are equal to the amount everyone was catching in the first place and are nontransferable, further entry has been curtailed, but the problems of economic inefficiency will not have been eliminated. The only gain will be that further entry and hence further overexploitation will be prevented or at least reduced. In order to obtain the full potential gains, it will be necessary to retire a portion of individual quotas through time.

In addition to the grandfathering system, it is also possible to auction the specified number of individual transferable quotas to the highest bidders. In this case, those vessels with the lowest costs will be able to pay the highest price by operating at the minimum of their average cost curves. Therefore, the final make-up of the fleet under an auction program will tend to be identical to that of a grandfather system with transferability. In both cases, only the most efficient boats will continue to operate. The rents from the fishery, however, would be collected by the government. Viewed in this light, the direct comparison between individual transferable quotas and taxes can clearly be seen.

The problem of the appropriate length of life of the individual transferable quotas is identical to that with licenses. Ideally, they should be permanent so that proper long-run planning is possible.

Effect of Regulations on Share Rate

In chapter 4 we discussed the share system of crew remuneration. Since all regulation programs will affect the profit position of vessels (indeed, that is how they change vessel behavior), regulation programs will also have an effect on the share rate. The purpose of this section is to describe exactly how the various regulations will affect the share rate. These effects can be most clearly demonstrated with the boat equilibrium and crew equilibrium curves, as reproduced in figure 6.7. Recall that the boat equilibrium curve represents the number of vessels that owners willingly operate at various share rates (see BEC_0), while the crew equilibrium curves represent the number of vessels that will be willingly crewed at various share rates (see CEC_0). The intersection of these curves determines the open-access equilibrium number of boats (N_0) and the natural share rate (S_0). Because the analysis is in terms of vessels each producing a constant amount of effort, it will not be possible to describe analytically the indirect inefficiencies in vessel operations caused by open-access regulations. However, it will be possible to trace out the general repercussions on share rates.

Consider first the case of gear restrictions. Gear restrictions that affect crew members, such as limits on the maximum hours worked per day per crew member, minimum crew sizes, or required training courses, will shift

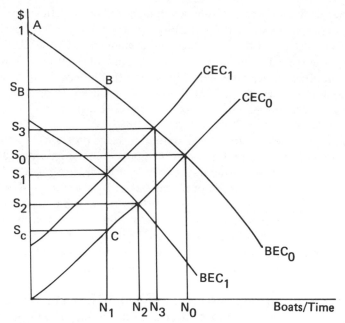

Figure 6.7. *Regulations and the Share Rate.*   Regulations that impose costs on boat owners will shift the *BEC* to the left, which will decrease the share rate. Regulations that impose costs on crew members will shift the *CEC* to the left, which will increase the share rate.

the crew equilibrium curve to the left, as from CEC_0 to CEC_1. These constraints increase the required labor costs of operating a boat, and hence each share rate will only provide enough crew profits for fewer boats. Therefore, there will be fewer boats willingly crewed at every share rate. It can be seen that, at the new equilibrium, the number of boats will be reduced to N_3 and the share rate will be increased to S_3.

     Similarly, those gear restrictions that fall completely on boat owners (limits on vessel power, etc.) will shift the boat equilibrium curve to the left, as from BEC_0 to BEC_1. In this case, it is more expensive for boat owners to operate, and therefore the amount of boat profits at each share rate will support fewer boats. The new equilibrium in this situation will also be at a smaller number of vessels (N_2), but the share rate will be reduced from S_0 to S_2. If both these gear restrictions on crew members and on boat owners are put into place simultaneously, the new equilibrium will be at the intersection of the CEC_1 and the BEC_1, which will result in a fleet size of N_1 and a share rate of S_1. The fleet size is reduced and the share rate is decreased. However, whether the share rate will go up or down in these situations will depend upon the relative size of the shift in the two curves. In this case, the shift of the BEC is greater, and so the share rate is decreased.

     If the gear restrictions fall on those inputs, the cost of which is shared by boats owners and crew members, both the *BEC* and *CEC* will shift to the left, but they will intersect at the same share rate. This will, therefore, result in a reduction in the fleet size, but there will be no change in share rate.

In summary, open-access regulations will always reduce the fleet size but will change the share rate according to which entity (boat owners or the crew members) bears most of the cost burden. If the crew bears all the costs, the share rate must go up to provide extra payments to them. In the reverse situation, the share rate must go down so as to leave more income in the hands of owners so that they can pay for their required inefficiencies. Similarly, if crew members suffer a relatively larger burden, the share rate will increase, but it will fall if the boat owners suffer more. Taxes will operate in the same manner, and the share rate will change according to which entity bears the tax.

The effect of individual transferable quotas on the share rate will depend upon which entity owns the quotas. Assume that individual transferable quotas are issued in numbers such that N_1 vessels can operate efficiently and that they are distributed to N_1 boat owners. This will make the boat equilibrium curve become a vertical line above N_1. That is, the new boat equilibrium curve can be measured by the line ABN_1. Boat owners will never wish to operate more than N_1 vessels because the extra catch could not be legally landed, given the limited number of individual quotas. The share rate in this instance will be S_C, the rate at which the line ABN_1 intersects the crew equilibrium curve.

Note, however, that boat owners would be willing to accept a share rate as high as S_B at a fleet size of N_1. The difference in what they would be willing to pay to the crew (S_B) and the amount that they have to pay (S_C) is an indication of the rent earned by the boat owners.

In the reverse case, where the individual transferable quotas are issued to crew members, the crew equilibrium curve will become a vertical line above N_1 (i.e., the new crew equilibrium curve is the line OCB). This line intersects the boat equilibrium curve at S_B, which will be the share rate under regulation. Note that crews would be willing to work for a share rate as low as S_C at this fleet size. The difference between what they actually earn in crew payments and what would be necessary to keep them at work represents the rent earned by crew members.

Two conclusions follow this analysis of individual transferable quotas. The ultimate number of vessels operating in the fleet with an individual transferable quota will be determined by the number of quotas issued. However, the share rate and, hence, who earns the rents, is a function of who owns them. If boats owners own the quotas, the share rate will be bid down by crews anxious to obtain work, and boat owners will earn the rent. On the other hand, if crew members own the individual quotas, share rates will be bid up by boat owners anxious to use their boats, and crew members will obtain the rents.

The Complete Economics of Regulation

The discussion thus far has focused on the biological effectiveness and the economic efficiency effects of fishery regulation techniques. These issues are important in determining practical regulation programs, but it is also necessary to consider institutional aspects of implementation. In addition to knowing what will happen if a particular regulation is adequately implemented, it is also necessary to understand what is really required in order to successfully implement a program (i.e., really change fishing behavior) and the degree to which it can realistically be accomplished. Equally important are government implementation costs and the costs imposed, directly or indirectly, on the industry. These issues can be usefully discussed by adopting the point of view of a fisheries management agency faced with the responsibility of designing and implementing a regulation program for a particular fishery. The analysis is drawn from Anderson (1985d) and Anderson and Lee (forthcoming). When judging the work of such agencies, the actual change in the behavior of industry participants and in market outputs is more critical than the theoretical possibilities of the management program selected. Therefore, it is important to realize that, although it is possible using the analysis discussed above, to describe an approximation of the economically efficient intertemporal harvest plan for a particular fishery, an agency cannot directly force a fleet of individual operators to follow this plan in the same way a corporate executive can plan the activities of his or her firm. The only things that agencies can directly control is type of regulation, the monitoring procedure, and in some cases the type of penalty for noncompliance, as well as the levels of each of these activities or instruments. The actual level of effort produced in any period of time is determined by the way individual firms react to market conditions, given the control instruments used and the way in which they are implemented. Therefore, fisheries agencies only indirectly determine the level of effort. To set the stage for the analysis to follow, it will be useful to discuss the items under agency control in more detail.

The first agency control variable is the choice of governing instrument or regulation type. Both limited entry and open-access regulations were discussed above. Once an instrument (or a combination of several) has been selected, it is also necessary to determine the level at which it is to be operated. For example: What should the total quota be? How many licenses should be issued?

However, determining the type and level of the governing instrument will not by itself change fishermen's behavior and therefore will not change the industry level of effort. The program must be monitored and steps must be taken to insure compliance. Hence, the second required agency control variable is a monitoring and enforcement procedure. Here again, there is a wide range from which to choose, and each will have different effects on government and industry costs and on the degree of compliance achieved. Dockside agents can inspect boats as they land, marine police or coast guard personnel can observe actual fishing at sea, auditors can review the firms' financial records, etc. Once a monitoring program has been selected, it is necessary to determine its extent of use, which usually is a decision on the amounts and types of resources that will be allocated to it.

Another necessary agency control variable is a penalty structure. Even with monitoring and enforcement, there will be no change in industry behavior if there is no penalty for deviant behavior. Possible choices are jail terms, boat or gear confiscations, forfeiture of catch, and fines. Each has different costs and different implications for compliance. Again, once the type of penalty has been chosen, it is necessary to determine the level. That is: How high should the fine be? How long should the jail sentence be?

In summary, fisheries agencies only indirectly control industry behavior, and they do so by selecting a combination of governing instrument, monitoring program, and penalty structure. The controls open to a management agency can be thought of as fixed and variable. The fixed controls are the particular governing instrument, monitoring program, and penalty structure, while the variable controls are the level at which each is set. The operational goal of a fisheries management agency should be to select the proper combination of fixed controls and to use them at the appropriate levels such that the optimum time path of effort will be produced. For purposes of this discussion, we will assume that this path can be described solely in terms of economic efficiency. The general results, however, apply to achieving any other desired harvest plan based on properly defined objectives. The real problem, of course, is to understand the indirect relationship between agency control and industry activity so that the proper control types can be set at the appropriate levels. And, as introduced above, the key to this is to understand how the profit position of individual firms is affected by the regulation program.

The motivating forces behind fishermen's behavior do not change under regulation. Each will still try to maximize profits. The only difference is that they must do so given the constraints imposed by the regulation program. The individual firm will continue to produce extra units of effort as long as it is privately profitable to do so, taking into account the way regulations affect revenues and costs. In addition, however, under regulation, firms also may find it profitable to undertake what may be called *regulation avoidance activities*, which make it more difficult for the agency to detect prohibited fishing behavior. Avoidance activities can be anything from underreporting catch to subterfuges to fishing or landing fish at night to using remote ports or fishing grounds. It is a separate activity from producing fishing effort, and firms will find it profitable to allocate resources to it as long as the returns (increased illegal catch or reduction in penalties) are greater than the costs of engaging in it.

Just because it can be profitable to engage in avoidance activities does not mean that all fishermen will react this way when the returns are in their favor. However, it would be naive to assume that this type of behavior never occurs, and a complete analysis must consider it. The amount of avoidance activity will probably vary inversely with the cohesiveness of the industry and the over-all acceptance of the need for regulation and of the perceived fairness of the particular program. For the analysis here, however, we will take the extreme case and assume that, given the nature of the existing regulation regime, indi-vidual fishing firms will select that combination of effort and avoidance activ-ities that maximizes profits.

It is important to realize, however, that the profit-maximizing behavior of regulated fishing firms is directly related to success of the monitoring pro-gram in detecting prohibited behavior. If nonadherence to regulation cannot be detected, industry production of effort will not change. Therefore, while certain management programs may look good on paper, they will not gener-ate the expected benefits unless the firms adhere to the regulation. But adher-ence will be highly unlikely unless nonadherence can be detected. Therefore, the phenomenon of detection must be considered a critical part of a regula-tion program. Let us consider it in more detail. In general, the amount of otherwise restricted fishing that is detected by the agency will be a function of how much is produced and the amount of avoidance activity (both under the control of individual firms) as well as the allowable level of fishing and the amount of monitoring activity (both under the control of the management agency). For purposes of discussion, this can be called a detection function and can be expressed as follows:

$$C^D = C^D (C, A, \bar{C}, m) \tag{6.8}$$

Let C^D be the amount of regulated activity that is detected, C the level that is actually produced by the fishery, and $\bar{C}$ the allowable level of the variable. For example, if the control variable is a quota, C^D would be the measured catch, C the actual catch, and $\bar{C}$ the allowable catch. The terms A and m refer to the amount of avoidance activity and monitoring, respectively. De-tected catch will likely increase with C and m but decrease with A and $\bar{C}^D$.

A key point to remember in devising management programs is that the detection function for different control instruments will be different. For ex-ample, catch restrictions are normally easier to monitor than are area clo-sures since they can be enforced on land at time of sale. Similarly, gear re-strictions can be quite difficult to enforce when more than one type of gear is allowed on the boat. These differences in detection functions emphasize an-other important aspect of management. In addition to the economic effi-ciency aspects of the various regulatory procedures, the ease with which non-compliance can be detected is also important.

The nature of the detection function will have significant effects on the way in which the individual fisherman chooses the profit-maximizing combi-nation of effort and avoidance activity. Just as some people observe posted highway speed limits simply because they believe in obeying the law, so will some commercial fishermen obey fishing regulations. Several important points are in order here, however. People obey the speed limits because they believe doing so will improve highway safety for themselves, their family, and other travelers. To the same degree, fishermen will obey fisheries regulations if they believe the regulations will result in benefits to themselves and their colleagues and if they think that they are being treated fairly with respect to other fishermen. However, continuing the analogy, many individuals speed on the highways, especially if they need to get from one place to another more rapidly than the law allows. This behavior is probably more prevalent when travelers are fairly sure that no traffic officers are around. Similarly, commercial fishermen will tend to disobey fisheries regulations if they can see a direct positive effect on their profits, and this behavior will be more prevalent in the absence of fisheries enforcement officers.

The penalties paid by the firm will be a function of the difference between the detected and the allowable amount of the control variable. Taking this into account, the fishing firm will produce extra units of effort as long as the value of the catch is greater than the sum of the harvesting cost and the expected penalty cost. At the same time, it will produce avoidance activities as long as the cost of the marginal unit of avoidance activity is less than the marginal reduction in penalty payments.

Given the above behavior on the part of individual firms, the aggregate regulated equilibrium level of effort and avoidance activity for the entire fishery will depend upon the allowable level of the control variable, the amount of monitoring, and the size of the penalty or fine. Therefore, if prices, costs, and technological and biological productivity of the fishery remain constant, it follows that the equilibrium-regulated level of effort and avoidance are indirectly determined by the actions of the agency. Letting K represent the size of the penalty but otherwise using the same notation as above, we can say that the agency directly controls $\bar{C}$, m, and K, and the individual firms choose their profit-maximizing combination of E and A accordingly. Therefore, the agency will indirectly control E and A, as represented in equations 6.9 and 6.10.

$$E = E\,(\bar{C},\, m,\, K) \tag{6.9}$$

$$A = A\,(\bar{C},\, m,\, K) \tag{6.10}$$

Effort will likely increase with $\bar{C}$ but decrease with m and K, while avoidance activity will likely decrease with $\bar{C}$ and increase with K. The effect of a change in m on avoidance activity is particularly interesting. In all likelihood avoidance will first increase but then decrease with m. Avoidance will be zero with no enforcement (noncompliance may be high, but there will be no incentive to distort the perceived amount of the control variable because there is no monitoring). It will initially increase with m, however, because monitoring increases the chances of detection and it may be privately productive to reduce the detected portion of the controlled output. Ultimately, however, avoidance activity will fall back to zero as monitoring increases because the increased chance of being caught will decrease the productivity of detection avoidance.

While little is known about the relationships between effort and avoidance and the control variables, if a fishery agency hopes to regulate with any degree of accuracy, it has to know what effects different policies will have on actual industry behavior. Knowledge of these relationships will help the agency to determine which control variables are more suitable to its particular problems.

Before continuing with the discussion, two comments concerning the importance of avoidance activity are in order. First, if economic efficiency is important in fisheries management, then it is necessary to take into account the degree to which any control program will encourage avoidance activity. The cost of such activities is really an implicit cost of the program in the sense that fishermen would not engage in them if there were no program. They are relevant costs in that the use of resources to engage in them precludes the production of goods and services elsewhere in the economy. However, the use of these resources is different in that they do not produce any off-setting benefits in terms of fishery output. They merely allow the industry to operate at a socially undesirable level of output, the problem that the control program is trying to correct. Second, avoidance activities are important because they can affect the general overall productivity of a management regime. That is, while they have no socially beneficial effects, the private benefit of reduced detection lowers the potential benefits to be gained from a management program.

In summary, the problem of developing a management plan is much more than determining what, if it could be achieved, would be an optimal harvest program, because the ability actually to achieve it and the direct and indirect costs involved are also important. In fact, consideration of these latter two issues redefines the concept of an optimal harvest time path.

The essence of this redefinition can be described in terms of figure 6.8. The top part is the familiar diagram (see figure 2.6), which demonstrates the difference between the open access and the efficient level of effort in a given period. The average revenue (AR) and the marginal revenue (MR) curves are defined for a particular stock size. If economic efficiency were the only criterion for management and if fishing could be costlessly regulated, it would be optimal to force the fishery to operate at E_1 during this time period. If effort is allowed to go beyond E_1, the marginal social cost (including harvest and user costs) of producing is greater than the marginal revenue of the catch, which with a constant price is equal to the value of the extra harvest. From the other way around, the marginal benefit from reducing effort from E_2 toward E_1 can be represented by the difference between the marginal social cost and the marginal revenue curves. Reductions in effort will result in a loss in marginal revenue, but until E_1 is reached, the reduction in marginal social cost is

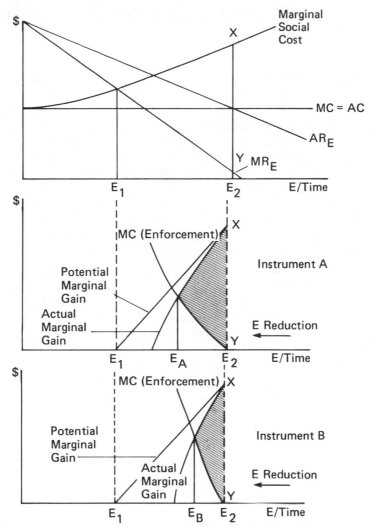

Figure 6.8. *Choice and Level of Regulatory Instrument.* The gains from regulation (effort reduction) are the reduction in open-access waste. How much of this potential is actually achieved depends, among other things, upon how the regulation affects the cost of producing effort. The optimal instrument is the one that maximizes the difference between actual gains achieved and the cost of enforcing them.

greater, and there will be potential net gains from reductions in effort.

In an overexploited fishery, the management agency's goal is to reduce effort and as such it can be quite useful to think in terms of benefits of reduced effort. This is graphically represented in figure 6.8, b and c, where the curves labeled potential marginal gain represent the difference between *MR* and marginal social cost in figure 6.8a. (The rest of the curves will be explained below.) Note that at E_2, the open-access level, potential marginal gain from effort reduction is equal to distance XY in all three graphs and that it falls to zero at E_1.

In terms of this diagram, the management problem is to determine a program that will achieve maximum potential benefits, net of all costs. This involves the selection of the proper combination of governing instrument, enforcement activity, and penalty structure and the optimal level at which to operate each of these control variables. While this is obviously a very complicated problem, most of the important issues can be demonstrated by focusing on the more restricted problem of choosing between two instruments, each at a set level with a predetermined penalty structure. To retain neutrality, the instruments will be called type A and type B. They could be taxes, individual quotas, gear restrictions, etc.

The difference between the two regulation types is demonstrated in figure 6.8, b and c by the curves labeled actual marginal gain. They represent the marginal regulatory gains that can actually be achieved from the particular instrument. The actual marginal gain is different from the potential marginal gain for at least two reasons. First, as described above, some regulatory types cause effort to be produced inefficiently. Second, regulations can encourage firms to engage in avoidance activity. The first increases the cost of producing effort while the second indirectly increases costs associated with fishing. Both affect the size of the actual gains that will be achieved with reductions in effort. Recall that the potential marginal gain curve is constructed as the difference between the marginal social cost curve and the marginal revenue-of-effort curve. This is because the benefit of reducing effort is the reduction in the marginal social cost of harvesting, while the cost is the foregone output of fish. The actual marginal gain curve takes into account the other costs associated with the way in which effort is reduced. The degree to which the actual marginal gain curves for different regulatory types will differ depends upon the specific incentives the particular instrument provides to produce inefficiently or to engage in avoidance activities. These incentives will depend in part on the nature of the detection function associated with the regulatory type.

The curves labeled marginal cost (enforcement) in figure 6.8, b and c represent the marginal cost of causing the industry to reduce effort from the open-access level, E_2, to any particular level of effort. It is enforcement that actually drives the system. With no enforcement activity, there will be no reduction in effort. However, as enforcement is increased, the equilibrium level of effort in the fishery will fall. Depending upon the nature of the detection function and the actual cost of particular enforcement activity, the cost of reducing effort can, and most likely will, vary between instruments. As such, the marginal cost of enforcement curves is drawn differently for the two regulatory types. The amount of avoidance activity also varies with the amount of enforcement, but this is accounted for in the difference between the potential and actual marginal gain curves.

In terms of this simplified example, the problem facing the agency is to determine which instrument type can achieve the highest net gains. In figure 6.8b, the optimal amount of enforcement with regulation type A is where effort is reduced from E_2 to E_A. At this point, the marginal enforcement cost of obtaining the last unit of effort reduction is just equal to the actual marginal gain of that reduction. At levels of effort higher than E_A, the actual marginal gains from a further reduction will be higher than the enforcement cost of obtaining it, and so it makes sense to continue reducing effort. The crosshatched area between the marginal cost of enforcement curve and the actual marginal gain curve from E_A to E_2 represents the total net gains for the current period. The optimal amount of effort and the total gain the next period will depend upon how the various curves will change, due to the change in stock size.

Similarly, the optimum level of effort for the current period, using the instrument type B, is E_B, and the yearly net gain is the crosshatched area in figure 6.8c. Notice that the optimal level of effort and the net actual gains for the same fishery vary with the type of instrument used. The size of the net gains will depend upon the loss in potential gains, which is a function of the inefficiencies in producing effort and the avoidance activities generated, and upon the marginal cost of enforcement, which is a function of the ease of detection, the cost of the enforcement activity, and the response of individual firms.

If the agency only had the choice between these two instruments at the specified levels, it appears as if instrument A would provide greater gains than would instrument B. However, in order to obtain these gains, the program should be enforced such that effort is reduced to E_A. The dual nature of this solution is critical. It involves the choice of the instrument and the way it should be used.

It should be emphasized, however, that the curves are drawn for a given level of the specified instruments, and so the nature of the real solution is even more complex. For example, if instrument type A is a tax that is set quite low, effort will only be reduced a small amount even with perfect enforcement and, hence, perfect adherence. However, a higher tax with perfect enforcement will reduce effort even further. Obviously, therefore, a complete analysis requires that the net gains for various levels of each instrument be determined. Which level is best for a particular regulatory type will depend upon how actual marginal gains and marginal enforcement costs are affected by changes in the level of the instrument. For example, the higher the tax, up to the optimal level, the higher will be the actual marginal gain curve because there will be a greater potential to eliminate excess capacity. At the same time, however, if the chance of detection and the level of enforcement are such that fishermen are encouraged to participate in avoidance activities, the actual marginal gain curve will be quite low. In any event, changing the level of a particular regulation type will potentially change both the actual marginal gain curve and the marginal cost (enforcement) curve. The optimal level for any instrument will be the place where the difference between the two curves, over the range of the optimal reduction in effort (as represented by the cross-hatched areas in figure 6.8, b and c), is a maximum.

Let us turn now to the more general discussion of determining an optimal fisheries management program. The goal is to determine the optimal combination of regulation instrument, enforcement activity, and penalty structure and the desired level of each. There are two steps in determining this optimal package. The first is to select likely combinations of the three main control variables. Since there are many types of governing instruments, monitoring programs, and penalty structures, the number of different combinations will be large, indeed. Some method will obviously have to be derived to filter out those combinations that would likely result in inferior management programs. For those that appear to have potential, however, it is necessary to determine at which level each variable should be set in this and future periods to obtain the maximum present value of gains. This is a simultaneous problem because industry reactions to the three control variables are interrelated. For example, the amount of adherence obtained by an increase in enforcement will depend upon the actual level of the tax and the size of the penalties. Once the desired level of each of the control variables is determined for each of the likely combinations, the second step is to select the combination that produces the highest net gain. If economic efficiency is the desired goal, this combination of instrument, enforcement activity, and penalty structure is the one that should be used. However, the maximum gains will not be achieved unless each is set at the appropriate level.

As a sidelight, it is possible to use the above discussion to focus in on another real-world management problem. Often management agencies have a limited capability to engage in enforcement activities. Therefore, it is necessary to determine how this capability can be used most advantageously. If it is possible to obtain information similar to that described in figure 6.8, b and c, this problem can be solved. The difference between the actual marginal gain and the marginal cost (enforcement) curves is the net gain per unit of effort reduction. Assume for the moment that the figures represent two different fisheries, both under the control of the same fisheries agency rather than as the same fishery operating under different controls as before. The problem is to determine how to allocate the enforcement capacity between the two fisheries. The gains from regulation will be maximized if the capacity is used first where the marginal net gains per unit of capacity are the greatest. Therefore, the capacity should be spread among the two fisheries such that the marginal gain from the last unit of capacity used in both fisheries is the same. For example, if 80 percent of capacity is used in one fishery and 20 percent is used in the other but the actual marginal gains, net of enforcement costs per unit of enforcement capacity for each fishery, are $1,500 and $2,000, respectively, the resources are not being used optimally. Shifting enforcement capacity from the low to the high return, the fisheries will increase the net benefits.

There will be a loss of $1,500 from removing the enforcement capacity from the first fishery, but there will be a gain of $2,000 by applying it to the second. Note, however, that with these shifts the marginal gain in the fishery receiving more attention will decrease while the return in the other will go up. Shifting the enforcement capacity will continue to be profitable, however, until the marginal returns become equal.

The information in this section can be of great assistance in determining an optimal fisheries management plan. In many instances, of course, it will not be possible to derive a detection function or the curves analogous to those in figure 6.8, a, b, and c. However, this analysis does provide an excellent framework for approaching the problem. It should be realized that, when adopting a management plan, there is a wide range of regulatory types from which to choose, and the actual gains achieved will depend upon how the industry responds to the particular instrument, monitoring plan, and penalty structure. Regulation can theoretically produce net benefits if overcapacity is reduced, but at the same time it generates enforcement costs as well as potential inefficiences in the production of effort and the encouragement of avoidance activities by fishermen. It is a complex procedure to select the appropriate combination of control variables, and the answer will differ from fishery to fishery. The economic, technological, and biological characteristics of the various fisheries will determine the nature of the detection function and the way in which firms react to various regulations in terms of effort produced, operating costs, and avoidance activity. Therefore, the optimal management program will have to be individually constructed for each fishery.

The Process of Developing Fisheries Management Policy

As indicated in the introduction, the rational exploitation of fisheries requires a multidisciplinary approach—biology, economics, management sciences, law, anthropology, sociology, etc. However, as promised, this discussion has focused exclusively on the economic aspects. The purpose of this section is to expand the discussion somewhat by suggesting a process by which fisheries management regulation programs can be properly developed. The discussion will be more general, and a goal will be to describe how and where the economic principles presented above fit into the whole picture.

Economic theory indicates that an unregulated fishery will result in the suboptimal utilization of the fish stock and the inputs used to harvest it. The first step in the management process, therefore, is to determine the current state of the fishery because, more than likely, the stock, the fleet, and the harvest will be nonoptimal in size and composition. Some of the questions that need to be answered to ascertain the state of the fishery are: What is stock size, annual recruitment, and stock growth rate? What are the relationships between these variables and the level and composition of total landings, and how do they vary with the behavior of other exploited and unexploited fish stocks? What is the size of the relevant fleet, and what determines its annual harvest—its growth? What are the production technicalities of harvest, processing, and marketing, and how are they affected by changes in biological and economic conditions and by the various regulatory measures? What is the income from the fishery, and how is it distributed? Once the current situation in the fishery is described and the basic nature of the interrelationships between the fleet and the stock is understood, it is possible to consider the question of how the fishery should be changed and by what means.

Depending upon the circumstances of the particular fishery, however, the ease of obtaining this information can vary quite significantly. Therefore, the policy development process must often start with whatever information is available. Programs to collect more and better information should be developed and implemented along with regulatory programs so that the new management programs can be developed as necessary as the fishery is better understood.

Once the above tasks are completed, it will be possible to give a more or less detailed description of the present state of both the fish stock or stocks and the industry. If no other possible state is preferred to the existing one and if it appears that no changes are likely, there is obviously no need for management. However, if other states are desired, the next step is to select appropriate management objectives as a guide to developing a management program.

Management objectives are the stated goal or goals to be achieved by a fisheries plan. They are a necessary part of the plan development process because they provide the only means of comparing the different potential regulatory schemes in order to select the one to be included in the plan. If objectives are to be useful in the comparison process, they must have an unambiguous interpretation. There are several important characteristics of such operational objectives. First, they must be stated such that criteria for success or failure can be quantified. The objective of improving fisheries may sound good, but it offers no real help in comparing policy alternatives. However, the goal of maximizing net revenues from the fishery is operational because earnings and costs can be measured and hence can provide an explicit means of comparison. While some important aspects of fisheries, such as equity, industry structure, etc. are difficult to quantify, they can still be appropriate considerations for management objectives. But, unless the objective is stated such that there is a viable method of determining that it has been met, comparisons of regulatory techniques will not be possible.

Related to the problem of quantification is the problem of the relative values to be given to conflicting objectives. There will almost always be more than one management objective, and hence there can be conflicts. In fact, if objectives are distinguishable from a management point of view, they will conflict. In cases where accomplishing one objective will also satisfy the others, there is really only one operational objective. It does not matter which one is selected as a basis for management; success in achieving one will guarantee success in the others. On the other hand, if there are analytically separate objectives, a policy that best achieves one will not achieve the other. To make objectives operational in these cases, it is necessary to specify the relative value of the various objectives so as to provide a means of comparing the positive and negative aspects of various regulatory options.

Consider a fishery where maximizing the net revenue of the entire fleet is an important goal, but due to income distributional considerations, it is desired to give special importance to income in a depressed port. If productivity in the depressed port is lower than elsewhere, the two objectives will conflict, because if the less efficient individuals from the depressed port are given preferential access to the stock the overall efficiency of the fishery will fall. The second objective can be achieved only at the expense of the other. One way to solve this problem is to place relative weights on these conflicting objectives. One alternative would be to maximize net revenues such that $1 in the depressed port is given a larger value, say $1.10, than $1 in other ports. In this way, policies favoring the depressed port would have larger weighted net revenues.

Constraints are another way of dealing with conflicting objectives. For example, in the previous case, if the management authority is not prepared to place relative weights on the net income to the various ports, it may be willing to set a minimum acceptable level of income for the depressed port. The appropriate objective would then be to maximize net revenue for the fishery such that net revenue in the less developed port is greater than or equal to a specified amount. Conceptually, determining the constraint is no different from assigning relative weights, but in some instances it may be an easier way to approach the problem.

A third important characteristic of operational objectives is the time frame. An objective of increased catch per unit of effort can be achieved more rapidly, all else equal, if harvest is stopped completely rather than if it is merely curtailed. The former will obviously have more arduous short-term effects on the profitability of the fleet, however. The trade-off between gains from management and the costs associated with the rate at which objectives are achieved is thus an important part of operational management objectives.

Also important is the range of issues under consideration (sometimes called the *accounting stance*) used in determining policy. For example, a narrow accounting stance would focus only on the existing harvesting sector in a particular fishery. A slightly broader stance would include potential entrants to the fleet, while a more general stance would consider the processing sector and perhaps various aspects of other related fisheries. The most general accounting stance would also include related industries such as boat building, net manufacturing, etc.

Specific fisheries management policies can have significant effects on the

harvesting and processing sectors and, depending on the technicalities involved, can even cause repercussions throughout the economy and society as a
whole. Adopting a narrow accounting stance will mean that only those effects
within the particular fishery will be considered. This makes policy development and implementation much simpler because it is only necessary to specify
objectives for those aspects of the fishery within the accounting stance. Therefore, there are likely to be fewer objectives and hence less potential for conflicts. Of course, it also increases the chances that some important variables
will be ignored and the policy selected will be inappropriate. The reverse argument holds for adopting a broader accounting stance. There are more issues that must be built into the objectives, which makes policy analysis more
difficult and, as a result, more expensive. However, it will lower the probability of selecting a suboptimal policy. The proper balance is to select an accounting stance that includes most of the relevant issues and where greater
detail is likely to increase policy analysis costs by more than the value of the
extra information.

    There is a wide range of relevant fisheries management objectives, but
there is no one combination that will be best for all fisheries at all times.
There are, however, certain points that are useful in selecting objectives.
First, for the most part, specific biological objectives are usually not necessary, and may in fact cloud the real issues behind management. For example,
an objective to achieve a standing stock of a specific size may be clear and
concise, but it begs the important question of why such a stock is beneficial.
Does this prevent extinction, keep catch per unit of effort high, etc.? These
things are important for the continued commercial success of the fishery, and
management objectives should address them directly. This does not mean
that the biology of the stock is not important. But achievement of properly
stated economic and social objectives will, of necessity, properly maintain the
stock.

    The efficiency aspects of fishery operation are important because the gen-
eral scarcity of resources requires that they be utilized effectively. It is vitally
important to consider the value of the harvest and the cost of the resources
used to obtain it. Managing such that the fishery achieves the maximum difference between value and cost of harvest will insure that resources are not
used in the fishery if they could be used more beneficially elsewhere in the
economy. Given resource scarcity, economic efficiency should be at least one
of the objectives used when selecting proper management strategies.
Granted, other issues are important also, and some of them may directly conflict with economic efficiency. (See the discussion of maximum social yield
above.) But the range of objectives selected and the relative weights assigned
to each should be such that the cost in terms of lost economic efficiency for
achieving other goals is directly considered. For example, while increased employment may be a valid objective, the gains from increased labor force par-

ticipation must be weighed against the economic efficiency costs of improper use of other resources due to overcapitalization. Further, while increased employment, which comes at the cost of reductions in total output, may be acceptable, it is likely that after some point the cost of continued increases in employment may become too high.

Another important economic aspect of management objectives is that, directly or indirectly, almost all will have income distributional implications. For example, the objective to increase total harvest may be obtained only by allowing individual fish to grow. Because of the size distribution of the stock and the make-up of the fleet, however, this may mean that only larger boats that work further from shore will be allowed to harvest. This may cause a redistribution of income from inshore to offshore vessels. Obviously, such a distribution will be an important aspect of the management policy, especially for the individuals involved. Management should therefore take these effects directly into account, and this can only be accomplished if distributional considerations are specified in an operational management objective.

The next step is to select the appropriate regulation package so as to best achieve the stated objectives. The previous section described how this could be done if economic efficiency were the only consideration. A similar procedure is appropriate when there are many objectives. It is first necessary to select a range of possible management programs (i.e., regulation type, enforcement program, and penalty structure) and then to find out which one, when operated correctly, most nearly achieves the stated objectives.

After implementing the appropriate management program, the next step is to monitor the fishery under the regulatory program. If the objectives have been stated properly, it will be possible to show in a quantifiable manner the degree to which they have been achieved. The purpose of this step is to monitor those critical elements of the fishery to see how they are changing as a result of the regulatory program. Using the results of the monitoring program, the next step is to determine if the objectives of management are being achieved. If the important parameters are being affected in the correct ways, then the management process is reduced to a continuation of current policy and continued monitoring to insure that the policy remains successful. If this is not the case, it is necessary to adjust the existing regulatory program or perhaps institute a completely new one. This decision should be based on a comparative study of how the fishery will react to the changes or the new program, considering what was learned from using the original program, and, in particular, why it did not perform as had been predicted.

The final step is periodically to reevaluate the fishery and the objectives of management. If the needs of the fishery change over time, due to better perceptions from improved information collected during the management process or to changes in the biological or economic conditions or because of the success of the regulatory program, it may be necessary to restate the objectives of management and begin the policy development process again. To see if this is the case, it is necessary occasionally to repeat the review and analysis of the whole fishery, which was the first step in the management process.

A Note on the Regulation of International Fisheries

Despite the recent changes in international law concerning a nation's right to manage the fisheries off its coasts, many stocks migrate between the fishing zones of more than one country. These fisheries face the same problems as any other, but they are further handicapped by the absence of any single authority with the power to institute regulations. No country engaged in fishing will delegate power to a central regulatory agency for fear that management decisions may dilute its national "rights." If the fish stock is in danger of being destroyed, nations may agree on gear restrictions or seasonal closures; these will, at least in the short run, be biologically beneficial to the fish stock without altering national advantages in the race to capture the fish. As pointed out earlier, however, effective long-run management must include some direct control over the total amount of effort, which will always involve a redistribution of the wealth of the fishery. Piecemeal reduction in effort will always result in inefficiently produced effort. Just as in the case of a nationally controlled fishery, some agreement on the distribution of the fishery must precede any economically optimal regulation policy.

In the discussion of maximum economic yield of an international fishery in chapter 4, it was concluded that the rights to the fishery, defined in terms of allowable effort, can be distributed in a mutually satisfactory way, the precise manner of division being immaterial to proper management. Where resources are mobile, however, some distribution will be possible whereby no country will be made worse off. Moreover, rights to the fishery should be freely transferable. In this way, those countries not able to produce effort as efficiently as others can either lease out their rights or hire effort from other countries to utilize those rights, with the result that the resource will provide maximum benefit and the fish will be harvested at minimum cost. In most cases, of course, the basic fishing license program will have to be supplemented with area closures, size limitations, and so forth, depending upon the specific biological and economic characteristics of the fishery.

The main difference between the management of a national and an international fishery is that the latter presents more prickly and more pressing distributional problems, adding to the highly complex job of managing any fishery. For interesting detailed analyses of the problems faced in international fisheries, see Cunningham et al. (1985) and Underdal (1980).

7

Practical Applications

Introduction

Thus far the discussion of the eonomics of fishery exploitation has for the most part been fairly theoretical. This last chapter aims to demonstrate in greater detail the practical utility of this theory. The first section consists of a brief description of several empirical studies of a particular fishery, showing the methods used and the nature of the results.

Empirical work on the New England lobster fishery derived from Bell (1970, 1972), Bell and Fullenbaum (1973), and Fullenbaum and Bell (1974) will be described in some detail so as to show exactly what types of data manipulations are required to do these sorts of studies. The results of other studies will be described in less detail to show what other types of real-world management questions can be answered and to what extent. A concluding section discusses practical applications of fisheries economics theory in more general terms. Because of the importance of applied research in putting the theory to work, this is also an appropriate concluding section to the book.

Examples of Empirical Models

Introduction

The purpose of this section is to demonstrate the applicability of some aspects of the preceding theoretical discussions. The work of Bell and others on the United States northern lobster fishery demonstrates that, using fairly accessible data, it is possible to obtain a rudimentary picture of open-access operation of a fishery and to recommend regulatory policies. Certainly much more work is needed before such studies can be perfected, and there is no claim that either the specific models that are used here or the estimated equations that are derived from them are the last word on the subject. A case in point is the lack of data on growth rates, which precludes any analysis of dynamic MEY. The first study to be discussed concentrates on revenue and cost

249

curves while the second, using only slightly more information, presents a general bioeconomic description of the fishery.

Lobster Revenue and Cost Models

Three pieces of information are needed for revenue and cost models: (1) an estimate of the sustainable yield curve, (2) an estimate of the average cost of effort, and (3) an estimate of the price of output. How each of these was obtained will be discussed in turn.

Following Schaefer (1954, 1957a, 1959), the sustainable yield curve, which has been diagrammed repeatedly throughout this book, can be expressed in mathematical terms as:

$$Y = cE - dE^2 \tag{7.1}$$

Using standard mathematical techniques, it can be shown that maximum sustainable yield will equal $c^2/4d$ and will be obtained when effort is equal to $c/2d$.

To apply equation 7.1 to a fishery, it is neccessary to obtain numerical estimates of the parameters, c and d. This can be accomplished in the following manner. It follows from the sustainable yield equation that average sustainable yield per unit of effort can be expressed as:

$$\frac{Y}{E} = c - dE \tag{7.2}$$

Therefore, if it is possible to get data on average catch and total effort over a period of years, estimates of c and d can be obtained, using ordinary least-squares regression techniques.

In the lobster fishery, seawater temperature is an important variable in the growth of the population; therefore, it is useful to modify the average catch equation as follows:

$$\frac{Y}{E} = c - dE + f\,(^{\circ}F) \tag{7.3}$$

This says that the average catch will depend upon seawater temperature (measured in degrees Fahrenheit) as well as upon the amount of effort used. In this way an important environmental variable can be built into the model.

Using data on average catch (measured in millions of pounds), effort (measured by the number of traps used), and seawater temperature for the years 1950 to 1966, the following equation for average catch was estimated as:

$$\frac{Y}{E} = -48.4 - .000024E + 2.126^{\circ}F \tag{7.4}$$

The estimates of the parameters were statistically significant at the 5 percent level, and there was no evidence of autocorrelation. According to these figures, an increase in effort of 100,000 traps will decrease annual catch per trap by 2.4 pounds, and an increase in temperature of one degree Fahrenheit will increase it by 2.126 pounds.

Using the 1966 average seawater temperature of 46 degrees Fahrenheit, which was close to the average of that over the past 65 years, the average catch equation becomes:

$$\frac{Y}{E} = 49.4 - .000024E$$

Multiplying through by E obtains the sustainable yield equation:

$$Y = 49.4E - .000024E^2 \qquad\qquad (7.5)$$

By use of the formulations derived earlier, the maximum sustainable yield is shown to be 25.459 million pounds, and it will be taken with 1,030,000 traps.

Industry data for the year 1966 allowed derivation of the following estimates of the cost of maintaining a lobster boat:

Operating Expenses		$ 4,965.16
Bait	$1,267.28	
Fuel	697.88	
Repair	3,000.00	
Fixed Expenses		$ 1,180.20
Depreciation	891.00	
Interest	289.20	
Returns to Capital and Labor		$ 5,925.48
Labor	5,202.48	
Capital	723.00	
TOTAL EXPENSES		$12,070.84

The total bait cost was estimated using the average number of traps fished per boat and the average bait cost per trap. Fuel cost was based on its unit price, the average number of trips, and the efficiency of the engines. The repair cost was determined directly from discussions with the fishermen.

The depreciation figures were based upon 10 percent of the hull value, 20 percent of the engine value, and 10 percent of the value of other equipment—percentages commonly accepted in the fishery. Interest was figured on the basis of 6 percent of the amount of indebtedness, that being the normal borrowing rate in 1966.

The return to labor was measured by the wages the fishermen could earn in other pursuits in the area. The rate of return to capital was estimated at a high 15 percent of the boat owner's equity because of the riskiness of the lobster fishery.

The total expenses of $12,070.84 per boat represent the opportunity cost of the vessel. The fisherman must earn at least this amount or, in the long run, it will be to his best advantage to cease fishing. Since the average boat carries 562.8 traps, the average opportunity cost of a trap is $21.43. Therefore, total cost can be expressed as a function of effort measured in traps:

$$TC = 21.43E \qquad (7.6)$$

It is now possible to obtain an equation for average cost in terms of output. We know that average cost is equal to total cost divided by total yield. Expressed in terms of E this is:

$$AC = \frac{21.43E}{49.4E - .000024E^2} \qquad (7.7)$$

This can be simplified to:

$$AC = \frac{21.43}{49.4 - .000024E} \qquad (7.7')$$

Solving equation 7.5 for E using the quadratic equation, we obtain:

$$E = \frac{-49.4 \pm \sqrt{[(49.4)^2 - 4(.000024)\,Y]}}{-2(.000024)} \qquad (7.8)$$

Substituting this into equation (7.7') yields:

$$AC = \frac{21.43}{\dfrac{49.4 \pm \sqrt{[(49.4)^2 - 4(.000024)\,Y]}}{2}}, \qquad (7.9)$$

which is an estimate of average cost in terms of total yield. It is also possible to get an estimate of marginal cost in terms of total yield by substituting equation (7.8) into equation (7.6) and taking the first derivative. This is:

$$MC = \frac{21.43}{\sqrt{[(49.4)^2 - 4(.000024)Y]}} \qquad (7.10)$$

Table 7.1, which was constructed using equations 7.5, 7.9, and 7.10, shows the relationship between total yield and average and marginal cost per pound. Notice that, as the number of traps increases, total yield eventually falls, but average cost per pound continues to rise because more money is being spent to obtain less yield. The marginal cost over this range of decreasing yield has no economic meaning.

It is beyond the scope of this book to explain how economists estimate demand curves, but suffice it to say that the following demand curve for the northern lobster fishery was estimated by way of standard economic tech-

Table 7.1. *Cost Data for Northern Lobster Fishery.*   This table shows the relationship between average and marginal cost of lobster and yield and effort in 1966.

Total Yield (Mill. lbs.)	Effort (Thous. traps)	Average Cost per Pound (Dollars)	Marginal Cost per Pound (Dollars)
1.0	20	.438	.443
5.0	107	.458	.484
10.0	227	.488	.557
15.0	370	.529	.677
20.0	553	.593	.937
25.0	892	.765	3.228
25.459*	1,030	.872	infinity
25.0	1,168	1.002	negative
20.0	1,507	1.616	negative
15.0	1,690	2.417	negative
10.0	1,833	3.930	negative
5.0	1,953	8.379	negative
1.0	2,039	43.743	negative

SOURCE: Bell (1970, table 1).
*Maximum sustainable yield.

niques and data comprising the ex-vessel price of northern inshore lobsters, aggregate U.S. personal income, U.S. population, the consumer price index, and total consumption, total imports, and total U.S. production of lobsters as well as production of northern inshore lobsters. The resultant equation,

$$\text{Price} = .9393 - .005705 \ Y, \tag{7.11}$$

states that, as the amount of northern lobsters harvested increases by a million pounds, the price will fall by a little more than one-half cent a pound.

This demand curve, together with the average and marginal cost curves from table 7.1, is plotted in the top half of figure 7.1; the lower half charts the sustainable yield curve as expressed in equation 7.5, the number of traps being measured in a downward direction. We know from the earlier analysis that open-access equilibrium will occur where the demand curve intersects the average cost curve. The diagram of this model predicts that the intersection will be reached at a price of $0.7952 and a total yield of 25.24 million pounds, obtained by using 933,000 traps. The actual figures for 1966 were $0.762, 25.6 million pounds and 947,113 traps.

Maximum economic yield occurs at the intersection of the marginal cost curve and the demand curve. According to the diagram this occurs at a price of $0.833 and a total yield of 18.57 million pounds obtained by using 490,000 traps. The average cost per pound while operating at this level of output is $0.571. The total economic rent earned at this point is the difference between the selling price and average cost multiplied by total yield, or $4,865,340.

The implications of these findings for economically efficient policy are as

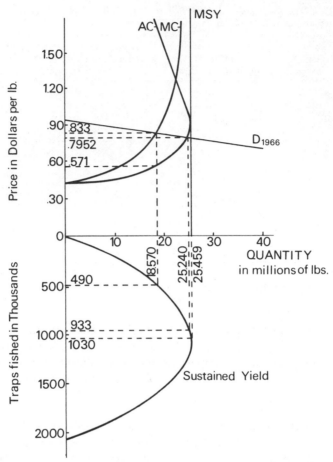

Figure 7.1. *Average Cost and Demand for the Northern Lobster Fishery in 1966.* Open-access equilibrium yield will occur at the intersection of the demand and the average cost curves. At this point price will be $0.7952 and total yield will be 25,459 million pounds, which can be harvested with 933,000 traps. Maximum economic yield occurs at the intersection of the demand and the marginal cost curves. At this point price will be $0.833 and total yield will be 18,570 million pounds, which can be harvested with 490,000 traps.

follows. Output in the fishery should be reduced from 25.24 to 18.57 million pounds by reducing the number of traps from 933,000 to 490,000. This will reduce average cost per pound from $0.7952 to $0.571, for a combined reduction in total cost of $9,467,378. Remembering the definition of opportunity cost, this reduction implies that goods worth that amount can now be produced in other parts of the economy. At the same time, however, the reduction in total yield, even though it will cause an increase in price, will cause the total value of lobsters consumed to fall from $20,070,848 to $15,468,810, for a loss of $4,602,038. Subtracting this from the increase in the production of goods in other areas, we find that a move to maximum economic yield has yielded to society a net benefit of $4,865,340. This is, of course, equal to the rent the fishery earns when operated at a static MEY. This conclusion holds for the year 1966, but for current policy decisions, the most recent data should be used to construct the curves for sustained yield, cost, and demand.

Interpreting the above in terms of dynamic analysis implies that effort should be reduced no more than to 490,000 traps. Precisely what this amount should be and how fast it should be approached depends upon the rate of growth of the lobster stock and the discount rate. Unfortunately, Bell did not extend the study to cover this aspect of regulation.

In a recent study Smith (1980) has shown that Bell overestimated the effect reductions in traps would have on the reduction in harvest, which means that the number of traps may have to be reduced to 25 percent rather than 50 percent of the open-access number. This demonstrates the importance of the basic economic product analysis on policy conclusions.

As a sidelight, it should be noted that, when no reliable demand curve can be obtained for the fishery, a simple fixed-price model can be used. For example, using the actual 1966 price of $0.762, the total revenue equation in terms of effort becomes:

$$TR = .762 \, (49.4E - .000024E^2) \tag{7.12}$$

The total cost equation in terms of effort has already been described in equation 7.6; plotting these two curves in figure 7.2, we can see that under these conditions, the open-access equilibrium occurs at 888,324 traps, while MEY occurs at 444,162 traps. Using this formulation, the derived estimate of dissipated rent is $3,612,000.

General Bioeconomic Equilibrium Model of Lobster

We have just seen how useful results can be obtained even with small amounts of data. But it is possible to expand the information by just slightly increasing the input of data. In particular, if it is possible to get an independent estimate of the size of the population at maximum sustainable yield, a general bioeconomic equilibrium model can be derived, which will, by the way, contain the essentials for dynamic analysis, as discussed in chapter 4. What follows is a description of such a study on the northern lobster fishery.

The main purpose of the study was to estimate equations for the population equilibrium curve and for the economic equilibrium curve. As explained earlier, the former establishes the combinations of population size and total effort that produce an equilibrium population; the latter comprises the combinations that produce an equilibrium level of effort. Graphical representations of these equations appear in figure 4.14. The equations themselves can be derived in the following manner.

Following Schaefer (1954, 1957a, 1959), the equation for the growth rate of a fish population (P) can be written as:

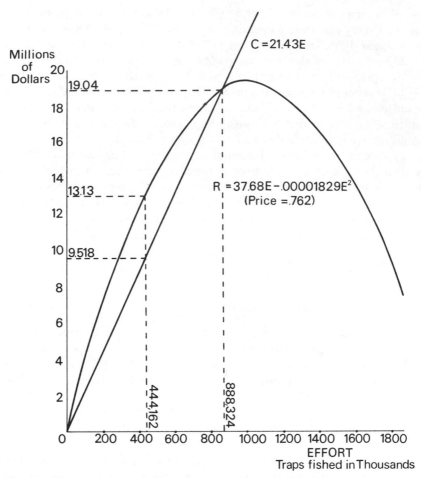

Figure 7.2. *Revenue and Cost in Terms of Effort.*   Using the 1966 price of $0.762, a total revenue curve can be derived from the sustained yield curve. Using this analysis, open-access equilibrium yield will occur at 888,324 traps, while MEY will be at 444,162 traps.

$$\frac{dP}{dt} = aP - bP^2 \qquad\qquad (7.13)$$

dP/dt represents the change in population size in weight per period of time, and a and b are constant parameters. It follows that the growth rate will be zero when the population size is zero and also when it is a/b. The latter will be the natural equilibrium population size for an unexploited stock. Growth, and therefore sustainable yield, will be a maximum when population is at $a/2b$.

The total harvest rate or catch rate at any point in time can be expressed as:

$$Y_t = rPE \tag{7.14}$$

This equation states that catch at any point in time depends upon the amount of effort used, the size of the population, and a "catchability" coefficient, r.

The population will be in equilibrium when the rate of catch equals the natural rate of growth. Mathematically, this can be expressed as:

$$aP - bP^2 - rPE = 0 \tag{7.15}$$

Solving for P yields:

$$P = \frac{a}{b} - \frac{r}{b} E, \tag{7.16}$$

which is the equation for the population equilibrium curve in this simplified model. It shows that, when E equals zero, the equilibrium population size will be a/b. As E increases, equilibrium will occur only at a smaller population size. How fast the equilibrium population size decreases as E increases depends upon the size of the growth coefficient, b, and the "catchability" coefficient, r.

On the economic side of the picture, an equilibrium level of effort in an open-access fishery will be reached when total revenue equals total cost. Recall from equation 7.11 that the general equation for a demand curve is of the form:

$$\text{Price} = \alpha - \beta Y_t \tag{7.17}$$

That is, price is a decreasing function of the quantity harvested. Y_t, however, can be expressed as rPE (see equation 7.14). Therefore, total revenue (or price times quantity harvested) becomes:

$$TR = (\alpha - \beta rPE)\, rPE \tag{7.18}$$

By letting π^* represent the per-unit opportunity cost of effort, the economic equilibrium condition for an open-access fishery (total revenue equals total cost) can be expressed as:

$$(\alpha - \beta rPE)\, rPE - \pi^* E \tag{7.19}$$

Solving this for E yields:

$$E = \frac{\alpha}{\beta rP} - \frac{\pi^*}{\beta r^2 P^2}, \tag{7.20}$$

which is the equation for the economic equilibrium curve. Although it is not subject to as simple an interpretation as is the population equilibrium equation, effort must change with changes in the population size in order to keep an equilibrium, and the equilibrium amount of effort for any population size will depend upon the sizes of α and β (the coefficients of the demand curve), upon the "catchability" coefficient r, and upon π^*, the unit opportunity cost of effort.

To use this model, it is necessary to obtain estimates of the following parameters: a, b, r, P, α, β, and π^*. All but the first four were estimated in the study previously discussed, and since an estimate of P is possible if a and b are known, the only new information that is needed for this study is estimates of a, b, and r. These can be obtained in a fairly straightforward manner, however. Substituting 7.16 into 7.14, we obtain an equation for the sustainable yield curve, because we have substituted the equation for the equilibrium population into the catch equation. This can be expressed as:

$$Y = \frac{ra}{b}E - \frac{r^2}{b}E^2 \tag{7.21}$$

This is the same as equation 7.1 except that:

$$d = \frac{r^2}{b} \tag{7.22}$$

and

$$c = \frac{ra}{b} \tag{7.23}$$

As demonstrated above, it is possible to obtain estimates of c and d (the parameters of the sustainable yield curve) by using past data on average catch and total effort. If an independent estimate of the population size at maximum sustainable yield can be obtained, then estimates can also be reached for a, b, and r by using equations 7.21, 7.22, and 7.23. Let P° be the population size at MSY. From the discussion above we know that:

$$P^\circ = \frac{a}{2b} \tag{7.24}$$

Therefore, it follows that:

$$\frac{a}{b} = 2P^\circ \tag{7.25}$$

Substituting this into equation 7.22 and solving for r, we obtain:

$$r = \frac{c}{2P^\circ} \tag{7.26}$$

Now from equations 7.22 and 7.23, we derive the following:

$$b = \frac{r^2}{d} \tag{7.27}$$

and

$$a = \frac{bc}{r} \qquad (7.28)$$

Because these three equations are in terms of parameters for which we can get estimates, it is possible by extension to obtain estimates for a, b, and r.

It has been estimated that $P°$ of the northern lobster fishery, when the seawater temperature is forty-six degrees Fahrenheit, is 31 million pounds. Use of that figure permits an estimate of the other three parameters and thus, construction of the population and economic equilibrium equations. Simultaneous solution of these gives predicted values for bioeconomic equilibrium population size and for the equilibrium amount of effort. These values, derived using data up to 1969, are listed in the top row of table 7.2. The model contains no explicit dynamic analysis, and so the speed at which this equilibrium is approached (if indeed it will be approached) cannot be determined.

Although it is not as easy to specify maximum economic yield via this model, it is very useful for comparative static analysis. Table 7.2 predicts the changes that will occur in the key variables as a result of adjustments in selected parameters. These new values are derived simply by changing the values of the appropriate parameters in equations 7.16 and 7.20. The model can also be used to study the impact of various management programs.

Table 7.2. *Comparative Static Analysis.* This table shows the effects on the crucial variables of selected changes in the parameters of the model.

	Traps (thousands)	Yield (million pounds)	Population (million pounds)
Initial equilibrium computed by model	1,069,000	28.56	28.62
Equilibrium values with the following parameter changes			
a) 25 percent increase in opportunity cost of labor	861,718	28.1	35.6
b) 25 percent increase in exogenous supply of lobsters	533,000	22.3	45.7
c) 5 percent increase in personal per capita income	1,228,310	27.4	28.0
d) 1°F decline in seawater temperature	1,041,710	26.8	29.0
e) Changes (a) through (d) simultaneously	509,356	20.7	45.9

SOURCE: Bell (1970, tables 1 and 2).

Other Empirical Studies

The detailed accounts of the lobster studies demonstrate some of the complexities and problems involved in estimating economically optimal harvest levels. The purpose of this section is to briefly describe the results of other studies in order to provide a more general description of the types of work that can be done. A careful review of such studies would provide specific suggestions as to how to undertake these difficult investigations. Such a review, while not possible here, is highly recommended, because to really understand fisheries economics and fisheries management, it is necessary to think in the context of specific fisheries with the realization that there are limits to what we can know about their biological and economic operations. Perhaps these brief comments will attract the reader's interest and encourage more detailed study.

Blomo et al. (1982) developed a model of the eastern Gulf of Mexico shrimp fishery and were able to derive a harvest program that would maximize current rents. They used a simulation model that accounted for biological and economic flucuations, including intraseasonal shrimp growth rates and differences in the price of shrimp at different sizes. Their results indicate that gains can be obtained by taking into account how the size and value of the harvest will change throughout the season as shrimp grow, migrate, and suffer natural mortality. Similarly, Warren et al. (1982) developed a bioeconomic model for managing fisheries off northwest Africa. They compared the open-access and optimal harvest levels and found that efficiency could be enhanced by reducing effort. To be specific, if effort is reduced by 40 percent, there would be an increase in the value of production of $184 million a year. Maximum gains of $222 million per year could be obtained with a 57 percent reduction in effort. Their preliminary investigations of fleet responsiveness showed that seasonal closures with fleet-size limitations could be used to achieve these gains.

In a similar study, Adu-Asamoah and Conrad (1982) developed a bioeconomic model for three species of tuna in the eastern tropical Atlantic. They were also able to show a difference between the open-access and optimal levels of fishing; in addition they demonstrated how the discount rule can affect the long-term equilibrium optimal amount of effort. Conrad (1982) derived an optimal harvest and age structure regulation program for a multicohort hard clam fishery. Under this plan, the steady-state optimum would call for exclusive harvesting of younger, more valuable cohorts (the littleneck clams) but would leave the older and less valuable "chowder" cohorts to produce young. See also Hsiao (1985) and Conrad (1985).

Townsend (1985) studied soft shell clam fisheries in Maine by comparing different management programs used in different parts of the state. Management for different stocks is under the control of various towns, and the programs run the gamut from open access to various forms of limited entry. He showed that yield per unit of effort was higher in the managed fisheries and that yield per recruit increased as entry was more tightly restricted. Townsend's results support the theory that limited entry improves economic welfare of fishermen. Agnello and Donnelley (1975a, 1976) had similar findings in their studies of oyster management.

There are several studies that deal directly with dynamic aspects of fisheries regulation. Acheson and Reidman (1982) studied the effect of raising the legal minimum size of lobsters over a five-year period. The purpose of such a regulation program was to increase egg production and recruitment and thus to reduce the likelihood of stock failure. Using a very imaginative analysis, they demonstrated that catch would fall in the five years over which the legal minimum size length is incrementally increased. Further, at the end of the period there would likely be fewer lobsters harvested, but there would be an increase in landed weight due to increases in average size. Further analysis, however, showed that the present value of catch would increase, however, because the loss over the five-year period would be more than made up for by the increases in later periods. In a similar investigation, Waters et al. (1980) studied a discard abatement policy for a shrimp fishery in North Carolina. They pointed out that regulations that would prevent fishing for brown shrimp during August and September on the grounds that too many small pink shrimp are harvested at that time do not appear to be worthwhile. The loss in brown shrimp harvested during the closure would likely be higher than any increase in the value of the pink shrimp fishing later in the season.

Henderson and Tugwell (1979) analyzed the dynamic aspects of harvesting two Canadian lobster fisheries in a way that is directly comparable to our theory. They show that the optimal harvest level, which considers both harvest and user costs, involves a 75 percent and 66 percent reduction in effort in the two fisheries. While this will decrease harvest in both, the reduction in harvest costs is such that the net annual savings are $202,000 and $180,000, respectively, which is in the range of 20 percent and 30 percent of the value of the open-access catch level. They also addressed the problem of the optimal harvest time path. Given the limitations of their data, they suggest as rapid as possible a decrease in effort from the open-access to the stationary optimum. However, they warn that, if the resources released from fishing cannot find employment elsewhere in the economy in the short run, then the optimal time path of harvest will involve a slower reduction in effort.

A dynamic analysis by Gallastegui (1983) provides similar information on a sardine fishery in Spain. Optimal utilization involves less harvest than is obtained by using less effort on a larger fish stock. Assuming full employment of resources, the optimal harvest path should allow for rapid increases in the stock by causing drastic reductions in harvest in the near term.

Concluding Comments on Practical Applications

The above descriptions help to provide an understanding of the problems involved and the types of results that follow from real-world applications of fisheries economics. The specific results, of course, are only of direct interest to those concerned with the particular fisheries involved. While there are studies on other fisheries, we are a long way from having current estimates of the economically optimal harvest levels of most fisheries throughout the world. Indeed, if management agencies want such an estimate for the fisheries under their jurisdiction, at best they will have to update existing studies using current economic and biological data, but more likely, they will have to start from scratch. Therefore, if the theoretical constructs developed in this book are to be used in practical fisheries management, much more applied research will be required. Such work is obviously beyond the scope of this book. Indeed, even a detailed review of existing work would be too big a task. The goals of this chapter have been much more modest. They were to show the types of things that can be done and to provide some insights as to how to go about doing it. Careful study of existing works and "hands on" experience will be required to really learn how to apply the theory and hence to really understand the optimal utilization of various fisheries.

To assist in reviewing such works, an extensive bibliography has been provided. While it contains references on both theoretical and applied aspects of fisheries economics, those studies with empirical content have been listed with an asterisk (*). It is interesting to note that those so marked are in the minority. There is a challenge to professional fisheries economists here. While one should always be careful of blocking paths of inquiry, it is likely that the returns to further refinements of theory are far less than would result if the same research effort were used to apply existing theory.

Study Questions

Chapter 2

1. Using the appropriate graphs, derive the sustainable yield curve. Make sure you define all terms and include a complete description of all steps and a proper definition of a sustainable yield curve.
2. Explain fully the differences and the relationship between the short-run yield curves and the sustainable yield curve.
3. Explain the process of obtaining a bioeconomic equilibrium in an open-access fishery.
4. Why does the fishing industry merit special attention? What are some of the peculiar results that occur in an unregulated fishery?
5. Using cost and revenue diagrams, differentiate between open-access equilibrium yield, maximum sustainable yield, and maximum economic yield. Make sure your discussion of the latter includes the opportunity cost of using inputs to utilize a fish stock, as well as the concept of user cost.
6. Explain why it is necessary to consider fisheries in terms of harvest patterns through time. Why will harvest go up or down through time in both open-access and maximum economic yield situations?

Chapter 3

1. Explain the relationship between the individual fisherman (vessel) and the fishery as a whole in terms of a constant cost fishery. Will effort be produced inefficiently? Will the proper amount of it be produced? Differentiate between open-access equilibrium yield and maximum economic yield in this analysis. Explain the relationship between the vessel-fishery diagram and the cost and revenue diagram.
2. Explain why there will be increasing long-run average cost curves in both highliner and congested fisheries. How would the answers to question 1 change if the analyses were done in terms of these types of fisheries?

3. How does the presence or absence of alternative uses or vessels affect the optimal harvest time path of a fishery?
4. How is the analysis of maximum economic yield affected when the assumption of a constant price of fish is dropped? Distinguish between the profit-maximization point and the maximum economic yield. What is being maximized at the latter point?
5. Distinguish between open access and stationary MEY in terms of the variable price of a fish model. Does it make sense to drive the stock below the size that generates maximum sustainable yield?
6. Using a production possibility curve and a set of social indifference curves, show why an unregulated open-access fishery will cause the economy to reach an equilibrium at a level of welfare that is lower than it need be.
7. How do population characteristics of the fish stock enter into the individual demand curve for recreational fishing and hence produce a bioeconomic analysis analogous to that for commercial fishing? Explain the difference between open access and maximum economic yield in a recreational fishery and describe the nature of the economic losses that occur under open access.
8. Explain the relationship between fisheries management and fishery development. Show why development without management will not produce maximum potential benefits and why, in some cases, it can actually result in economic losses.

Chapter 4

1. Using the same basic analysis introduced in chapter 2, derive the asymptotic and forward-bending sustainable yield curves. What effects can these types of curves have on open-access equilibrium yield?
2. Explain the difference between the Schaefer logistic growth model and dynamic pool models.
3. Explain the sustainable yield curve for regenerative species.
4. Explain the concept of eumetric fishing. How is the proper combination of effort and mesh size determined?
5. What are the differences between growth overfishing and recruitment overfishing?
6. Describe the concept of a maximum social yield. What can the economist add to a discussion of this concept?
7. Describe fully the meaning of an international maximum economic yield, including a full discussion of the three criteria that must be simultaneously fulfilled if one is to be met. Explain why the international distribution of the property rights to the fish stock is so critical here and why it is impossible to define a priori one point as an international MEY.
8. Explain how population equilibrium curves and economic equilibrium

curves can be used to describe the way in which a fishery will or will not achieve an open-access equilibrium.

9. Why has the share system of remuneration been almost universally accepted among fishing industries in the world? How is the share rate determined, and how can the differences in the specific make-up of share systems between fisheries be explained?

Chapter 5

1. Describe the nature of the open-access and the maximum economic yield positions for the six classifications of fisheries described in this chapter.
2. Explain why the use of the boat as well as the number of boats in the fleet is an important aspect of both the open-access and optimal utilization of many complex fisheries.
3. Explain why it is sometimes the case that the stationary MEY point of biologically interdependent fisheries will necessitate an increase in the level of effort applied to one of the stocks. Are similar situations possible for other classifications of fisheries as well?

Chapter 6

1. Discuss the possible goals of a fishery regulation program.
2. Give a brief description of the components of effort and the ways various methods of reducing effort can affect the cost of producing it.
3. Discuss those fishery regulations that are aimed at selecting the size of first capture. When are they biologically justified? When are they economically justified?
4. Discuss the economic efficiency and biological efficacy aspects of various types of regulations.
5. Discuss the possibilities of obtaining net economic efficiency gains from some open-access regulations.
6. What are the economic efficiency advantages of the so-called limited entry regulations?
7. Discuss the income distribution problems of fishery management in general and of various types of regulations in particular.
8. Explain the economic aspects of actually operating a fishery management program. Show why the costs of implementation and enforcement as well as avoidance activities undertaken by vessel owners should be considered in determining optimal regulation schemes.
9. List the steps that should be followed in the process of developing a fisheries management policy.

Bibliography

Abgrall, J. 1978. "Fishing Industry: In Support of a Single Manager." *Canadian Journal of Agricultural Economics* 26:35–42.

Acheson, J. M. 1975a. "Fisheries Management and the Social Context: The Case of the Maine Lobster Fishery." *Transactions of the American Fisheries Society* 104 (4): 653–68.

———. 1975b. "The Lobster Fiefs: Economic and Ecological Effects: Maine." *Human Ecology* 3, no. 3: 183–207.

———. 1981. "Anthropology of Fishing." *Annual Review of Anthropology* 10:275–316.

*Acheson, J., and R. Reidman. 1982. "Biological and Economic Effects of Increasing the Minimum Legal Size of American Lobster in Maine." *Transactions of the American Fisheries Society* 111:1–12.

Adasiak, A. 1979. "Alaska's Experience with Limited Entry." *Journal of the Fisheries Research Board of Canada* 36 (7): 770–82.

*Adu-Asamoah, R., and J. M. Conrad. 1982. "Fishery Management: The Case of Tuna in the Eastern Tropical Atlantic." Cornell Agricultural Economics Staff Paper, #82-15, 26 pp.

*Agnello, R. J., and L. G. Anderson. 1977. "Production Relationships among Interrelated Fisheries." In *Economic Impacts of Extended Fisheries Jurisdiction*, ed. L. G. Anderson, 157–94. Ann Arbor: Ann Arbor Science Publishers.

*———. 1983. "Production Responses for Multi-Species Fisheries." *Canadian Journal of Fisheries and Aquatic Sciences* 38 (11): 1393–1404.

*Agnello, R., and L. Donnelley. 1975a. "Prices and Property Rights in the Fisheries." *Southern Economic Journal* 42, no. 2: 253–62.

*———. 1975b. "Property Rights and Efficiency in the U.S. Oyster Industry." *Journal of Law and Economics* 18:521–33.

*———. 1975c. "The Interaction of Economic, Biological, and Legal Forces in the Middle Atlantic Oyster Industry." *Fishery Bulletin* 73 (2): 256–61.

*———. 1976. "Externalities and Property Rights in the Fisheries." *Land Economics* 52 (4): 518–29.

---

*As indicated in chapter 7, the works marked with an asterisk have empirical content.

*————. 1977. "Externalities and Property Rights in the Fisheries: A Reply." *Land Economics* 53 (4): 492-95.

*————. 1984. "Regulation and the Structure of Property Rights: The Case of the U.S. Oyster Industry." *Research in Law and Economics* 6:267-81.

Allen, R. 1980. "Fishing for a Common Policy." *Journal of Common Market Studies* 19 (2): 123-39.

Andersen, P. 1982. "Commercial Fisheries under Price Uncertainty." *Journal of Environmental Economics and Management* 9 (1): 11-28.

Andersen, P., and J. G. Sutinen. 1983. "Fisheries Law Enforcement and International Trade in Fisheries." In *Proceedings of the International Seafood Trade Conference*, Alaska Sea Grant Report #83-2:509-16.

————. 1984. "Stochastic Bioeconomics: A Review of Basic Methods and Results." *Marine Resource Economics* 1 (2): 117-36.

Anderson, J. L. 1985. "Market Interactions between Aquaculture and the Common-Property Commercial Fishery." *Marine Resource Economics* 2 (1): 1-24.

Anderson, L. G. 1973. "Optimum Economic Yield of a Fishery Given a Variable Price of Output." *Journal of Fisheries Research Board of Canada* 30:509-18.

————. 1974. "Economic Aspects of Fisheries Utilization in the Law of the Sea Negotiations." *San Diego Law Review* 11, no. 3: 656-78.

————. 1975a. "Analysis of Open-Access Commercial Exploitation and Maximum Economic Yield in Biologically and Technologically Interdependent Fisheries." *Journal of Fisheries Research Board of Canada* 32:1825-42.

————. 1975b. "Optimum Economic Yield of an Internationally Utilized Common Property Resource." *Fishery Bulletin* 70 (January): 51-66.

————. 1975c. "Criteria for Maximum Economic Yield of an Internationally Exploited Fishery." In *The Future of International Fisheries Management*, ed. H. Knight. St. Paul: West Publishing.

————. 1976. "The Relationship between Firm and Fishery in Common Property Fisheries." *Land Economics* 52:180-91.

————. 1977a. "A Classification of Fishery Management Problems to Aid in the Analysis and Proper Formulation of Management." *Ocean Development and International Law Journal* 4 (2): 113-20.

————, ed. 1977b. *Economic Impacts of Extended Fisheries Jurisdiction.* Ann Arbor: Ann Arbor Science Publishers.

————. 1978a. "Production Functions for Fisheries: Comments." *Southern Economic Journal* 44 (3): 661-66.

————. 1978b. "The Relationship between Firm and Fishery in Common Property Fisheries: Reply." *Land Economics* 54:104-5.

————. 1980a. "A Comparison of Limited Entry Fisheries Management Schemes." In *ACMRR Working Party on the Scientific Basis of Determining Management Measures*, FAO Fisheries Report 236:47-74. Rome: FAO.

————. 1980b. "An Economic Analysis of Joint Recreational and Commercial Fisheries." In *Allocation of Fishery Resources*, Proceedings of the Technical Consultation, Vichy, France, 1980, ed. J. H. Grover, 16-26. Rome: FAO.

————. 1980c. "Estimating the Benefits of Recreation under Conditions of Congestion: Comments and Extension." *Journal of Environmental Economics and Management* 7(4):401-6.

————. 1980d. "Necessary Components of Economic Surplus in Fisheries Economics." *Canadian Journal of Fisheries and Aquatic Sciences* 37 (5): 858–70.

*————. 1981. *Economic Analysis for Fisheries Management Plans.* Ann Arbor: Ann Arbor Science Publishers.

————. 1982a. "Marine Fisheries." In *Current Issues in Natural Resource Policy*, ed. P. Portney. Washington, D.C.: Resources for the Future.

————. 1982b. "Optimal Utilization of Fisheries with Increasing Costs of Effort." *Canadian Journal of Fisheries and Aquatic Sciences* 39:211–14.

————. 1982c. "Optimum Effort and Rent Distribution in the Gulf of Mexico Shrimp Fishery: Comment." *American Journal of Agricultural Economics* 64 (1): 157–59.

————. 1982d. "The Economics of Multipurpose Fleet Behavior." In *Essays in the Economics of Natural Resources*, ed. L. J. Mirman and D. F. Spulber. Amsterdam: North Holland.

————. 1982e. "The Share System in Open-Access and Optimally Regulated Fisheries." *Land Economics* 58 (4): 435–49.

————. 1983a. "Economics and the Fisheries Management Development Process." In *Global Fisheries: Perspectives for the 1980s*, ed. B. J. Rothschild. New York: Springer-Verlag.

————. 1983b. "The Demand Curve for Recreational Fishing with an Application to Stock Enhancement Activities." *Land Economics* 59 (3): 279–86.

————. 1983c. "Exploitation of the Lobster Fishery: Comment." *Journal of Environmental Economics and Management* 10:180–83.

————. 1984. "Uncertainty in the Fisheries Management Process." *Marine Resource Economics* 1 (1): 77–88.

————. 1985a. "The Economical Management of Multispecies Fisheries: Comment." *Land Economics* 61 (3): 319–22.

————. 1985b. "Potential Economic Benefits from Gear Restrictions and License Limitation in Fisheries Regulation." *Land Economics* 61 (4): 409–18.

————. 1985c. "The Pendulum Swings: A Public Choice Historical Perspective of East Coast Groundfisheries Management." In *Fisheries Management: Issues and Options*, ed. T. Frady. Fairbanks: Alaska Sea Grant Report No. 85-2:235–54.

————. 1985d. "A Management Agency Perspective of the Economics of Regulation." In *Proceedings of the Second Conference of the International Institute of Fisheries Economics and Trade*, vol. 1, ed. R. Johnston. Corvallis: Oregon State University Sea Grant College Program.

————. 1986. "Economically Optimal Total Allowable Catches in the Absence of Stock Recruitment Relationships." In *Natural Resource Policy and Management: Essays in Honor of James A. Crutchfield*, ed. E. Miles, R. Pealy, and R. Stocks. Seattle: University of Washington Press.

*Anderson, L. G., and A. Ben-Israel. 1981. "Modelling and Simulation of Interdependent Fisheries, and Optimal Effort Allocation Using Mathematical Programming." In *Applied Operations Research in Fisheries*, ed. K. B. Haley. New York: Plenum Press.

Anderson, L. G., and D. Lee. Forthcoming. "Optimal Governing Instrument, Operation Level, and Enforcement in Natural Resource Regulation: The Case of the Fishery." *American Journal of Agricultural Economics.*

Arnold, V., and D. Bromley. 1970. "Social Goals, Problem Perception, and Public Intervention: The Fishery." *San Diego Law Review* 7 (3): 469–87.

Asada, Y. 1973. "License Limitation Regulations: The Japanese System." *Journal of the Fisheries Research Board of Canada* 30:2085-95.

Austin, C. B. 1977. "Incorporating Economic Considerations into Practical Fishery Policies." In *Economic Impacts of Extended Fisheries Jurisdiction*, ed. L. G. Anderson. Ann Arbor: Ann Arbor Science Publishers.

Balasubramanian, S. 1981. "Fishery Provisions of the ICNT: Part I." *Marine Policy* 5 (5): 313-21.

———. 1982. "Fishery Provisions of the ICNT: Part II." *Marine Policy* 6 (1): 27-42.

Baltzo, C. H. 1959. "Enforcement of Alaska Fisheries Regulations." In *Biological and Economic Aspects of Fisheries Management*, ed. J. Crutchfield, 104-7. Seattle: University of Washington Press.

Beddington, J. R. et al. 1975. "Optimal Cropping of Self-Reproducible Natural Resources." *Econometrica* 43 (4): 789-802.

Beddington, J. R., and C. W. Clark. 1984. "Allocation Problems between National and Foreign Fisheries with a Fluctuating Fish Resource." *Marine Resource Economics* 1 (2): 137-54.

Beddington, J. R., and R. May. 1977. "Harvesting Natural Populations in a Randomly Fluctuating Environment." *Science* 197:463-5.

Beddington, J. R., and R. B. Rettig. 1984. *Approaches to the Regulation of Fishing Effort*, FAO Fisheries Technical Paper #243. Rome: FAO.

Bell, F. W. 1959. "Economic Effects of Regulations of the Pacific Halibut Fishery." In *Biological and Economic Aspects of Fisheries Management*, ed. J. Crutchfield, 51-75. Seattle: University of Washington Press.

*———. 1966. *The Economics of the New England Fishing Industry: The Role of Technological Change and Government Aid*. Research Report No. 31 to the Federal Reserve Bank of Boston. Boston: Federal Reserve Bank of Boston.

*———. 1968. "The Pope and the Price of Fish." *American Economic Review* 58 (December): 1346-50.

*———. 1970. "Estimation of the Economic Benefits to Fishermen, Vessels and Society from Limited Entry to the Inshore U.S. Lobster Fishery." Working Paper No. 36, Bureau of Commercial Fisheries (now National Marine Fisheries Service). Washington, D.C.: NMFS.

*———. 1972. "Technological Externalities and Common Property Resources: An Empirical Study of the U.S. Northern Lobster Fishery." *Journal of Political Economy* 80:148-58.

———. 1977. "World-Wide Economic Aspects of Extended Fishery Jurisdiction Management." In *Economic Impacts of Extended Fisheries Jurisdiction*, ed. L. G. Anderson. Ann Arbor: Ann Arbor Science Publishers.

———. 1978. *Food from the Sea: The Economics and Politics of Ocean Fisheries*. Boulder, Colo.: Westview Press.

*———. 1979. "Recreational versus Commercial Fishing in Florida: An Economic Impact Analysis." Policy Sciences Program, Florida State University, 11 pp.

*Bell, F. W., and R. F. Fullenbaum. 1973. "The American Lobster Fishery: Economic Analysis of Alternative Management Strategies." *Marine Fisheries Review* 35 (August): 1-6.

Bell, F. W., and J. E. Hazelton. 1967. *Recent Developments and Research in Fisheries Economics*. Dobbs Ferry, N.Y.: Oceana Publications.

*Bell, F. W., and R. Kinoshita. 1973. "Productivity Gains in U.S. Fisheries." *Fishery Bulletin* 71, no. 4: 911-19.

Berck, P. 1981. "Optimal Management of Renewable Resources with Growing Demand and Stock Externalities." *Journal of Environmental Economics and Management* 8:105-17.

Beverton, R., and S. Holt. 1957. *On the Dynamics of Exploited Fish Populations.* London: Ministry of Agriculture, Fisheries and Food, Fisheries Investigations Series 2(19).

Bishop, B., and K. Samples. 1980. "Sport and Commercial Fisheries Conflicts: A Theoretical Analysis." *Journal of Environmental Economics and Management* 7:220-33.

Bishop, R. C. 1973. "Limitation of Entry in the U.S. Fishing Industry: An Economic Proposal." *Land Economics* 49, no. 4: 381-90.

———. 1975. "Limitation of Entry in the U.S. Fishing Industry: A Reply." *Land Economics* 51, no. 1: 182-85.

———. 1978. "Endangered Species and Uncertainty: The Economics of a Safe Minimum Standard." *American Journal of Agricultural Economics* 60 (1): 10-18.

Blomo, V. 1981. "Conditional Fishery Status as a Solution to Overcapitalization in the Gulf of Mexico Shrimp Fishery." *Marine Fisheries Review* 43 (7): 20-24.

*Blomo, V., J. P. Nichols, W. L. Griffin, and W. E. Grant. 1982. "Dynamic Modeling of the Eastern Gulf of Mexico Shrimp Fishery." *American Journal of Agricultural Economics* 64 (3): 475-82.

*Bockstael, N. E., and J. J. Opaluch. 1983. "Discrete Modelling of Supply Response under Uncertainty: The Case of the Fishery." *Journal of Environmental Economics and Management* 10 (3): 125-37.

*———. 1984. "Behavioral Modeling and Fisheries Management." *Marine Resource Economics* 1 (1): 105-15.

*Booth, D. E. 1972. "A Model for Optimal Salmon Management." *Fishery Bulletin* 70 (April): 497-506.

*Botsford, L. W., R. D. Methot, and W. E. Johnson. 1983. "Effort Dynamics of the Northern California Dungeness Crab (*Cancer magister*) Fishery." *Canadian Journal of Fisheries and Aquatic Sciences* 40 (3): 337-46.

Bottemanne, C. 1959. *Principles of Fisheries Development.* Amsterdam: North Holland.

Boyd, J. 1966. "Optimization and Suboptimization in Fishery Regulation: Comment." *American Economic Review* 56:511-17.

*Briggs, H., R. Townsend, and J. Wilson. 1982. "An Input-Output Analysis of Maine's Fisheries." *Marine Fisheries Review* 44 (1): 1-7.

Bromley, D., and R. Bishop. 1977. "From Economic Theory to Fisheries Policy." In *Economic Aspects of Extended Fisheries Jurisdiction*, ed. L. G. Anderson, 281-302. Ann Arbor: Ann Arbor Science Publishers.

*Brown, B. E. et al. 1975. *The Effect of Fishing on the Marine Finfish Biomass in the Northwest Atlantic from the Eastern Edge of the Gulf of Maine to Cape Hatteras.* International Commission for the Northwest Atlantic Fisheries Research Document, 75/18.

Brown, G., Jr. 1974. "An Optimal Program for Managing Common Property Resources with Congestion Externalities." *Journal of Political Economy* (January/February): 163-73.

Brown, G., Jr., and J. H. Goldstein. 1984. "A Model for Valuing Endangered Species." *Journal of Environmental Economics and Management* 11 (4): 303–9.

Burkenroad, M. 1953. "Theory and Practice of Marine Fishery Management." *Journal du Conseil International pour l'Exploration de la Mer* 18:300–310.

Butlin, J. 1975. "Optimal Depletion of a Replenishable Resource: An Evaluation of Recent Contributions to Fisheries Economics." In *The Economics of Natural Resource Depletion*, ed. D. Pearce and J. Rose, 85–114. New York: Wiley.

Campbell, B. A. 1971. "Problems of Over-expansion in the Salmon Fleet in British Columbia." Reprint of three articles from *Western Fisheries*, October and November 1970, January 1971. Vancouver: Canada Department of Fisheries and Forestry.

———. 1972a. "Limited Entry in the Salmon Fishery: The British Columbia Experience." PASGAP 6. Vancouver, B.C.: Fisheries Programs, Centre for Continuing Education, University of British Columbia.

———. 1972b. "Licence Limitation Regulations: Canada's Experience." *Journal of the Fisheries Research Board of Canada* 30:2070–76.

———. 1973. "A Review of the Economic Theories of Licence Limitation in a Common Property Resource as They Relate to the Experience of the Salmon Vessel Licence Control Program in British Columbia." Section IV of the British Columbia Salmon Vessel Licence Control Program, a report prepared for the Fisheries and Marine Service of the Department of the Environment, Canada.

Campbell, D. 1984. "Individual Transferable Catch Quotas: Their Role, Use, and Application." Fishery Report No. 11, Department of Primary Production. Canberra: Department of Primary Producta.

*Carlson, E. 1975. "The Measurement of Relative Fishing Power Using Cross Section Production Functions." In *Measurement of Fishing Effort*, ed. J. Pope. Rapports et Proces-verbaux des Reunions du Conseil International pour l'Exploration de la Mer 168:84–98.

Carroz, J., and M. Savini. 1979. "The New International Law of Fisheries Emerging from Bilateral Agreements." *Marine Policy* 3 (2): 79–98.

Cauvin, D. 1980. "The Valuation of Recreational Fisheries." *Canadian Journal of Fisheries and Aquatic Sciences* 37:1321–27.

Chan, K. 1978. "The Economic Consequences of the 200-Mile Seabed Zone." *Canadian Journal of Economics* 11:314–18.

Charles, A. T. 1983a. "Optimal Fisheries Investment: Comparative Dynamics for a Deterministic Seasonal Fishery." *Canadian Journal of Fisheries and Aquatic Sciences* 40:2069–79.

———. 1983b. "Optimal Fisheries Investment under Uncertainty." *Canadian Journal of Fisheries and Aquatic Sciences* 40:2080–91.

Charles, A. T., and G. R. Munro. 1985. "Irreversible Investment and Optimal Fisheries Management: A Stochastic Analysis." *Marine Resource Economics* 1 (3): 247–64.

Chen, T-N., and D. L. Hueth. 1983. "Welfare Considerations in the Development of a Joint Venture Policy." In *Proceedings of the International Seafood Trade Conference*, Alaska Sea Grant Report #83-2:461–72.

Cheng, K., C. Lin, and A. Wang. 1981. "Analysis of Modified Model for Commercial Fishing with Possible Extinction of Fishery Resources." *Journal of Environmental Economics and Management* 8 (2): 151–55.

Christy, A. 1974. "A Market for Fishery Resources?" In *Fisheries Conflicts in the*

North Atlantic: Problems of Management and Jurisdiction, ed. G. Pontecorvo, 91–94. Cambridge, Mass.: Ballinger.

Christy, A., and A. Scott. 1965. *The Common Wealth of Ocean Fisheries.* Baltimore: Johns Hopkins Press.

Christy, F. T., Jr. 1969. "Fisheries Goals and the Rights of Property." *Transactions of the American Fisheries Society* 98 (April): 369–78.

———. 1970. "New Dimensions for Transnational Marine Resources." *American Economic Review* 60 (May): 109–13.

———. 1973a. *Alternative Arrangements for Marine Fisheries: An Overview.* Washington, D.C.: Resources for the Future.

———. 1973b. "Northwest Atlantic Fisheries Arrangements: A Test of the Species Approach." *Ocean Development and International Law Journal* 1, no. 1: 65–91.

———. 1977. "Limited Access Systems under the Fishery Conservation and Management Act of 1976." In *Economic Impacts of Extended Fisheries Jurisdiction*, ed. L. G. Anderson, 141–56. Ann Arbor: Ann Arbor Science Publishers.

———. 1980. "Comment on Quantitative Rights as an Instrument for Regulating Commercial Fisheries." *Canadian Journal of Fisheries and Aquatic Sciences* 37 (5): 902–3.

———. 1982. "Territorial Use Rights in Marine Fisheries." Fisheries Technical Paper 227, CIDA/CECAF/FAO Workshop, 1980. Rome: FAO.

Churchill, R. 1977. "The EEC Fisheries Policy—Towards a Revision." *Marine Policy* 1 (1): 26–36.

Cicin-Sain, B., J. Moore, and A. Wyner. 1978. "Limiting Entry to Commercial Fisheries: Some Worldwide Comparisons." *Ocean Management* 4 (1): 21–49.

Clark, C. W. 1973a. "The Economics of Overexploitation." *Science* 181:630–34.

———. 1973b. "Profit Maximization and Extinction of Animal Species." *Journal of Political Economy* 81:950–61.

———. 1973c. "Economic Theory of the Multi-species Fishery." Unpublished manuscript. Department of Mathematics, University of British Columbia.

———. 1974a. "Possible Effects of Schooling on the Dynamics of Exploited Fish Populations." *Journal du Conseil International pour l'Exploration de la Mer* 36:7–14.

———. 1974b. "Supply and Demand Relationships in Fisheries Management." Unpublished manuscript. Department of Mathematics, University of British Columbia.

———. 1976. *Mathematical Bioeconomics: The Optimal Management of Renewable Resources.* New York: Wiley.

———. 1977. "Control Theory in Fisheries Economics: Frill or Fundamental?" In *Economic Impacts of Extended Fisheries Jurisdiction*, ed. L. G. Anderson, 317–30. Ann Arbor: Ann Arbor Science Publishers.

———. 1980. "Towards a Predictive Model for the Economic Regulation of Commercial Fisheries." *Canadian Journal of Fisheries and Aquatic Sciences* 37:1111–29.

———. 1981. "Fisheries Management and Fishing Rights." In *ACMRR Working Party on the Scientific Basis of Determining Management Measures*, FAO Fisheries Report 236:101–13. Rome: FAO.

———. 1985a. *Bioeconomic Modelling and Fisheries Management.* New York: Wiley.

———. 1985b. "The Effect of Fishermen's Quotas on Expected Catch Rates." *Marine Resource Economics* 1 (4): 419–27.

Clark, C. W., A. T. Charles, J. R. Beddington, and M. Mangel. 1985. "Optimal Capacity Decisions in a Developing Fishery." *Marine Resource Economics* 2 (1): 25-54.

Clark, C. W., C. Clark, and G. Munro. 1975. "The Economics of Fishing and Modern Capital Theory: A Simplified Approach." *Journal of Environmental Economics and Management* 2:92-106.

Clark, C. W., F. Clarke, and G. Munro. 1979. "The Optimal Exploitation of Renewable Resource Stocks: Problems of Irreversible Investment." *Econometrica* 47 (1): 25-47.

Clark, C. W., G. Edwards, and M. Friedlaender. 1973. "Beverton-Holt Model of a Commercial Fishery: Optimal Dynamics." *Journal of Fisheries Research Board of Canada* 30:1629-40.

*Clark, C. W., and G. P. Kirkwood. 1979. "Bioeconomic Model of the Gulf of Carpentaria Prawn Fishery." *Journal of the Fisheries Research Board of Canada* 36 (11): 1304-12.

*Clark, C. W., and R. Lamberson. 1982. "An Economic History and Analysis of Pelagic Whaling." *Marine Policy* 6 (2): 103-20.

Clark, C. W., and M. Mangel. 1979. "Aggregation and Fishery Dynamics: A Theoretical Study of Schooling and the Purse Seine Tuna Fisheries." *Fishery Bulletin* 77 (2): 317-37.

Clark, C., and G. Munro. 1978. "Renewable Resource Management and Extinction." *Journal of Environmental Economics and Management* 5 (2): 198-205.

———. 1980. "Fisheries and the Processing Sector: Some Implications for Management Policy." *The Bell Journal of Economics* 7:603-16.

*Comitini, S. 1977. "An Economic Analysis of the State of the Hawaiian Skipjack Tuna Fishery." The University of Hawaii Sea Grant Technical Report, November.

*Comitini, S., and D. S. Huang. 1967. "A Study of Production and Factor Shares in the Halibut Fishing Industry." *Journal of Political Economy* 75 (August): 366-72.

*Conrad, J. M. 1982. "Management of a Multiple Cohort Fishery: The Hard Clam in Great South Bay." *American Journal of Agricultural Economics* (August):463-74.

*Conrad, J. M. 1985. "Management of a Multiple Cohort Fishery: Reply." *American Journal of Agricultural Economics* 67 (3): 676-78.

Copes, P. 1970. "The Backward-bending Supply Curve of the Fishing Industry." *Scottish Journal of Political Economy* 17:69-77.

———. 1972. "Factor Rents, Sole Ownership, and the Optimum Level of Fisheries Exploitation." *The Manchester School of Social and Economic Studies* 40:145-63.

———. 1977. "Instituting a Management Regime for the Prawn Fishery of the Northern Territory of Australia." In *Economic Impacts of Extended Fisheries Jurisdiction*, ed. L. G. Anderson, 267-80. Ann Arbor: Ann Arbor Science Publishers.

———. 1981. "The Impact of UNCLOS III on Management of the World's Fisheries." *Marine Policy* 6 (3): 217-28.

Copes, P., and B. Cook. 1982. "Rationalization of Canada's Pacific Halibut Fishery." *Ocean Management* 8 (2): 157-75.

Copes, P., and J. Knetsch. 1981. "Recreational Fisheries Analysis: Management Modes and Benefit Implications." *Canadian Journal of Fisheries and Aquatic Sciences* 38:559-70.

Cropper, M. et al. 1979. "The Optimal Extinction of a Renewable Resource." *Journal of Environmental Economics and Management* 6:341-49.

Crutchfield, J. A. 1956. "Common Property Resources and Factor Allocation." *Canadian Journal of Economics and Political Science* 22:292-300.

————, ed. 1959. *Biological and Economic Aspects of Fisheries Management.* Seattle: University of Washington Press.

————. 1961. "An Economic Evaluation of Alternative Methods of Fishery Regulations." *Journal of Law and Economics* 4 (October): 131-43.

————. 1962. "Valuation of Fishery Resources." *Land Economics* 38:145-54.

————. 1965a. "Economic Objectives of Fishery Management." In *The Fisheries: Problems in Resource Management*, ed. J. A. Crutchfield, 43-64. Seattle: University of Washington Press.

————. 1965b. "International Fisheries Management: A Plan for Action." *Gulf and Caribbean Fisheries Institute* 17 (November): 12-18.

————, ed. 1965c. *Biological and Economic Aspects of Fishery Management.* Seattle: University of Washington Press.

————. 1967. "Management of the North Pacific Fisheries: Economic Objectives and Issues." *Washington Law Review* 43:283-307.

————. 1968. "Overcapitalization of Fishing Effort." In *The Future of the Sea's Resources*, ed. L. M. Alexander. Kingston: University of Rhode Island.

————. 1969. "National Quotas for the North Atlantic Fisheries: An Exercise in Second Best." In *The Law of the Sea: International Rules and Organization of the Sea*, ed. L. M. Alexander. Kingston: University of Rhode Island.

————. 1970. "Economic Aspects of International Fishing Conventions." In *Economics of Fishery Management: A Symposium*, ed. A. D. Scott. Vancouver: Institute of Animal Resource Ecology, University of British Columbia.

————. 1973. "Economic and Political Objectives in Fishery Management." *Transactions of the American Fisheries Society* 102 (April): 481-91.

————. 1975. "An Economic View of Optimum Sustainable Yield." In *Optimum Sustainable Yield as a Concept in Fisheries Management*, ed. P. Roedel, 13-20. Washington, D.C.: American Fisheries Society.

————. 1979a. "Economic and Social Implications of the Main Policy Alternatives for Controlling Fishing Effort." *Journal of Fisheries Research Board of Canada* 36 (7): 742-52.

————. 1979b. "Marine Resources—The Economics of U.S. Ocean Policy." *American Economic Review* 69 (2): 266-71.

Crutchfield, J. A., and R. Lawson. 1974. *West African Marine Fisheries: Alternatives for Management.* Washington, D.C.: Resources for the Future.

Crutchfield, J. A., and G. Pontecorvo. 1969. *The Pacific Salmon Fisheries.* Baltimore: Johns Hopkins Press.

Crutchfield, J. A., and A. Zellner. 1962. "Economic Aspects of the Pacific Halibut Fishery." *Fishery Industrial Research* 1:1-73. Washington, D.C.: U.S. Department of Interior.

Crutchfield, S. R. 1983a. "A Bioeconomic Model of an International Fishery." *Journal of Environmental Economics and Management* 10 (4): 310-28.

————. 1983b. "Estimation of Foreign Willingness to Pay United States Fishery Resources: Japanese Demand for Alaska Pollock." *Land Economics* 59 (1): 16-23.

Cunningham, S. 1980. "EEC Fisheries Management: A Critique of Common Fisheries Policy Objectives." *Marine Policy* 4 (3): 229-35.

―――. 1981. "The Evolution of the Objectives of Fisheries Management during the 1970s." *Ocean Management* 6 (4): 251-78.

―――. 1983. "The Increasing Importance of Economics in Fisheries Regulation." *Journal of Agricultural Economics* 34 (1): 69-78.

Cunningham, S., M. R. Dunn, and D. Whitmarsh. 1985. *Fisheries Economics: An Introduction.* New York: St. Martin's Press.

Cunningham, S., and D. Whitmarsh. 1980. "Fishing Effort and Fisheries Policy." *Marine Policy* 4 (4): 309-16.

―――. 1981. "When Is Overfishing Underfishing?" *Environmental Management* 5 (5): 377-84.

Cunningham, S., and J. Young. 1983. "The EEC Common Fisheries Policy: Retrospect and Prospect." *National Westminster Bank Quarterly Review* (May):2-13.

Cushing, D. 1977a. "The Atlantic Fisheries Commissions." *Marine Policy* 1 (3): 230-38.

―――. 1977b. "The Problems of Stock and Recruitment." In *Fish Population Dynamics*, ed. J. Gulland. Chichester: Wiley.

Dasgupta, P. S., and G. M. Heal. 1979. *Economic Theory and Exhaustible Resources.* London: Cambridge University Press.

DeVoretz, D., and R. Schwindt. 1985. "Harvesting Canadian Fish and Rents: A Partial Review of the Report of the Commission on Canadian Pacific Fisheries Policy." *Marine Resource Economics* 1 (4): 347-67.

Dickie, L. 1962. "Effects of Fishery Regulation on the Catch." In *The Economic Effects of Fishery Regulation*, ed. R. Hamlisch, FAO Fisheries Report 5:104-33. Rome: FAO.

*Dow, R. L., F. W. Bell, and D. M. Harriman. 1975. "Bioeconomic Relationships of Maine Lobster Fishery and Alternative Management Schemes." *NOAA Technical Report, NMFS*, SSRF-683. Seattle: U.S. Department of Commerce.

*Dudley, N., and G. Waugh. 1980. "Exploitation of a Single-Cohort Fishery under Risk: A Simulation-Optimization Approach." *Journal of Environmental Economics and Management* 7:234-55.

*Duncan, A. J. 1984. "The Hauraki Gulf Controlled Fishery: A Preliminary Economic Analysis." New Zealand Fishing Industry Board, 49 pp.

Dwyer, J. F., and M. D. Bowes. 1978. "Concepts of Value for Marine Recreational Fishing." *American Journal of Agricultural Economics* 60:1008-12.

FAO. 1980. *Working Party on the Scientific Basis of Determining Management Measures*, FAO Fisheries Report No. 236. Rome: FAO.

*Ferris, J. S., and C. G. Plourde. 1982. "Labour Mobility, Seasonal Unemployment Insurance, and the Newfoundland Inshore Fishery." *Canadian Journal of Economics* 15 (3): 426-41.

Fisheries of the United States. 1984. *Current Fishery Statistics*, No. 8360. April 1985. Washington, D.C.: National Oceanic and Atmospheric Administration.

Flaaten, O. 1983. "The Optimal Harvesting of a Natural Resource with Seasonal Growth." *Canadian Journal of Economics* 16 (3): 447-62.

*Flagg, V. G. 1977. "Optimal Output and Economic Rent of the Eastern Tropical Tuna Fishery: An Empirical Analysis." *American Journal of Economics and Sociology* 36:19-32.

Food and Agriculture Organization of the United Nations. 1973. *Report of The Technical Conference on Fishery Management and Development*, Vancouver, Canada,

13-23 February 1973 (FID/R134[En]). Rome: FAO. (contains a bibliography of the 69 papers prepared for the conference)

Fox, W. 1970. "An Exponential Surplus Yield Model for Optimizing Exploited Fish Populations." *Transactions of the American Fisheries Society* 99:80-88.

*Fraidenburg, M. E., and G. G. Bargmann. 1982. "Estimating Boat-Based Fishing Effort in a Marine Recreational Fishery." *North American Journal of Fisheries Management* 4:351-58.

Fraser, G. 1979. "Limited Entry: Experience of the British Columbia Salmon Fishery." *Journal of Fisheries Research Board of Canada* 36 (7): 754-63.

Frick, H. 1957. "The Optimum Level of Fisheries Exploitation." *Journal of Fisheries Research Board of Canada* 14:683-88.

Fullenbaum, R. F. 1972. "On Models of Commercial Fishing: A Defense of the Traditional Literature." *Journal of Political Economy* 80 (July/August): 761-68.

*Fullenbaum, R. F., and F. W. Bell. 1974. "A Simple Bioeconomic Fishery Management Model: A Case Study of the American Lobster Fishery." *Fishery Bulletin* 72 (January): 13-25.

Fullenbaum, R. F., E. W. Carlson, and F. W. Bell. 1971. "Economics of Production from Natural Resources: Comment." *American Economic Review* 61 (June): 483-87.

Gaither, N. 1980. "A Stochastic Constrained Optimization Model for Determining Commercial Fishing Seasons." *Management Science* 26 (2): 143-54.

*Gallastegui, C. 1983. "An Economic Analysis of Sardine Fishing in the Gulf of Valencia (Spain)." *Journal of Environmental Economics and Management* 10 (2): 138-50.

Gates, J. M. 1974. "Demand Price, Fish Size, and the Price of Fish." *Canadian Journal of Agricultural Economics* 22 (3): 1-12.

———. 1984. "Principal Types of Uncertainty in Fishing Operations." *Marine Resource Economics* 1 (1): 31-49.

*Gates, J. M., and V. J. Norton. 1974. *The Benefits of Fisheries Regulation: A Case Study of the New England Yellowtail Flounder Fishery*, University of Rhode Island Marine Technical Report No. 21. Kingston, R.I.: University of Rhode Island.

Gertenbach, L. 1973. "Licence Limitation Regulations: The South African System." *Journal of the Fisheries Research Board of Canada* 30:2077-84.

Ginter, J. J. C., and Rettig, R. B. 1978. "Limited Entry Revisited." In *Limited Entry as a Fishery Management Tool*. Seattle: Washington Sea Grant Publication.

Gordon, H. 1953. "An Economic Approach to the Optimum Utilization of Fishery Resources." *Journal of the Fisheries Research Board of Canada* 10 (7): 442-57.

———. 1954. "The Economic Theory of the Common Property Resource: The Fishery." *Journal of Political Economy* 62 (2): 124-42.

———. 1957. "Obstacles to Agreement on Control in the Fishing Industry." In *The Economics of Fisheries*, ed. R. Turvey and J. Wiseman, 65-72. Rome: FAO.

Gould, J. R. 1972a. "Extinction of a Fishery by Commercial Exploitation: A Note." *Journal of Political Economy* 80:1031-38.

———. 1972b. "Externalities, Factor Proportions, and the Level of Exploitation of Free Access Resources." *Economica*, n.s. 39 (November): 383-402.

Griffin, W. L., R. D. Lacewell, and J. P. Nichols. 1976. "Optimum Effort and Rent Distribution in the Gulf of Mexico Shrimp Fishery." *American Journal of Agricultural Economics* 58:644-52.

Grover, J. H., ed. 1982. *Allocation of Fishery Resources*, Proceedings of the Technical Consultation, Vichy, France, 1980. Rome: FAO/AFS.

Gulland, J. A. 1968. *The Concept of the Maximum Sustainable Yield and Fishery Management*, FAO Fisheries Technical Paper No. 70 (FRs/T70). Rome: FAO.

———. 1969. *Fisheries Management and the Limitation of Fishing*, FAO Fisheries Technical Paper No. 92 (FRs/T92[En]). Rome: FAO.

———. 1972. *Population Dynamics of World Fisheries*. Seattle: University of Washington Press.

———. 1974. *The Management of Marine Fisheries*. Seattle: University of Washington Press.

———. 1977. *Fish Population Dynamics*. New York: Wiley.

———. 1980. *Some Problems of the Management of Shared Stocks*, FAO Fisheries Technical Paper No. 206. Rome: FAO.

———. 1984. "Fisheries: Looking Beyond the Golden Age." *Marine Policy* 8 (2): 137-50.

Gulland, J. A., and L. Boerema. 1973. "Scientific Advice on Catch Levels." *Fishery Bulletin* 71 (2): 325-35.

Gulland, J. A., and J. E. Carroz. 1968. "Management of Fishery Resources." *Advances in Marine Biology* 6:1-71.

Gulland, J. A., and M. Robinson. 1973. "Economics of Fishery Management." *Journal of the Fisheries Research Board of Canada* 30:2042-50.

Haefele, E. T., ed. 1974. *The Governance of Common Property Resources*. Baltimore: The Johns Hopkins University Press.

Hamlisch, R., ed. 1962. *The Economic Effects of Fishery Regulation*, FAO Fisheries Report No. 5. Rome: FAO.

Hannesson, R. 1974a. *Economics of Fisheries: Some Problems of Efficiency*. Lund, Sweden: Student litteratur.

———. 1974b. "Relation between Reproductive Potential and Sustained Yield of Fisheries." *Journal of the Fisheries Research Board of Canada* 31:359-62.

*———. 1975. "Fishery Dynamics: A North Atlantic Cod Fishery." *Canadian Journal of Economics* 8:151-73.

———. 1978a. "A Note on the Welfare Economic Consequences of Extended Fishing Limits." *Journal of Environmental Economics and Management* 5 (2): 187-97.

———. 1978b. *Economics of Fisheries*. Bergen, Norway: Universitetsforlaget.

*———. 1983a. "Bioeconomic Production Function in Fisheries: Theoretical and Empirical Analysis." *Canadian Journal of Fisheries and Aquatic Sciences* 40 (7): 968-82.

———. 1983b. "Optimal Harvesting of Ecologically Interdependent Fish Species." *Journal of Environmental Economics and Management* 10 (4): 329-45.

———. 1984. "Fisheries Management and Uncertainty." *Marine Resource Economics* 1 (1): 89-96.

———. 1985. "The Effects of a Fishermen's Monopoly in the Market for Unprocessed Fish." *Marine Resource Economics* 2 (1): 75-86.

*Henderson, J., and M. Tugwell. 1979. "Exploitation of the Lobster Fishery: Some Empirical Results." *Journal of Environmental Economics and Management* 6:287-96.

Herfindahl, O. C., and A. V. Knesse. 1974. *Economic Theory of Natural Resources*. Columbus, Ohio: Charles E. Merrill.

*Hilborn, R. 1985. "Fleet Dynamics and Individual Variation: Why Some People Catch More Fish than Others." *Canadian Journal of Fisheries and Aquatic Science* 42:2–13.

*Hilborn, R., and M. Ledbetter. 1979. "Analysis of the British Columbia Salmon Purse-seine Fleet: Dynamics of Movement." *Journal of the Fisheries Research Board of Canada* 36:384–91.

Hildebrandt, J. 1976. "Interactive Fisheries: A Two Species Schaefer Model." *Rapports et Proces-verbaux des Reunions du Conseil International pour l'Exploration de la Mer* 168:64–66.

Hite, J. C., and J. M. Stepp. 1969. *Economic Analysis of the Development Potential of the Commercial Fisheries of the Coastal Plains Region*, Economics of Marine Resources, No. 1. Clemson, S.C.: Clemson University.

*Hsiao, Y-M. 1985a. "Management of a Multiple Cohort Fishery: Comment." *American Journal of Agricultural Economics* 67 (3): 674–75.

———. 1985b. "Economic Analysis of the Hard Clam Fishery Management in North Carolina." Ph.D. diss., Department of Economics and Business, North Carolina State University, Raleigh, N.C.

Huang, D., and B. S. Lee. 1972. "The Underlying Production Relation of the Japanese Tuna Long Line Fishery." Paper read at the Econometric Society Meeting, Toronto, December 1972.

Huppert, D. 1979. "Implications of Multipurpose Fleets and Mixed Stocks for Control Policies." *Journal of the Fisheries Research Board of Canada* 36(7):845–54.

*Huson, R. M., D. Rivard, W. G. Doubleday, and W. D. McKone. 1984. "Impact of Varying Mesh Size and Depth of Fishing on the Financial Performance of 14 Integrated Harvesting/Processing Operations for Redfish in the Northwest Atlantic." *North American Journal of the Fisheries Management* 4:32–47.

Hutchings, H. M. 1967. "Assessment of Our Capability for Management of Common Property Resources." Issue Paper No. 4. Washington, D.C.: U.S. Bureau of Commercial Fisheries.

Jackson, R. 1982. "Extended National Fisheries Jurisdiction: Palliative or Panacea?" Seattle: Washington Sea Grant, McKerman Lecture, 1981.

James, M. 1959. "Political and Social Limitations of Fishery Management." In *Biological and Economic Aspects of Fisheries Management*, ed. J. Crutchfield. Seattle: University of Washington Press.

Johnson, B. 1975. "A Review of Fisheries Proposals Made at the Caracas Session of UNCLOS III." *Ocean Management* 2:285–314.

*Johnson, R. N., and G. D. Libecap. 1982. "Contracting Problems and Regulation: The Case of the Fishery." *American Economic Review* 72 (5): 1005–22.

*Jonsson, S. 1983. "The Icelandic Fisheries in the Pre-Mechanization Era, c. 1800–1905: Spatial and Economic Implications of Growth." *The Scandinavian Economic History Review* 31 (2): 132–50.

Joseph, J. 1977. "The Management of Highly Migratory Species: Some Important Concepts." *Marine Policy* 1 (4): 275–88.

Joseph, J., and J. Greenough. 1979. *International Management of Tuna, Porpoise, and Billfish*. Seattle: University of Washington Press.

Kaczynski, W. 1979a. "Responses and Adjustments of Foreign Fleets to Controls Imposed by Coastal Nations." *Journal of the Fisheries Research Board of Canada* 36 (7): 800–10.

————. 1979b. "Joint Ventures in Fisheries between Distant-Water and Developed Coastal Nations: An Economic View." *Ocean Management* 5 (1): 39–48.

*Kahn, J. R., and W. M. Kemp. 1985. "Economic Losses Associated with the Degradation of an Ecosystem: The Case of Submerged Aquatic Vegetation in Chesapeake Bay." *Journal of Environmental Economics and Management* 12:246–63.

Karpoff, J. 1984. "Low-Interest Loans and the Markets for Limited Entry Permits in the Alaska Salmon Fisheries." *Land Economics* 60 (1): 69–80.

Kasahara, H. 1973. "Problems of Allocation as Applied to the Exploitation of the Living Resources of the Sea." In *Needs and Interests of Developing Countries*, ed. L. M. Alexander. Kingston: University of Rhode Island.

Kasahara, H., and W. Burke. 1973. *North Pacific Fisheries Management*. Washington, D.C.: Resources for the Future.

Kellogg, R. L. 1985. "A Bioeconomic Model for Determining the Optimal Timing of Harvest with Application to Two North Carolina Fisheries." Ph.D. diss., Department of Economics and Business, North Carolina State University, Raleigh, N.C.

Kesteven, G. L. 1973. *Manual of Fisheries Science*, FAO Fisheries Technical Paper No. 118 (FRIM/T118). Rome: FAO.

Kim, C. 1983. "Optimal Management of Multi-Species North Sea Fishery Resources." *Weltwirtschaftliches Archiv* 119 (1): 138–51.

King, D. 1979. "International Management of Highly Migratory Species—Centralised versus Decentralised Economic Decision-Making." *Marine Policy* 3 (4): 264–77.

Kirby, M. 1982. *Navigating Troubled Waters: A New Policy for Atlantic Fisheries*. Report on the Task Force on Atlantic Fisheries, Minister of Supply and Services, Canada.

Knight, H. G., ed. 1975. *The Future of International Fisheries Management*. St. Paul: West Publishing.

Koenig, E. F. 1984a. "Controlling Stock Externalities in a Common Property Fishery Subject to Uncertainty." *Journal of Environmental Economics and Management* 11 (2): 124–38.

————. 1984b. "Fisheries Regulation under Uncertainty: A Dynamic Analysis." *Marine Resource Economics* 1 (2): 193–208.

Koers, A. W. 1973. *International Regulation of Marine Fisheries*. Surrey, England: Fishing News (Books).

*Koslow, J. A. 1982. "Limited Entry Policy and the Bristol Bay, Alaska Salmon Fishermen." *Canadian Journal of Fisheries and Aquatic Sciences* 39 (3): 415–25.

Larkin, P. 1963. "Interspecific Competition and Exploitation." *Journal of the Fisheries Research Board of Canada* 20:647–78.

————. 1966. "Exploitation in a Type of Predator-Prey Relationship." *Journal of the Fisheries Research Board of Canada* 23:349–56.

————. 1977. "An Epitaph for the Concept of Maximum Sustained Yield." *Transactions of the American Fisheries Society* 106 (1): 1–11.

Larkins, H. 1980. "Management Under FCMA—Development of a Fishery Management Plan." *Marine Policy* 4 (3): 170–82.

Lawson, R. M. 1984. *Economics of Fisheries Development*. New York: Praeger Publishers.

Lawson, R., and M. A. Robinson. 1983. "Artisanal Fisheries in West Africa: Problems of Management Implementation." *Marine Policy* 7:183–91.

*Lett, P., and C. Kohler. 1976. "Recruitment: A Problem of Multispecies Interaction and Environmental Perturbations, with Special Reference to Gulf of St. Lawrence Atlantic Herring (*Clupea harengus harengus*)." *Journal of the Fisheries Research Board of Canada* 33:1353-71.

Leung, A., and A. Y. Wang. 1976. "Analysis of Models for Commercial Fishing: Mathematical and Economical Aspects." *Econometrica* 44 (2): 295-303.

Levhari, D., and L. Mirman. 1980. "The Great Fish War: An Example Using a Dynamic Cournot-Nash Solution." *Bell Journal of Economics* 11 (1): 322-34.

Levhari, D., R. Michener, and L. J. Mirman. 1981a. "Dynamic Models of Fishing Competition." *American Economic Review* 71 (4): 649-61.

―――. 1981b. "Dynamic Programming Models of Fishing: Monopoly." In *Essays in the Economics of Renewable Resources*, ed. L. J. Mirman and D. Spulber, 175-86. Amsterdam: North Holland.

Lewis, T. R. 1977. "Optimal Fishery Management under Conditions of Uncertainty." In *Economic Impacts of Extended Fisheries Jurisdiction*, ed. L. G. Anderson, 349-78. Ann Arbor: Ann Arbor Science Publishers.

―――. 1980. *Optimal Resource Management under Conditions of Uncertainty: The Case of an Ocean Fishery*. Seattle: University of Washington Press.

Lewis, T. R., and P. Schmalensee. 1977. "Nonconvexity and Optimal Exhaustion of Renewable Resources." *International Economic Review* 18 (3): 535-52.

Lokken, H. 1959. "The Political and Sociological Limitations of the Halibut Programme." In *Biological and Economic Aspects of Fisheries Management*, ed. J. Crutchfield, 80-83. Seattle: University of Washington Press.

Lucas, K. 1980. "How Changes in Fish Resources and in the Regime of the Sea Are Affecting Management, Development, and Utilization." In *Advances in Fish Science and Technology*, ed. J. Connell. Farnham, Surrey: Fishing News (Books).

Ludwig, D. 1980. "Harvesting Strategies for a Randomly Fluctuating Population." *Journal du Conseil International pour l'Exploration de la Mer* 39:168-74.

*McCarl, B. A., and R. G. Rettig. 1983. "Influence of Hatchery Smolt Releases on Adult Salmon Production and Its Variability." *Canadian Journal of Fisheries and Aquatic Sciences* 40:487-95.

McConnell, K. E. 1979. "Values of Marine Recreational Fishing: Measurement and Impact of Measurement." *American Journal of Agricultural Economics* 61:921-25.

McConnell, K. E., and I. E. Strand. 1981a. "Some Economic Aspects of Managing Marine Recreational Fishing." In *Economic Analysis for Fisheries Management Plans*, ed. L. G. Anderson, chap. 11. Ann Arbor: Ann Arbor Science Publishers.

*―――. 1981b. "Measuring the Cost of Time in Recreation Demand Analysis: An Application to Sport Fishing." *American Journal of Agricultural Economics* 63 (1): 153-56.

McConnell, K., and J. Sutinen. 1979. "Bioeconomic Models of Marine Recreational Fishing." *Journal of Environmental Economics and Management* 6:127-39.

McEvoy, A. F., and H. N. Scheiber. 1984. "Scientists, Entrepreneurs, and the Policy Press: A Study of the Post-1945 California Sardine Depletion." *Journal of Economic History* 44 (2): 393-406.

McGaw, R. L. 1981. "The Supply of Effort in a Fishery." *Applied Economics* 13: 245-53.

McGoodwin, J. R. 1980. "Mexico's Marginal Inshore Pacific Fishing Cooperatives." *Anthropological Quarterly* 53 (1): 42-51.

McKelvey, R. 1981. "Economic Regulation of Targeting Behavior in a Multispecies Fishery." University of British Columbia Program in Natural Resources Economic Research Paper No. 75, 21 pp.

————. 1983. "The Fishery in a Fluctuating Environment: Coexistence of Specialist and Generalist Fishing Vessels in a Multipurpose Fleet." *Journal of Environmental Economics and Management* 10 (4): 287–309.

MacKenzie, W. 1979. "Rational Fishery Management in a Depressed Region: The Atlantic Groundfishery." *Journal of the Fisheries Research Board of Canada* 36 (7): 811–26.

Mangel, M., and R. E. Plant. 1985. "Regulatory Mechanisms and Information Processing in Uncertain Fisheries." *Marine Resource Economics* 1 (4): 389–418.

Marasco, R., and J. Terry. 1982. "Controlling Incidental Catch: An Economic Analysis of Six Management Options." *Marine Policy* 6 (2): 131–39.

May, R. et al. 1979. "Management of Multispecies Fisheries." *Science* 205:267–77.

McKenzie, W. 1959. "Biology and Economics in Fishery Management." In *Biological and Economic Aspects of Fisheries Management*, ed. J. Crutchfield, 17–21. Seattle: University of Washington Press.

*Meany, T. 1979. "Limited Entry in the Western Australian Rock Lobster and Prawn Fisheries: An Economic Evaluation." *Journal of the Fisheries Research Board of Canada* 36 (7): 789–96.

Mendelssohn, R. 1979. "Determining the Best Trade-Off between Expected Economic Return and the Risk of Undesirable Events When Managing a Randomly Varying Population." *Journal of the Fisheries Research Board of Canada* 36:939–47.

Miller, J. R., and F. C. Menz. 1979. "Some Economic Considerations for Wildlife Preservation." *Southern Economic Journal* 46 (3): 718–29.

Miller, M., and J. Johnson. 1981. "Hard Work and Competition in the Bristol Bay Salmon Fishery." *Human Organization* 40 (2): 131.

Miller, M., and J. Van Maanen. 1979. "Boats Don't Fish, People Do: Some Enthnographic Notes on the Federal Management of Fisheries in Gloucester." *Human Organization* 38 (4): 377.

————. 1982. "Getting into Fishing: Observations on the Social Identities of New England Fishermen." *Urban Life* 11 (1): 27–54.

Miles, E. 1974. *Organizational Arrangements to Facilitate Global Management of Fisheries*. Washington, D.C.: Resources for the Future.

Mirman, L. J. 1979. "Dynamic Models of Fishing: A Heuristic Approach." In *Control Theory in Mathematical Economics*, ed. P. T. Liu and J. G. Sutinen, 39–73. New York: Marcel Dekker.

Mishan, E. J. 1982. *Cost-Benefit Analysis*, 3d ed. London: George, Allen, and Unwin.

Mitchell, C. 1979. "Bioeconomics of Commercial Fisheries Management." *Journal of the Fisheries Research Board of Canada* 36:699–704.

*Mohring, H. 1974. "The Costs of Inefficient Fishery Regulation: A Partial Study of the Pacific Coast Halibut Industry." Paper read at the American Economic Association Meeting, San Francisco, December.

Moloney, D., and P. Pearse. 1979a. "Quantitative Rights as an Instrument for Regulating Commercial Fisheries." *Journal of the Fisheries Research Board of Canada* 36 (7): 859–66.

————. 1979b. "Quantitative Rights—A Reply." *Canadian Journal of Fisheries and Aquatic Sciences* 37:903–4.

Morehouse, T. A. 1972. "Limited Entry in the British Columbia Salmon Fisheries." In *Alaska Fisheries Policy*, ed. A. R. Tussing, T. A. Morehouse, and J. D. Babb, Jr. Fairbanks: Institute of Social, Economic, and Government Research.

Morey, E. R. 1980. "Fisheries Economics: An Introduction and Review." *Natural Resources Journal* 20:827–51.

*————. 1984. "A Generalized Harvest Function for Fishing: Allocating Effort among Common Property Cod Stocks." Boulder, Colo.: University of Colorado. Manuscript.

Munro, G. R. 1979. "The Optimal Management of Transboundary Renewable Resources." *Canadian Journal of Economics* 12:355–76.

————. 1980. *A Promise of Abundance: Extended Fisheries Jurisdiction and the Newfoundland Economy.* Minister of Supply and Services, Canada.

————. 1982. "Fisheries, Extended Jurisdiction and the Economics of Common Property Resources." *Canadian Journal of Economics* 15:405–25.

Munro, G. R., and A. D. Scott. 1984. "The Economics of Fisheries Management," Discussion Paper 84-09. University of British Columbia, 96 pps.

Needler, A. 1979. "Evolution of Canadian Fisheries Management towards Economic Rationalization." *Journal of the Fisheries Research Board of Canada* 36:716–24.

Neher, P. 1974. "Notes on the Volterra-Quadratic Equation." *Journal of Economic Theory* 8:39–49.

*Noetzel, B. G., and V. J. Norton. 1969. *Costs and Earnings in the Boston Large-Trawler Fleet*, Bulletin 400. Kingston, R.I.: URI Agricultural Experiment Station.

Organization for Economic Co-operation and Development. 1972. *Economic Aspects of Fish Production.* Paris: OECD.

————. 1982. *International Trade in Fish Products: Effects of the 200 Mile Limit.* Paris: OECD.

*O'Rourke, D. 1971. "Economic Potential of the California Trawl Fishery." *American Journal of Agricultural Economics* 53 (November): 583–92.

Owers, J. 1975. "Limitation of Entry in the United States Fishing Industry: A Comment." *Land Economics* 51, no. 1: 177–78.

Paulik, G., A. Hourston, and P. Larkin. 1967. "Exploitation of Multiple Stocks by a Common Fishery." *Journal of the Fisheries Research Board of Canada* 24:2527–37.

Pauly, D. 1979. "Theory and Management of Tropical Multispecies Stocks: A Review, with Emphasis on the Southeast Asian Demersal Fisheries," ICLARM Studies and Reviews No. 1. Manila: International Center for Living Aquatic Resources Management, 35 pp.

Pearse, P. H. 1972. "Rationalization of Canada's West Coast Salmon Fishery, An Economic Evaluation." In *Organization for Economic Cooperation and Development, Economic Aspects of Fish Production*, 172–202. Paris: OECD.

————. 1979a. "Impact of Canada's Pacific Salmon Fleet Control Program." *Journal of the Fisheries Research Board of Canada* 36:764–69.

————. 1979b. "Symposium on Policies for Economic Rationalization of Commercial Fisheries." *Journal of the Fisheries Research Board of Canada* 36 (7): 711–866.

————. 1981. "Fishing Rights, Regulations, and Revenues." *Marine Policy* 5 (2): 135–46.

————. 1982. *Turning the Tide: A New Policy for Canada's Pacific Fisheries*. Commission on Pacific Fisheries Policy, Minister of Supply and Services, Canada.

Pella, J., and P. Tomlinson. 1969. "A Generalized Stock Production Model." *Inter-American Tropical Tuna Commission Bulletin* 13:421–58.

*Perrin, W. F., and B. G. Noetzel. 1971. "Economic Study of San Pedro Wetfish Boats." *Fishery Industrial Research* 6, no. 2: 105–38.

Peterson, S., and L. J. Smith. 1982. "Risk Reduction in Fisheries Management." *Ocean Management* 8:65–79.

Plourde, C. 1970. "A Simple Model of Replenishable Resource Exploitation." *American Economic Review* 60:518–22.

————. 1971. "Exploitation of a Common-Property Replenishable Natural Resource." *Western Economic Journal* 9:256–66.

————. 1979. "Diagrammatic Representations of the Exploitation of Replenishable Natural Resources: Dynamic Iterations." *Journal of Environmental Economics and Management* 6 (2): 119–26.

Plourde, C., and R. Bodell. 1984. "Uncertainty in Fisheries Economics: The Role of the Discount Rate." *Marine Resource Economics* 1 (2): 155–70.

Pontecorvo, G., ed. 1974. *Fisheries Conflicts in the North Atlantic*. Cambridge, Mass.: Ballinger.

Quin, J. 1983. "E.E.C. Fisheries Policy." *Journal of Agricultural Economics* 34 (3): 337–47.

Quirk, J., and V. Smith. 1970. "Dynamic Economic Models of Fishing." In *Economics of Fisheries Management: A Symposium*, ed. A. Scott. Institute of Animal Resource Ecology, University of British Columbia, 3–32.

Radovich, J. 1975. "Application of Optimum Sustainable Yield Theory to Marine Fisheries." In *Optimum Sustainable Yield as a Concept in Fisheries Management*, ed. P. Roedel, 21–28. Washington, D.C.: American Fisheries Society.

Reed, W. 1974. "A Stochastic Model for the Economic Management of a Renewable Resource." *Mathematical Biosciences* 22:313–37.

————. 1979. "Optimal Escapement Levels in Stochastic and Deterministic Harvesting Models." *Journal of Environmental Economics and Management* 6:350–63.

Rettig, R. 1973. "Multiple Objectives for Marine Resource Management." In *Ocean Fishery Management: Discussions and Research*, ed. A. Sokoloski. NOAA Technical Report, NMFS Circular 371.

Rettig, R. B., and J. C. C. Ginter, eds. 1978. *Limited Entry as a Fishery Management Tool*. Seattle: University of Washington Press.

Ricker, W. E. 1954. "Stock and Recruitment." *Journal of the Fisheries Research Board of Canada* 11:559–623.

————. 1958. "Maximum Sustained Yields from Fluctuating Environments and Mixed Stocks." *Journal of the Fisheries Research Board of Canada* 15 (May): 991–1006.

————. 1975. *Computation and Interpretation of Biological Statistics of Fish Populations*. Ottawa: Fisheries and Marine Service.

Robinson, M. 1980. "World Fisheries to 2000." *Marine Policy* 4 (1): 19–32.

Roedel, P., ed. 1975. *Optimum Sustainable Yield as a Concept in Fisheries Management*. Washington, D.C.: American Fisheries Society.

Rogers, G. 1979. "Alaska's Limited Entry Program: Another View." *Journal of the Fisheries Research Board of Canada* 36 (7): 783-88.

Rothschild, B. J., ed. 1972a. *World Fisheries Policy.* Seattle: University of Washington Press.

———. 1972b. "An Exposition on the Definition of Fishing Effort." *Fishery Bulletin* 70:671-79.

———. 1973. "Questions of Strategy in Fishery Management and Development." *Journal of the Fisheries Research Board of Canada* 30:2017-30.

———. 1977. "Fishing Effort." In *Fish Population Dynamics*, ed. J. Gulland, chap. 5. London: Wiley Interscience.

Rothschild, B. J., and J. W. Balsiger. 1971. "A Linear-Programming Solution to Salmon Management." *Fishery Bulletin* 69 (January): 117-39.

Rothschild, B. J., J. M. Gates, and A. M. Carlson. 1977. "Management of Marine Recreational Fisheries." In *Marine Recreational Fisheries*, ed. H. Clepper, 149-72. Washington, D.C.: Sport Fishing Institute.

Roy, N., W. E. Schrank, and E. Tsoa. 1982. "The Newfoundland Groundfishery: Some Options for Renewal." *Canadian Public Policy* 8 (2): 222-338.

Royce, W. F. 1972. *Introduction to the Fishery Sciences.* New York: Academic Press.

*Russell, C. S., and W. J. Vaughan. 1982. "The National Recreational Fishing Benefits of Water Pollution Control." *Journal of Environmental Economics and Management* 9 (4): 328-54.

Saila, S. B., and K. W. Hess. 1975. "Some Applications of Optimal Control Theory to Fisheries Management." *Transactions of the American Fisheries Society* 104 (3): 620-29.

Saila, S. B., and V. J. Norton. 1974. *Tuna: Status, Trends, and Alternative Management Arrangements.* Washington, D.C.: Resources for the Future.

*Samples, K. C., and R. C. Bishop. 1985. "Estimating the Value of Variations in Anglers' Success Rates: An Application of the Multiple-Site Travel Cost Method." *Marine Resource Economics* 2 (1): 55-74.

Sancho, N., and C. Mitchell. 1975. "Economic Optimization in Controlled Fisheries." *Mathematical Biosciences* 27:1-7.

*———. 1977. "Optimal Fishing Effort of Canada's Offshore Groundfish Fisheries— An Application of Economic Optimization Techniques." *Mathematical Biosciences* 34:157-66.

Schaefer, M. 1954. "Some Aspects of the Dynamics of Populations Important to the Management of the Commercial Marine Fisheries." *Bulletin of the Inter-American Tropical Tuna Commission* 1:25-56.

———. 1957a. "Some Considerations of the Population Dynamics and Economics in Relation to the Management of the Commercial Marine Fisheries." *Journal of the Fisheries Research Board of Canada* 14:669-81.

*———. 1957b. "A Study of the Dynamics of the Fishery for Yellowfin Tuna in the Eastern Tropical Pacific." *Bulletin of the Inter-American Tropical Tuna Commission* 2:247-85.

———. 1959. "Biological and Economic Aspects of the Management of the Commercial Marine Fisheries." *Transactions of the American Fisheries Society* 88:100-104.

Schnute, J. 1977. "Improved Estimates from the Schaefer Production Model: Theoretical Considerations." *Journal of the Fisheries Research Board of Canada* 34:583–603.

————. 1979. "A Revised Schaefer Model." *Investigacion pesquera* 43:31–40.

Schnute, J., and J. Sibert. 1983. "The Salmon Terminal Fishery: A Practical, Comprehensive Timing Model." *Canadian Journal of Fisheries and Aquatic Sciences* 40 (7): 835–53.

Schworn, W. E. 1983. "Monopsonistic Control of a Common Property Renewable Resource." *Canadian Journal of Economics* 16 (2): 275–87.

Scott, A. 1955. "The Fishery: The Objectives of Sole Ownership." *Journal of Political Economy* 63 (2): 116–24.

————. 1957. "Optimal Utilization and the Control of Fisheries." In *The Economics of Fisheries*, ed. R. Turvey and J. Wiseman, 42–56. Rome: FAO.

————. 1962. "The Economics of Regulating Fisheries." In *The Economic Effects of Fishery Regulation*, ed. R. Hamlisch, F.A.O. Fisheries Report 5:25–61. Rome: FAO.

Scott, A. D., ed. 1970. *Economics of Fishery Management: A Symposium*. Vancouver: Institute of Animal Resource Ecology, University of British Columbia.

————. 1979. "Development of Economic Theory on Fisheries Regulation." *Journal of the Fisheries Research Board of Canada* 36 (7): 725–41.

————. 1983. "Property Rights and Property Wrongs." *Canadian Journal of Economics* 16 (4): 555–73.

Shepherd, J. G. 1981. "Matching Fishing Capacity to the Catches Available: A Problem in Resource Allocation." *Journal of Agricultural Economics* 32 (3): 331–40.

Shyam, M. 1982. "The New International Economic Order and the New Regime for Fisheries Management." *Ocean Management* 8:51–64.

Silvert, W. 1977. "The Economics of Over-Fishing." *Transactions of the American Fisheries Society* 106:121–30.

————. 1982. "Optimal Utilization of a Variable Fish Supply." *Canadian Journal of Fisheries and Aquatic Sciences* 39 (2): 462–68.

Sissenwine, M. P. 1977. "A Compartmentalized Simulation Model of the Southern New England Yellowtail Flounder, *Limanda ferruginea*, Fishery." *Fishery Bulletin* 75 (3): 465–82.

————. 1978. "Is MSY an Adequate Foundation for Optimum Yield?" *Fisheries* 3 (6): 22–4, 37–42.

————. 1984. "The Uncertain Environment of Fishery Scientists and Managers." *Marine Resource Economics* 1 (1): 1–30.

Sissenwine, M. P., and Kirkley, J. E. 1982. "Fishing Management Techniques: Practical Aspects and Limitations." *Marine Policy* 6 (1): 43–57.

Smith, C. L. 1981. "Satisfaction Bonus from Salmon Fishing: Implications for Economic Evaluation." *Land Economics* 57 (2): 181–94.

Smith, F. 1975. *The Fisherman's Business Guide*. Ann Arbor: UMI Publications.

Smith, I. R. 1981. "Improving Fishing Incomes When Resources Are Overfished." *Marine Policy* 5 (1): 17–22.

Smith, J. B. 1980. "Replenishable Resource Management under Uncertainty: A Reexamination of the U.S. Northern Fishery." *Journal of Environmental Economics and Management* 7 (3): 209–19.

————. 1985. "A Discrete Model of Replenishable Resource Management under Uncertainty." *Marine Resource Economics* 1 (3): 283–308.

Smith, P. E., and T. O. Wisley. 1982. "Optimal Harvesting of a Replenishable Resource in a Model with Logistic Growth." *Journal of Economic Development* 7 (2): 7-16.

Smith, V. L. 1968. "Economics of Production from Natural Resources." *American Economic Review* 58:409-31.

———. 1969. "On Models of Commercial Fishing." *Journal of Political Economy* 77:181-98.

———. 1971. "Economics of Production from Natural Resources: Reply." *American Economic Review* 61 (June): 488-91.

———. 1972. "On Models of Commercial Fishing: The Traditional Literature Needs No Defenders." *Journal of Political Economy* 80 (July/August): 776-78.

———. 1977. "Control Theory Applied to Natural and Environmental Resources: An Exposition." *Journal of Environmental Economics and Management* 4:1-24.

Sokoloski, A. A., ed. 1973. *Ocean Fishery Management: Discussions and Research.* Seattle: National Oceanic and Atmospheric Administration Technical Report NMFS CIRC-371.

Southey, C. 1969. "Studies in Fisheries Economics." Ph.D. diss., University of British Columbia, Vancouver.

———. 1971. "The International Fishery: A Proposal Based on the New Welfare Economics." In *The United Nations and Ocean Management*, ed. L. M. Alexander. Kingston: University of Rhode Island.

———. 1972. "Policy Prescriptions in Bionomic Models: The Case of the Fishery." *Journal of Political Economy* 80:769-75.

Spence, A. M. 1973. "Blue Whales and Applied Control Theory." *The Economics Series*, Technical Report No. 108. Stanford, Calif.: Institute for Mathematical Studies in the Social Sciences.

Spulber, D. F. 1985. "The Multicohort Fishery under Uncertainty." *Marine Resource Economics* 1 (3): 265-82.

Stokes, R. L. 1979. "Limitation of Fishing Effort—An Economic Analysis of Options." *Marine Policy* 3 (4): 289-301.

———. 1981a. "Economics of Development and Management: The Alaskan Groundfish Case." In *Economic Analysis for Fisheries Management Plans*, ed. L. G. Anderson, 267-88. Ann Arbor: Ann Arbor Science Publishers.

———. 1981b. "The New Approach to Foreign Fisheries Allocation: An Economic Appraisal." *Land Economics* 57 (4): 568-82.

———. 1982. "The Economics of Salmon Ranching." *Land Economics* 58 (4): 464-77.

Strand, I. E., and D. Heuth. 1977. "Optimal Control in Multispecies Fisheries." In *Economic Impacts of Extended Fisheries Jurisdiction*, ed. L. G. Anderson. Ann Arbor: Ann Arbor Science Publishers.

Sturgess, N., and T. Meany. 1982. *Policy and Practice in Fisheries Management*, Proceedings of the National Fisheries Seminar held in Melbourne, 1980. Canberra: Australian Government Publishing Service.

Sutinen, J. G. 1979. "Fishermen's Remuneration Systems and Implications for Fisheries Development." *Scottish Journal of Political Economy* 26:147-62.

———. 1982. "Economic Principles of Allocation in Recreational and Commercial Fisheries." In *Allocation of Fishery Resources*, Proceedings of the Technical Consultation, Vichy, France, 1980, ed. J. H. Grover, 432-42. Rome: FAO.

Swierzbinski, J. 1985. "Statistical Methods Applicable to Selected Problems in Fisheries Biology and Economics." *Marine Resource Economics* 1 (3): 209–33.

Talbot, L. 1975. "Maximum Sustainable Yield: An Obsolete Management Concept." *Transactions of the North American Wildlife and Natural Resources Conference* 40:91–96.

*Taylor, T. G., and F. J. Prochaska. 1985. "Fishing Power Functions in Aggregate Bioeconomic Models." *Marine Resource Economics* 2 (1): 87–108.

*Terry, J. M., and J. W. Balsiger. 1981. "A Bioeconomic Simulation Model for Sablefish in the Gulf of Alaska." Seattle: National Marine Fisheries Service (December), 34 pp.

*Tettey, E., C. Pardy, W. Griffin, and A. N. Swartz. 1984. "Implications of Investing under Different Economic Conditions of the Profitability of Gulf of Mexico Shrimp Vessels Operating out of Texas." *Fishery Bulletin* 82 (2): 365–73.

Tomlinson, J. W. C., and J. Vertinsky. 1975. "International Joint Ventures in Fishing and 200 Mile Economic Zones." *Journal of the Fisheries Research Board of Canada* 32:2569–79.

*Townsend, R. E. 1985. "An Economic Evaluation of Restricted Entry in Maine's Soft-Shell Clam Industry." *North American Journal of Fisheries Management* 5:57–64.

*Tsoa, E., W. E. Schrank, and N. Roy. 1982. "U.S. Demand for Selected Groundfish Products, 1967–80." *American Journal of Agricultural Economics* 64 (3): 483–9.

Turvey, R. 1964. "Optimization and Suboptimization in Fishery Regulation." *American Economic Review* 54:64–76.

Turvey, R., and J. Wiseman, eds. 1957. *The Economics of Fisheries*. Rome: FAO.

Tussing, A. R., R. A. Hiebert, and J. G. Sutinen. 1974. *Fisheries of the Indian Ocean*. Washington, D.C.: Resources for the Future.

Tussing, A. R., T. A. Morehouse, and J. D. Babb, Jr., eds. 1972. *Alaska Fisheries Policy*. Fairbanks: Institute of Social, Economic, and Government Research.

Underdal, A. 1980. *The Politics of International Fisheries Management: The Case of the North-East Atlantic*. Oslo: Universitetsforlaget.

U.S. Department of Commerce. 1984. *Fisheries of the United States, 1983*. Washington, D.C.

Van Maanen, J., M. Miller, and R. Johnson. 1982. "An Occupation in Transition: Traditional and Modern Forms of Commercial Fishing." *Work and Occupations* 9 (2): 193–216.

*Van Meir, L. 1969. "An Economic Analysis of Policy Alternatives for Managing the Georges Bank Haddock Fishery," Working Paper No. 21, Bureau of Commercial Fisheries, Division of Economic Research. May 1969.

*Vaughan, W. J., and C. S. Russell. 1982. "Valuing a Fishing Day: An Application of a Systematic Varying Parameter Model." *Land Economics* 58 (4): 450–63.

Villegas, L., A. C. Jones, and R. F. Labisky. 1982. "Management Strategies for the Spiny Lobster Resources in the Western Central Atlantic: A Cooperative Approach." *North American Journal of Fisheries Management* 2:216–23.

Visgilio, G. 1978. "The Relationship between Firm and Fishery in Common Property Fisheries: Comment." *Land Economics* 54:100–103.

Walker, K. D., R. B. Rettig, and R. Hilborn. 1983. "Analysis of Multiple Objectives in Oregon Coho Salmon Policy." *Canadian Journal of Fisheries and Aquatic Sciences* 40 (5): 580–87.

Walters, C., and R. Hilborn. 1976. "Adaptive Control of Fishing Systems." *Journal of the Fisheries Research Board of Canada* 33:145–59.

Wang, A., and K-S. Cheng. 1978. "Dynamic Analysis of Commercial Fishing Models." *Journal of Environmental Economics and Management* 5 (2): 113–27.

Wang, D. H., L. Goodreau, and J. Mueller. 1981. "Economics of the Atlantic Sea Scallop Management." Manuscript prepared for Eastern Economic Association, 8th Annual Convention, 1982.

Warren, J. P., W. L. Griffin, and W. E. Grant. 1982. "Regional Fish Stock Management: A Model for North-West Africa." *Marine Policy* 6 (2): 121–30.

*Waters, J. R., J. E. Easley, Jr., and L. E. Danielson. 1980. "Economic Trade-Offs and the North Carolina Shrimp Fishery." *American Journal of Agricultural Economics* 62:124–29.

Watt, K. 1956. "The Choice and Solution of Mathematical Models for Predicting and Maximizing the Yield of a Fishery." *Journal of the Fisheries Research Board of Canada* 13:613–45.

Waugh, G. 1984. *Fisheries Management: Theoretical Developments and Contemporary Applications.* Boulder, Colo.: Westview Press.

Waugh, G., and P. Calvo. 1974. "Economics of Exhaustible Resources: The Fishery." *Economic Record* 50:423–29.

Westrheim, S. J. 1983. "A New Method for Alloting Effort to Individual Species in a Mixed Species Trawl Fishery." *Canadian Journal of Fisheries and Aquatic Sciences* 40 (3): 352–60.

Wilen, J. E. 1979. "Fisherman Behaviour and the Design of Efficient Fisheries Regulation Programmes." *Journal of the Fisheries Research Board of Canada* 36 (7): 855–58.

———. 1985. "Towards a Theory of the Regulated Fishery." *Marine Resource Economics* 1 (4): 369–88.

Wilson, J. A. 1982. "The Economical Management of Multispecies Fisheries." *Land Economics* 58 (4): 417–34.

———. 1985. "The Economical Management of Multispecies Fisheries: Reply." *Land Economics* 61 (3): 323–26.

Wilson, J., and F. Olson. 1975. "Limitation of Entry in the United States Fishing Industry: A Second Comment." *Land Economics* 51 (2): 179–81.

Wyner, W. E., A. J. Moore, and B. Cicin-Sain. 1977. "Politics and Management of the California Abalone Fishery." *Marine Policy* 1 (4): 326–39.

Yohe, G. W. 1984. "Regulation under Uncertainty: An Intuitive Survey and Application to Fisheries." *Marine Resource Economics* 1 (2): 171–92.

Zoeteweij, H. 1956. "Fishermen's Remuneration." In *The Economics of Fisheries*, ed. R. Turvey and J. Wiseman. Rome: FAO.

Index

Multispecies fisheries (*cont.*)
  maximum economic yield, 166; population equilibrium curve for, 164;
  and predator-prey stocks, 180; relative prices of each species in, 170; and
  sustainable yield curve and MSY, 164
Munro, G. R., xiii, xvi, 33, 42, 70

Negotiations in international fisheries
  for mutually beneficial redistributions
  of the fishing rights, 143
Neher, P., 42
Nichols, J. P., 157
Noncommercially exploitable fishery, 50,
  53
Northern lobster fishery, 249
Norton, V. J., xiii

Open-access equilibrium yield, 46-50,
  76-79, 83-85, 94-96, 98-101, 115,
  159; and change in costs, 50; and
  change in price, 54; and change in
  productivity, 52; compared to MEY,
  46; definition of, 21-29; and determination of share rate, 159; eumetric
  yield curve, 128; and extinction and
  economic destruction, 151; with forward-bending population equilibrium
  curve, 112, 115; and the individual
  boat; 56-61; in international fishery,
  137; and multiple equilibria, 77; multipurpose fleet, seasonally fished stocks,
  173-77; and northern lobsters, 253;
  one fleet, multiple independent-stock
  fishery, 171-73; one fleet, multiple
  joint-stock fishery, 164-71; the paradox of fisheries development, 98; process of achieving, 30, 151, 180; and
  rate at which new technologies are
  introduced, 211; recreational fishing,
  94; revenue maximization point of,
  87; and shrimp fisheries, 124; in terms
  of whole economy, 83-87; two fleets,
  biological interdependence, 180-84;
  two fleets, technological interdependence, 185-87; two fleets, one stock,
  189-90; and variable price of fish, 74-77
Open-access regulation types, 195;
  effect on share rate, 233
Opportunity cost: defined, 11; and other
  sources of employment, 27; and regulation, 205; effect of, on share rate, 160
Optimal allocation of resources, xvii, 10,
  32
Optimal utilization of fishery: in any
  period of time, 34; complete destruc-

tion of the fish stock, 42; discount
  rate, 41; dynamic nature, 35
Optimal yield and distribution line for
  an international fishery, 141
Overexploitation, two types, 47
Overfishing: growth, 130; recruitment,
  130

Penalty structure for regulations, 234
Plourde, C., 148
Pollution and bioeconomic equilibrium,
  32
Pontecorvo, G., xiii
Population equilibrium curve: asymptotic, 109; derivation of, 22; and dynamic analysis, 149; equation for,
  257; forward-bending, 109, 111; and
  interdependent fisheries, 164, 167,
  168, 169; and northern lobster fishery,
  255; and regenerative species, 120,
  122; and shape of the sustained yield
  curve, 108; upward-rising, 122
Population size, natural equilibrium of,
  20
Predator-prey relationship in interdependent fisheries, 180, 183
Present value, explanation of, 16
Price: changes in, and effect on MEY,
  44; changes in, and open-access equilibrium yield, 51-53; equals marginal
  cost, 6; uncertainty of, and MEY, 45
Processing and marketing sectors, effect
  of regulation on, 202
Production function: definition of, 4;
  difference between short-run and
  long-run, 24; in a fishery, 20-25
Production possibility (PP) curve: definition of, 10-13; and effect of regulation, 205-7; and effort and other
  goods, 84; and fish and other goods,
  84, 85, 105; and gear restrictions, 205;
  interdependent, 135; and maximization of revenue, 86
Productivity, changes in, and open-
  access equilibrium yield, 52
Profit: definition of, 6, 9; rent to stock,
  81. *See also* Scarcity rent
Profit-maximizing output, 6
Property-right indifference curve and
  international fisheries, 139
Pulse fishing, 42

Quirk, J., 148
Quotas: and amelioration of detrimental
  side effects, 195; description of, 204;
  similarity of, with closed seasons and
  areas, 199; three inefficiencies of,
  202; transferable individual, 215ff.

Taxes: capture rent, 221; effect on share rate, 233; as means of regulation, 219; on only one of the components of effort, 221; practical problems in the implementation of, 224; that will achieve MEY, 221, 223

Technological interdependence: discussion of, 185; and maximum economic yield, 187

Total cost. *See* Cost, total

Total revenue. *See* Revenue, total

Townsend, R. E., 260

Tugwell, M., 47, 261

Tuna, 260

Uncertainty and MEY, 45

United Nations Convention of the Law of the Sea, xv

Unregulated fishery. *See* Open-access equilibrium yield

User cost: defined, 34; expression for, 225; individual boat, 63; of fish, 79. *See also* Scarcity rent

Value, determination of, xvii

Wang, A., 148

Warren, J. P., 260

Waters, J. R., 261

Waugh, G., 119, 129

Whitemarsh, D., xv

Yield: for specified levels of population, 25; two levels of cost for each, 75

Zoeteweij, H., 156

About the Author

Lee G. Anderson is professor of economics and marine studies at the University of Delaware. The first edition of *The Economics of Fisheries Management* was published by Johns Hopkins in 1977.

The Johns Hopkins University Press

The Economics of Fisheries Management,
Revised and enlarged edition

This book was set in English 49 text and Helios display type by Action Comp
Co., Inc. It was printed on 50-lb. Sebago Eggshell Cream paper and bound in
Roxite A by the Maple Press Company.